Linux
Kernel
Programming

*Developing kernel architecture and device drivers for
character, block, USB, and network interfaces*

THIERRY GAYET

bpb

www.bpbonline.com

First Edition 2025

Copyright © BPB Publications, India

ISBN: 978-93-65897-364

To View Complete
BPB Publications Catalogue
Scan the QR Code:

Dedicated to

My wife, **Yuniati Gayet**

My children, **Angela Gayet** *and* **Luca Gayet**

About the Author

THIERRY GAYET currently works as a senior developer for TIXEO, a company that has developed an ultra-secure French video conferencing system validated by the country's security authority.

He holds a DEST (postgraduate diploma) in computer science, specializing in artificial intelligence, which he obtained in the late 1990s from CNAM (University of Le Mans).

With over 30 years of experience in Linux development, he has extensively explored software development. His expertise has also extended to fields such as artificial intelligence, cybersecurity, and quantum physics.

Dynamic and dedicated to Linux and system hacking, he participates in repair cafés and continues to design systems based on embedded Linux or IoT.

In the 1990s, when the internet had not yet taken off as much as it does today, he created a Linux user association or group with the aim of helping to better understand and popularize the use of Linux.

Author of numerous articles in Linux Magazine and Misc, he has also presented numerous professional training sessions, conferences, and lectures in various topical areas. In this book, he shares his knowledge and insights to help you better understand the Linux kernel and develop your own drivers.

About the Reviewers

❖ **Austin Kim** has more than 14 years of experience in embedded Linux **Board Support Package** (**BSP**) development. He has worked on many tasks such as board bring-up, crash and performance troubleshooting, and bootloader development for Arm-based devices. He has strong skills in reverse engineering and debugging binaries using tools like TRACE32, Crash-Utility, and ftrace.

Currently, Austin works as a Linux kernel BSP engineer at LG Electronics. He enjoys sharing practical skills in reverse engineering and debugging through courses about Armv8-A, RISC-V architecture, and kernel crash debugging.

❖ **Martin Yanev** is a highly accomplished software engineer with nearly a decade of experience across diverse industries, including aerospace and medical technology. Over his illustrious career, Martin has carved a niche for himself in developing and integrating cutting-edge software solutions for critical domains such as air traffic control and chromatography systems. Renowned as an esteemed instructor and computer science professor at Fitchburg State University, he possesses a deep understanding of the full spectrum of OpenAI APIs and exhibits mastery in constructing, training, and fine-tuning AI systems. As a widely recognized author, Martin has shared his expertise to help others navigate the complexities of AI development. With his exceptional track record and multifaceted skill set, Martin continues to propel innovation and drive transformative advancements in the field of software engineering.

Acknowledgement

I would like to express my sincere gratitude to everyone who contributed to the completion of this book, especially my wife, Yuniati, who encouraged me, and finally, my children, who helped and supported me throughout the writing process.

I am extremely grateful to BPB Publications for their guidance and expertise in the completion of this book. Their support and assistance were invaluable in navigating the complexities of the publication process.

I would also like to thank the reviewers, technical experts, and editors who provided valuable comments and helped improve this manuscript. Their ideas and suggestions significantly improved the quality of the book. Finally, I would like to express my gratitude to the readers who expressed interest in our book. Your support and encouragement were greatly appreciated.

Thank you to everyone who contributed to the completion of this book.

Preface

Understanding the fundamentals of an operating system can be relatively complex. This book has taken on the challenge of popularizing and exploring the various concepts implemented within the GNU/Linux kernel.

Composed of 13 in-depth chapters, this book covers a wide range of topics essential to understanding this kernel.

We will begin with a brief introduction to the history and evolution of this kernel. Then, we will take a block-by-block look at the kernel structure itself, which will form the basis for the subsequent chapters.

Chapter 4 will describe in detail the device model used to structure files in sysfs and used within the kernel itself, among other things, by udev.

Chapter 5 will introduce us to the world of character drivers to develop drivers for keyboards, mice, and many other devices. Chapter 6 will cover another category of drivers: block drivers used for local or remote network mass storage. At this point, you will have the tools to develop your own file system if you wish.

Chapter 7 will then follow, describing how to develop drivers for your USB devices.

Chapter 8 will detail the intricacies of the network stack with the various hooks related to Netfilter. This will be followed by a detailed look at the LSM used to secure a Linux system through numerous system hooks.

The remaining chapters will finally detail memory, communications systems often linked to hardware, process management, and debugging.

Through practical examples, comprehensive explanations, and a structured approach, this book aims to provide the reader with a solid understanding of the GNU/Linux kernel. Whether you are a novice or an experienced user, I hope this book will be useful for exploring the fundamentals of this operating system and will help you develop it further by developing your own extensions or drivers.

Chapter 1: History of the GNU/Linux Kernel - This chapter provides a historical overview of the kernel's evolution, its inspirations, and the key players who brought this famous kernel to life.

Chapter 2: Introduction to the Linux Kernel - After providing a historical overview, the first part will provide a detailed presentation of the kernel architecture. This will then serve as a key chapter for the rest of the book.

Chapter 3: Introduction to Device Drivers - In the second part, we will explore the development of a Hello World driver and discuss various compilation techniques, inter-driver dependency management, and module loading and unloading.

Chapter 4: Linux Device Model - This chapter lays the foundation for the various registration and declaration processes between drivers, which will be used throughout the book.

Chapter 5: Character Device Drivers - This chapter covers the development of the first type of character-based driver.

Chapter 6: Block Drivers and Virtual Filesystem - This second type of block-based driver is used to manage SATA or network drives.

Chapter 7: USB drivers and libusb - This chapter details the drivers used to control devices via the USB protocol.

Chapter 8: Network Drivers - The network, at the heart of today's communications, will be discussed through the implementation of a network card driver. Details of the Netfilter architecture will also be presented for filtering or your own firewall.

Chapter 9: Linux Security Modules - Like all operating systems, maximum security is essential. This is what the NSA initiated with SELinux in late 2000 by proposing system-level hooks allowing precise access control. This chapter will provide a behind-the-scenes understanding and, perhaps, the opportunity to develop your own LSM.

Chapter 10: Kernel Memory and DMA - This chapter details the physical and virtual memory management modes. Direct or DMA access without going through the CPU will also be covered, including NUMA management.

Chapter 11: Navigating Linux Communication Interfaces - Whether it is an embedded device or a standard motherboard, different hardware communication protocols are used, such as I2C, to manage peripherals.

Chapter 12: Process Management - Since the GNU/Linux kernel is a multi-tasking, multi-user system, a scheduler is used to properly schedule the various tasks in the kernel or user space. Without it, the kernel would be single-tasking.

Chapter 13: Debugging GNU/Linux Kernel and Drivers - Developing is one thing, but being able to fine-tune a driver or a specific part of the kernel is another. Indeed, due to their relative complexity, the Linux kernel has seen the development of specific tools that complement each other. The reader will be given a brief overview of the various tools.

Code Bundle and Coloured Images

Please follow the link to download the
Code Bundle and the *Coloured Images* of the book:

https://rebrand.ly/27joie2

The code bundle for the book is also hosted on GitHub at
https://github.com/bpbpublications/Linux-Kernel-Programming.
In case there's an update to the code, it will be updated on the existing GitHub repository.

We have code bundles from our rich catalogue of books and videos available at
https://github.com/bpbpublications. Check them out!

Errata

We take immense pride in our work at BPB Publications and follow best practices to ensure the accuracy of our content to provide with an indulging reading experience to our subscribers. Our readers are our mirrors, and we use their inputs to reflect and improve upon human errors, if any, that may have occurred during the publishing processes involved. To let us maintain the quality and help us reach out to any readers who might be having difficulties due to any unforeseen errors, please write to us at :

errata@bpbonline.com

Your support, suggestions and feedbacks are highly appreciated by the BPB Publications' Family.

Piracy

If you come across any illegal copies of our works in any form on the internet, we would be grateful if you would provide us with the location address or website name. Please contact us at **business@bpbonline.com** with a link to the material.

If you are interested in becoming an author

If there is a topic that you have expertise in, and you are interested in either writing or contributing to a book, please visit **www.bpbonline.com**. We have worked with thousands of developers and tech professionals, just like you, to help them share their insights with the global tech community. You can make a general application, apply for a specific hot topic that we are recruiting an author for, or submit your own idea.

Reviews

Please leave a review. Once you have read and used this book, why not leave a review on the site that you purchased it from? Potential readers can then see and use your unbiased opinion to make purchase decisions. We at BPB can understand what you think about our products, and our authors can see your feedback on their book. Thank you!

For more information about BPB, please visit **www.bpbonline.com**.

Join our book's Discord space

Join the book's Discord Workspace for Latest updates, Offers, Tech happenings around the world, New Release and Sessions with the Authors:

https://discord.bpbonline.com

Table of Contents

CHAPTER 1

History of the GNU/Linux Kernel

Introduction

This first chapter describes the origin and the evolution of the functionalities of the Linux kernel to better understand not only what the kernel is but also the way in which it has evolved structurally.

Structure

The chapter covers the following topics:

- Inspirations
- Linux kernel history
- Evolutions of the several features by release/milestones
- License of the GNU/Linux

Objectives

This chapter is an important preamble to understanding where Linux comes from, its history, and why we need to study this operating system, which owes its fame in part to the openness of its code, its robustness, and its performance. At the end of this chapter, you will have an overview of what the Linux kernel is. *Linux Torvald,* the inventor of

Linux, did not invent everything from scratch but was inspired by what existed at the time, whether he owned it or not. It is, therefore, useful to know these inspirations for a good understanding.

Inspirations

In the 1960s and 1970s, Unix was an operating system developed at AT&T's Bell Labs. It was known for its modular design, stability, and efficiency. Unix (often written in capital letters, **UNIX**, particularly when it is the official trademark) is an operating system created by Bell Labs in 1969 as an interactive time-sharing system.

The name **Unix** is a play on words, combining **uniplexed** (meaning single or one at a time) and **multics** (referring to an earlier operating system project). Unix was developed as a successor to the Multics operating system.

Ken Thompson and *Dennis Ritchie* are considered the inventors of Unix.

In 1974, Unix became the first operating system developed in the C language. *Linus Torvalds*, the creator of the Linux kernel, was a Unix user during his university days and was inspired by Unix's concepts of multi-user, multitasking, and resource management (see *Figure 1.1*). The following figure shows us a concentric view or onion model of a Unix system:

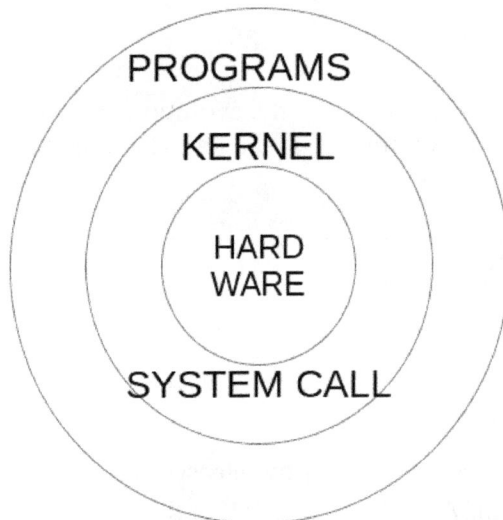

Figure 1.1: *Onion view of the UNIX system*

Unix is often considered to be based on an onion model.

The model proposed by the Unix systems is layered, going from the hardware to the user via the kernel, which controls it and the software that provides utilities via several kinds of software. The following figure shows us a vertical view of the onion model:

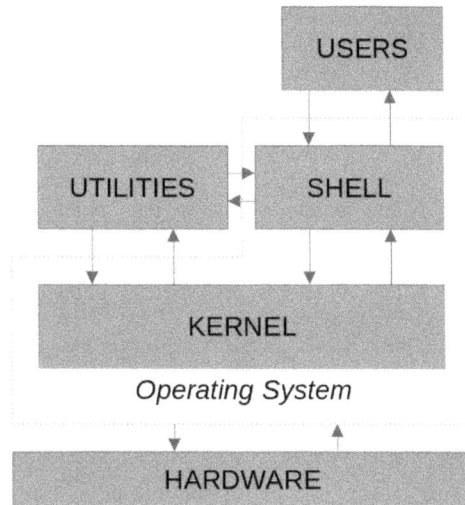

Figure 1.2: *Another view of a UNIX system layered view*

View of the architecture of a Unix System is similar to an actual Linux in outline.

As we will explore, Linux distributions are numerous, and they inspire each other. With Unix systems, it was the same because when we talk about Unix systems (for those who knew them), we talk about IBM AIX, HP UX, Irix, Solaris, UnixWare, Ultrix, Microsoft Xenix, SCO Unix, Net/OpenBSD, and many others.

All these systems have evolved and contributed to developing the modern systems we know today in their own way. The following figure shows us the countless versions of Unix systems that were common at the time and that for the most part, have been replaced today by the Linux system:

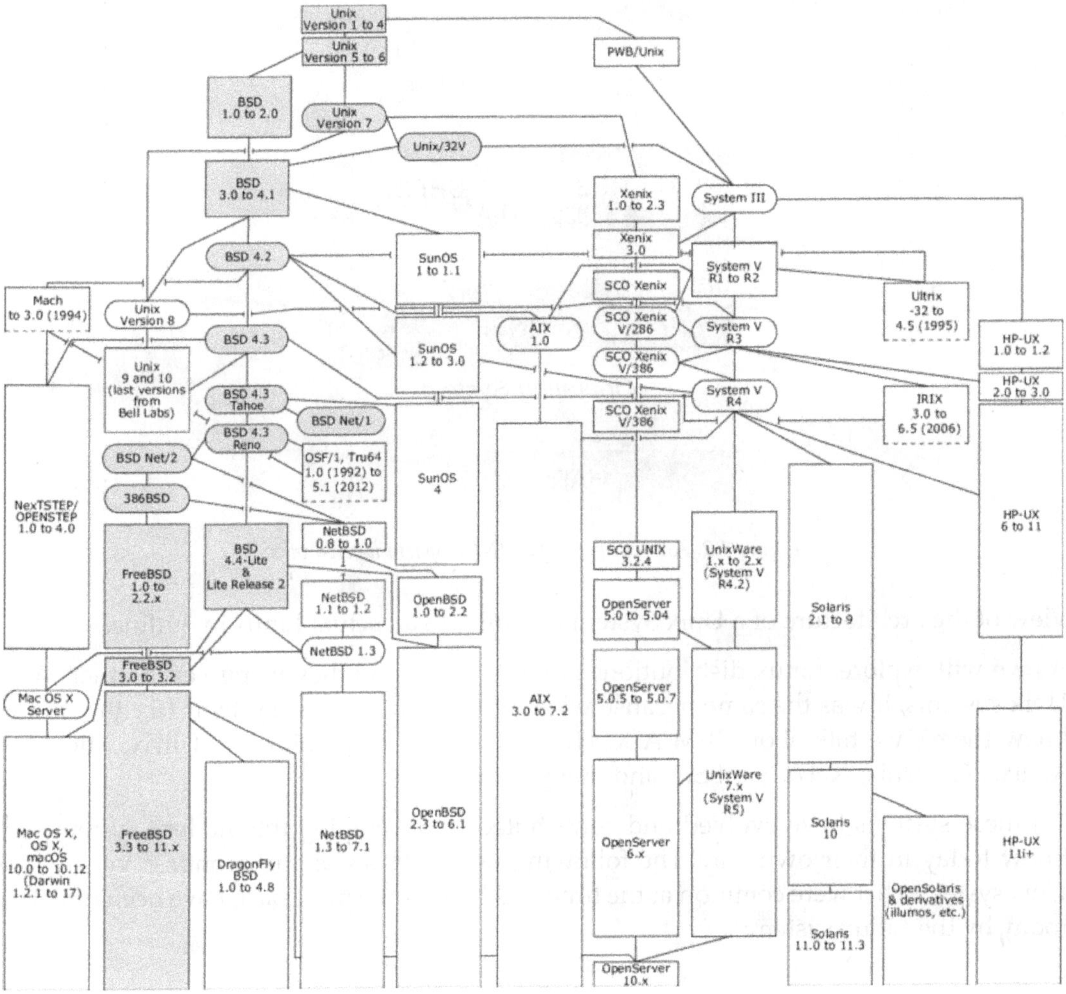

Figure 1.3: History and dependencies of Unix systems

Many of the commands in 1972's Unix 2nd edition are still used in today's Linux.

Another inspiration was Minix (for mini-UNIX), an educational and experimental operating system, created by *Andrew S. Tanenbaum* (also known as AST) in 1984 for students to dissect a real OS. Indeed, AT&T had banned the use of Unix for educational purposes and forbids its use for teaching.

MINIX was a microkernel written in the C programming language to reimplement V7. It was designed for the IBM PC (with 256KB RAM, 360KB 5.25-inch floppy disk). It was structured in a more modular way than UNIX and is compatible with it from a user point of view, but completely different from the kernel side.

Its goals were to deliver an open-source, clean design that students can understand, a small microkernel, the rest of the OS is user processes, and communicate using synchronous message passing. Many of the basic programs, such as **cat, grep, ls, make, ...,** and the shell are present and perform the same functions as UNIX MINIX requires 20 MB of hard disk partition. MINIX is not as efficient as UNIX because it is designed to be readable. The following figure clearly shows the positioning of controllers in user space and no kernel, which will be seen by Linux as an inefficient approach in the following figure:

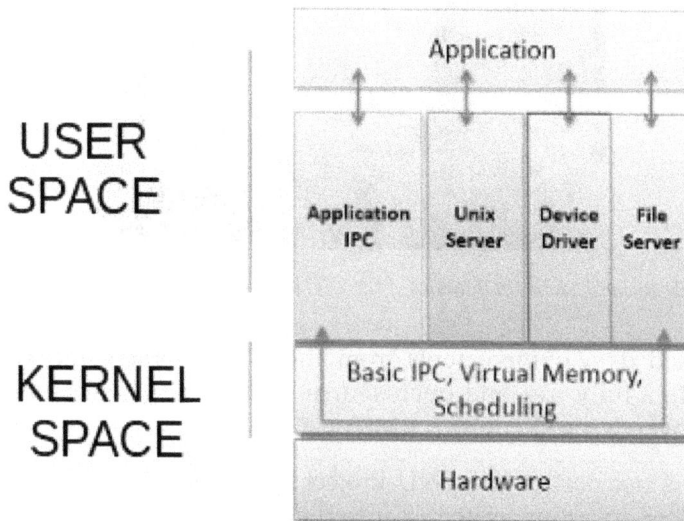

Figure 1.4: Architecture of a microkernel kernel

The kernel is the core part of an operating system; it manages the system resources. It is like a bridge between the application and the hardware of the computer. In a monolithic kernel, user services and kernel services are both kept in the same address space.

Linus Torvalds worked on Minix for a period, gaining practical experience in operating system design. However, he found that Minix had limitations in terms of performance and features, which motivated him to create his own kernel, which gave birth to the Linux kernel a few years later. The initial version was crashing after an hour following a heat problem.

We should not forget one of the latest and important inspirations that made the Linux kernel what it has become today. This owes its current name to it, namely GNU/Linux, which derives from the rights of the GPL to which it is attached.

GNU is a free operating system created in 1983 by *Richard Stallman* (as shown in *Figure 1.5*), maintained by the GNU Project. GNU covers the concepts and operation of UNIX. This project already has a kernel called HURD, which is a play on words, as it is intended to sound like **herd** (as in a herd of animals) and represents a desire to move away from the Unix monolithic kernel model. It entered competition with Linux, which overshadowed it.

Figure 1.5: Richard Stallman, founder of the GNU Project and Free Software Foundation

Linus Torvalds used development tools from the **GNU's Not Unix (GNU)** Project, an initiative to create a fully free and open-source operating system launched IN 1983 by *Richard Stallman*, who is also known as RMS.

Although Linux is not part of the GNU Project, it has been combined with GNU tools to create a complete operating system, hence the term **GNU/Linux**. GNU tools played a crucial role in the early development of Linux.

As we have seen, Linux was not born without taking inspiration from what existed at the time, but *Linus Torvald*, its creator, knew how to create a monolithic kernel taking the advantages of one and leaving the disadvantages of others. Linux can therefore be considered an amalgamation of concepts that already in the 70s/80s, were considered avant-garde and modern. Unlike Minix, the following figure clearly shows the movement of a large part of the controllers in the kernel address space:

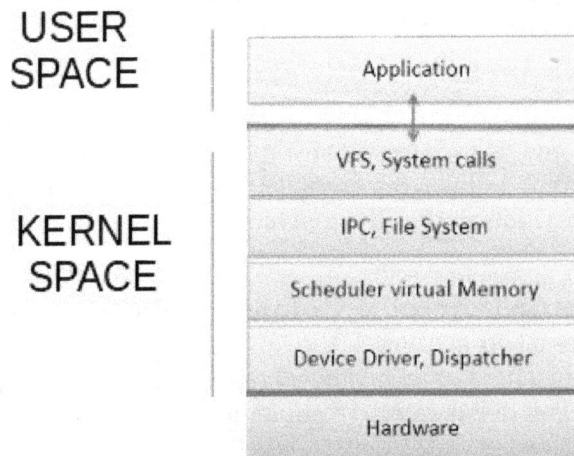

Figure 1.6: Architecture of a monolithic kernel architecture of a monolithic kernel as Linux has become

Linus Torvalds was influenced by the concept of open source and code sharing. It has chosen to release its kernel source code under the **GNU General Public License (GPL)**, which encourages collaboration and contributions from developers around the world.

These inspirations led to the creation of the Linux kernel, which was developed with open-source principles, modularity, and efficiency in mind. It is built on best practices from existing UNIX systems while introducing continuous innovation and improvement.

Linux kernel history

Once upon a time, there was a project called Linux that started at the *University of Helsinki* in 1991 as a personal project born out of Finnish *Linus Torvald's* thesis to create a new monolithic free operating system kernel.

He wrote the program specifically for the hardware he was using and independently of an operating system because he wanted to use the functions of his new PC equipped with an 80386 processor. Development was carried out on MINIX using the GNU C compiler.

The resulting Linux kernel has been marked by steady growth throughout its history from its initial release of its source code in 1991, it has grown from a small number of licensed C files prohibiting commercial distribution to the version 4.15 in 2018 with more than 23.3 million lines of source code, not including comments, under the GNUv2 label.

In April 1991, *Linus Torvalds*, then a 21-year-old computer science student at the University of Helsinki, Finland, started working on some simple ideas for a UNIX-inspired operating system for a personal computer. It all started with an Intel 80386 assembly language task switcher and terminal driver.

On July 3, 1991, in an effort to implement UNIX system calls in his project, *Linus Torvalds* attempted to obtain a digital copy of the POSIX standards documentation by submitting a request to the `comp.os.minix` newsgroup. However, he was unable to find this documentation, so he first resorted to determining system calls from university-owned SunOS documentation for use in operating his *Sun Microsystems* server. He also learned some system calls from Tenenbaum's MINIX text, which was part of the Unix course.

On August 25, 1991, Torvalds posted the following to `comp.os.minix`, a Usenet newsgroup. Here is what *Linux Torvald* posted on this date on the forum:

Hello everybody out there using minix -

I'm doing a (free) operating system (just a hobby, won't be big and professional like gnu) for 386(486) AT clones. This has been brewing since april, and is starting to get ready. I'd like any feedback on things people like/dislike in minix, as my OS resembles it somewhat (same physical layout of the file-system (due to practical reasons) among other things).

I've currently ported bash (1.08) and gcc (1.40), and things seem to work. This implies that I'll get something practical within a few months, and I'd like to know

> *what features most people would want. Any suggestions are welcome, but I won't promise I'll implement them.*

> *And yes - it's free of any minix code, and it has a multi-threaded fs. It is NOT portable (uses 386 task switching etc), and it probably never will support anything other than AT-harddisks, as that's all I have.*

> —Linus Torvalds

On September 17, 1991, *Torvalds* released Linux version 0.01 and installed the **ftp.funet. fi**–FTP server of the **Finnish University and Research Network** (**FUNET**). It was not executable since its code needed Minix to compile and test it.

On October 5, 1991, *Torvalds* announced the first **official** version of Linux, version 0.02. At this point, Linux was able to run Bash, GCC, and a few other GNU utilities:

> *[As] I mentioned a month ago, I'm working on a free version of a Minix-lookalike for AT-386 computers. It has finally reached the stage where it's even usable (though may not be depending on what you want), and I am willing to put out the sources for wider distribution. It is just version 0.02...but I've successfully run bash, gcc, gnu-make, gnu-sed, compress, etc. under it.*

```
79      void main(void)          /* This really IS void, no error here. */
80      {                        /* The startup routine assumes (well, ...) this */
81      /*
82       * Interrupts are still disabled. Do necessary setups, then
83       * enable them
84       */
85              time_init();
86              tty_init();
87              trap_init();
88              sched_init();
89              buffer_init();
90              hd_init();
91              sti();
92              move_to_user_mode();
93              if (!fork()) {          /* we count on this going ok */
94                      init();
95              }
96      /*
97       *  NOTE!!   For any other task 'pause()' would mean we have to get a
98       * signal to awaken, but task0 is the sole exception (see 'schedule()')
99       * as task 0 gets activated at every idle moment (when no other tasks
100      * can run). For task0 'pause()' just means we go check if some other
101      * task can run, and if not we return here.
102      */
103             for(;;) pause();
104     }
```

Figure 1.7: The main function in the Linux 0.0.1 source code

Despite the limited features of the first versions, Linux quickly won the hearts of developers and users. Many people have contributed to the code for the project, including some developers from the MINIX community.

For version 0, Linux indicated that it was primarily intended for testing and not for productive use. Version 0.11, released in December 1991, was the first self-hosted Linux because it could be compiled by a computer running the same kernel.

According to *Torvald*, Linux began to gain prominence in 1992 after the X Window System was ported to Linux by *Orest Zborowski*, which allowed Linux to support a GUI for the first time. Having remained a system usable on the command line for a long time, like the MS-DOS system had been in its time, X Windows was finally able to give the Linux system a graphical interface, which made it possible to popularize it:

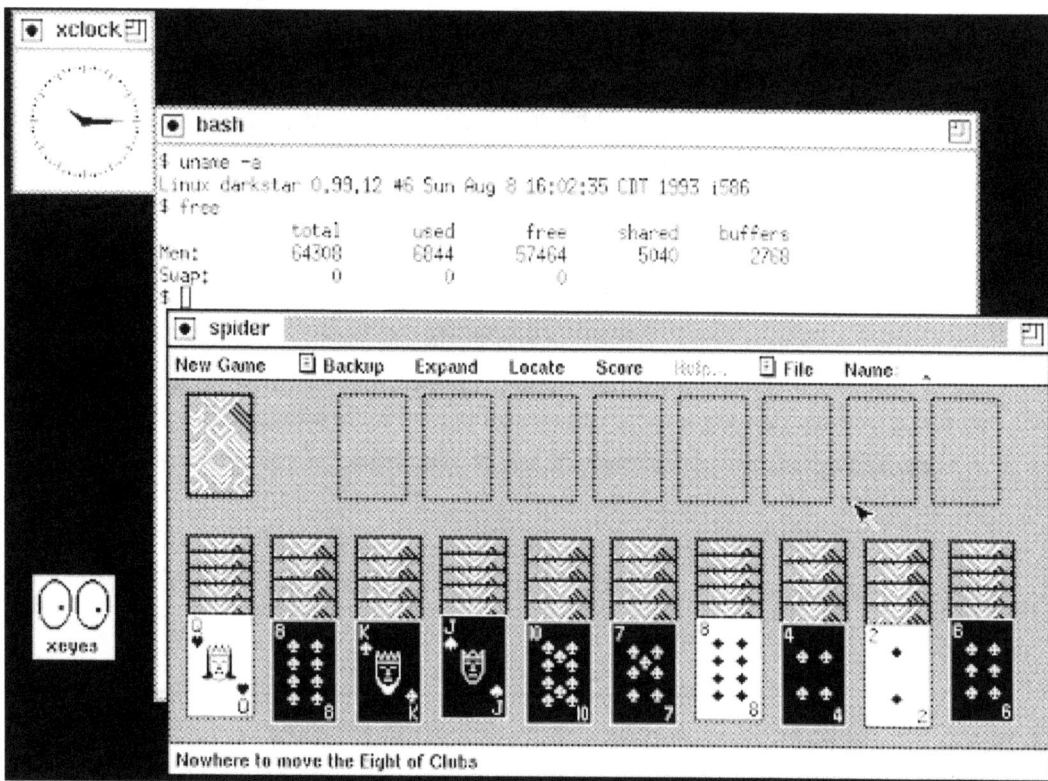

Figure 1.8: *An early version of Slackware with Linux kernel 0.99 and the X Window System*

It was from there that the Linux adventure began, giving life to an ever-increasing number of distributions which, as we saw with the chronology of Unix versions, were inspired by each other. to give the best of what we can have today.

Linux now appears (as shown in *Figure 1.9* in green) among the biggest names in *nix:

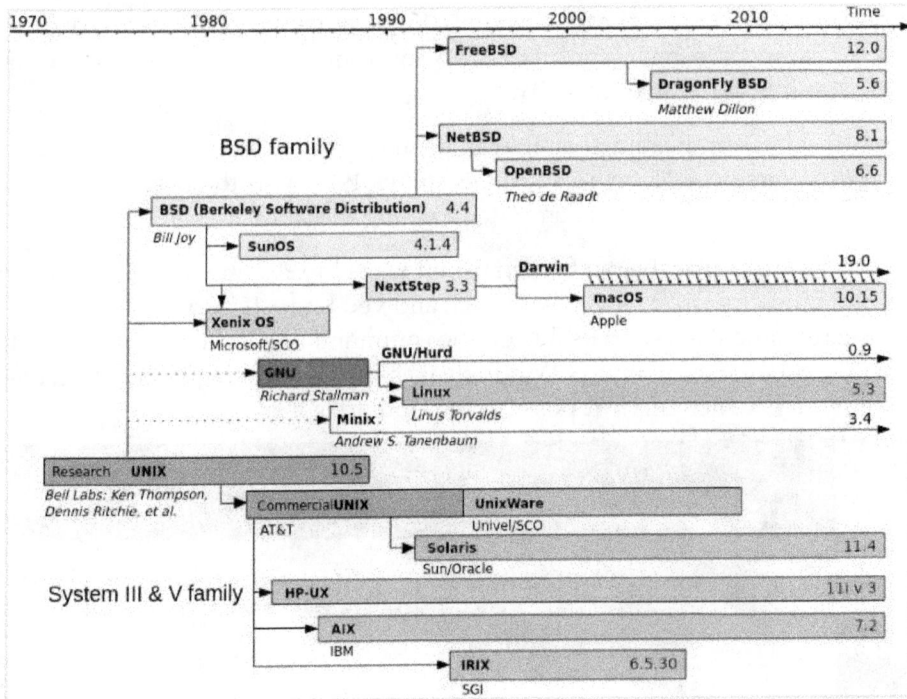

Figure 1.9: *The Unix family tree*
Source: *wikimedia.org*

It was also an adventure among the different distributions that we can meet today. Some had their day and they now no longer exist; others still persist to this day, as shown in the figure:

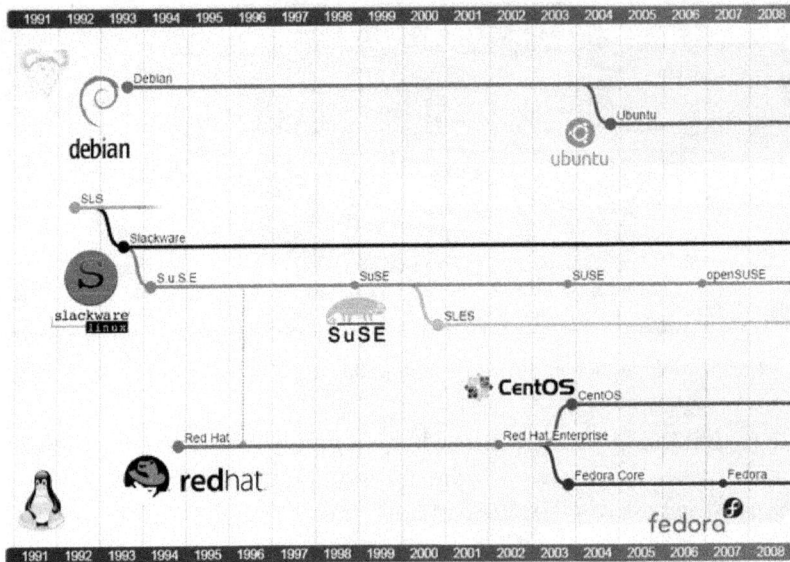

Figure 1.10: *The Linux distribution*
Source: *http://futurist.se/gldt/*

Evolutions of the several features by release/ milestones

It is important to keep in mind the different stages of the development of the Linux kernel in terms of functionalities because this allows you to know how it has evolved over time. In the following sections, we will see in detail the important points of each release that the Linux kernel has experienced.

Early development (1991-1993)

Notable developments are:

- **1991**: Linus Torvalds announces the Linux project.
- **1992**: The first public release, Linux 0.01, supports only the Intel 386 processor.
- **1993**: Linux 0.99.1 is released under the GNU GPL, marking the official open-source nature of the project.

Early versions of the GNU/Linux kernel, such as Linux 0.01 and Linux 0.99, were quite minimal and had limited functionality compared to later versions. These early releases were more like proof-of-concept releases and focused primarily on providing essential features for a basic operating system. Some key features of these early Linux kernel releases include:

- **Basic hardware support**: These early versions had rudimentary support for the Intel 386 processor architecture. The focus was on getting the kernel to run on this hardware platform.
- **Multitasking**: Linux 0.01 introduced basic multitasking capabilities, allowing multiple processes to run concurrently.
- **Memory management**: These early versions included basic memory management, such as paging and memory allocation for processes. However, it was far from the advanced memory management seen in later versions.
- **File system**: A simple filesystem was implemented for file storage, but it lacked the rich filesystem support found in later versions.
- **Shell and basic utilities**: Linux 0.01 included a simple shell and a few basic utilities to interact with the system.
- **No networking**: Networking support was absent in these early versions. It was added gradually in subsequent releases.
- **No modules**: The concept of loadable kernel modules, which allows for dynamic kernel extension, was not present in these early versions.

Early versions of the Linux kernel were very limited in terms of features and hardware support. They were primarily created as a hobby project by *Linus Torvalds*, and their simplicity was intentional to keep development manageable. Later versions of the Linux kernel added many features, expanded hardware support, and improved performance, making Linux a versatile and powerful operating system.

Kernel version 1.0 (1994)

In 1994, Linux 1.0 was released, signifying stability and maturity, and although it did not introduce any specific revolutionary features, it marked an important milestone in the development of the Linux kernel.

Linux 1.0 had seen several earlier releases and incremental improvements, and by the time version 1.0 was released, it had achieved a level of reliability and robustness that made it suitable for a wider range of applications. Its stability and maturity were essential in gaining the trust of users and the broader software community.

The release of version 1.0 also signaled that Linux was a viable and stable alternative to proprietary Unix-like operating systems. It has attracted more attention from developers, businesses, and organizations, which has contributed to the rapid growth of the Linux ecosystem and its adoption in various fields.

Kernel version 2.0 (1996)

In 1996, Linux 2.0 was released, introducing better hardware support and improved performance. This release marked a crucial step forward in making Linux a more robust and versatile operating system. Some of the key features and advancements in Linux 2.0 included:

- **Enhanced hardware support**: Linux 2.0 added support for a broader range of hardware platforms and devices, making it more accessible for a variety of computer systems.

- **Symmetric Multiprocessing (SMP)**: SMP support was introduced, allowing Linux to run on multiprocessor systems. This feature significantly improved system scalability and performance on machines with multiple CPUs.

- **Improved networking**: Linux 2.0 included enhanced networking capabilities, making it suitable for server applications. Features like TCP/IP stack improvements, support for more network devices, and better network performance were integrated.

- **Better memory management**: The memory management subsystem was enhanced, providing better utilization of system memory and improved performance.

- **Virtual file system (VFS)**: The introduction of the VFS layer allowed for greater filesystem flexibility and easier integration of various filesystem types, such as ext2, NFS, and more.

- **Expanded filesystem support**: Support for additional filesystems was added, including **Second Extended File System (ext2)**, which became the default filesystem for Linux.

- **Increased system stability**: Linux 2.0 brought increased system stability and reliability, making it suitable for a wider range of production environments.

- **Improved kernel modules**: Kernel modules, a way to dynamically load and unload kernel components, were introduced. This allowed for easier expansion of kernel functionality without the need for recompilation.

- **Broader software compatibility**: The improved hardware support and stability of Linux 2.0 made it more compatible with a wider range of software applications, attracting more developers and users.

Overall, Linux 2.0 was a significant step forward in the development of the Linux kernel, expanding its capabilities and making it a more mature and reliable choice for servers and desktops. This release laid the foundation for the continued growth and popularity of the Linux operating system.

Kernel version 2.2 (1999)

In 1999, Linux 2.2 was released, enhancing stability, performance, and hardware support. This version marked a substantial improvement over its predecessor and made Linux more suitable for a wider range of applications. Some of the key features and advancements in Linux 2.2 include:

- **Stability and bug fixes**: Linux 2.2 included numerous bug fixes and stability improvements, addressing issues present in earlier versions. This contributed to a more reliable and robust operating system.

- **Enhanced hardware support**: Continued expansion of hardware support, including better compatibility with a variety of processors, chipsets, and peripheral devices.

- **Improved networking**: Further enhancements to networking capabilities, including support for more network devices and protocols, as well as better performance and scalability for network-intensive applications.

- **Advanced filesystems**: Introduction of features like the journaling file system (ext3) as an option, improving filesystem robustness and recovery in case of system crashes or power failures.

- **Kernel preemption**: Kernel preemption support was introduced, allowing for more responsive system behavior and real-time application support.

- **USB support**: Initial support for **Universal Serial Bus (USB)** devices, laying the groundwork for broader USB support in later versions.

- **Improved scalability**: Performance improvements and optimizations that made Linux more scalable for larger and more complex workloads, making it suitable for enterprise environments.

- **PCMCIA support**: It provides better support for **Personal Computer Memory Card International Association** (**PCMCIA**) devices, commonly used in laptops and other portable systems.

- **Memory management enhancements**: Further refinements to memory management, including improvements in memory allocation and utilization.

- **Kernel module enhancements**: Ongoing development of the kernel module system for dynamically loading and unloading kernel components.

Linux 2.2 was a crucial release that solidified Linux's reputation as a stable, high-performance operating system for a wide range of applications. Its improved hardware support, improved performance, and increased stability have attracted more users and developers to the Linux ecosystem. This release also served as a springboard for future developments of the Linux kernel.

Kernel version 2.4 (2001)

In 2001, Linux 2.4 was released with significant improvements in memory management and file system support. This release introduced several key features and improvements that made Linux more suitable for a wide range of applications. Some of the key features of Linux 2.4 included:

- **Advanced memory management**: Linux 2.4 introduced substantial improvements in memory management, including better support for large amounts of RAM and improved virtual memory handling. These enhancements made Linux more capable of handling memory-intensive tasks.

- **Extensible page tables (high memory support)**: This version introduced the concept of extensible page tables, also known as **high memory support**, which allowed Linux to address more than 1 GB of physical memory on 32-bit systems.

- **Improved SMP Scalability**: Further enhancements to **Symmetric Multiprocessing** (**SMP**) support, making Linux 2.4 more scalable and efficient on multi-CPU systems.

- **Enhanced filesystem support**: Introduction of journaling filesystems, including ext3, which provided improved data integrity and faster filesystem recovery after system crashes or power failures. XFS and ReiserFS were also supported as optional filesystems.

- **Improved networking stack**: Enhancements to the networking stack, including support for larger numbers of network devices, better IPv6 support, and improved network performance.

- **Firewall and IP filtering**: Introduction of the Netfilter framework, which allowed for the implementation of powerful firewall and IP packet filtering capabilities, enabling administrators to secure their systems more effectively.

- **USB support**: Continued development of USB support, making it more robust and extending compatibility with a wider range of USB devices.

- **Enhanced driver support**: Additional device drivers and hardware support, making Linux compatible with a broader array of hardware components.

- **Improved performance**: Numerous performance optimizations and efficiency improvements throughout the kernel, resulting in faster system operation and response times.

- **Kernel preemption**: Further refinements to kernel preemption, allowing for more responsive behavior and real-time application support.

Linux 2.4 was an important release that solidified Linux's position as a mature and capable operating system, particularly for server and enterprise environments. Its improved memory management, file system improvements, and networking improvements have contributed to its widespread adoption in a variety of computing scenarios.

Kernel version 2.6 (2003)

In 2003, Linux 2.6 was released, bringing substantial performance and resource management enhancements. The main feature of Linux 2.6 was the emphasis on scalability, performance, and improved support for various hardware platforms. Some of the key features of this release included:

- **Improved scalability**: Linux 2.6 included numerous enhancements to improve its scalability on multi-processor systems and larger server configurations. These improvements allowed Linux to handle more concurrent users and processes efficiently.

- **New I/O schedulers**: This version introduced several I/O schedulers, including the **Completely Fair Scheduler** (**CFS**) and the anticipatory scheduler. These schedulers improved disk I/O performance and responsiveness.

- **Enhanced power management**: Linux 2.6 featured better support for advanced power management features, making it more suitable for laptops and mobile devices. **Advanced Configuration and Power Interface** (**ACPI**) support was enhanced, enabling improved power management.

- **Udev**: The introduction of udev simplified device management and made it easier to handle dynamically detected hardware devices.

- **Kernel-based asynchronous I/O**: This feature allowed asynchronous I/O operations directly within the kernel, improving performance for I/O-bound applications.

- **Kernel preemption**: Further improvements to kernel preemption and real-time support made Linux 2.6 more responsive and suitable for real-time and high-performance computing applications.

- **Large file support**: Increased support for very large files, addressing the needs of enterprise and scientific computing.

- **Security enhancements**: Security features like **Security-Enhanced Linux (SELinux)** and capabilities-based security were introduced, enhancing the overall security of the Linux system.

- **Inotify**: The introduction of inotify provided a mechanism for monitoring changes to files and directories, making it useful for various applications like file synchronization and monitoring.

- **IPv6 improvements**: Linux 2.6 continued to improve IPv6 support, reflecting the increasing importance of the IPv6 protocol.

- **New filesystems**: The introduction of new filesystems, such as JFS, XFS, and the introduction of the **Extended 4 (ext4)** filesystem, which brought significant improvements in scalability, performance, and robustness to the Linux filesystem stack.

- **Enhanced networking**: Ongoing improvements to networking, including better network stack performance, **quality of service (QoS)** support, and enhanced protocol support.

Overall, Linux 2.6 was a major step in the development of the Linux kernel, making it more adaptable, scalable, and performance-oriented for a wide range of computing environments, from desktops to servers and embedded systems.

Kernel version 3.0 (2011)

Linux 3.0 is released, mainly for version numbering simplification; it does not introduce major technical changes. The main feature of the GNU/Linux kernel version 3.0, released in 2011, was primarily a change in version numbering rather than the introduction of revolutionary features or architectural changes. It is important to note that Linux 3.0 did not introduce any significant new technical features or changes to core kernel functionality compared to Linux 2.x versions. Instead, the version number change was largely symbolic, intended to simplify the numbering system. Here are some key points about Linux 3.0:

- **Version numbering simplification**: The primary reason for transitioning from the 2.x series (for example, Linux 2.6.x) to version 3.0 was to simplify the version numbering system. The kernel maintainers decided to increment the major version number to reflect the kernel's maturity and stability rather than introduce major architectural changes. Functionally, Linux 3.0 was very similar to Linux 2.6.x.

- **Stability and incremental improvements**: While the major version number changed, Linux 3.0 continued to receive incremental improvements in various areas, including performance enhancements, driver updates, and bug fixes. These improvements contributed to the overall stability and reliability of the kernel.

- **Symbolic change**: The version number change served as a symbolic gesture to acknowledge the kernel's maturity and the fact that it had evolved significantly since the days of Linux 1.0. However, it did not represent a major shift in kernel development or architecture.

- **Continued development**: Despite the version number change, Linux development continued as usual, with subsequent releases (for example, Linux 3.1, 3.2, etc.) introducing new features and improvements in a gradual and evolutionary manner.

In summary, Linux 3.0 was primarily a change in version numbering to reflect the maturity of the kernel rather than the introduction of a specific revolutionary feature. It continues the tradition of continuous development and refinement of the Linux kernel, with improvements in performance, hardware support, and overall stability. Later versions build on this foundation with new features and improvements.

Kernel version 4.0 (2015)

Linux 4.0 is released, focusing on performance and stability improvements. Released in 2015, it was not a single revolutionary feature, but rather a series of incremental improvements, bug fixes, and optimizations aimed at improving overall performance, stability, and support. Kernel hardware. Some notable aspects of Linux 4.0 include:

- **Kernel Mode Setting (KMS)**: While not introduced in version 4.0, this version marked a milestone in Linux graphics with the widespread adoption of **Kernel Mode Setting (KMS)**. KMS improved graphics support, including better display resolution management and enhanced graphics hardware support.

- **Improved hardware support**: Linux 4.0 continued to expand its support for new hardware components, including support for more processors, chipsets, graphics cards, and peripherals.

- **Kernel live patching**: Kernel live patching support was introduced in this version, allowing critical security patches to be applied to a running kernel without requiring a system reboot. This was a significant advancement in system uptime and security.

- **Intel's Skylake architecture support**: Enhanced support for Intel's Skylake microarchitecture, providing better compatibility and performance for systems using Skylake processors.

- **Faster filesystem mounting**: Improved filesystem mounting performance, particularly for filesystems like Btrfs and NFS, which resulted in faster system boot times and overall responsiveness.

- **Improved power management**: Power management features continued to evolve, improving energy efficiency for laptops and mobile devices.

- **New hardware drivers**: Addition of new hardware drivers for better support of various devices and peripherals.

- **Performance optimizations**: General performance optimizations and enhancements throughout the kernel codebase.

- **Security patches**: Continued efforts to address security vulnerabilities and improve system security, including the mitigation of vulnerabilities like Spectre and Meltdown.

It is important to note that Linux kernel development follows an incremental approach, with each release building on the foundations of the previous release. Although Linux 4.0 did not introduce a single major feature, it contributed to the overall stability, performance, and hardware compatibility of the Linux kernel, making it a solid choice for a wide range of computing environments. Subsequent kernel versions continued to add new features and improvements.

Kernel version 5.0 (September 2021)

The Linux kernel 5 introduced several important features and improvements. Please note that there may have been later versions with additional features and improvements beyond what we can provide here. Here are some of the main features and improvements of the Linux 5 Kernel:

- **Faster performance**: Kernel 5 introduced various performance improvements, including reduced latency and better resource utilization, making it more efficient for both desktop and server workloads.

- **Improved hardware support**: Kernel 5 included support for new hardware components and platforms, such as AMD Navi GPUs, Intel Icelake CPUs, and Raspberry Pi 4. It also improved support for existing hardware.

- **Security enhancements**: The kernel continued to receive security enhancements to protect against various vulnerabilities and threats. This includes improvements in mitigating Spectre and Meltdown vulnerabilities.

- **I/O improvements**: The introduction of I/O optimizations, such as the `io_uring` interface, improved disk and network I/O performance.

- **Real-time preemption**: Real-time preemption patches were merged into the mainline kernel, making it more suitable for real-time and low-latency applications.

- **File system updates**: The **ext4** file system received several improvements and optimizations. Btrfs, XFS, and other file systems also received updates and bug fixes.

- **Graphics and GPU support**: Linux kernel 5 brought support for new AMD and Intel GPUs. There were also improvements in the open-source Nouveau driver for NVIDIA GPUs.

- **Energy efficiency**: Kernel 5 included various power management enhancements to improve energy efficiency on laptops and other devices.

- **Wireless and networking**: Improvements were made to the networking stack, including support for new wireless chipsets and enhanced network performance.

- **Improved hardware monitoring**: The kernel added support for new sensors and hardware monitoring features, making it easier for system administrators to monitor and manage hardware health.

- **Security and hardening**: Ongoing work in the kernel focused on improving security through features like **Kernel Address Space Layout Randomization** (**KASLR**) and other hardening measures.

- **New system calls and APIs**: Kernel 5 introduced new system calls and APIs, enabling developers to create more sophisticated applications and services.

Kernel version 6.0 (October 2022)

On October 2, 2022, Linus Torvalds announced Linux 6.0 as an update with many changes, especially regarding the number of commits. Although he clarified that a change in major version number does not necessarily result in major fundamental changes:

> *So, as it is hopefully clear to everybody, the major version number change is more about me running out of fingers and toes than it is about any big fundamental changes.*

> *But of course, there's are various changes in 6.0 — we've got over 15k non-merge commits in there in total, after all, and as such 6.0 is one of the bigger releases at least in numbers of commits in a while.*

> — *Linus Torvalds*

Here are some of the new features and improvements included in the Linux 6.0 kernel:

- Support for Intel's 4th generation Xeon Sapphire Rapids processors and 13th generation Raptor Lake core chips.

- PCI support for the OpenRISC and LoongArch architecture.

- Intel SGX2 support.

- Qualcomm Snapdragon 8xc Gen3 support.

- AMD temperature monitoring for upcoming AMD CPUs.

- Scheduler changes, including improved NUMA balancing for AMD Zen.

- Support for NVMe in-band authentication.

- The RISC-V architecture includes a new default configuration capable of running Docker from the start.

- Several runtime verifications.

- The ext4 filesystem supports new `ioctl()` operations: `EXT4_IOC_GETFSUUID` and `EXT4_IC_SETFSUUID`.

- Raspberry Pi V3D kernel driver support for Raspberry Pi 4.

- Better energy utilization thanks to the removal of the energy-margin heuristics that limited process migration across CPUs.

Since kernel version 6.1, in December 2022, it became the first language other than C and assembly to be supported in the development of the Linux kernel.

To have more details on the different supports added in the Linux kernel, there is a summary by commit on this website **https://Kernelnewbies.org/LinuxChanges**.

License of the GNU/Linux

Initially, *Torvalds* released Linux under a license that prohibited any commercial use.

This was changed in version 0.12 following a move to the GNU General Public License version 2 (GPLv2). This license authorizes the distribution and sale of possibly modified and unmodified versions of Linux but requires that all such copies be released under the same license and be accompanied, or, upon request, in open access, with the complete corresponding source code. *Torvalds* described licensing Linux under GPLv2 as, *the best thing I've ever done*.

The Linux kernel is explicitly licensed under the GNU General Public License version 2 only (GPL-2.0 only) with an explicit system call exception (`linux-syscall-note`), without offering the licensee the option to choose a later version. Contributed code must be available under a GPL compatible license.

GNU General Public License version 2 (GPL-2.0) is a widely used open-source software license that was developed by the **Free Software Foundation (FSF)**. Here is a short summary of its key points:

- **Distribution and modification**: The GPL-2.0 allows anyone to use, modify, and distribute software covered by the license. You have the freedom to modify the code to suit your needs and share those modifications.

- **Copyleft**: GPL-2.0 is a copyleft license, which means that if you distribute a modified version of the software, you must also make the modified source code available to others under the same GPL-2.0 terms. In other words, it ensures that the software and its derivatives remain open source.

- **Commercial use**: You can use GPL-2.0-licensed software for commercial purposes. There are no restrictions on charging for distribution, support, or services related to the software.

- **Attribution**: When you distribute GPL-2.0-licensed software or its derivatives, you must retain the original copyright notices, disclaimers, and a copy of the GPL-2.0 license itself.

- **Compatibility**: GPL-2.0 is not compatible with some other open-source licenses, particularly those with more permissive terms. When you combine GPL-2.0-licensed code with code under incompatible licenses, the resulting work must be licensed entirely under the terms of the GPL-2.0.

- **No warranty**: The GPL-2.0 includes a disclaimer that states the software is provided **as is** without any warranties. Users and distributors are responsible for any risks associated with their use.

- **Termination**: If you violate the terms of the GPL-2.0, your rights to use and distribute the software can be terminated. However, you can regain those rights by coming into compliance with the license.

It is important to note that GPL-2.0 is a legal document, and its terms are legally binding. Developers and organizations using or distributing software under this License should read and understand its provisions carefully to ensure compliance with its requirements. Additionally, GPL-2.0 has been widely used in the open-source community, contributing to the growth of free and open-source software.

For more information about the licence GPLv2 only, you may access **https://spdx.org/licenses/GPL-2.0-only.html**.

There has been considerable debate about how easily the license could be changed to use later GPL versions (including version 3), and whether this change is even desirable. Torvalds himself specifically stated when releasing version 2.4.0 that his own code is only released under version 2. However, the terms of the GPL state that if no version is specified, then no version can be used, and Alan Cox pointed out that very few other Linux contributors have specified a particular version of the GPL.

In September 2006, a survey of 29 key kernel programmers indicated that 28 of them preferred GPLv2 to the current version of GPLv3. Torvalds commented, *I think a number of outsiders...thought that personally I was just a weird guy because I was not publicly a big fan of GPLv3*. This group of top kernel developers, including Torvalds, Greg Kroah-Hartman, and Andrew Morton, commented in the media on their objections to GPLv3. They referenced clauses regarding DRM/tivoization, patents, **additional restrictions,** and warned against balkanization of the **Open-Source Universe** by the GPLv3. *Linus Torvalds*, who decided not to adopt GPLv3 for the Linux kernel, reiterated his criticism even years later.

Conclusion

In this first chapter, we were able to see the historical context of the creation of the Linux kernel, which was able to become a complete distribution with the tools of the GNU Project. We were also able to see the influences of the technologies of the time, which pushed the developments, the innovations to circumvent the constraints and to adopt the positive points to give in the end the system as we know it today.

In the next chapter, we will go into detail about the structure of the Linux system, but especially the kernel itself, which is the initial goal of this book.

We are ready to take the next train that will take us to the inner universe of the Linux kernel.

Join our book's Discord space

Join the book's Discord Workspace for Latest updates, Offers, Tech happenings around the world, New Release and Sessions with the Authors:

https://discord.bpbonline.com

CHAPTER 2
Introduction to the Linux Kernel

Introduction

This chapter will present the internal structure of the Linux kernel architecture and will guide us to a first experience by first retrieving the code sources, defining the configuration of the modules to be built, building the kernel itself, and then finally, its execution using a QEMU virtual machine.

Structure

This chapter covers the following topics:

- Preparing the work environment
- Introduction to the kernel
- Downloading the GNU/Linux kernel sources to recompile them
- Downloading official tarball from kernel.org
- Configuring a custom kernel and modules
- Building your own kernel
- Installation
- Execution and boot sequence
- Coding styles

Objectives

By the end of this chapter, you will be able to understand the structuring of the GNU/Linux kernel tree as well as the workflow for generating a Linux kernel, which will then allow us to begin the actual development of the drivers.

Preparing the work environment

To be in line with the rest of the commands, all of the commands cited in this book have been validated on a Linux distribution, Ubuntu 22.04.3 X86_64 LTS. However, with sometimes a few adaptations, the whole thing will be transposable without problem to all Linux distributions.

Several useful packages will, therefore, need to be installed for the rest of this chapter:

```
$ sudo apt install git build-essential curl qemu-system-gui qemu-system-utils
qemu-system-x86 gnupg2 bison flex libncurses5-dev libglade2-dev libglade2-0
libgtk2.0-0 libgtk2.0-dev libglib2.0-0 libglib2.0-dev
```

This book focuses on the GNU/Linux kernel; we will inspect it step by step throughout the chapters. However, we will need a Linux system (often called **rootfs** for the **userspace** part), which will allow us to validate a kernel across the board.

For that purpose, we will generate an archive in **ext2** format using the Buildroot project (**https://buildroot.org**) often used in the embedded world.

The following are the project sources on the default branch (master/HEAD):

```
$ git clone --depth 1 https://git.busybox.net/buildroot/ && cd buildroot/
Cloning into 'buildroot'...
remote: Enumerating objects: 17248, done.
remote: Counting objects: 100% (17248/17248), done.
remote: Compressing objects: 100% (16360/16360), done.
remote: Total 17248 (delta 888), reused 11876 (delta 446), pack-reused 0
Receiving objects: 100% (17248/17248), 7.96 MiB | 8.20 MiB/s, done.
Resolving deltas: 100% (888/888), done.

$ git branch
* master

$ git log
commit d797ecc6f026e1f0af17f91df33e8cd44731a97f (grafted, HEAD -> master,
origin/master, origin/HEAD)
Author: Thomas Petazzoni <thomas.petazzoni@bootlin.com>
(...)
```

Next, we will have to define a **rootfs** configuration, a sort of identity card for the build that will indicate what will be included and how it should be built. We can inject the following configuration. You define a configuration adapt for the **x86_64** architecture:

```
$ nano   .config
# Select a target architecture (e.g., x86_64)
BR2_x86_64=y
# Set the system hostname
BR2_TARGET_GENERIC_HOSTNAME="bpb"
# Configure the root filesystem (initramfs)
BR2_TARGET_ROOTFS_INITRAMFS=y


# Skip the Linux kernel build (since you don't want to build a kernel)
BR2_LINUX_KERNEL=n
# select ext2 for the target image
BR2_TARGET_ROOTFS_EXT2=y
BR2_TARGET_ROOTFS_EXT2_2=y
BR2_TARGET_ROOTFS_EXT2_2r1=y
BR2_TARGET_ROOTFS_EXT2_GEN=2
BR2_TARGET_ROOTFS_EXT2_REV=1
BR2_TARGET_ROOTFS_EXT2_LABEL="rootfs"
BR2_TARGET_ROOTFS_EXT2_SIZE="250M"
BR2_TARGET_ROOTFS_EXT2_INODES=0
BR2_TARGET_ROOTFS_EXT2_INODE_SIZE=256
BR2_TARGET_ROOTFS_EXT2_RESBLKS=5
BR2_TARGET_ROOTFS_EXT2_MKFS_OPTIONS="-O ^64bit"
BR2_TARGET_ROOTFS_EXT2_NONE=y
```

In Buildroot, a **defconfig** (short for default configuration) refers to a configuration file that specifies the default settings and options for building a root filesystem and cross-compilation environment for an embedded Linux system. The **defconfig** file contains a set of configuration parameters, such as which packages to include, kernel options, target architecture settings, and more.

```
$ make defconfig
```

The configuration should be something like this:

```
$ cat .config | grep -v "#" | grep -v '^$'
(...)
BR2_HAVE_DOT_CONFIG=y
BR2_HOST_GCC_AT_LEAST_4_9=y
```

```
BR2_HOST_GCC_AT_LEAST_5=y
BR2_HOST_GCC_AT_LEAST_6=y
BR2_HOST_GCC_AT_LEAST_7=y
BR2_HOST_GCC_AT_LEAST_8=y
BR2_HOST_GCC_AT_LEAST_9=y
BR2_USE_MMU=y
BR2_i386=y
BR2_ARCH_HAS_TOOLCHAIN_BUILDROOT=y
BR2_ARCH="i686"
BR2_NORMALIZED_ARCH="i386"
BR2_ENDIAN="LITTLE"
BR2_GCC_TARGET_ARCH="i686"
BR2_BINFMT_SUPPORTS_SHARED=y
BR2_READELF_ARCH_NAME="Intel 80386"
BR2_x86_i686=y
(...)
```

If you want to customize the final **rootfs** by adding more tools, you can launch the n-curse configurator:

```
$ make menuconfig
```

Next comes the generation step. The estimated time for construction will depend on the power of your computer, but also on the bandwidth of your internet connection. However, on a modern model and a fiber optic internet connection, it will take around 30 minutes or more:

```
$ time make
make 5540,18s user 583,48s system 308% cpu 33:07,71 total
```

In the end, we, therefore, have a **rootfs** in several formats:

```
$ ls -alh output/images
total 12M
drwxr-xr-x 2 tgayet tgayet 4,0K sept. 30 22:01 .
drwxrwxr-x 6 tgayet tgayet 4,0K sept. 30 21:53 ..
-rw-r--r-- 1 tgayet tgayet  60M sept. 30 22:01 rootfs.ext2
-rw-r--r-- 1 tgayet tgayet 4,2M sept. 30 22:01 rootfs.tar
```

It is still great to get a complete Linux system with just a size of 60 Megabytes, which explains why the Buildroot and Yocto builds are used in the embedded world.

The **Filesystem Hierarchy Standard** (**FHS**) is a set of guidelines and conventions that specify the directory structure and organization of files and directories on a Linux system.

The following figure shows us the hierarchical detail of the structure of a file system of a Linux distribution:

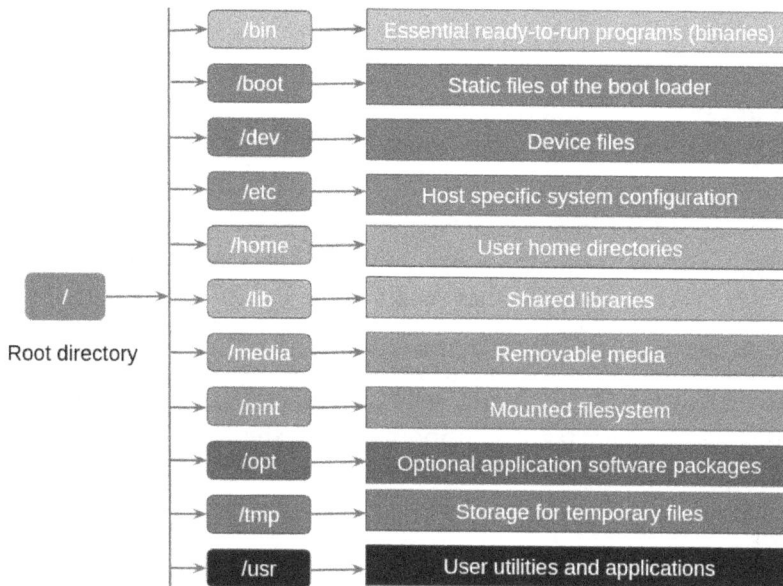

Figure 2.1: *The Filesystem Hierarchy Standard*

The FHS is not a formal standard, but it is widely adopted by Linux distributions to ensure consistency and compatibility between different distributions. This is because the **/boot** directory contains bootloader-related files that are necessary for system startup, such as Kernel **initrd** (initial RAM disk image), **vmlinuz** (Virtual Memory LINUx gZip—compressed Linux kernel executable) and **grub** (Grand Unified Bootloader).

Note: This is a vmlinuz and not a vmlinux, vmlinuz–LINUX virtual memory, uncompressed Linux kernel executable.

To test and validate our **rootfs**, we will use the kernel of our distribution:

```
$ ls -alh /boot | grep $(uname -r)
-rw-r--r--  1 root root 270K sept.  7 09:11 config-6.2.0-33-generic
lrwxrwxrwx  1 root root   27 sept. 19 13:30 initrd.img -> initrd.img-6.2.0-
33-generic
-rw-r--r--  1 root root  72M sept. 19 13:31 initrd.img-6.2.0-33-generic
-rw-------  1 root root 7,7M sept.  7 09:11 System.map-6.2.0-33-generic
lrwxrwxrwx  1 root root   24 sept. 19 13:30 vmlinuz -> vmlinuz-6.2.0-33-
generic
-rw-------  1 root root  14M sept.  7 10:18 vmlinuz-6.2.0-33-generic
```

The running kernel release is **6.2.0-33-generic** and it can be found using the **uname** command:

```
$ uname -r
```

```
6.2.0-33-generic
```

Thanks to **qemu**, we can test the kernel that we will generate, but we can do it now with our Linux distribution. For access reasons, we will first make a copy of the pre-built kernel in a temporary directory before testing it.

```
$ sudo cp /boot/vmlinuz-$(uname -r) /tmp/vmlinuz-$(uname -r)
```

```
$ sudo chmod 777 /tmp/vmlinuz-$(uname -r)
```

```
$ qemu-system-x86_64 -kernel /tmp/vmlinuz-$(uname -r) -hda  output/
images/rootfs.ext2 -nographic -append root="/dev/sda console=ttyS0" -net
nic,macaddr=00:11:22:33:44:55 -net user
```

Details of the arguments used with the **qemu** command:

- **-append**: Specifies kernel parameters. In this example, **root=/dev/hda** indicates that the root system uses a supported filesystem (**ext2**), and **console=ttyS0** specifies the serial console for the kernel traces.

- **-nographic**: Disable graphics output, which is useful for booting in text mode.

- **-net nic,macaddr=00:11:22:33:44:55**: Specifies the Mac address of the virtual network interface.

- **-net user**: Configures a user interface to access the virtual machine over the network.

The following figure shows the execution of the kernel of a distribution using the previously generated **rootfs**:

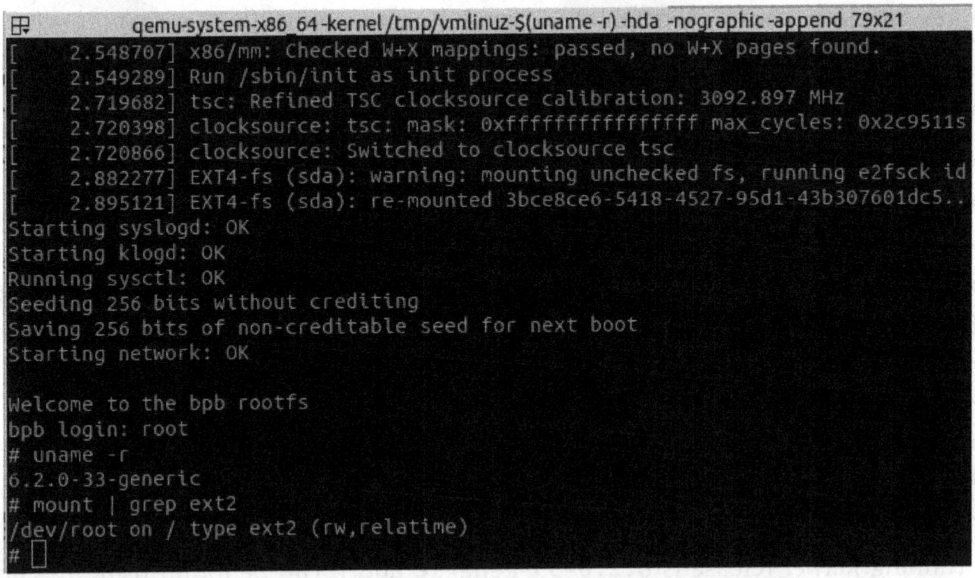

Figure 2.2: Testing the GNU/Linux kernel via qemu

We will use these **rootfs** as well as **qemu** to test the kernel that we will generate.

The login for this **rootfs** is root and does not have a password.

We can confirm that the version of the kernel used corresponds to that of the kernel of our distribution, **namely: 6.2.0-33-generic**. In addition, the **rootfs** are well mounted at the root **/** with the **ext2** file system.

Although we have detailed how to generate a custom **rootfs**, a ready-to-use **rootfs** (**rootfs.etx2**) can be downloaded from the GitHub associated with this book.

Note: The tool used for the configuration and the build is exactly the same as that used in the GNU/Linux kernel project.

Introduction to the kernel

As seen in *Chapter 1, History of the GNU/Linux Kernel*, the GNU/Linux kernel is a monolithic kernel that includes several layers and several modules and has seen its architecture evolve over time. Linux is a monolithic kernel with a modular, modern design (it can insert and remove loadable kernel modules at runtime), supporting most features previously available only in closed kernels of non-free operating systems.

The following figure shows us the architecture of the GNU/Linux kernel:

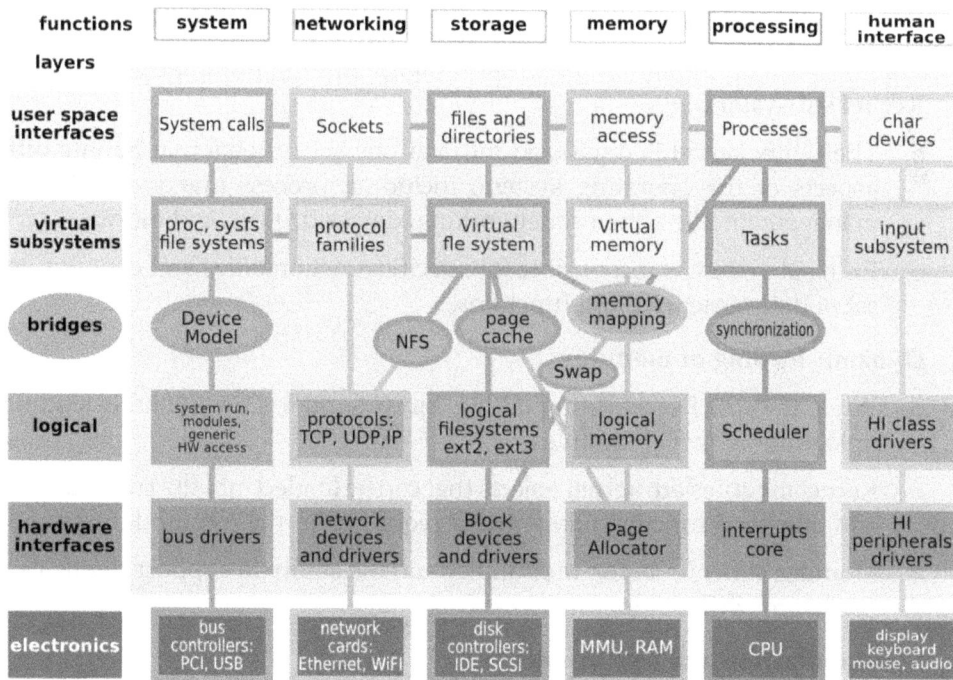

Figure 2.3: The Linux kernel architecture

Here are some technical characteristics of a GNU/Linux kernel:

- **Monolithic kernel architecture:**
  - The Linux kernel follows a monolithic architecture, where the entire operating system kernel runs as a single, privileged process in kernel space.
  - Kernel space is a protected part of memory that is inaccessible to user-space processes.
  - Simultaneous computation of multiple processes at once, each of which has one or more threads executing on SMP and NUMA.

- **Single address space:**
  - In a monolithic kernel, all kernel components share a single address space.
  - This means that kernel modules and subsystems can directly call each other's functions and access each other's data structures without needing to go through well-defined APIs.

- **High privilege level:**
  - The kernel code runs in the highest privilege level of the CPU, often referred to as *kernel mode*.
  - This allows the kernel to execute sensitive and privileged operations, such as managing hardware resources and controlling the execution of user-space processes.

- **Kernel subsystems:**
  - The Linux kernel is organized into various subsystems that handle different aspects of the operating system, including process management, memory management, file systems, networking, device drivers, and more.
  - Each subsystem is responsible for specific functionalities and contains its own set of data structures and functions.

- **Dynamic loading of modules:**
  - While the core kernel is monolithic, Linux supports the dynamic loading and unloading of kernel modules.
  - Kernel modules are kernel objects that can be loaded into the running kernel to add or extend functionality without requiring kernel recompilation.
  - Modules allow for better modularity and the ability to support a wide range of hardware without bloating the kernel image.

- **Synchronization and concurrency:**
  - Monolithic kernels must carefully manage concurrency and synchronization since all kernel code runs in a single address space.

o Techniques such as locks, semaphores, and spinlocks are used to protect shared data structures and ensure thread safety.

- **Extensive device support:**

  o Monolithic kernels often have extensive built-in device driver support for various hardware devices.

  o Device drivers are part of the kernel and can directly interact with hardware, providing efficient access.

- **Efficient function calls:**

  o Kernel functions can be directly called with minimal overhead since they are in the same address space.

  o Function calls within the kernel are similar to regular function calls in user-space programs.

- **Kernel panics:**

  o In the event of a critical error or unrecoverable fault, a monolithic kernel can trigger a *kernel panic*, which halts the system to prevent further damage.

  o Kernel panics typically involve generating a stack trace and diagnostic information for debugging.

- **Complexity:**

  o Monolithic kernels tend to be more complex due to the inclusion of a wide range of subsystems and device drivers.

  o This complexity can make it challenging to understand and maintain the kernel codebase.

- **High performance:**

  o Monolithic kernels often provide high performance because they eliminate the overhead associated with **inter-process communication** (**IPC**) in microkernel architectures.

  o Kernel functions can be optimized for low-level hardware access.

- **Size and boot time:**

  o Monolithic kernels may have larger sizes compared to microkernels due to the inclusion of many subsystems and drivers.

  o The kernel size and boot time can be affected by the number of enabled features and device drivers.

Device drivers run in kernel space (ring 0 in many CPU architectures) with full, privileged access to the hardware. However, there are certain modules that have been designed to run in user space: this is the case of modules based on file systems with FUSE/CUSE and certain parts of UIO or USB modules with the **libusb** library. The X Window System and Wayland, the window system and display server protocols used in Linux, do not run in the kernel.

Unlike standard monolithic kernels, device drivers are easily configurable as modules and can be loaded or unloaded while the system is running, and can also be preempted under certain conditions to properly handle hardware interrupts and better support symmetric multiprocessing. Linux, therefore, does not have a stable device driver application binary interface.

Linux usually enables memory protection and virtual memory and can also handle non-uniform memory access. The μClinux project, which also allows Linux to be run on microcontrollers, works without virtual memory.

The hardware is represented in the file hierarchy in **ramfs**. User applications, therefore, interact by convention with device drivers via entries in the **/dev** or **/sysfs** directories. Process information is also mapped to the file system through the **/procfs** directory.

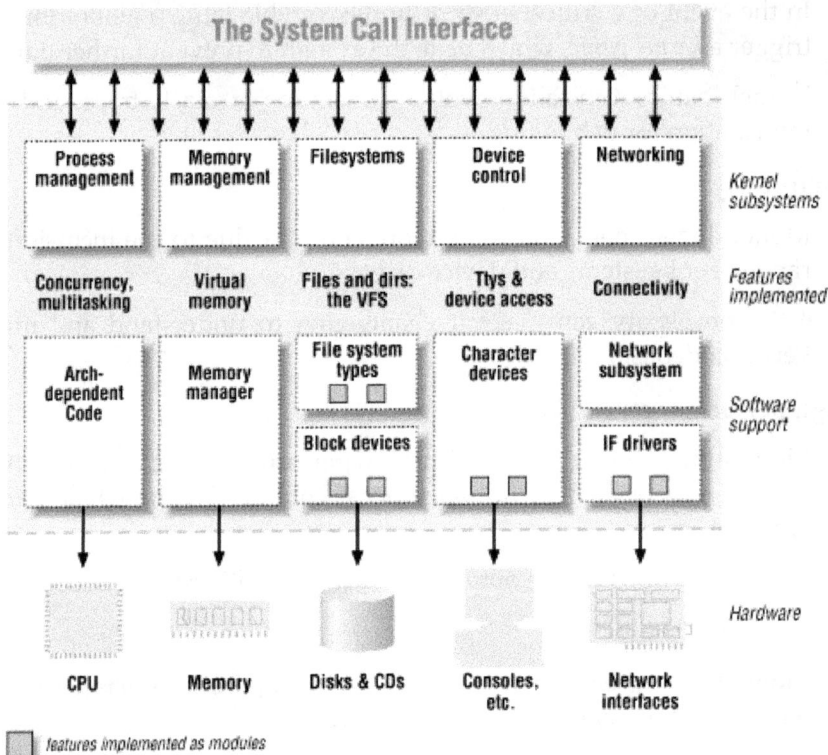

Figure 2.4: Architecture of the kernel by layers

This modular view will be useful to us later, we will have to keep it in mind for the configuration part, which will allow us to select the contents of the kernel.

The steps to build a Linux kernel are as follows:

1. Obtaining sources and, if it is a tarball, validating the authenticity of the archive.

2. Configuration of the build to determine the static part and the dynamic modules to generate.

3. Build the kernel and dynamic modules.

4. Installation

5. Test the kernel using **qemu** with the prebuilt **rootfs** (**rootfs.ext2**).

We will go over all these steps in detail one by one.

Downloading the GNU/Linux kernel sources to recompile them

In this section, we will learn how to retrieve GNU/Linux kernel sources in different ways.

Using distributions' packages

The first solution to modify the configuration of your current kernel is to start from the installed sources via a separate package in the **/usr/src/** directory. Each kernel version will have a directory prefixed with **linux-headers** followed by its version and extraversion. For a given version, there are, therefore, several packages, the kernel runtime and its sources (**linux-headers**):

```
$ apt-cache search `uname -r`
linux-buildinfo-6.2.0-33-generic - Linux kernel buildinfo for version 6.2.0
on 64 bit x86 SMP
linux-cloud-tools-6.2.0-33-generic - Linux kernel version specific cloud
tools for version 6.2.0-33
linux-headers-6.2.0-33-generic - Linux kernel headers for version 6.2.0 on
64 bit x86 SMP
linux-image-6.2.0-33-generic - Signed kernel image generic
linux-image-unsigned-6.2.0-33-generic - Linux kernel image for version
6.2.0 on 64 bit x86 SMP
linux-modules-6.2.0-33-generic - Linux kernel extra modules for version
6.2.0 on 64 bit x86 SMP
linux-modules-extra-6.2.0-33-generic - Linux kernel extra modules for
version 6.2.0 on 64 bit x86 SMP
linux-modules-ipu6-6.2.0-33-generic - Linux kernel ipu6 modules for version
6.2.0-33
```

`linux-modules-ivsc-6.2.0-33-generic - Linux kernel ivsc modules for version 6.2.0-33`

`(...)sure that your code is accepted into the mainline kernel.`

These rules will be important for us to start from the beginning with good habits.

Once the source packages are installed, they are available in the **/usr/src/linux-headers-<version>** directory:

```
$ ls -ald /usr/src/linux-headers*
drwxr-xr-x  7 root root 4096 sept.  5 13:41 /usr/src/linux-headers-6.2.0-
32-generic
drwxr-xr-x  7 root root 4096 sept. 19 13:26 /usr/src/linux-headers-6.2.0-
33-generic
$ cd /usr/src/linux-headers-$(uname -r)
$ pwd
/usr/src/linux-headers-6.2.0-33-generic
$ ls -alh
total 2,3M
drwxr-xr-x  7 root root 4,0K sept. 19 13:26 .
drwxr-xr-x 17 root root 4,0K sept. 19 14:11 ..
drwxr-xr-x  3 root root 4,0K sept. 19 13:26 arch
lrwxrwxrwx  1 root root   39 sept.  7 09:11 block -> ../linux-hwe-6.2-
headers-6.2.0-33/block
lrwxrwxrwx  1 root root   39 sept.  7 09:11 certs -> ../linux-hwe-6.2-
headers-6.2.0-33/certs
-rw-r--r--  1 root root    0 sept.  7 09:11 .checked-atomic-arch-fallback.h
-rw-r--r--  1 root root    0 sept.  7 09:11 .checked-atomic-instrumented.h
-rw-r--r--  1 root root    0 sept.  7 09:11 .checked-atomic-long.h
-rw-r--r--  1 root root 270K sept.  7 09:11 .config
lrwxrwxrwx  1 root root   40 sept.  7 09:11 crypto -> ../linux-hwe-6.2-
headers-6.2.0-33/crypto
lrwxrwxrwx  1 root root   47 sept.  7 09:11 Documentation -> ../linux-hwe-
6.2-headers-6.2.0-33/Documentation
lrwxrwxrwx  1 root root   41 sept.  7 09:11 drivers -> ../linux-hwe-6.2-
headers-6.2.0-33/drivers
lrwxrwxrwx  1 root root   36 sept.  7 09:11 fs -> ../linux-hwe-6.2-
headers-6.2.0-33/fs
-rw-r--r--  1 root root   39 sept.  7 09:11 .gitignore
drwxr-xr-x  4 root root 4,0K sept. 19 13:26 include
lrwxrwxrwx  1 root root   38 sept.  7 09:11 init -> ../linux-hwe-6.2-
```

```
headers-6.2.0-33/init
lrwxrwxrwx  1 root root   42 sept.  7 09:11 io_uring -> ../linux-hwe-6.2-
headers-6.2.0-33/io_uring
lrwxrwxrwx  1 root root   37 sept.  7 09:11 ipc -> ../linux-hwe-6.2-
headers-6.2.0-33/ipc
lrwxrwxrwx  1 root root   40 sept.  7 09:11 Kbuild -> ../linux-hwe-6.2-
headers-6.2.0-33/Kbuild
lrwxrwxrwx  1 root root   41 sept.  7 09:11 Kconfig -> ../linux-hwe-6.2-
headers-6.2.0-33/Kconfig
drwxr-xr-x  2 root root 4,0K sept. 19 13:26 kernel
lrwxrwxrwx  1 root root   37 sept.  7 09:11 lib -> ../linux-hwe-6.2-
headers-6.2.0-33/lib
-rw-r--r--  1 root root  71K sept.  7 09:11 Makefile
-rw-r--r--  1 root root 1,3K sept.  7 09:11 .missing-syscalls.d
lrwxrwxrwx  1 root root   36 sept.  7 09:11 mm -> ../linux-hwe-6.2-
headers-6.2.0-33/mm
-rw-r--r--  1 root root 1,9M sept.  7 09:11 Module.symvers
lrwxrwxrwx  1 root root   37 sept.  7 09:11 net -> ../linux-hwe-6.2-
headers-6.2.0-33/net
lrwxrwxrwx  1 root root   47 sept.  7 09:11 rust -> ../linux-hwe-6.2-lib-
rust-6.2.0-33-generic/rust
lrwxrwxrwx  1 root root   41 sept.  7 09:11 samples -> ../linux-hwe-6.2-
headers-6.2.0-33/samples
drwxr-xr-x  7 root root  12K sept. 19 13:26 scripts
lrwxrwxrwx  1 root root   42 sept.  7 09:11 security -> ../linux-hwe-6.2-
headers-6.2.0-33/security
lrwxrwxrwx  1 root root   39 sept.  7 09:11 sound -> ../linux-hwe-6.2-
headers-6.2.0-33/sound
drwxr-xr-x  4 root root 4,0K sept. 19 13:26 tools
lrwxrwxrwx  1 root root   40 sept.  7 09:11 ubuntu -> ../linux-hwe-6.2-
headers-6.2.0-33/ubuntu
lrwxrwxrwx  1 root root   37 sept.  7 09:11 usr -> ../linux-hwe-6.2-
headers-6.2.0-33/usr
lrwxrwxrwx  1 root root   38 sept.  7 09:11 virt -> ../linux-hwe-6.2-
headers-6.2.0-33/virt
```

As for the configuration of the kernel itself, it is in two locations:

- first time in the above directory with the .config file (/usr/src/ linux-headers-$(uname -r)/.config (see above)
- second time in the /boot directory:

```
$ ls -alh /boot/config-`uname -r`*
-rw-r--r-- 1 root root 270K sept.  7 09:11 /boot/config-6.2.0-33-
generic
```

Downloading official tarball from kernel.org

If you want to compile a different version of the current kernel, the simplest method is to retrieve the sources for a given kernel version from the official **kernel.org** website:

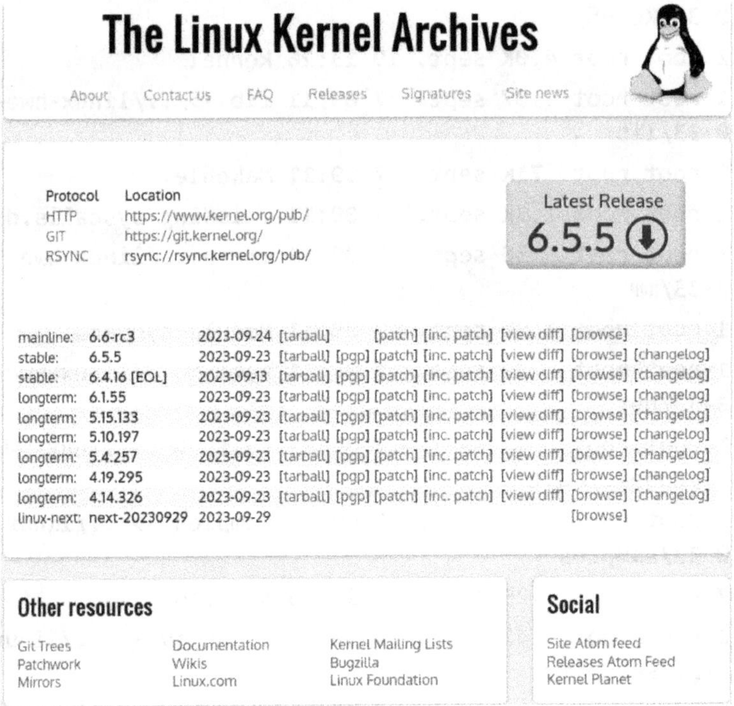

Figure 2.5: Official GNU/Linux kernel development page

This site now only supports four protocols compared to eight in the past: HTTPS, GIT, and RSYNC. As we can see, the site mentions several kernel versions: stable, **end of life** (**EOL**), or long-term. Indeed, when a kernel moves from the mainline branch to the stable branch, two things can happen:

- **Mainline kernels**: Latest releases from the GNULinux kernel developer community. These versions generally have a shorter support life and are quickly replaced by new versions.

- **Long Term Support (LTS) kernels**: Some Linux kernels are tagged as LTS, meaning they have an extended support period. LTS releases are maintained and receive security patches and maintenance updates for several years, typically between 2 to 6 years or more, depending on the specific kernel.

- **End of Life (EOL)kernels**: After several bugfix reviews, the kernel maintainers will not release any more bugfixes for this kernel version. If the kernel version is marked EOL, you have to plan to upgrade to the next major and stable release.

Note the XML and JSON Files, which are updated with each new kernel delivery:

- o XML: **https://www.kernel.org/feeds/kdist.xml**

- o JSON: **https://www.kernel.org/releases.json**

To download the source tarball, we can use the **curl** command:

```
$ curl -OL https://cdn.kernel.org/pub/linux/kernel/v6.x/linux-
6.5.5.tar.xz
  % Total    % Received % Xferd  Average Speed   Time    Time
Time  Current
                                 Dload  Upload   Total   Spent
Left  Speed
100  132M  100  132M    0       0  5208k       0  0:00:26  0:00:26 --:-
-:-- 3713k
```

Download the Linux kernel sources, but it may be necessary to confirm the source of the latter to guarantee traceability. Indeed, it is very useful in DevSecOps; it helps protect against malicious code. To do this, the tarballs coming from the **kernel.org** site are associated with a GPG fingerprint allowing this control:

```
$ curl -OL https://cdn.kernel.org/pub/linux/kernel/v6.x/linux-
6.5.5.tar.sign
         % Total    % Received % Xferd  Average Speed   Time    Time
Time  Current
                                 Dload  Upload   Total   Spent   Left
Speed
         100   987  100   987    0       0  3005       0 --:--:-- --:--
:-- --:--:-- 3009
```

We now need to import the two **gpg** public keys associated with the official maintainers of the GNU/Linux project via the following command:

```
$ gpg2 --locate-keys torvalds@kernel.org gregkh@kernel.org
gpg: key 38DBBDC86092693E: public key "Greg Kroah-Hartman
<gregkh@kernel.org>" imported
gpg: Total number processed: 1
gpg:                imported: 1
gpg: key 79BE3E4300411886: public key "Linus Torvalds <torvalds@kernel.
org>"
 imported
gpg: Total number processed: 1
```

```
gpg:                    imported: 1
pub   rsa4096 2011-09-23 [SC]
      647F28654894E3BD457199BE38DBBDC86092693E
uid           [ unknown] Greg Kroah-Hartman <gregkh@kernel.org>
sub   rsa4096 2011-09-23 [E]


pub   rsa2048 2011-09-20 [SC]
      ABAF11C65A2970B130ABE3C479BE3E4300411886
uid           [ unknown] Linus Torvalds <torvalds@kernel.org>
```

You will observe that signing is done on the uncompressed version of the archive, so that only one signature is required for the compressed **.gz** and **.xz** versions of the release. You must therefore start by decompressing the archive first using **unxz** in our case:

```
$ unxz linux-6.5.5.tar.xz
```

Now, verify the **.tar** archive against the signature:

```
$ gpg2 --verify linux-6.5.5.tar.sign
gpg: assuming signed data in 'linux-6.5.5.tar'
gpg: Signature made sam. 23 sept. 2023 11:16:13 CEST
gpg:                 using RSA key 647F28654894E3BD457199BE38DBBDC86092693E
gpg: Good signature from "Greg Kroah-Hartman <gregkh@kernel.org>"
[unknown]
gpg: WARNING: This key is not certified with a trusted signature!
gpg:          There is no indication that the signature belongs to the
owner.
Primary key fingerprint: 647F 2865 4894 E3BD 4571 99BE 38DB BDC8 6092 693E
```

It was also possible to combine these two steps into a one-liner:

```
$ xz -cd linux-6.5.5.tar.xz | gpg2 --verify linux-6.5.5.tar.sign –
```

Note: The existence of a script allowing you to authenticate an official kernel: https://git. kernel.org/pub/scm/linux/kernel/git/mricon/korg-helpers.git/tree/get-verified-tarball

Cloning the official Git repo

Another method highly coveted by developers is retrieving from the official GIT repo:

```
    $ git clone git://git.kernel.org/pub/scm/linux/kernel/git/torvalds/
linux.git
Cloning into 'linux'...
remote: Enumerating objects: 9721192, done.
remote: Counting objects: 100% (120/120), done.
```

```
remote: Compressing objects: 100% (63/63), done.
remote: Total 9721192 (delta 74), reused 75 (delta 57), pack-reused 9721072
Receiving objects: 100% (9721192/9721192), 2.69 GiB | 16.76 MiB/s, done.
Resolving deltas: 100% (7970513/7970513), done.
Updating files: 100% (81757/81757), done.
```

To find out the list of available tags:

```
$ git tag --list
(…)
v6.5
v6.5-rc1
v6.5-rc2
v6.5-rc3
v6.5-rc4
v6.5-rc5
v6.5-rc6
v6.5-rc7
v6.6-rc1
v6.6-rc2
v6.6-rc3
(...)
```

We can search for the tag closest to that of our Ubuntu Linux distribution, namely **6.2.0-33-generic,** which corresponds to a **v6.2** release:

```
$ git tag --list |grep 6.2
```

To switch to a specific release/tag from the **v6.2** tag in a **linux_6.2** branch:

```
$ git checkout -b linux_6.2  v6.2
```

We are ready to move on to the Linux kernel configuration step.

Configuring a custom kernel and modules

The purpose of the configuration step is to define the GNU/Linux kernel feature identity map. This will enable a number of features either statically in the monolithic kernel (static part) or in dynamic modules (dynamic part).

The purpose of a configurator is to generate a **.config** file, which will summarize all the features to be activated. A **.config** file is like an ID card of the build.

Configurators are invoked by passing specific target names to the main makefile. The configuration brick is identical to that used in many other projects like Builldroot, Ptxdist, crosstool-ng, etc. It was redeveloped a few years ago by *Yann Morin*.

Different types of configurators exist:

- **config**: Updates the configuration using a text interface
- **nconfig**: Updates the configuration using a **ncurse** interface (light black and white version)
- **menuconfig**: Updates configuration using a **ncurse** interface (color version)
- **xconfig**: Updates configuration using a QT interface
- **gconfig**: Updates configuration using a GTK interface
- **oldconfig**: Updates the configuration using the `.config` file present in the kernel sources
- **localmodconfig**: Updates the current configuration by deactivating unloaded dynamic modules
- **localyesconfig**: Updates the configuration by integrating dynamic modules into the static part of the kernel
- **silentoldconfig**: Same as `oldconfig` but updates dependencies `silently`
- **defconfig**: Updates the configuration, taking the default settings for a given architecture
- **savedefconfig**: Saves the current configuration as config. Minimal by default
- **allnoconfig**: Creates a new configuration where all options are set to **no**
- **allyesconfig**: Creates a new configuration where all options are set to **yes**
- **allmodconfig**: Creates a new configuration where all options are
- **alldefconfig**: Creates a new configuration where all options requested are set to their default value
- **randconfig**: Defines a new configuration by responding randomly for enabling options
- **listnewconfig**: List new options
- **olddefconfig**: Same as `silentoldconfig` but sets new symbols to their default value

The following figure contains some screenshots of the different types of configurators:

Figure 2.6: Several screenshots of the configurator

The configuration of a GNU/Linux kernel is a crucial step in customizing the behavior and features of the kernel to suit your specific requirements.

Each menu can have up to three states: selected in the static part of the kernel (y), selected as a dynamic module (m), and not selected.

The following figure gives an example with the QT configurator:

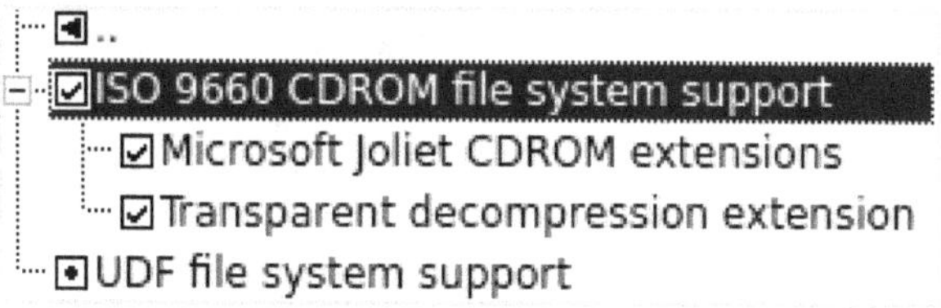

Figure 2.7: View of the QT configurator

Description of activations for feature management with dependency management. Each activation can be either included in the static part of the kernel itself or separately, when possible, in a dynamically loadable module:

- **ISO9660 CDROM file system support**: Will be included in a dynamic **.ko** module separate from the kernel; if this configuration is selected, this will enable both sub dependencies.

- **UDF file system support**: Will be included in the static part of the Linux kernel.

The resulting configuration file will ultimately have one line per feature following the following rules:

- Any line prefixed with a number and ending with *is not set* will not be taken into account.

- Any line ending with **=m** will generate a dynamic module.

- Any line ending with **=y** will include the functionality in the static part of the kernel.

Extraction of a **.config** file:

```
(...)
## CD-ROM/DVD Filesystems
#CONFIG_ISO9660_FS=m
CONFIG_JOLIET=y
CONFIG_ZISOFS=y
CONFIG_UDF_FS=y
CONFIG_UDF_NLS=y
## DOS/FAT/NT Filesystems
## CONFIG_MSDOS_FS is not set
#CONFIG_VFAT_FS is not set
CONFIG_NTFS_FS=m
# CONFIG_NTFS_DEBUG is not set
CONFIG_NTFS_RW=y
(...)
```

The kernel configuration includes a system of dependencies between options. For example, enabling a network driver activates the network stack. There are two types of dependencies:

- **Dependency on dependencies**: An option A on which B depends remains invisible as long as B is not activated.

- **Dependency selection**: With an option A dependent on B, when A is activated, B is automatically activated as well.

Make **xconfig** display all options, even the ones that are not active. In this version, the inactive options are just grayed out.

This configuration phase is essential for choosing the drivers to include in the kernel:

- We must avoid leaving unnecessary drivers because this increases the size of the kernel.

- The share of drivers compiled statically versus dynamic modules must be taken into account regarding the loading time of the kernel into memory. The same goes for initialization.

- Too many statically compiled drivers include a long loading phase unless XIP and AXFS are used (eXecute In Place).

The kernel configuration is typically performed using tools like **make menuconfig, make nconfig**, or **make xconfig**, which provide a user-friendly interface for modifying various configuration options.

The following are several key topics that you can configure when customizing a Linux kernel:

- **Code maturity**: Allows you to hide or reveal options that are still in development and therefore, considered unstable (often useful to say yes here if you want to be able to benefit from the latest advances in the kernel).

- **General setup**: A set of general options on your system (unless you want to compile for very specific architectures) is as follows:
  - Kernel version and identification
  - Kernel architecture (e.g., 32-bit or 64-bit)
  - Kernel compression method
  - Kernel command line
  - Kernel timer frequency
  - Kernel preemption model

- **Block layer**: The inputs/outputs on your motherboard (can be removed for on-board use)

- **Loadable module support**: Options concerning module management (the default is almost always correct for regular use)
  - Enable or disable the ability to load kernel modules at runtime
  - Configure module versioning and symbol information

- **Processor type and features**: Options relating to the processor(s): type (x86, Sparc, ...), hyper-thread, dual-core, SMP, etc.

- o   Processor family and microarchitecture optimization
- o   Support for symmetric multiprocessing (SMP)
- o   CPU frequency scaling (e.g., CPU governors)
- o   Virtualization options (e.g., KVM, Xen, VirtualBox)

- **Power management and ACPI**: Options regarding power saving, standby, and ACPI/APM
  - o   CPU idle states and power-saving features
  - o   **Advanced Configuration and Power Interface (ACPI)** support
  - o   ACPI sleep states (e.g., Suspend to RAM)

- **Bus options (PCI, USB, I2C, etc.)**: Management of all the places where you could plug cards (PCI, PCMCIA, ISA, etc.)
  - o   Configure support for various bus types and controllers (e.g., PCI, USB, SCSI)
  - o   Enable or disable specific device drivers and controller support

- **Device drivers**: Options concerning all hardware drivers (this is often where we spend the most time)
  - o   Configure support for various hardware devices and peripherals
  - o   Enable or disable support for specific network cards, storage devices, sound cards, graphics cards, and more
  - o   Support for filesystems (e.g., ext4, NTFS, CIFS)
  - o   Input devices (e.g., keyboards, mice, touchpads)
  - o   Storage drivers (e.g., SATA, NVMe, SCSI)
  - o   Networking options (e.g., Ethernet, Wi-Fi, Bluetooth)
  - o   USB support and device drivers

- **Executable file formats**: Management of executable files (ELF support must always be at *Y*);

- **File systems**: Options regarding file systems managed by your kernel (you will have to take a look)
  - o   Enable support for various filesystems (e.g., ext4, Btrfs, XFS)
  - o   Network filesystems (e.g., NFS, CIFS)
  - o   Disk quota support
  - o   Filesystem-related options (e.g., extended attributes, file locking)

- **Kernel features:**
  - ○ Real-time support (PREEMPT-RT)
  - ○ Task scheduler options (e.g., Completely Fair Scheduler, Round Robin)
  - ○ POSIX compatibility options
  - ○ Kernel debugging and tracing (e.g., kprobes, ftrace, perf)
  - ○ Security options (e.g., SELinux, AppArmor, seccomp)
- **Networking support**: Options concerning the network protocols managed by your kernel (the default is often sufficient, but take a look at it in case)
- Networking protocols and options (e.g., IPv4, IPv6, TCP, UDP)
- Networking stack options (e.g., QoS, IPsec, netfilter/iptables)
- Virtual networking (e.g., TUN/TAP support)
  - ○ Packet filtering and routing options
- **Instrumentation support**: Kernel profiling option (no need to enable it).
- **Security options**: Options concerning the security model of your kernel (the default is sufficient)
  - ○ **Mandatory Access Control** (**MAC**) frameworks (e.g., SELinux, Smack)
  - ○ Secure computing mode (seccomp)
  - ○ Kernel hardening options [e.g., **Address Space Layout Randomization (ASLR)**]
  - ○ Cryptographic options (e.g., cryptographic API, encryption algorithms)
- **Security options**: Options concerning the security model of your kernel (the default is sufficient)
- **Cryptographic options**: Cryptographic algorithms that can be implemented in the kernel (the default is sufficient)
- **Library routines**: Common kernel libraries (the default is sufficient)
  - ○ PeKernel performance counters (e.g., perf_events)
  - ○ Profiling support (e.g., OProfile, perf)
  - ○ Hardware performance monitoring [e.g., Intel **Performance Monitoring Unit (PMU)**]

Kernel documentation: Enable or disable kernel documentation (useful for kernel development)

These are just some of the key topics you can configure in the Linux kernel. The specific options and their availability may vary depending on the kernel version and your hardware. When configuring the kernel, it is essential to carefully consider your system's requirements and constraints to create a customized kernel that meets your needs while minimizing unnecessary features.

Unlike a packaged version (**.deb**, **.rpm**, etc.), sources from a tarball from kernel.org do not natively provide a default configuration. On a Linux distribution, it is necessary to recover the current kernel configuration file.

First, it is necessary to check the current kernel version with the uname command:

```
$ uname -a
Linux tgayet-DS87D 6.2.0-33-generic #33~22.04.1-Ubuntu SMP PREEMPT_DYNAMIC
Thu Sep  7 10:33:52 UTC 2 x86_64 x86_64 x86_64 GNU/Linux
```

To start from the configuration of the kernel packaged by a given distribution, you must copy the .config configuration file to the root of the Linux kernel sources or from the /boot directory:

```
$ cp /boot/config-`uname -r`* .config
```

Or,

```
$ cp /usr/src/linux-headers-$(uname -r)/.config .config
```

For this **.config** configuration file to be taken into account, you must use the **oldconfig** target or **alldefconfig**:

```
$ make oldconfig
```

Note that if the current kernel is compiled with the pseudo filesystem **/proc/config.gz**, it will be possible to *hot* regenerate this file from the current kernel config:

```
$ zcat /proc/config.gz > .config
```

To do this, the kernel must have been compiled with the following configuration:

```
CONFIG_IKCONFIG=y
```

```
CONFIG_IKCONFIG_PROC=y
```

Then activated from the following menu in the kernel:

General setup `--->[*] Kernel .config support[*]` Enable access to **.config** through **/proc/config.gz**

Once the configuration phase is complete, a **.config** file should be located at the root of the sources. It should be noted that this functionality is less and less activated in current kernels.

Before starting the generation phase, it may be useful to identify the kernel. A set of variables located at the start of the **makefile** is used for this:

```
VERSION = 6
PATCHLEVEL = 2
SUBLEVEL = 0
EXTRAVERSION = -bpb
NAME = Kernel linux for bpb book
```

Another way to append an extra version is to add a **CONFIG_LOCALVERSION** within the **.config** file. It must start with a hyphen to make the transition between the version and the defined extra string:

```
CONFIG_LOCALVERSION = -custom
```

For example, if you added **-custom** as the extra version label, the kernel version might look like **5.14.0-custom** when you check it with **uname -r**.

Building your own kernel

Once our kernel is configured, we will need to build it.

Before moving on to the generation stage, you will need to check if you have all the necessary tools:

Software	Minimal version	Command to check version
Gnu C	2.95.3	gcc --version
Gnu make	3.78	make --version
binutils	2.12	ld -v
util-linux	2.10o	fdformat --version
module-init-tools	0.9.10	depmod -V
e2fsprogs	1.29tune2fs	tune2fs
jfsutils	1.1.3	fsck.jfs -V
reiserfsprogs	3.6.3	reiserfsck -V 2>&1 | grep reiserfsprogs
xfsprogs	2.1.0	xfs_db -V
pcmcia-cs	3.1.21	cardmgr -V
quota-tools	3.09	quota -V
PPP	2.4.0	pppd --version
isdn4k-utils	3.1pre1	isdnctrl 2>&1 | grep version
nfs-utils	1.0.5	showmount --version
procps	3.1.13	ps --version
oprofile	0.5.3	oprofiled –version

Table 2.1: Necessary tools required to build your own kernel

The generation of the GNU / Linux kernel is carried out in two steps:

1. The static part of the kernel compressed or not (**vmlinux**, **bzimage**, etc.)
2. The dynamic part of the **drivers/modules/kernel** objects (***.ko**)

Generating a GNU/Linux kernel from command-line sources

Now, let us go through each step-by-step procedure, from getting the sources, configuring them, compiling them, and finally installing them.

> **Note: The most basic target is the one defined by scripts!**

```
$ make scripts
  HOSTCC   scripts/genksyms/genksyms.o
  YACC     scripts/genksyms/parse.tab.[ch]
  HOSTCC   scripts/genksyms/parse.tab.o
  LEX      scripts/genksyms/lex.lex.c
  HOSTCC   scripts/genksyms/lex.lex.o
  HOSTLD   scripts/genksyms/genksyms
  HOSTCC   scripts/selinux/genheaders/genheaders
  HOSTCC   scripts/selinux/mdp/mdp
  HOSTCC   scripts/kallsyms
  HOSTCC   scripts/sorttable
  HOSTCC   scripts/asn1_compiler
  HOSTCC   scripts/sign-file
  HOSTCC   scripts/insert-sys-cert
```

To do this, a simple make allows you to launch the generation, taking into account the configuration defined in the **.config** file:

```
$ make
```

By default, source generation is quite silent, meaning there will only be one line per action (compilation, link editing, etc.). A detail is only displayed in the event of a fatal error. To switch from this silent mode to verbose mode, it is possible to change mode via the *V* parameter. An example of using both modes is as follows:

```
$ make V=1 # for verbose mode
```

Or,

```
$ make V=0 # for silent mode; by default, therefore, equivalent to a simple make
```

Also, note the existence of the *V=2* mode. Other parameters like *C* or *W* exist.

If the machine compiling the sources has more than one processor or core, it is possible to parallelize the generation using the **j / --jobs** and **-l / --load-average** parameters.

The **-j** option sets the maximum number of parallel tasks that can be executed by the **makefile**, and the **-l** option prevents any new parallel tasks from starting unless the load is below the specified quota. The reason why the number of tasks is set higher than the number of processors is to help ensure saturation of processor usage.

To find out how much can be parallelized, a simple calculation like the following is easy to do:

```
$ export NBCORE=$(($(grep -c processor /proc/cpuinfo)+1))
```

Or,

```
$ export NBCORE=$(($(cat /proc/cpuinfo|grep processor|wc -l)+1))
```

For an INTEL core I7, this gives 9, and for an INTEL core I3, this gives 5. To have a generation that can optimally adapt to the machine where the Linux kernel sources are compiled, the following commands can be used:

```
$ export NBCORE=$(($(cat /proc/cpuinfo | grep processor | wc -l)+1))
$ make –jobs=$((NBCORE+1)) –load-average=${NBCORE}
```

Also, note that the generation can be launched even if you are not in the source's directory. Indeed, like any GNU **Makefile**, the **-C** parameter allows you to specify the source path where the **Makefile** is located:

```
$ make -j 9 -C=~/linux_src/
```

The build generates several main files:

- **./vmlinux**: uncompressed Linux kernel used for debugging
- **./System.map**: table of symbols contained in the static part
- **./arch/<ARCH>/boot/bzImage**: compressed Linux kernel

The compressed kernel name is the ELF **vmlinux** file, which can be used for debugging or profiling. This is rarely the file loaded in RAM because we prefer a compressed version called **bzImage**:

```
$ file vmlinux
vmlinux: ELF 64-bit LSB executable, x86-64, version 1 (SYSV), statically
linked, BuildID[sha1]=faed1aa89d999a80ea62b816311a4b55cc49b866, not
stripped

$ file  arch/x86/boot/bzImage
arch/x86/boot/bzImage: Linux kernel x86 boot executable bzImage, version
6.2.0-bpb-dirty (tgayet@tgayet-DS87D) #1 SMP PREEMPT_DYNAMIC Sun Oct  1
20:21:24 CEST 2023, RO-rootFS, swap_dev 0XB, Normal VGA
```

Note: The i386 architecture is redirected to x86:

arch/i386/boot/bzImage: symbolic link to `../../x86/boot/bzImage'

Once the build is complete, we cannot wait to test our kernel just built using **qemu** and the **rootfs** generated at the very beginning of this chapter:

```
$ qemu-system-x86_64 -kernel ./arch/x86/boot/bzImage -hda ./
rootfs.ext2 -nographic -append root="/dev/sda console=ttyS0" -net
nic,macaddr=00:11:22:33:44:55 -net user
```

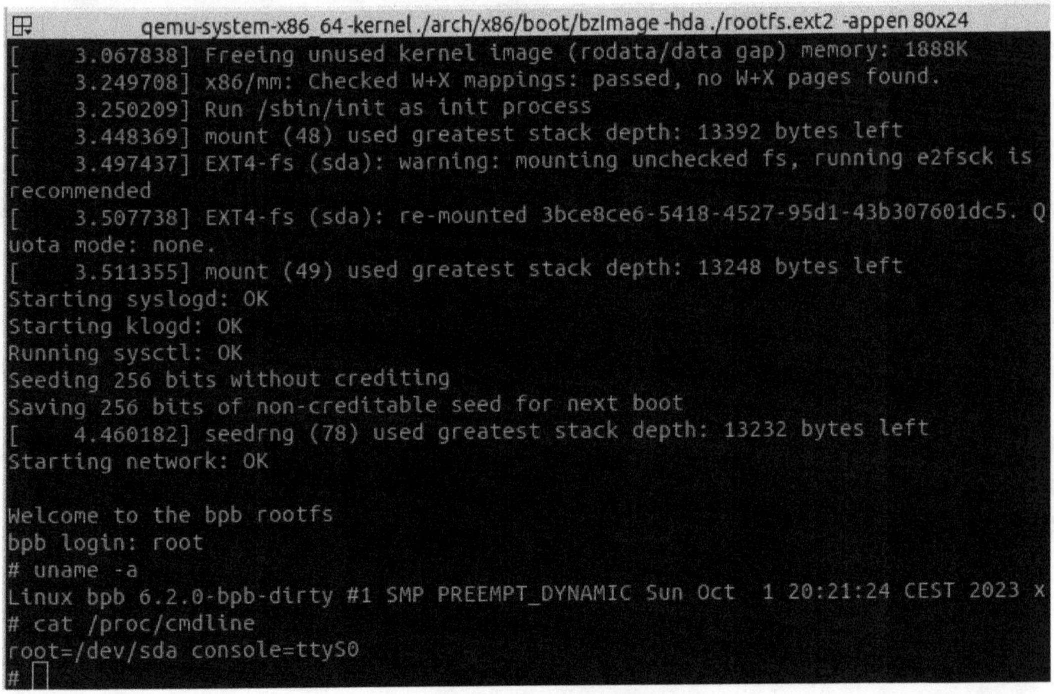

Figure 2.8: Test of the new kernel built

We can both confirm that this is our kernel with the suffix provided by **EXTRAVERSION**, and also by looking at the parameters given to the kernel (accessible via **/proc/cmdline**).

In the context of a Linux kernel, the term **dirty** does not refer to the cleanliness or state of the kernel's code or data. Instead, it has a specific technical meaning related to memory management and caching.

In the Linux kernel, the **dirty** state is used to indicate that a page of memory (usually a page in RAM) has been modified since it was last read from storage (e.g., from a disk). When data in memory is modified, it is marked as **dirty** to indicate that it no longer matches the data stored on disk. This information is important for the following few reasons:

- **Write efficiency**: The kernel can optimize writes to storage by only writing back pages that are marked as dirty. This helps reduce the number of write operations and improves overall I/O performance.

- **Caching**: The kernel may keep frequently accessed data in memory (caches) for faster access. When this cached data is modified, it is marked as dirty, and the kernel will eventually write it back to storage to ensure data consistency.

- **Data integrity**: Tracking `dirty` pages is crucial for data integrity. It ensures that changes made to data in memory are eventually persisted to storage, so that in the event of a system crash or power failure, the system can recover without losing critical data.

The term `dirty` is commonly used in computer science and operating systems to describe this concept of modified data that needs to be synchronized with non-volatile storage. It is essentially a flag indicating that certain data in memory needs to be written back to disk to maintain data consistency.

In contrast, `clean` pages are those that have not been modified since they were read from storage and are in sync with their on-disk counterparts. The kernel's memory management system keeps track of these states to efficiently manage data and ensure data integrity in the system.

Generating a DEB package for Ubuntu/Debian/ Mint

Building a kernel package for Ubuntu or Debian involves several steps, including configuring the kernel, compiling it, creating Debian packages, and installing them. The steps are as follows:

1. Before you begin, make sure you have the necessary build tools and dependencies installed:

   ```
   $ sudo apt-get install build-essential fakeroot kernel-package
   libncurses5-dev bison flex
   ```

2. Obtain the kernel source code. You can download it from the official **kernel.org** website or use a package manager to fetch the source package.

   For example, to download the kernel source package for Ubuntu:

   ```
   $ sudo apt-get source linux-image-$(uname -r)
   ```

3. Enter the kernel source directory:

   ```
   $ cd linux-<version>  # Replace <version> with the actual kernel
   version
   ```

4. For a text-based configuration menu:

   ```
   $ make menuconfig
   ```

5. For a graphical configuration menu:

   ```
   $ make xconfig
   ```

6. Configure the kernel as needed, including any custom settings or features you require.

   Build the kernel and create a Debian package using the following commands:

   ```
   $ fakeroot make-kpkg --initrd --append-to-version=<custom_version>
   kernel_image kernel_headers
   ```

7. Replace `<custom_version>` with your desired version label, which will be appended to the kernel version.

   After successfully building the kernel package, you can install it:

   ```
   $ sudo dpkg -i ../linux-image-<custom_version>_amd64.deb  # Replace
   with the actual package name
   ```

8. You may also need to install the corresponding `linux-headers` package:

   ```
   $ sudo dpkg -i ../linux-headers-<custom_version>_amd64.deb  #
   Replace with the actual package name
   ```

9. Update the bootloader configuration to recognize the new kernel. For GRUB, you can update the configuration using:

   ```
   $ sudo update-grub
   ```

10. Reboot your system to load the new kernel:

    ```
    $ sudo reboot
    ```

11. After the system has rebooted, you can verify that the new kernel is active:

    ```
    $ uname -r
    ```

    This should display the kernel version with your custom version label.

Packaging for Fedora Core/Red Hat/SUSE

Building a kernel package for Fedora Core, Red Hat, or SUSE Linux typically involves creating a custom **Red Hat Package Manager** (**RPM**) package.

Each of these distributions has its own packaging and build processes, so the following is an overview of each one:

To generate an RPM package for Fedora Core/Red Hat, follow the given steps:

1. Ensure you have the necessary development tools installed:

   ```
   $ sudo dnf install rpm-build redhat-rpm-config gcc make
   ```

2. Download the kernel source code from the official Fedora or Red Hat repositories. You can use tools like **dnf** or **yum**:

   ```
   $ sudo dnf download --source kernel
   ```

3. Set up the RPM build environment:

   ```
   $ rpmdev-setuptree
   ```

   This will create the **rpmbuild** directory structure.

4. Copy the downloaded kernel source **RPM** into the **SOURCES** directory:

   ```
   $ cp kernel*.src.rpm ~/rpmbuild/SOURCES/
   ```

5. Extract the source RPM:

   ```
   $ rpm -i ~/rpmbuild/SOURCES/kernel*.src.rpm
   ```

   You can apply custom patches or modifications to the kernel source at this point.

6. Configure the kernel as needed, including any custom settings or features you require:

   ```
   $ cd ~/rpmbuild/SPECS
   $ rpmbuild -bp kernel.spec
   ```

7. Build the kernel RPM package:

   ```
   $ rpmbuild -bb kernel.spec
   ```

8. Install the generated RPM package:

   ```
   $ sudo dnf install ~/rpmbuild/RPMS/<architecture>/kernel-*.rpm
   ```

9. Update the GRUB configuration and reboot your system to load the new kernel:

   ```
   $ sudo grub2-mkconfig -o /boot/grub2/grub.cfg  # For GRUB2
   $ sudo reboot
   ```

Follow these steps for generating an RPM package for SUSE Linux:

1. Ensure that you have the necessary development tools installed:

   ```
   $ sudo zypper install rpm-build gcc make
   ```

2. Download the kernel source code from the official SUSE repositories.

3. Set up the RPM build environment:

   ```
   $ rpmdev-setuptree
   ```

   This will create the **rpmbuild** directory structure.

4. Copy the downloaded kernel source RPM into the SOURCES directory:

   ```
   $ cp kernel*.src.rpm ~/rpmbuild/SOURCES/
   ```

5. Extract the source RPM:

   ```
   $ rpm -i ~/rpmbuild/SOURCES/kernel*.src.rpm
   ```

   You can apply custom patches or modifications to the kernel source at this point.

6. Configure the kernel as needed, including any custom settings or features you require:

```
$ cd ~/rpmbuild/SPECS
$ rpmbuild -bp kernel.spec
```

7. Build the kernel RPM package:

```
$ rpmbuild -bb kernel.spec
```

8. Install the generated RPM package:

```
$ sudo zypper install ~/rpmbuild/RPMS/<architecture>/kernel-*.rpm
```

9. Update the GRUB configuration and reboot your system to load the new kernel:

```
$ sudo grub2-mkconfig -o /boot/grub2/grub.cfg  # For GRUB2
$ sudo reboot
```

Please replace **<architecture>** with your system's architecture (e.g., **x86_64**). Keep in mind that building and installing custom kernels can be complex, and it is essential to have proper backups and recovery plans in place when working with system-critical components like the kernel.

Installation

Once the generation phase is complete, the parts can be installed separately.

The installation can be carried out using the default paths or be redefined as given in the following table:

Name of the Makefile parameter	Description	Default value of the path	Associated target
INSTALL_PATHS	Specifies where to install the kernel and mapping (system map)	/boot	Install
INSTALL_MOD_PATH	Specifies where to install native dynamic modules to kernel sources	/lib/ modules/$(KERNELRELEASE)/ kernel	modules_ install
INSTALL_MOD_DIR	Specifies where to install dynamic modules extra to sources	/lib/ modules/$(KERNELRELEASE)/ extra	modules_ install
INSTALL_FW_ PATH	Specifies where to install firmware in the dynamic module tree	$(INSTALL_MOD_PATH)/lib/ firmware	firmware_ install

Table 2.2: GNU/Linux kernel Makefile parameter

The installation can be modified by specifying a prefix to the **rootfs** root. This is particularly useful for installing the kernel itself, which is often done in the path where the bootloader is located:

```
$ make INSTALL_PATH=<kernel_path> install
```

As for dynamic modules:

```
$ make INSTALL_MOD_PATH=<dynamic_modules_path> modules_install
```

For firmware:

```
$ make INSTALL_FW_PATH=<dynamic_modules_path> firmware_install
```

Once the kernel is installed, you will need to ask grub to update:

```
$ sudo update-grub2
[sudo] password for tgayet:
Generating grub.cfg ...
Found linux image: /boot/bzImage-6.2.0-bpb
Found initrd image: /boot/bzImage-6.2.0-bpb
```

If all goes well, at this step, the kernel is added to the list of bootable kernels at startup.

Execution and boot sequence

The **vmlinux** file is a statically linked executable containing the Linux kernel in ELF/COFF formats. It may be required for kernel debugging, **system.map** symbol table generation, or other operations, but must be made bootable before use as an operating system kernel by adding a multiboot header, a boot sector, and configuration routines. On older UNIX platforms, the kernel image was named **/unix**. With the use of virtual memory, kernels supporting this feature were given the prefix **vm** to differentiate them. The name **vmlinux** is a concatenation of **vmunix**, while in **vmlinuz** the letter **z** at the end indicates that it is compressed (e.g., **gzipped**).

Traditionally, when creating a bootable kernel image, the kernel is also compressed using **gzip** or, since Linux 2.6.30, using **LZMA** or **bzip2**, which requires the inclusion of a very small decompression stub in the resulting image. The stub unpacks the kernel code, on some systems prints dots to the console to indicate progress, then continues the boot process. Support for **LZO**, **xz**, **LZ4,** and **zstd** compression was added later.

The decompression routine is a negligible factor in startup time, and before the arrival of **bzImage**, the size constraints of certain architectures were extremely limiting, particularly under **x86**, making compression mandatory.

Decompression at boot of a compressed Linux kernel:

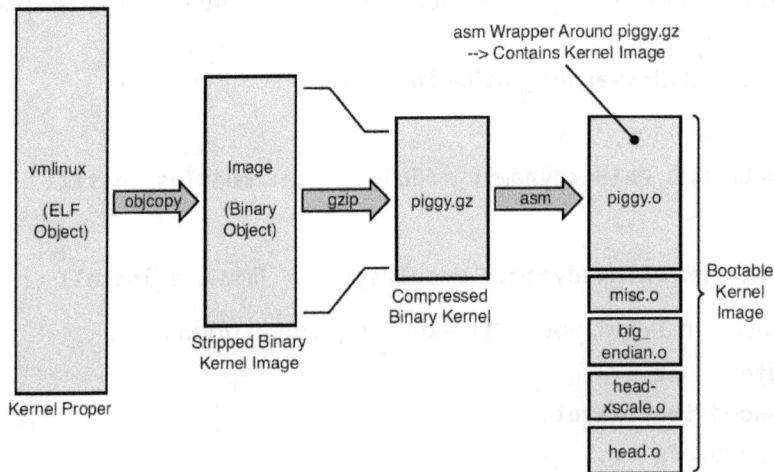

Figure 2.9: Linux kernel boot and decompression process

The file name of the boot image is not important, but most distributions use **vmlinuz** as the image.

As the Linux kernel has evolved, the size of user-generated kernels has exceeded the limits imposed by some architectures, where the space available to store compressed kernel code is limited. The bzImage (big zImage) format was designed to overcome this limitation by dividing the kernel into non-contiguous memory regions.

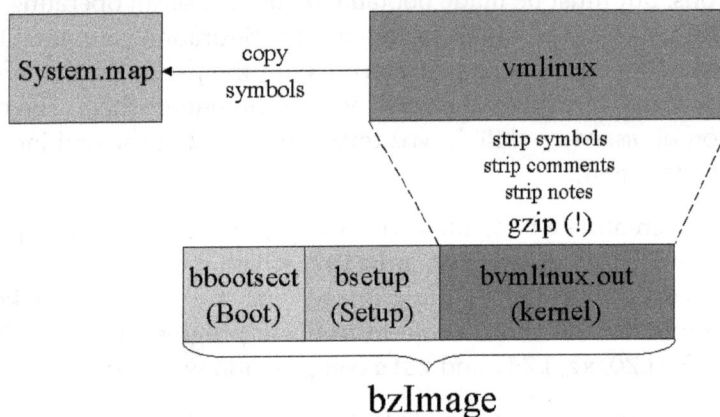

Figure 2.10: Anatomy of a bzImage

The **bzImage** was compressed using **gzip** until Linux 2.6.30, which introduced more algorithms. Although the **bz** prefix might make you think that **bzip2** compression is used, this is not the case. (**bzip2** is often distributed with tools prefixed with **bz**, such as **bzless**, **bzcat**, and many more.)

The **System.map** file is also generated when the Linux kernel is compiled. It is a symbol table used by the kernel. A table is a lookup between symbol names and their addresses in memory. A symbol name can be the name of a variable or the name of a function. It is required when the address of a symbol name or the symbol name of an address is needed during debugging process. It is particularly useful for debugging kernel panics and errors. The kernel does the address-to-name translation itself when **CONFIG_KALLSYMS** is enabled, so tools like **ksymoops** are not required.

The **bzImage** file follows a specific structure: **bootsect.o + setup.o + misc.o + piggy.o concatenated**. **piggy.o** contains the **gzipped vmlinux** file in its data section. The extract-**vmlinux** script in the **scripts/** directory in the kernel sources extracts a GNU/Linux kernel image.

Some distributions may provide a **kernel-debuginfo** package that contains the **vmlinux** file for the corresponding kernel RPM, and it is usually installed under **/usr/lib/debug/ lib/modules/`** uname -r` **/vmlinux, /usr /lib/debug/lib64/modules/`uname -r`/vmlinux**, or **/boot**.

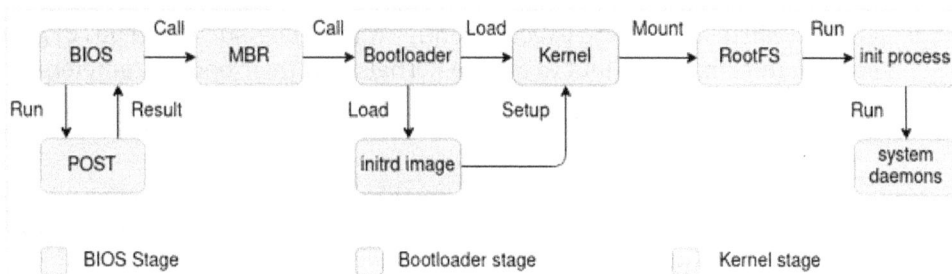

Figure 2.11: *The boot sequence in three steps*

The process of booting a Linux kernel from the BIOS, **Master Boot Record** (**MBR**), GRUB2, and **initial RAM disk** (**initrd**) involves a sequence of steps that the system follows during startup.

In the previous run with **qemu**, **qemu** replaces the BIOS and bootloader (**qemu** or another).

Here is an overview of the startup process of a Linux OS:

- **BIOS initialization**:
  - When you power on or reset a computer system, the **Basic Input/Output System** (**BIOS**) is the first software that runs.
  - The BIOS performs hardware checks, initializes devices, and locates a bootable device to load the boot loader.
  - The BIOS typically looks for bootable devices in a predefined order, such as the hard drive, CD/DVD drive, USB drive, or network boot, depending on the BIOS settings.

- **Master boot record**:

  o If the bootable device is a hard drive, the BIOS looks for the **Master Boot Record (MBR)**, which is the first sector (512 bytes) of the bootable storage device.

  o The MBR contains the primary boot loader code, which is a small program responsible for loading the secondary boot loader, such as GRUB2.

- **Secondary Boot Loader (GRUB2)**:

  o **Grand Unified Boot Loader (GRUB2)** is a popular secondary boot loader used in many Linux distributions.

  o When the MBR code executes, it loads the secondary boot loader's core image, typically located in a specific partition known as the **/boot** partition.

  o GRUB2 presents a menu to the user (if configured) and allows the selection of a specific kernel to boot.

  o GRUB2 can also load and execute configuration files, such as **grub.cfg**, which contain information about available kernels and their boot parameters.

  o In the embedded world, the **qemu** bootloader is very widely used.

- **Linux Kernel load**:

  o Once a specific kernel is selected, GRUB2 loads the Linux kernel image (e.g., **vmlinuz**) into memory.

  o GRUB2 also specifies the kernel command line parameters, including the root filesystem and the location of the **initrd** image.

- **Initrd (Initial RAM Disk)**:

  o The **initrd** is an initial RAM disk that contains essential drivers and utilities needed to mount the root filesystem.

  o The kernel loads the **initrd** into memory and extracts its contents.

  o The **initrd** is particularly useful for systems where the root filesystem is stored on complex storage devices, such as **Logical Volume Manager (LVM)** or software RAID arrays.

  o It allows the kernel to access the necessary drivers before mounting the actual root filesystem.

- **Root Filesystem mounting**:

  o With the help of the **initrd**, the kernel mounts the root filesystem, typically located on the hard drive.

- o Once the root filesystem is mounted, the kernel transitions control to the **init** process, which is the first user-space process and the ancestor of all other processes.

- o The **init** process initializes the rest of the user-space components, services, and applications.

The **initrd** is often used as a temporary workaround to ensure the system can boot when more complex storage or device configurations are involved. Once the root filesystem is mounted, the kernel no longer needs the **initrd**. The exact details of the boot process can vary depending on the distribution and configuration, but this overview provides a general understanding of how a Linux kernel boots from BIOS to **initrd**.

You can select a kernel and even modify it with additional kernel parameters. Optionally, you can use a command line shell for greater manual control over the startup process.

With the second stage bootloader in memory, the file system is consulted and the default kernel image and **initrd** image are loaded into memory. Once the images are ready, the bootloader from *Step 2* calls the kernel image.

Next, we come to the GNU/Linux kernel itself. At this stage, the kernel is not yet truly executed; First of all, the kernel configuration part needs to do some things like memory management related stuff. After all these things, the kernel will be unpacked and can finally run.

Coding styles

The Linux kernel community follows a well-defined coding style to maintain consistency and readability across the codebase. Adhering to these coding style guidelines is essential when contributing code to the Linux kernel.

The primary coding style rules are outlined in the **Linux Kernel Coding Style document**, which is accessible in the kernel source tree under **Documentation/process/coding-style.rst**.

Here are some of the key coding style guidelines for writing code within the Linux kernel:

- **Indentation**:
  - o Use tabs for indentation, not spaces. Each tab is equal to eight spaces.
- **Line length**:
  - o Limit lines to 80 characters in length for code and comments.
  - o **Exception**: You can go up to 100 characters for explanatory comments.
- **Braces:**
  - o Use the *Kernighan and Ritchie* style for braces, where the opening brace is on the same line as the statement or function declaration:

```
    if (condition) {
                /* code here */
        } else {
                /* code here */
        }
```

- **Functions and variables**:
  - o Function names are in lowercase with underscores (e.g., `function_name()`).
  - o Variable names are in lowercase with underscores (e.g., `variable_name`).
  - o Use descriptive variable and function names.

- **Structures**:
  - o Structure names are in lowercase with underscores, and field names are lowercase with underscores (e.g., `struct my_struct { int field_name; }`).

- **Comments**:
  - o Use `/* ... */` for comments rather than `//`.
  - o Comments should be concise and explain the *why* rather than the *what*.
  - o Document function parameters, return values, and global variables.
  - o Place comments before the code they describe.

- **Headers and includes**:
  - o Organize include statements alphabetically, with system headers first, followed by kernel headers, and then local headers.
  - o Avoid using `#include` inside header files to reduce dependency issues.

- **Whitespace and blank lines**:
  - o Use a single space after a comma.
  - o No trailing whitespace at the end of lines.
  - o Use blank lines to separate logical sections of code, but not excessively.

- **Switch statements**:
  - o Use `case` labels are indented at the same level as the `switch` statement, without additional indentation.

- **Return statements**:
  - o Avoid using complex expressions in return statements.
  - o Do not use parentheses around the return value unless necessary.

- **Error handling**:
  - Use negative error codes (e.g. **ENOMEM**) for error returns.
  - Avoid using **goto** for error handling; use structured error handling instead.

- **Macros**:
  - Use macros sparingly and prefer inline functions for simple tasks.
  - Macros should be named in uppercase with underscores (e.g., **#define MACRO_ NAME**).

- **Enums and constants**:
  - Enumerations are preferred over **#define** for constants.
  - Constants should be named in uppercase with underscores (e.g., **#define CONSTANT_NAME**).

- **Typecasting**:
  - Avoid unnecessary typecasting.
  - Use C99 types when appropriate (e.g., **int32_t**, **uint64_t**).

- **Headers for license and copyright**:
  - Include the appropriate license and copyright headers in source files.

These are some of the primary coding style guidelines used in the Linux kernel. Adhering to these guidelines helps maintain the readability and consistency of the codebase, making it easier for developers to collaborate and maintain the kernel.

When contributing to the Linux kernel, it is essential to follow these coding style rules to ensure that your code is accepted into the mainline kernel.

These rules will be important for us to start from the beginning with good habits.

Conclusion

This chapter was an important step in understanding the different parts of a GNU/Linux kernel, but also in understanding the different stages of generating a custom kernel.

For the moment, we have not yet written any code or modified anything; we have just taken the sources as is. However, in the next chapter, we will begin to put our hands into the heart of the system by developing its first drivers from scratch.

Join our book's Discord space

Join the book's Discord Workspace for Latest updates, Offers, Tech happenings around the world, New Release and Sessions with the Authors:

https://discord.bpbonline.com

## CHAPTER 3

Introduction to Device Drivers

Introduction

In the previous chapter, we saw how to configure a GNU/Linux kernel from sources, build it, and then execute it. In this chapter, we are going to focus on the kernel space and the user space, and focus on all the specificities of the drivers to start implementing them ourselves. This is a key chapter for getting started with drivers.

Structure

This chapter covers the following topics:

- User space, kernel space, and syscalls interface
- Driver's compilation within or outside the kernel
- Compilation inside Buildroot
- Compilation inside Yocto
- Kernel facilities and helper functions
- Error handling
- Installing modules
- Loading and unloading dynamic modules

- Modules dependencies
- Modules parameters
- Modules licensing
- Modules logging
- Dynamic kernel module support

Objectives

The main objective will be to better understand and assimilate the different interactions between the user space and the kernel itself. In addition, we will establish the foundations that will serve us throughout the book for writing drivers. By the end of this chapter, you will, therefore, be able to write simple drivers, compile them, and load them into the GNU/Linux kernel.

User space, kernel space, and syscalls interface

Linux is mainly divided into the unprivileged user space and kernel space. These two components interact through a **system called interface**, which is a predefined and mature interface to the Linux kernel for userspace applications.

The following figure will give you a basic understanding of the layer division between user space and kernel space:

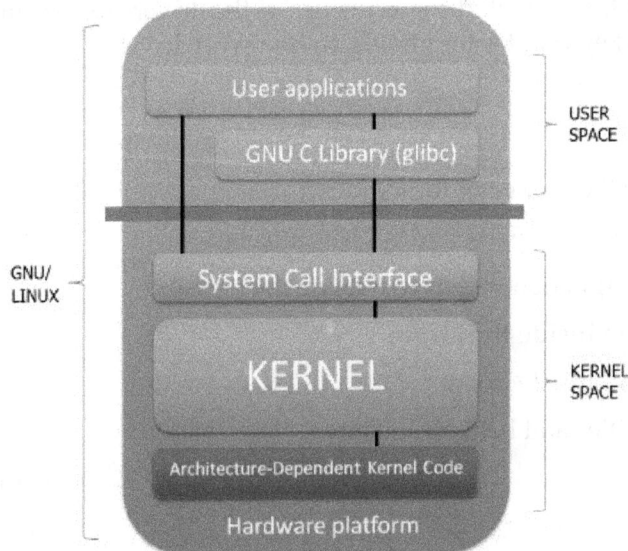

Figure 3.1: Interactions between user space and kernel via sci

Here is a description of each layer:

- **Userspace**:

    o   Userspace refers to the part of a computer's memory and processing power where user-level applications and processes run.

    o   User-level applications include things like text editors, web browsers, media players, and any software that a typical user interacts with directly.

    o   Userspace applications have limited access to hardware and system resources. They rely on the operating system's kernel to perform privileged operations, such as reading from and writing to hardware devices or managing memory.

- **Kernelspace**:

    o   Kernelspace is the part of the computer's memory and processing power where the operating system's kernel runs.

    o   The kernel is the core component of the operating system that manages system resources, schedules tasks, controls hardware devices, and enforces security.

    o   Kernelspace is considered privileged and has direct access to the hardware. The kernel handles hardware interrupts and system calls, making it a crucial part of the operating system.

- **System call interface:**

    o   The **system call interface (SCI)** is a set of functions and mechanisms that allow user-level applications in the userspace to request services provided by the kernel in the kernelspace.

    o   System calls are a standardized way for applications to interact with the kernel. They provide a bridge between the two spaces, allowing user-level applications to perform tasks that require privileged operations, such as file I/O, process management, and hardware access.

    o   Some common system calls include **open()/close()**, **read()**, **write()**, **fork()**, **exec()**, **exit()**, and so on.

    o   User-level applications make system calls using specific libraries and language constructs provided by the operating system. For example, in C, you can use functions like **open()**, **read()**, and **write()** to make system calls.

The sequence of events when a system call is made typically involves the following:

- The user-level application invokes a system call by using a function provided by the operating system's libraries (e.g., the C standard library).

- The library function prepares the arguments and triggers a software interrupt (e.g., using assembly instructions).

- The CPU switches from userspace to kernelspace and begins executing the kernel code.

- The kernel processes the system call, performs the requested operation, and returns the result to the user-level application.

- The CPU switches back to userspace, and the user-level application continues its execution.

The following figure shows the sequence of steps involved in calling one of the C standard library functions, **fwrite** (from the C library called **libc** or **glibc**):

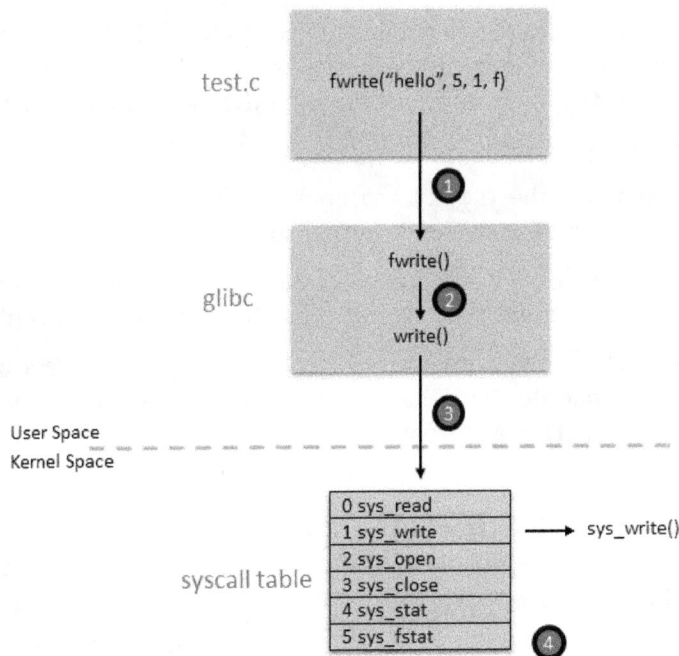

Figure 3.2: Tracing a system call from user space to the Linux kernel

Here are the steps in the process:

1. The **fwrite()** function (from the standard C library) is used within the **test.c** source code and is implemented in the **glibc*** which is one of the main components of Linux.

2. **fwrite()** is a wrapper for the **write()** function.

3. **write()** will load the ID for the **sys_write()** system call and its arguments into the processor registers, then perform a context switch to give control to the kernel level.

4. The way of the execution depends on the processor architecture, and sometimes the processor model. For example, x86 processors are typically called **interrupt 80**, while x64 processors use the syscall processor instruction. The processor, now running in kernel space, passed the system call ID to the system call table and called the function **sys_write()**.

The userspace, kernelspace, and system call interface are essential components of the GNU/Linux operating system's architecture, allowing it to provide a safe and controlled environment for running applications while efficiently managing system resources and hardware access.

Linux's SCI is largely POSIX compliant, although there are some Linux-specific variations and extensions. **Portable Operating System Interface (POSIX)** is a specification that defines a set of system interfaces, libraries, and programming standards for Unix-like operating systems aimed at ensuring the portability of applications across various Unix platforms.

Linux, as a Unix-like operating system, was designed based on POSIX principles and standards. As a result, many functions and system calls available in Linux follow POSIX specifications. This means that applications developed according to POSIX standards are generally compatible with Linux and other Unix-like operating systems.

However, it is essential to note that Linux also has its own specific extensions and features that are not covered by POSIX. Application developers should be aware of these differences and, in some cases, may need to adapt their applications to take advantage of Linux-specific features.

Drivers are no exception to the rule and interact with the binary via system calls. Only the kernel does nothing and does not make it an operating system. It needs processes, and therefore, the SCI is used as a standard communication interface.

All drivers are structured with two callbacks. The first callback, **init_module()**, is called during its loading to initialize and reserve all resources, and the second one, **cleanup_module()** to clean it up or deallocate during unloading.

The following figure details the dynamic loading of a kernel module into the GNU/Linux kernel. It shows the driver's input and output hooks:

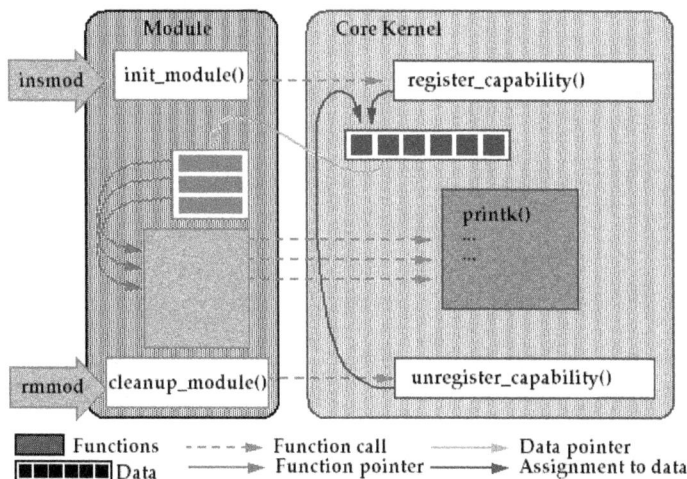

Figure 3.3: Dynamic (un)link of a driver in the kernel

To get started, we will use this simple code as hello world:

```
/*

 * The simplest hello-world kernel module
 */
#include <linux/init.h>    /* Needed for the macros */
#include <linux/module.h> /* Needed by all modules */
#include <linux/printk.h> /* Needed for pr_info()  */

static int __init hello_init(void)
{
        pr_info("Hello, world\n");
        return 0;
}

static void __exit hello_exit(void)
{
        pr_info("Goodbye, world\n");
}

module_init(hello_init);
module_exit(hello_exit);
MODULE_LICENSE("GPL");
```

Performed when loading the driver, the initialization callback is used to record and reserve the resources necessary for the proper functioning of the driver (capabilities). Conversely, the cleanup callback is used to free all unnecessary resources when unloading the driver.

We will use this code skeleton to highlight the different points of this chapter.

Driver's compilation within or outside the kernel

Now that we have a minimalist driver, we want to compile it so we can play with it.

For this, there are several possibilities depending on whether the code is already in the Linux kernel sources. In *Chapter 2, Introduction to the Linux Kernel*, we saw how to retrieve the sources of a GNU/Linux kernel, and now it will be useful to us because the **makefile** at the root of the project sources is the engine to generate a driver.

Compilation within the GNU/Linux kernel

The goal is to customize the GNU/Linux kernel sources and add an entry that can be viewed via the commands: **make menuconfig**

Here are the files needed in the **drivers/helloworld/** directory, with, of course, the **helloworld.c**:

```
drivers/helloworld/
├── helloworld.c
├── Kconfig
└── Makefile
```

All drivers are located in the **drivers/** directory of the Linux kernel sources. At this stage, we will go to the root of the source code.

We have to add first the following line at the end of the **drivers/Makefile** file so that it is known from the sources:

```
obj-$(CONFIG_HELLOWORLD) += helloworld/
```

To edit the **drivers/Kconfig** file, add the following line before the **endmenu** line:

```
source "drivers/helloworld/Kconfig"
```

From there, we will create a new directory that will contain our hello world driver:

```
$ mkdir -p helloworld/
```

Create the **drivers/helloworld/Kconfig** file and edit it:

```
menu "HELLOWORLD support"
config HELLOWORLD
        tristate "HELLOWORLD Support"
        default m
        help
        Say Y to enable HELLOWORLD support, M to compile it as a module
endmenu
```

Finally, create the **drivers/helloworld/Makefile** file:

```
obj-${CONFIG_HELLOWORLD} := helloworld.o
```

We can, therefore, (re)configure our kernel with the **.config** file (o reload) corresponding to the current kernel of your development machine. Check that the configuration interface displays your new driver and allows you to select it as a module. Select the device drivers menu, then go to the bottom:

```
$ make menuconfig
```

The following figure shows the possible selection of our module in the GNU/Linux kernel configuration step. The arrow indicates a sub-part:

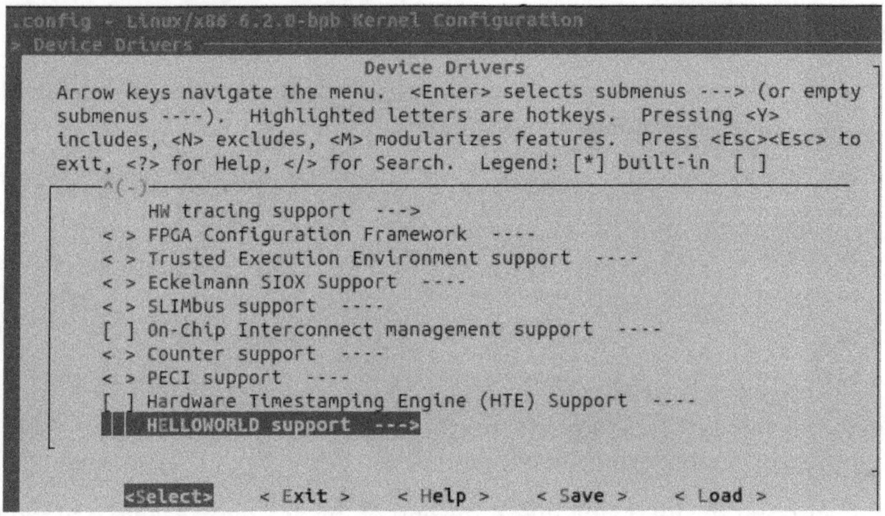

Figure 3.4: *Selection of our new module*

In the **drivers/helloworld/Makefile** file, we select **"tristate"** with the following states:

- **State 1**: Not selected.

- **State 2 or M**: Compiled as drivers; this will generate a **.ko** file.

- **State 3 or ***: Compiled in the static part of the Linux kernel.

We can change the state using the spacebar.

The following figure shows the sub-part of our sub-menu allowing the tri-state selection as seen previously (If this remains empty, the module will not be compiled):

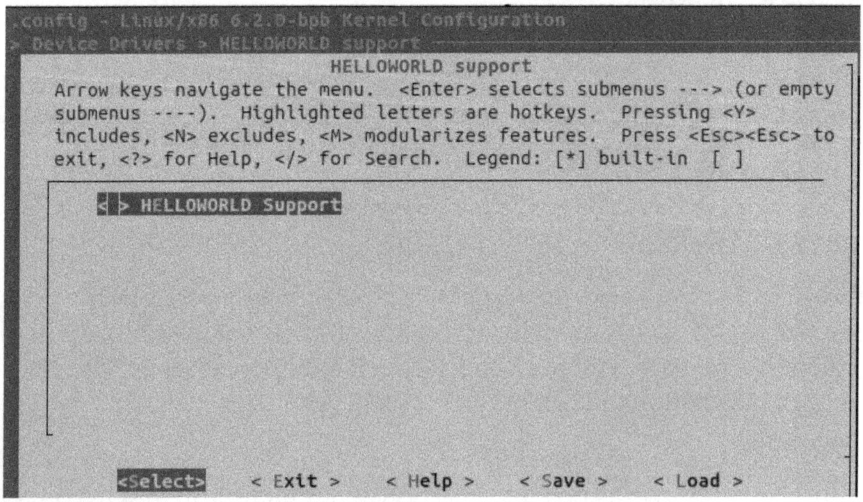

Figure 3.5: *Driver not selected in the kernel config*

The following figure shows the selection of our driver in the dynamic module (M):

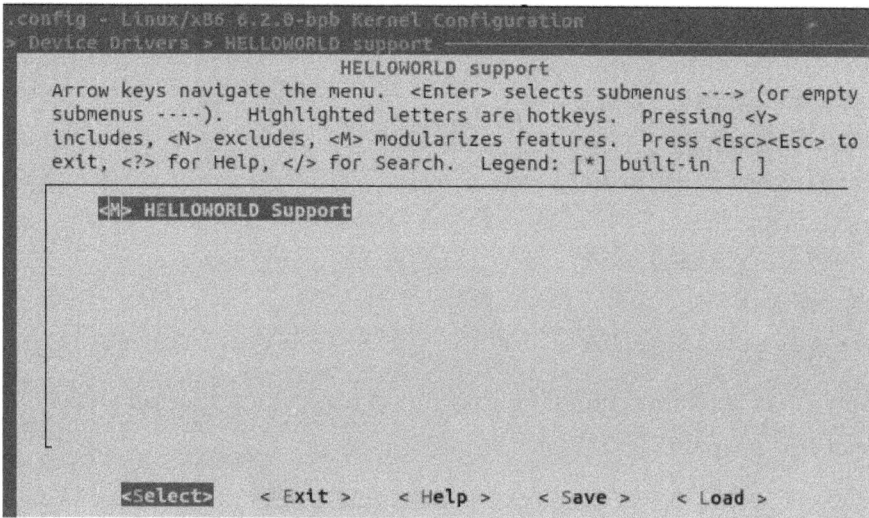

Figure 3.6: Driver selected to be compiled as a dynamic module

The following figure shows the selection of our driver in the static part of the kernel itself:

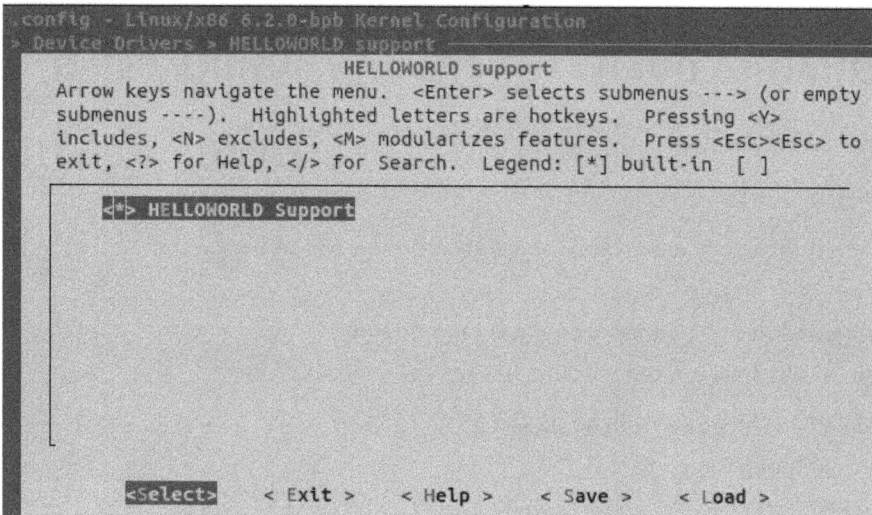

Figure 3.7: Driver selected to be compiled in the static part of the kernel

The **HELLOWORLD** driver should appear at the end of the device drivers list:

```
$ cat .config |grep -i helloworld
# HELLOWORLD support
CONFIG_HELLOWORLD=m
# end of HELLOWORLD support
```

We can therefore start compiling the module:

```
$ make
[...]
LD drivers/helloworld/builtin.
o
CC [M] drivers/helloworld/helloworld.o
MODPOST vmlinux
Building modules, stage 2.
MODPOST 1 modules
CC drivers/helloworld/helloworld.mod.
```

Note: Sometimes the kernel must be ready for modules compilation with:

```
$ make modules_prepare
```

Adding a driver in this way is very rare because of its presence in the kernel sources; it is contaminated by the GPL license of the GNU/Linux kernel! This is why the majority of cases are compiled externally using the Makefile from the sources. This is what we will see now. We will study another external approach, which consists of relocating the sources of a driver outside the kernel source code.

Compilation outside the GNU/Linux kernel

The difference with the previous compilation is that the sources of our drivers are not those of the GNU/Linux kernel. We will therefore need a Makefile, which will be written to remotely invoke the one located at the root of the kernel sources:

Let us create a directory called **helloworld** with the following two files:

```
helloworld
├── helloworld.c  : source code of our driver
└── Makefile main file used to build/install our driver
```

Our **makefile** will have the following content:

```
obj-m := helloworld.o
KERNEL_DIRECTORY := /lib/modules/$(shell uname -r)/build

all:
        make helloworld-C $(KERNEL_DIRECTORY modules
    modinfo ./helloworld.ko

load:
        insmod ./helloworld.ko
```

```
        dmesg

unload:
        rmmod ./helloworld.ko
        dmesg

install:
    make M=$(shell pwd)-C $(KERNEL_DIRECTORY) modules_install
    /sbin/depmod -a

clean:
    make M=$(shell pwd)-C $(KERNEL_DIRECTORY) clean
```

For this step, you must have installed the sources of a Linux kernel whose path will be pointed to by the **KERNEL_DIRECTORY** variable!

Let us build the driver:

```
$ make
make M=/home/tgayet/Documents/bpb/03-introduction-to-the-device-
drivers-27-10-2023/helloworld -C /lib/modules/6.2.0-35-generic/build
modules
make[1]: Entering directory '/usr/src/linux-headers-6.2.0-35-generic'
  CC [M]  /home/tgayet/Documents/bpb/03-introduction-to-the-device-
drivers-27-10-2023/helloworld/helloworld.o
  MODPOST /home/tgayet/Documents/bpb/03-introduction-to-the-device-
drivers-27-10-2023/helloworld/Module.symvers
  CC [M]  /home/tgayet/Documents/bpb/03-introduction-to-the-device-
drivers-27-10-2023/helloworld/helloworld.mod.o
  LD [M]  /home/tgayet/Documents/bpb/03-introduction-to-the-device-
drivers-27-10-2023/helloworld/helloworld.ko
make[1]: Leaving directory '/usr/src/linux-headers-6.2.0-35-generic'
```

It must generate all the following files:

```
$ ls -al
total 344
drwxrwxr-x  2 tgayet tgayet    4096 oct.  23 19:54 .
drwxrwxr-x 10 tgayet tgayet    4096 oct.  23 19:54 ..
-rw-rw-r--  1 tgayet tgayet     436 oct.  23 19:35 helloworld.c
-rw-rw-r--  1 tgayet tgayet  109288 oct.  23 19:54 helloworld.ko
-rw-rw-r--  1 tgayet tgayet     497 oct.  23 19:54 .helloworld.ko.cmd
```

```
-rw-rw-r--   1 tgayet tgayet     100 oct.   23 19:54 helloworld.mod
-rw-rw-r--   1 tgayet tgayet     891 oct.   23 19:54 helloworld.mod.c
-rw-rw-r--   1 tgayet tgayet     364 oct.   23 19:54 .helloworld.mod.cmd
-rw-rw-r--   1 tgayet tgayet   93368 oct.   23 19:54 helloworld.mod.o
-rw-rw-r--   1 tgayet tgayet   39157 oct.   23 19:54 .helloworld.mod.o.cmd
-rw-rw-r--   1 tgayet tgayet   17336 oct.   23 19:54 helloworld.o
-rw-rw-r--   1 tgayet tgayet   38181 oct.   23 19:54 .helloworld.o.cmd
-rw-rw-r--   1 tgayet tgayet     326 oct.   23 19:31 Makefile
-rw-rw-r--   1 tgayet tgayet     100 oct.   23 19:54 modules.order
-rw-rw-r--   1 tgayet tgayet     326 oct.   23 19:54 .modules.order.cmd
-rw-rw-r--   1 tgayet tgayet       0 oct.   23 19:54 Module.symvers
-rw-rw-r--   1 tgayet tgayet     371 oct.   23 19:54 .Module.symvers.cmd
```

We can check our new **helloworld** driver:

$ file helloworld.ko

```
helloworld.ko: ELF 64-bit LSB relocatable, x86-64, version 1 (SYSV),
BuildID[sha1]=8b3236f53f04a0c4dddd0358f110e79b7aa36c83, with debug_info,
not stripped
```

$ modinfo helloworld.ko

```
filename:        /home/tgayet/Documents/bpb/03-introduction-to-the-device-
drivers-27-10-2023/helloworld/helloworld.ko
license:         GPL
srcversion:      80158CC88F1748420B63317
depends:
retpoline:       Y
name:            helloworld
vermagic:        6.2.0-35-generic SMP preempt mod_unload modversions
```

The drivers are well adapted to our kernel version thanks to **"uname -r"**. It can therefore be loaded dynamically without any problem:

$ insmod ./helloworld.ko

We can check that the module is well-loaded:

$ cat /proc/modules|grep -i helloworld

```
helloworld 16384 0 - Live 0x0000000000000000 (OE)
```

or

$ lsmod|grep -i helloworld

```
helloworld              16384  0
```

Finally, we can unload it:

```
$ rmmod ./helloworld.ko
```

The kernel traces will display a message from the driver:

```
$ dmesg -w
[20429.883271] Hello, world
[20624.543701] Goodbye, world
```

Here, we are with our **helloworld** drivers, which we will evolve over time.

If you need to split the source code into several files (**helloworld.c**, **start.c**, **stop.c**), you may have to adapt the above **makefile** as follows:

```
obj-m += helloworld.o
obj-m += startstop.o
startstop-objs := start.o stop.o
PWD := $(CURDIR)


all:
        make M=$(shell pwd) -C /lib/modules/$(shell uname -r)/build
modules


clean:
        make M=$(shell pwd) -C /lib/modules/$(shell uname -r)/build
```

For uses in the embedded world, we will quickly discuss the compilation of drivers in a Buildroot or Yocto environment. There are many build systems, unfortunately, we cannot describe them all, but the two discussed are the most common.

Compilation inside Buildroot project

In your Buildroot project, create the **helloworld** directory inside the package one.

```
package/
       └── helloworld
          ├── Config.in
          ├── helloworld.mk
          └── helloworld.c
```

Add the above **helloworld.c** source code into the **helloworld** directory.

In this directory, create a **Config.in** file. This file is used to configure the kernel driver package and enable it in the Buildroot configuration:

```
config BR2_PACKAGE_HELLOWORLD
    bool "Helloworld driver"
    depends on BR2_PACKAGE_HELLOWORLD_LOADABLE
    help
      My custom kernel driver

config BR2_PACKAGE_HELLOWORLD_LOADABLE
    bool "Enable helloworld Driver"
    default y
    help
      Enable building and loading of helloworld Driver
```

Create a **helloworld.mk** makefile that defines how to build and install your kernel driver. This makefile should specify the package name, source location, build instructions, and any other relevant details.

HELLOWORLD_VERSION = 1.0

HELLOWORLD_SOURCE = $(TOPDIR)/path/to/your/source

HELLOWORLD_SITE = file://$(HELLOWORLD_SOURCE)

HELLOWORLD_INSTALL_TARGET = YES

$(eval $(kernel-module))

Adjust the **HELLOWORLD_VERSION**, **HELLOWORLD_SOURCE**, and other variables to match your specific kernel driver. The **$(eval $(kernel-module))** line is used to instruct Buildroot to build it as a kernel module.

To include your custom kernel driver package in your Buildroot build, go to your Buildroot configuration (usually found in **configs/**) and enable your package under the "**Target packages**" section. You can do this either through the **menuconfig** interface or by directly editing the **.config** file.

After configuring your package, build your Buildroot project using the make command:

$ make

Once the Buildroot build is complete, you can find your kernel driver module inside the output directory. Install and load it on your target device as needed.

Compilation inside Yocto project

Yocto recipes are typically organized into layers. You should navigate to the Yocto layer in which you want to create the recipe. The meta-directory is commonly used to organize Yocto layers.

Inside your layer, create a directory to contain your kernel driver recipe. The directory structure should look like this:

```
meta-yourlayer/
├── recipes-kernel/
│   ├── helloworld/
│   │   ├── helloworld.bb
│   │   └── helloworld.c
```

In the helloworld's directory, create a **helloworld.bb** recipe file to define your kernel driver's recipe. The content of the **.bb** file should look like the following:

```
DESCRIPTION = "Helloworld Driver"
LICENSE = "CLOSED"  # Specify the appropriate license
SRC_URI = "file://path/to/your/source.tar.gz"
S = "${WORKDIR}"


# Define your build dependencies
DEPENDS = "linux-yocto"


# Specify the target kernel version
COMPATIBLE_MACHINE = "your-target-machine"


do_compile() {
    # Add your build instructions here
}


do_install() {
    # Define installation instructions (if needed)
}
FILES_${PN} += "${libdir}/modules/${KERNEL_VERSION}/extra/*"
```

Yocto works with templates; it will be enough to customize certain variables like the URL of the git repository containing the source of our driver, its license, and its dependencies:

- **Description**: Brief description of your kernel driver.

- **LICENSE**: Specify the appropriate license.

- **SRC_URI**: Source URI pointing to your driver source code.

- **DEPENDS**: Define any build dependencies. In this case, we specified **linux-yocto** as an example.

- **COMPATIBLE_MACHINE**: Specify the target machine for your driver.

- **do_compile()**: Add build instructions specific to your kernel driver.
- **do_install()**: Define installation instructions if required.
- **FILES_${PN}**: Specify the location to install the kernel module files.

To include your custom driver in your Yocto image, you will need to add it to your image recipe. You can do this by modifying your custom image recipe in the Yocto project's configuration. Here is a simplified example of how to add it to your image recipe:

```
IMAGE_INSTALL_append = " helloworld"
```

This line tells Yocto to include your **helloworld** package in the image.

After defining your kernel driver recipe and adding it to your image, you can build the Yocto image using the **bitbake** command:

```
$ bitbake your-image
```

After the build process, you will find your kernel driver module in the deployment directory specified in your Yocto configuration. You can deploy and load it on your target device as needed.

Kernel facilities and helper functions

Kernel facilities and helper functions in the Linux kernel are critical components for driver development and low-level system operations.

These facilities and functions provide various services and abstractions to manage hardware, perform common tasks, and interact with the kernel's core. Here are some of the key kernel facilities and helper functions:

- **Kernel modules (loadable kernel modules)**:
  - **module_init() and module_exit()**: Functions used to specify initialization and cleanup functions for kernel modules.
  - **EXPORT_SYMBOL() and EXPORT_SYMBOL_GPL()**: Macros are used to export symbols from a module for use by other modules.
- **Kernel logging**:
  - **printk()**: The primary function for logging messages to the kernel log.
  - **pr_<level>()**: Macros for logging at specific log levels, such as **pr_err()**, **pr_info()**, etc.
- **Memory allocation and deallocation**:
  - **kmalloc(), kzalloc(), kcalloc(), and kfree()**: Functions for dynamic memory allocation and deallocation.
  - **vmalloc(), vfree()**: Functions for allocating and freeing large chunks of memory from the kernel's virtual memory pool.

- **Device registration and management**:
  - ○ **alloc_chrdev_region()**: Allocate a range of character device numbers.
  - ○ **cdev_init() and cdev_add()**: Initialize and add a character device to the kernel.
  - ○ **register_chrdev_region()**: Register a range of character device numbers.

- **Kernel synchronization and locking**:
  - ○ **spin_lock() and spin_unlock()**: Functions for implementing spin locks.
  - ○ **mutex_init(), mutex_lock(), and mutex_unlock()**: Functions for using mutex locks.
  - ○ **semaphore_init(), down() and up()**: Functions for using semaphores.
  - ○ **atomic_t and related atomic operations**: Tools for atomic operations on variables.

- **File operations**:
  - ○ **file_operations structure:** Contains function pointers for handling file operations, such as open, read, write, and close.

- **Kernel timers**:
  - ○ **init_timer() and add_timer()**: Functions for working with kernel timers.
  - ○ **jiffies**: A variable that represents the number of timer ticks since system startup.

- **Work queues and work items**:
  - ○ **queue_work(), queue_delayed_work(), and related functions**: Used for deferred work execution.
  - ○ **struct work_struct**: A data structure representing a work item.

- **Interrupt handling**:
  - ○ **request_irq() and free_irq()**: Functions for requesting and releasing interrupt handlers.
  - ○ **irqreturn_t and related types**: Used for interrupt handler functions.
  - ○ **atomic_t and atomic_inc()/atomic_dec()**: Atomic operations for managing shared data in an interrupt context.

- **Power management**:
  - ○ **pm_runtime_get(), pm_runtime_put(), and related functions**: Used for managing power states of devices.

- **Device trees**:
  - ○ **of_get_property()**: Function for retrieving properties from the device tree.

- o **of_platform_populate()**: Function to populate the platform bus with devices based on device tree information.

- **Miscellaneous helper functions**: Various helper functions for string manipulation, list management, bit manipulation, etc., are available in the Linux kernel libraries.

These facilities and helper functions play a crucial role in kernel driver development and in implementing various aspects of the kernel.

They provide a standardized way to interact with the kernel's core and manage hardware devices, ensuring stability and compatibility across different hardware platforms.

Error handling

Handling errors in a Linux driver is crucial for maintaining system stability and ensuring the proper operation of hardware or software components.

Error handling can be complex and depends on the specific context of the driver. Here are the general guidelines for handling errors in a Linux driver:

- **Return values:** In C code, it is common to use return values to indicate errors. Functions that can fail typically return an error code or a negative value. For example, the standard convention is to return 0 for success and a negative value for failure, with negative error codes indicating specific error conditions.

- **Error codes:** Use predefined error codes to make error handling more explicit and meaningful. In the Linux kernel, error codes are defined in header files like **errno.h** and can be used in your driver code.

- **Log errors:** When an error occurs, log the details to the kernel log using functions like **pr_err()**, **dev_err()**, or **printk()**. This allows system administrators and developers to diagnose problems.

  Example:

  ```
  if (error_condition) {
      pr_err("Error message: %s\n", error_description);
      return -ENODEV; // Return an appropriate error code
  }
  ```

- **Cleanup resources:** If your driver has allocated resources (memory, I/O ports, etc.), make sure to release them when an error occurs. This can involve freeing memory, unregistering devices, or undoing any setup your driver has done.

- **Return appropriate error codes:** When returning error codes, make sure to use meaningful codes that indicate the specific error condition. Linux provides a wide range of error codes (e.g., -ENOMEM for out-of-memory, -EIO for I/O errors). Choose the most appropriate code to describe the problem.

- **Recovery**: Consider whether your driver can recover from certain errors. For example, if there is a communication error with hardware, you might attempt to reset the device or recover gracefully.

- **Avoid kernel panics**: Make every effort to avoid kernel panics. If an error is so severe that the system cannot continue to operate safely, it might be better to unload the driver or disable the hardware rather than crash the kernel.

- **Testing and validation**: Rigorously test your driver under various conditions to ensure it handles errors correctly. This includes negative test cases to trigger error conditions.

- **Documentation**: Document the error handling strategies used in your driver code so that other developers can understand and maintain the code effectively.

- **User-friendly messages**: If your driver is providing messages to userspace, ensure that error messages are clear and provide helpful information about what went wrong.

- **Code review**: Have your code reviewed by experienced developers. They may identify potential error scenarios or suggest improvements in error handling.

- **Use debugging tools**: The Linux kernel offers various debugging tools and frameworks (e.g., **kprobes**, **kdump**, **kexec**) that can help diagnose and troubleshoot driver issues.

Error handling in kernel drivers is a critical aspect of kernel development. Understanding the expected error scenarios and how to respond to them is essential for creating reliable and stable drivers.

This topic will be discussed more extensively in *Chapter 13, Debugging GNU/Linux Kernel and Drivers*.

Installing modules

Installing a driver is done via the initial makefile using the **modules_install** target of the main Makefile of the GNU Linux kernel:

```
$ make  modules_install
```

The **depmod** command is used to generate a cache of module dependencies. This information is crucial for the kernel to efficiently manage and (un)load kernel modules dynamically. To do this, simply use the **depmod** command after installing a module:

```
$ depmod -a
```

The main purposes of **depmod** are as follows:

- **Dependency resolution**:
    - One of the primary purposes of **depmod** is to analyze kernel modules and determine their dependencies on other modules.

o Kernel modules often depend on other modules to function correctly. **depmod** identifies these dependencies, which may include other kernel modules or symbols, and creates a database of this information.

- **Module loading**:

  o The kernel uses the dependency information generated by **depmod** when loading modules using commands like **modprobe** or during the system's boot process.

  o When a module is requested for loading, the kernel checks the dependency information to ensure that all required modules are loaded first.

- **Preventing symbol conflicts**:

  o Kernel modules can define and use symbols (functions or variables) that may be common across multiple modules.

  o **depmod** helps avoid symbol conflicts by maintaining a record of which symbols are used by which modules. This prevents modules from using the same symbol name in conflicting ways.

- **Efficient module loading**:

  o **depmod** creates a file named **modules.dep** that stores the module dependencies in a format that is easily parsed by the kernel.

  o This allows the kernel to load modules efficiently, as it can quickly determine the required order of loading based on dependencies.

- **Updating module dependencies**:

  o The dependency information is updated whenever new modules are installed, existing modules are modified, or the kernel is updated.

  o When the system's kernel is updated, it is common to run **depmod** to ensure that the module dependencies are current and in sync with the new kernel version.

In summary, **depmod** plays a vital role in managing and loading kernel modules in a Linux system by generating and maintaining module dependency information. This information helps ensure the proper functioning of the kernel and the modules it relies on. It is an essential tool for module management and system stability.

This command updates the file **/lib/modules/`uname -r`/modules.dep** which is used mainly for loading and dynamic loading with **modprobe**:

```
$ cat /lib/modules/`uname -r`/modules.dep
updates/dkms/sysdig-probe.ko:
kernel/zfs/znvpair.ko: kernel/zfs/spl.ko
```

```
kernel/zfs/spl.ko:
misc/vboxnetadp.ko: misc/vboxdrv.ko
(...)
```

The most important cache files are generally:

- **/lib/modules/`uname -r`/modules.dep**: This file contains a list of modules and their dependencies.

- **/lib/modules/`uname -r`/modules.alias**: This file contains aliases for modules, allowing a module to be loaded using different names.

Loading and unloading dynamic modules

There are two methods of loading or unloading drivers under Linux, one *manual* (**isnmod** / **rmmod**) and the other *automatic* (**modprobe**), as we saw with the **depmod** command during installation.

You can load a module using the **insmod** or **modprobe** command. Use **insmod** to load a module manually. Replace **<module_name>** with the name of your module file without the **.ko** extension:

```
$ sudo insmod /path/to/your/module_name.ko
```

To unload a module manually, use the following command with **rmmod**, replacing **<module_name>** with the name of the module you want to unload:

```
$ sudo rmmod module_name
```

The **modprobe** command is the recommended command for loading modules because it handles dependencies. If the module has dependencies, **modprobe** will load them automatically. Use it like this:

```
$ sudo modprobe module_name
```

To unload a module with **modprobe**, use the following command with the **-r** option, replacing **<module_name>** with the name of the module you want to unload:

```
$ sudo modprobe -r module_name
```

The **-r** option tells **modprobe** to remove the specified module.

If the module has dependencies, **modprobe** will also unload any modules that depend on it. Be cautious when unloading modules, as this can affect the functionality of your system.

Modules dependencies

It is common for a driver to serve as a function for another driver by exporting useful and factorable functions.

The dependency of one driver on another is based on symbols shared between them. For example, we will see a module exporting a symbol (a function), which will be used (via an import) in another separate module:

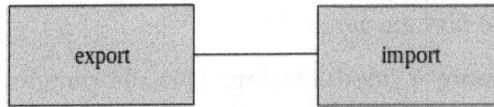

Figure 3.8: Two drivers with dependency

To centralize the exported and shared function(s), it is common to use a **.h** file, which centralizes their prototypes:

```
#ifndef EXPORT_SYMBOLE_H
#define EXPORT_SYMBOLE_H
void fonction_hello(int numero);
#endif
```

The code of the first **export** driver is that of the driver exporting the **function_hello** function. We notice the use of the **export_api.h** header:

```
#include <linux/module.h>
#include "export_api.h"

static int __init export_chargement(void)
{
        printk(KERN_ALERT "Hello, world\n");
        return 0;
}

static void __exit export_dechargement(void)
{
      printk(KERN_ALERT "Goodbye, cruel world\n");
}

void fonction_hello(int numero)
{
        printk (KERN_INFO "Hello, le numero est %d\n", numero);
}

EXPORT_SYMBOL(fonction_hello);
MODULE_LICENSE("GPL");
module_init(export_chargement);
module_exit(export_dechargement);
```

The code of the second **import** driver is that of the driver importing the **function_hello** function. We can also notice the use of the **"export_api.h"** header:

```
#include <linux/module.h>
#include "export_api.h"


static int __init import_chargement(void)
{
        printk(KERN_ALERT "Hello, world\n");
        fonction_hello(10); // inported function
        return 0;
}


static void __exit import_dechargement(void)
{
        fonction_hello(20); // imported function
        printk(KERN_ALERT "Goodbye, cruel world\n");
}


module_init(import_chargement);
module_exit(import_dechargement);
MODULE_LICENSE("GPL");
```

During the compilation phase, two interdependent drivers will be generated:

```
$ make
make M=/home/tgayet/Documents/bpb/03-introduction-to-the-device-
drivers-27-10-2023/code_3_dependencies -C /lib/modules/6.2.0-35-generic/
build modules
make[1]: Entering directory '/usr/src/linux-headers-6.2.0-35-generic'
warning: the compiler differs from the one used to build the kernel
  The kernel was built by: x86_64-linux-gnu-gcc-11 (Ubuntu
11.4.0-1ubuntu1~22.04) 11.4.0
  You are using:            gcc-11 (Ubuntu 11.4.0-1ubuntu1~22.04) 11.4.0
  CC [M]  /home/tgayet/Documents/bpb/03-introduction-to-the-device-
drivers-27-10-2023/code_3_dependencies/export.o
  CC [M]  /home/tgayet/Documents/bpb/03-introduction-to-the-device-
drivers-27-10-2023/code_3_dependencies/import.o
  MODPOST /home/tgayet/Documents/bpb/03-introduction-to-the-device-
drivers-27-10-2023/code_3_dependencies/Module.symvers
  CC [M]  /home/tgayet/Documents/bpb/03-introduction-to-the-device-
```

```
drivers-27-10-2023/code_3_dependencies/export.mod.o
   LD [M]   /home/tgayet/Documents/bpb/03-introduction-to-the-device-
drivers-27-10-2023/code_3_dependencies/export.ko
   BTF [M] /home/tgayet/Documents/bpb/03-introduction-to-the-device-
drivers-27-10-2023/code_3_dependencies/export.ko
Skipping BTF generation for /home/tgayet/Documents/bpb/03-introduction-
to-the-device-drivers-27-10-2023/code_3_dependencies/export.ko due to
unavailability of vmlinux
   CC [M]   /home/tgayet/Documents/bpb/03-introduction-to-the-device-
drivers-27-10-2023/code_3_dependencies/import.mod.o
   LD [M]   /home/tgayet/Documents/bpb/03-introduction-to-the-device-
drivers-27-10-2023/code_3_dependencies/import.ko
   BTF [M] /home/tgayet/Documents/bpb/03-introduction-to-the-device-
drivers-27-10-2023/code_3_dependencies/import.ko
Skipping BTF generation for /home/tgayet/Documents/bpb/03-introduction-
to-the-device-drivers-27-10-2023/code_3_dependencies/import.ko due to
unavailability of vmlinux
make[1]: Leaving directory '/usr/src/linux-headers-6.2.0-35-generic'
modinfo ./export.ko
filename:        /home/tgayet/Documents/bpb/03-introduction-to-the-device-
drivers-27-10-2023/code_3_dependencies/./export.ko
license:         GPL
srcversion:      FA57E7778C239436BA6A952
depends:
retpoline:       Y
name:            export
vermagic:        6.2.0-35-generic SMP preempt mod_unload modversions
modinfo ./import.ko
filename:        /home/tgayet/Documents/bpb/03-introduction-to-the-device-
drivers-27-10-2023/code_3_dependencies/./import.ko
license:         GPL
srcversion:      A6734BD1D5BFFB086A3B429
depends:         export
retpoline:       Y
name:            import
vermagic:        6.2.0-35-generic SMP preempt mod_unload modversions
```

With manual loading, it becomes complicated because you obviously have to export the module that exports its function before loading the one that needs it.

If we try to manually load the second driver without loading the first, we observe that the loading fails due to the absence of the symbol not found:

```
$ sudo insmod import.ko
[sudo] password for thierryg:
insmod: error inserting 'import.ko': -1 Unknown symbol in module
```

If we load the module **export.ko** first, and then the module **import.ko**, it goes better:

We can start with loading the first module:

```
$ sudo insmod export.ko
```

It is possible to check the presence of the symbol within the kernel:

```
$ cat /proc/kallsyms | grep function_hello
f7c5709c r __ksymtab_function_hello [export]
f7c570a4 r __kstrtab_function_hello [export]
f7c57000 T hello_function [drv_export]
```

We can now load the second module successfully:

```
$ sudo insmod import.ko
```

For unloading, the first module **export.ko** cannot be unloaded because it is used by the second **import.ko**:

```
$ sudo rmmod export.ko
$ sudo rmmod import.ko
```

If done in this order, it will generate the following error: **"Module export is in use by import"**.

To do this, you must unload the second module, then the first:

```
$ sudo rmmod import.ko
$ sudo rmmod export.ko
```

As for dynamic (un)loading, this is where it is easy to use thanks to the dependency file generated by **depmod**; everything is done by itself:

To load a module dynamically:

```
$ sudo modprobe export
$ lsmod | grep import
$ lsmod | grep export
```

Due to the dependencies **/lib/modules/`uname -r`/modules.dep**, **modprobe** will have loaded the first module **export.ko** then **import.ko**.

Unloading is just as easy:

```
$ sudo modprobe -r export
```

Modprobe will unload the **import.ko** module, then if it is no longer used, it will also unload the export module.

Modules parameters

A driver is like a binary; it can manage parameters that will condition its loading and be used at the time of its initialization.

The following is an example of a driver that can manage a parameter:

```c
#include <linux/init.h>
#include <linux/module.h>
#include <linux/moduleparam.h>

MODULE_LICENSE("Dual BSD/GPL");

static char* whom    = "world";
static int   howmany = 1;

module_param(howmany, int,    S_IRUGO);
module_param(whom,     charp, S_IRUGO);

static int param_init(void)
{
        int i;
        for (i = 0 ;  i <= howmany ;   i++)
        {
                printk(KERN_ALERT "(%d) Hello, %s\n", i, whom);
        }
        return 0;
}


static void param_exit(void)
{
        printk(KERN_ALERT "Goodbye, cruel world\n");
}


module_init(param_init);
module_exit(param_exit);
```

Compile the drivers using the previous **makefile** and test the driver with **modinfo** which should show the parameters:

```
$ make
make M=/home/tgayet/Documents/bpb/03-introduction-to-the-device-
drivers-27-10-2023/code_3_parameters -C /lib/modules/6.2.0-35-generic/build
modules
make[1]: Entering directory '/usr/src/linux-headers-6.2.0-35-generic'
warning: the compiler differs from the one used to build the kernel
  The kernel was built by: x86_64-linux-gnu-gcc-11 (Ubuntu
11.4.0-1ubuntu1~22.04) 11.4.0
  You are using:                gcc-11 (Ubuntu 11.4.0-1ubuntu1~22.04) 11.4.0
  CC [M]  /home/tgayet/Documents/bpb/03-introduction-to-the-device-
drivers-27-10-2023/code_3_parameters/param.o
  MODPOST /home/tgayet/Documents/bpb/03-introduction-to-the-device-
drivers-27-10-2023/code_3_parameters/Module.symvers
  CC [M]  /home/tgayet/Documents/bpb/03-introduction-to-the-device-
drivers-27-10-2023/code_3_parameters/param.mod.o
  LD [M]  /home/tgayet/Documents/bpb/03-introduction-to-the-device-
drivers-27-10-2023/code_3_parameters/param.ko
  BTF [M] /home/tgayet/Documents/bpb/03-introduction-to-the-device-
drivers-27-10-2023/code_3_parameters/param.ko
Skipping BTF generation for /home/tgayet/Documents/bpb/03-introduction-
to-the-device-drivers-27-10-2023/code_3_parameters/param.ko due to
unavailability of vmlinux
make[1]: Leaving directory '/usr/src/linux-headers-6.2.0-35-generic'
modinfo ./param.ko
filename:       /home/tgayet/Documents/bpb/03-introduction-to-the-device-
drivers-27-10-2023/code_3_parameters/./param.ko
license:        Dual BSD/GPL
srcversion:     7A66826FBC8FB7CDB8F5059
depends:
retpoline:      Y
name:           param
vermagic:       6.2.0-35-generic SMP preempt mod_unload modversions
parm:           howmany:int
parm:           whom:charp
```

We observe two parameters here:

```
$ tree  /sys/module/param/parameters
/sys/module/param/parameters
├── howmany
└── whom
```

As we can see, these two values are read-only and cannot be modified:

```
$ ls -alh /sys/module/param/parameters/
total 0
drwxr-xr-x 2 root root     0 oct.  26 21:51 .
drwxr-xr-x 6 root root     0 oct.  26 21:51 ..
-r--r--r-- 1 root root 4,0K oct.  26 21:51 howmany
-r--r--r-- 1 root root 4,0K oct.  26 21:51 whom
```

We can load our module without any parameters (use of the default context):

```
$ sudo insmod param.ko
$ lsmod | grep param
param                 16384  0
$ dmesg
[ 7658.068510] (0) Hello, world
```

We will test each loading combination with the parameters. Between each, you will have to remember to unload the driver:

```
$ sudo rmmod param
```

Without parameters or when a parameter is not marked, a default value must be set.

Then, with a single parameter:

```
$ sudo insmod param.ko howmany=5
$ dmesg
[ 7404.087814] (0) Hello, world
[ 7404.087821] (1) Hello, world
[ 7404.087822] (2) Hello, world
[ 7404.087823] (3) Hello, world
[ 7404.087824] (4) Hello, world
[ 7404.087825] (5) Hello, world
```

Finally, with another parameter:

```
$ sudo insmod param.ko whom=bpb
$ dmesg
[ 7470.763580] (0) Hello, bpb
```

Finally, with the two parameters:

```
$ sudo insmod param.ko howmany=10 whom=bpb
$ dmesg
[ 7600.566090] (0) Hello, bpb
[ 7600.566096] (1) Hello, bpb
[ 7600.566097] (2) Hello, bpb
[ 7600.566099] (3) Hello, bpb
[ 7600.566100] (4) Hello, bpb
[ 7600.566101] (5) Hello, bpb
[ 7600.566102] (6) Hello, bpb
[ 7600.566103] (7) Hello, bpb
[ 7600.566104] (8) Hello, bpb
[ 7600.566105] (9) Hello, bpb
[ 7600.566106] (10) Hello, bpb
```

As we have seen, it is possible to load a driver dynamically with **modprobe**:

```
$ sudo modprobe param howmany=10
```

If we use unknown parameters, they are just ignored:

```
$ sudo insmod ./param.ko  wrongparam=45
$ dmesg
```

If a parameter name provided at load time is incorrect, the following message will be displayed via **dmesg**:

```
[ 7560.515786] param: unknown parameter wrongparam ignored
```

Note the need for administrator rights for loading dynamic modules into the kernel.

Modules licensing

A license is very important to specify the rights of the modules loaded in order to be sure that the kernel is secure. Indeed, we can have such a message when loading a dynamic module:

```
$ sudo insmod xxxxxx.ko

loading out-of-tree module taints kernel.
module license 'unspecified' taints kernel.
```

Several macros to indicate the license for a module are available, such as: GPL, GPL v2, GPL and additional rights, Dual BSD/GPL, Dual MIT/GPL, Dual MPL/GPL and Proprietary.

They are defined within **include/linux/module.h**.

To reference what license, you can use the MODULE_LICENSE's macro.

Here is an example:

```
#include <linux/init.h> /* Needed for the macros */
#include <linux/module.h> /* Needed by all modules */
#include <linux/printk.h> /* Needed for pr_info() */


MODULE_LICENSE("GPL");
MODULE_AUTHOR("bpb");
MODULE_DESCRIPTION("A sample driver with a GPL license");


static int __init init_hello(void)
{
        pr_info("Hello, world\n");
        return 0;
}


static void __exit cleanup_hello(void)
{
        pr_info("Goodbye, world\n");
}


module_init(init_hello);
module_exit(cleanup_hello);
```

In a GNU/Linux kernel, taints refer to the kernel's state of being tainted. When the Linux kernel is tainted, it means that it has encountered a situation or condition that might compromise its integrity, security, or supportability. A tainted kernel is one that has been marked as potentially unreliable for various reasons.

The Linux kernel can be tainted for a variety of reasons, and each reason is represented by a unique taint flag. The taint flags are typically represented as one or more letters that indicate the reason for the tainting. Some common reasons for tainting the kernel include:

- **Proprietary modules**: When proprietary or closed-source kernel modules are loaded, the kernel is tainted with the *P flag*. Proprietary modules may not adhere to open-source principles and can potentially cause issues or instability.

- **Firmware issues**: If the kernel encounters problems related to firmware, it may be tainted with the *F flag*. Firmware issues can affect hardware compatibility and functionality.

- **Out-of-tree modules**: Modules that are not part of the mainline kernel source tree, such as third-party or custom modules, can taint the kernel with the *O flag*. These modules might not be as well-tested or reliable as in-tree modules.

- **Forced load**: The *X flag* indicates that a module was forcibly loaded into the kernel, possibly bypassing safety checks.

- **Unsigned modules**: If the kernel loads unsigned modules without a proper digital signature, it may be tainted with the *U flag*. This can be a security concern as unsigned modules may be untrusted.

- **Hardware issues**: Certain hardware errors or issues can taint the kernel with the *H flag*. Hardware problems can lead to instability or unpredictable behavior.

- **Userspace issues**: Errors originating from user space, such as invalid syscalls or corrupted system files, can taint the kernel with the *A flag*. This indicates that userspace processes may be causing problems.

- **GPL violations**: Loading kernel modules that violate the GNU **General Public License** (**GPL**) can taint the kernel with the *g flag*. Regularly check the kernel's taint status using tools like **dmesg** or **cat /proc/sys/kernel/tainted**. If the kernel is tainted, investigate the cause and take appropriate action.

The presence of these taint flags makes it easier to diagnose kernel issues and determine potential sources of problems. However, running a tainted kernel can have consequences, and in some cases, support from the Linux community or vendors may be limited when the kernel is tainted.

Note: While a tainted kernel can be useful for identifying issues, it is generally recommended to use open-source modules and adhere to best practices to maintain the stability and security of the Linux kernel.

Modules logging

In the beginning, there was **printk**, usually followed by a priority such as **KERN_INFO** or **KERN_DEBUG**. More recently, this can also be expressed in shorthand using a set of print macros, such as **pr_info** and **pr_debug**. It just avoids crazy keyboard strokes and looks a little neater. They can be found in the following header: **#include/linux/printk.h**

printk() is one of the best-known functions in the Linux kernel. This is the standard tool we have for printing messages, and generally the most basic way of tracing and debugging.

Usage: **printk(LOGLEVEL "Message: %s\n", arg);**

Example: **pr_info("Hello, world 4\n");**

Where **LOGLEVEL** is one of the log levels.

Note: It is concatenated to the format string; the log level is not a separate argument.

The available log levels are:

Loglevel	String	Alias function
KERN_EMERG	"0"	pr_emerg()
KERN_ALERT	"1"	pr_alert()
KERN_CRIT	"2"	pr_crit()
KERN_ERR	"3"	pr_err()
KERN_WARNING	"4"	pr_warn()
KERN_NOTICE	"5"	pr_notice()
KERN_INFO	"6"	pr_info()
KERN_DEBUG	"7"	pr_debug() and pr_devel() if DEBUG is defined
KERN_DEFAULT	""	
KERN_CONT	"c"	pr_cont()

Table 3.1: *log level synthesis per macro*

For instance, the kernel **printk.h** has:

```
#define pr_info(fmt,arg...) \
        printk(KERN_INFOfmt,##arg)
```

Just like its name, **pr_info()** is **printk()** with priority **KERN_INFO**.

You can configure the log level of the **dmesg** command by filtering the kernel log messages based on their severity level. The log level is managed through the **klogd** service, which is part of the system's logging infrastructure. Here is how to configure the log level of **dmesg**:

You can check the current log level by running **dmesg** without any options. This command displays the kernel log messages according to their severity levels. The most severe messages are displayed by default.

```
$ dmesg
```

Or,

```
$ dmesg -w (to watch the log in real-time)
```

You can use the **-n** option with **dmesg** to set the log level temporarily. For example, to display messages with a log level of *warning* (level 4) or higher, you can use:

```
$ dmesg -n 4
```

Adjust the log level as needed for your debugging or monitoring purposes.

With some kernel settings, we have to allow the command without being root:

```
$ sudo sysctl -w kernel.dmesg_restrict=0
```

The **kernel.printk sysctl** configuration controls the verbosity of kernel log messages in Linux. It consists of four numerical values, each representing a different log level. These values are used to filter and control which messages are displayed on the system console and logged. The format for **kernel.printk** is: **console_loglevel console_loglevel console_loglevel debug_loglevel**.

Here are the possible values for each part of **"kernel.printk"**:

- **console_loglevel (console log level for console messages)**:
  - This value sets the log level for messages that are displayed on the system console.
  - Valid values are from 0 to 7, corresponding to log levels:
    - **0**: KERN_EMERG (emergency)
    - **1**: KERN_ALERT (alert)
    - **2**: KERN_CRIT (critical)
    - **3**: KERN_ERR (error)
    - **4**: KERN_WARNING (warning)
    - **5**: KERN_NOTICE (notice)
    - **6**: KERN_INFO (informational)
    - **7**: KERN_DEBUG (debug)
- **console_loglevel (console log level for console log buffer)**: This value sets the log level for messages that are recorded in the console log buffer. Valid values are from 0 to 7, following the same log levels as mentioned previously.
- **console_loglevel (console log level for messages displayed on console)**: This value sets the log level for messages that will be displayed on the system console. Valid values are from 0 to 7, with the same log levels.
- **debug_loglevel (debug log level)**: This value sets the log level for debug messages. Valid values are from 0 to 7, using the same log levels as listed above.

Dynamic kernel module support

This is a trend that tends to be confirmed. More and more manufacturers are providing **dynamic kernel module support** (**DKMS**) to their drivers (**virtualbox**, **ndiswrapper**, **lttng**, **fglrx**, etc.) in order to guarantee continuity of service as developments evolve. versions of the GNU/Linux kernel, but also the drivers themselves.

On Fedora and derivatives such as RedHat, **AutoKernel Modules (akmods)** are commonly used, although similar to DKMS. We will only see DKMS, which is more cross-platform and less specific to a Linux distribution.

Each time a kernel version is changed, made by the package manager, a trigger is automatically launched in the post-installation actions of the RPM, DEB, etc. packages. The same action is performed when a driver is updated.

It must, therefore, be recompiled from the driver sources while using the current kernel API, guaranteeing a certain consistency.

DKMS was developed by the company *Dell*, mainly in Bash and perl language in order to respond to this problem. It is freely distributed as open-source under the GPLv2 license.

The DKMS architecture is made up of different parts:

- **Module sources: /usr/src/<drv_name>-<version>/**

- **The kernel module tree: /lib/modules/`uname -r`/:** DKMS will replace or add the modules that we are going to make it manage

- **The DKMS tree /var/lib/dkms, containing**:

    o   The directories where the modules will be built

    (/var/lib/dkms/<drv_name>/<version>/build/)

    o   The original modules saved

    o   Modules compiled by DKMS

The following figure shows the important paths used by DKMS:

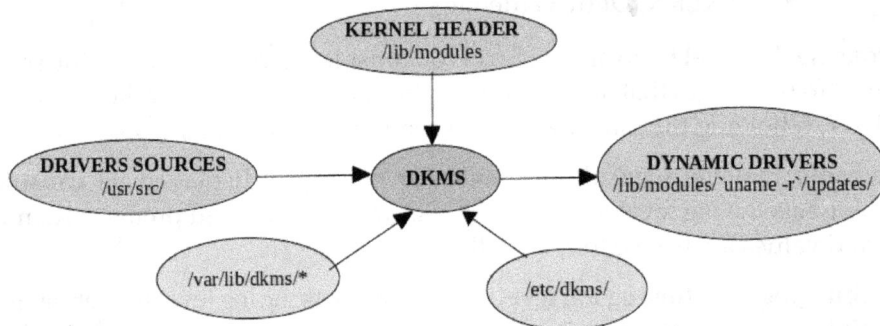

Figure 3.9: Main files used by DKMS

Concerning DKMS itself, we distinguish the first part linked to its configuration (**/etc/ dkms**) and its internal working part (**/var/lib/dkms/***).

The second part includes the driver sources, the headers by GNU/Linux kernel version, and finally, the dynamic modules built.

Installation

Dkms has become an essential brick, and it is officially packaged for a certain number of GNU/Linux distributions:

- **Debian/Ubuntu:** `$ sudo apt-get install dkms dh-modaliases`
- **OpenSuse:** `$ sudo zypper install dkms`
- **Fedora core:** `$ sudo yum install dkms`
- **From the official GIT repo sources:** `$ git clone git://linux.dell.com/dkms.git`

For packages, the dependencies will be **"make"**, **"linux-headers-generic"**, and **"linux-headers"**.

On the other hand, the DKMS sources do not offer an installer. The files are a bit scattered all over the file system. You must therefore copy the files by hand. This remains the least practical method, rather than installing it using your favorite package system.

If we do a search in the repos, we see the list of drivers external to the kernel arriving with DKMS support, increasing little by little over the years.

Configuration

The core of DKMS can be configured quite simply via a configuration file located in **/etc/dkms/framework.conf** in which all the paths in force in DKMS are defined:

```
## This configuration file modifies the behavior of
## DKMS (Dynamic Kernel Module Support) and is sourced
## in by DKMS every time it is run.

## Source Tree Location (default: /usr/src)
source_tree="/usr/src"

## DKMS Tree Location (default: /var/lib/dkms)
dkms_tree="/var/lib/dkms"

## Install Tree Location (default: /lib/modules)
install_tree="/lib/modules"

## tmp Location (default: /tmp)
tmp_location="/tmp"
```

```
## verbosity setting (verbose will be active if you set it to a non-null
value)
# verbose="1"
```

Supporting Secure Boot with UEFI with DKMS involves a few key steps to ensure that custom kernel modules are signed and can be loaded when Secure Boot is enabled. Here is a step-by-step guide:

1. Install dependencies:

   ```
   $ sudo apt install dkms openssl mokutil linux-headers-$(uname -r)
   ```

2. You may check that you are using a secure boot:

   ```
   $ sudo mokutil --sb-state
   SecureBoot enabled
   If not enabled, please set the secure mode first!
   ```

3. Create a directory to store your key pair:

   ```
   $ mkdir -p /var/lib/dkms/mok
   ```

   ```
   $ cd /var/lib/dkms/mok
   ```

4. Option #1, generate a private key and a self-signed public certificate:

   ```
   $ openssl req -new -x509 -newkey rsa:2048 -keyout MOK.priv -outform
   DER -out MOK.der -nodes -days 36500 -subj "/CN=Custom DKMS Module
   Signing/"
   ```

   It will generate the following files:

   a. **MOK.priv**: The private key used for signing kernel modules.

   b. **MOK.der**: The self-signed certificate in DER format, which will be imported into Secure Boot using **mokutil;** it will also used by dkms for signing drivers on post build step.

5. Option #2, validate the DER certificate with a certification authority (PKI):

   If your company has a certification authority (PKI), it will be necessary to proceed in two stages:

   Instead of generating a self-signed certificate, create a Certificate Signing Request (CSR), which will be signed by your PKI CA:

   ```
   $ openssl req -new -newkey rsa:2048 -keyout MOK.priv -out MOK.csr
   -nodes -subj "/CN=Custom DKMS Module Signing/"
   ```

   At this stage, you need to submit **MOK.csr** to your organization's PKI Certificate Authority (like Microsoft AD CS, FreeIPA, or an external CA). Example command for signing the CSR with a local CA:

   ```
   $ openssl x509 -req -in MOK.csr -CA CA.crt -CAkey CA.key
   -CAcreateserial -out MOK.pem -days 36500 -sha256
   ```

Once you receive a signed certificate (**MOK.pem**), convert it to DER format:

```
$ openssl x509 -in MOK.pem -outform DER -out MOK.der
```

6. Make new certificate:

```
$ sudo mokutil –enable-validation
```

—> At this step, a password will be requested; it will be requested again after the reboot.

7. Enroll the key into the **Machine Owner Key (MOK)** list. Use **mokutil** to import the key to the **MOK** list, which will be used by the kernel to verify signed modules:

```
$ sudo mokutil --import MOK.der
To check that the import was successful:
    $ sudo mokutil --list-new
```

Follow the prompts to set a password. You will need to confirm the enrollment after a reboot.

8. **Reboot and enroll the key**: During the boot process, you will be prompted to enroll the key. Follow the on-screen instructions and use the password you set earlier.

You can confirm the import of the new key within the UEFI BIOS:

```
$ sudo mokutil --list-enrolled | grep "Custom DKMS Module Signing"
```

9. **Configure DKMS to use the signing key**: Edit or create the DKMS configuration file to include signing commands.

```
$ sudo nano /etc/dkms/framework.conf
Add the following lines:
mok_signing_key=/var/lib/dkms/mok/MOK.priv
mok_certificate=/var/lib/dkms/mok/MOK.der
```

10. To verify that the module is properly signed and can be loaded with Secure Boot enabled, you can check the module signature using:

```
$ modinfo -F sig_id /lib/modules/$(uname -r)/updates/dkms/example-
module.ko
```

You should see an output indicating the module is signed.

In this step, you are able to load/unload the dynamic module:

```
$ modprobe   example-module
$ modprobe -r   example-module
```

In case of a signature problem, an error would be reported.

Functioning

DKMS works like a state machine. The first step is to add the drivers via a configuration file. Then, once known in the DKMS database, it is possible to ask it to compile the module on one or more GNU/Linux kernel versions, then to install it in **/lib/module/<kernel-version> /...**

Each step is separate, so it is possible to add a driver without it being built or installed.

The installation can be automatic, depending on the settings:

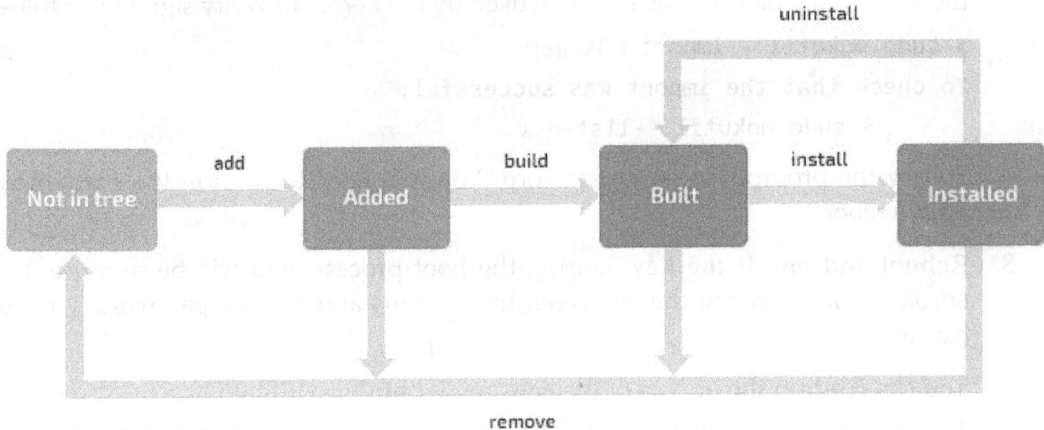

Figure 3.10: State machine for DKMS

Each configuration file relies on a set of variables propagated by DKMS:

- **kernelver**: This variable contains the kernel version for which the module is being built. This is particularly useful in defining the **MAKE** command, e.g., **MAKE[0]="make INCLUDEDIR=/lib/modules/${kernelver}/build/include"**

- **dkms_tree**: This variable indicates where the DKMS tree is located on the local system. By default, it is **/var/lib/dkms**, but this value should not be hardcoded in **dkms.conf** in case the user has changed this on their system (such a setting is made by using **/etc/dkms/framework.conf** or adding the **–dkmstree** option when calling).

- **source_tree**: This variable indicates where DKMS stores the module sources on the system. By default, this is **/usr/src**, but this value should not be hard-coded in **dkms.conf** in case the user has changed this on their system (using **/etc/dkms/ framework.conf** or adding the **–source tree** option when calling).

- **kernel_source_dir**: This variable contains the path to the kernel sources for which the module is built. This is typically **/lib/modules/$kernelver/build** unless another path has been specified with the **--kernel-sourcedir** option.

Adding DKMS support for a driver

To show how the integration of an external driver into the DKMS kernel sources is done, we will start with the sources of a small, simple character driver.

It will consist of the following files in **/usr/src/helloworld-0.1**:

```
/usr/src/helloworld-0.1
├── dkms.conf
├── helloworld.c
└──Makefile
```

Let us first create a directory in **/usr/src/** including the name of the package and its version, separated by a hyphen:

```
$ sudo mkdir -p /usr/src/helloworld-0.1
```

Then, let us add to this directory a **dkms.conf** file used by DKMS to specify the paths and names of the different elements associated with the driver:

```
$ sudo vim /usr/src/helloworld-0.1/dkms.conf
```

With the following content:

```
PACKAGE_NAME="helloworld"
PACKAGE_VERSION="0.1"
MAKE[0]="make -C ${kernel_source_dir} SUBDIRS=${dkms_tree}/${PACKAGE_
NAME}/${PACKAGE_VERSION}/build modules"
CLEAN=" make -C ${kernel_source_dir} SUBDIRS=${dkms_tree}/${PACKAGE_
NAME}/${PACKAGE_VERSION}/build clean"
BUILT_MODULE_NAME[0]= helloworld
BUILT_MODULE_LOCATION[0]=.
DEST_MODULE_LOCATION[0]=/updates
REMAKE_INITRD="no"
AUTOINSTALL="yes"
```

For the **CLEAN** target, it is possible to make it simpler: **CLEAN="rm -f *.*o"**

We will use the source of the module **"helloworld.c"** described above and save it in the following directory: **/usr/src/helloworld-0.1/**

It is also necessary to attach a simple Makefile in the following **path/usr/src/helloworld-0.1/**:

```
obj-m:= helloworld.o
KDIR := ${kernel_source_dir}
all:
        make -C $(KDIR) M=$(shell pwd) modules
```

```
install:
        make -C $(KDIR) M=$(shell pwd) modules_install
clean:
        make -C $(KDIR) M=$(shell pwd) clean
```

Still in the **/usr/src/helloworld-0.1** path, adding dkms support for a module is as simple as the following command:

```
$ sudo dkms add -m helloworld -v 0.1
Creating symlink /var/lib/dkms/helloworld/0.1/source ->
                 /usr/src/helloworld-0.1
DKMS: add completed.
```

Apart from this path, it will be necessary to specify the path containing the **dkms.conf** configuration file via the **-c** parameter:

```
$ sudo dkms add -m helloworld -v 0.1 -c /usr/src/helloworld-0.1/dkms.conf
Creating symlink /var/lib/dkms/helloworld/0.1/source ->
                 /usr/src/helloworld-0.1
DKMS: add completed.
```

By default, **dkms** will opt for support for the current kernel version, but to specify another version, the **-k** parameter can be used:

```
$ sudo dkms add -m helloworld -v 0.1 -k `uname -r`
Creating symlink /var/lib/dkms/helloworld/0.1/source ->
                 /usr/src/helloworld-0.1
DKMS: add completed.
```

Once added, a tree structure is created in **/var/lib/dkms/helloworld/0.1/**:

```
$ tree /var/lib/dkms/helloworld/0.1/
/var/lib/dkms/helloworld/0.1/
├──build
└── source -> /usr/src/helloworld-0.1
```

Let us also check the module status in DKMS regarding this module:

```
$ dkms status | grep  helloworld
helloworld, 0.1: added
```

To know from a general point of view, the modules that are compatible with a specific kernel version, the **dkms status** command supports the **-k** parameter, to which it is possible to specify a GNU/Linux kernel version:

```
$ dkms status -k `uname -r`
backfire, 0.73-1: added
helloworld, 0.1, 6.2.0-35-generic, x86_64: installed
vboxhost, 4.3.0, 6.2.0-35-generic, x86_64: installed
```

When adding, if the module is already known by dkms, it will indicate the following error message:

```
$ sudo dkms add -m helloworld -v 0.1
```

In the case of adding a module, a check is made to see if it has not already been inserted beforehand. Otherwise, the following error message will be displayed:

```
DKMS tree already contains: helloworld-0.1
You cannot add the same module/version combo more than once.
```

Generation for the current kernel

Let us check the version of my currently loaded GNU/Linux kernel:

```
$ uname -a
Linux tgayet-DS87D 6.2.0-35-generic #35~22.04.1-Ubuntu SMP PREEMPT_DYNAMIC
Fri Oct  6 10:23:26 UTC 2 x86_64 x86_64 x86_64 GNU/Linux
$ uname -r
6.2.0-35-generic
```

We can list the currently installed kernels:

```
$ dpkg --list | grep linux-image
(...)
amd64           Signed kernel image generic
ii  linux-image-6.2.0-34-generic                                6.2.0-
34.34~22.04.1                            amd64           Signed kernel image
generic
ii  linux-image-6.2.0-35-generic                                6.2.0-
35.35~22.04.1                            amd64           Signed kernel image
generic
ii  linux-image-generic-hwe-22.04                               6.2.0.35.35
~22.04.13                               amd64           Generic Linux kernel image
```

The author's kernel headers are located in a standard directory:

```
$ ls -al /lib/modules/`uname -r`/
```

The step of generating the dynamic module for my kernel version is done using the **build** parameter of the **dkms** command:

```
$ sudo dkms build -m helloworld/0.1
```

Kernel preparation is unnecessary for this kernel. Building module:

```
cleaning build area....
make KERNELRELEASE=3.8.0-32-generic -C /lib/modules/3.8.0-32-generic/build
SUBDIRS=/var/lib/dkms/helloworld/0.1/build modules....
```

```
cleaning build area....
DKMS: build completed.
```

The generation can be done either with the current kernel (default) or with a specific version:

```
$ sudo dkms build -m helloworld/0.1 -k `uname -r`
Kernel preparation is unnecessary for this kernel. Skipping...
Building module:
cleaning build area....
make KERNELRELEASE=3.8.0-32-generic -C /lib/modules/3.8.0-32-generic/build
SUBDIRS=/var/lib/dkms/helloworld/0.1/build modules....
cleaning build area....
DKMS: build completed.
```

The result of the build will have generated the following tree:

```
$ tree /var/lib/dkms/helloworld/0.1/
/var/lib/dkms/helloworld/0.1/
├── 3.8.0-32-generic
│   └── x86_64
│   ├── log
│   │   └── make.log
│   └── Arial module
│       └── helloworld.ko
├──build
│   ├── dkms.conf
│   ├── Makefile
│   └── helloworld.c
└── source -> /usr/src/helloworld-0.1
```

During this step, a log file is created named **make.log**:

```
$ cat /var/lib/dkms/helloworld/0.1/`uname -r`/x86_64/log/make.log
```

```
DKMS make.log for helloworld-0.1 for kernel 3.8.0-32-generic (x86_64)
Monday, November 18, 2013, 10:01:14 (UTC+0100)
make: entering directory "/usr/src/linux-headers-3.8.0-32-generic"
   CC [M] /var/lib/dkms/helloworld/0.1/build/helloworld .o
/var/lib/dkms/helloworld/0.1/build/helloworld .c: In function '__check_buf_
size':
/var/lib/dkms/helloworld/0.1/build/helloworld .c:16:1: warning: return from
incompatible pointer type [enabled by default]
```

```
/var/lib/dkms/helloworld/0.1/build/helloworld .c: In function 'k_read':
/var/lib/dkms/helloworld/0.1/build/helloworld .c:34
```

The module has been generated, and its identity card can be viewed with the **modinfo** command:

```
$ modinfo /var/lib/dkms/helloworld/0.1/`uname -r`/x86_64/module/helloworld
.ko
filename: /var/lib/dkms/helloworld
/0.1/6.2.0-35-generic/x86_64/module/helloworld.ko
license: GPL
author: bpb
description: ex-drv-char-dkms
srcversion: 3853BD18B15DD07DE2E4338
depends:
vermagic: 6.2.0-35-generic SMP mod_unload modversions
parm: major:Static major number (none = dynamic) (int)
parm: buf_size:Buffer size (int)
```

We can also notice that the **status** of the module has changed in DKMS:

```
$ dkms status | grep helloworld
helloworld, 0.1, 3.8.0-32-generic, x86_64: built
```

As the module has been generated for the current kernel, let us perform a quick loading test:

```
$ sudo insmod /var/lib/dkms/helloworld/0.1/`uname -r`/x86_64/module/
helloworld.ko
$ dmsg -w
(…)
[261032.273926] char: allocated to 64 bytes buffer
[261032.273932] char: successfully loaded with major 250
$ lsmod | grep helloworld
helloworld 12868 0
$ rmmod ./helloworld.ko
```

Installing a module managed by DKMS

The installation of a **dkms** module is also done by passing the **install** parameter:

```
$ dkms install -m helloworld -v 0.1
helloworld:
Running module version sanity check.
```

```
   - Original module
     - No original module exists within this kernel
   - Facility
     - Installing to /lib/modules/3.8.0-32-generic/updates/dkms/
depmod....
DKMS: install completed.
```

Just like the addition or generation phase, it is possible to use a specific kernel version rather than the current version:

```
$ sudo dkms install -m helloworld -v 0.1 -k `uname -r`
helloworld:
Running module version sanity check.
   - Original module
     - No original module exists within this kernel
   - Facility
     - Installing to /lib/modules/3.8.0-32-generic/updates/dkms/
depmod....
DKMS: install completed.
```

The status can be checked because it must be changed to installed:

```
$ sudo dkms status | grep helloworld
helloworld, 0.1, 3.8.0-32-generic, x86_64: installed
```

The installation will install our module in the **/update/dkms/** directory of the tree linked to the current kernel modules:

```
$ ls -al /lib/modules/`uname -r`/updates/dkms/
total 608
drwxr-xr-x 2 root root 4096 Nov 18 10:52 .
drwxr-xr-x 3 root root 4096 Oct 22 12:00..
-rw-r--r-- 1 root root 8544 Nov 18 10:52 helloworld.ko
-rw-r--r-- 1 root root 504640 Nov 10 03:21 vboxdrv.ko
-rw-r--r-- 1 root root 14896 Nov 10 03:21 vboxnetadp.ko
-rw-r--r-- 1 root root 38320 Nov 10 03:21 vboxnetflt.ko
-rw-r--r-- 1 root root 36656 Nov 10 03:21 vboxpci.ko
```

As we noticed, the **depmod** command was launched, which updated the **modules.dep** dependency file.

```
$ cat /lib/modules/`uname -r`/modules.dep | grep helloworld
updates/dkms/helloworld.ko:
```

This allows the module to be loaded dynamically via the **modprobe** command:

```
$ sudo modprobe helloworld
$ lsmod | grep helloworld
helloworld 12868 0
$ sudo modprobe -r helloworld
```

If ever an installation was requested while the build phase was not carried out, then **dkms** will carry out the build phase first by dependency:

```
$ dkms install -m helloworld -v 0.1
```

Kernel preparation is unnecessary for this kernel. Skipping...

Building module:

```
cleaning build area....
make KERNELRELEASE=3.8.0-32-generic -C /lib/modules/3.8.0-32-generic/build
SUBDIRS=/var/lib/dkms/helloworld/0.1/build modules....
cleaning build area....
DKMS: build completed.
helloworld.ko:
Running module version sanity check.
  - Original module
    - No original module exists within this kernel
  - Facility
    - Installing to /lib/modules/3.8.0-32-generic/updates/dkms/
depmod....
DKMS: install completed.
```

Uninstalling a driver managed by DKMS

As we would have guessed, the uninstallation will be done without necessarily expanding on it.

```
$ sudo dkms uninstall -m helloworld -v 0.1 -k `uname -r`
```

No need to go into too much detail about this step, which only removes the previously installed driver **/lib/modules/<kernel-release>/updates/dkms/**

Removing

For removing the dkms support for all kernel versions, this is quite similar to adding a stage:

```
$ sudo dkms remove -m helloworld -v 0.1 --all
-------- Uninstall Beginning --------
Module: helloworld
Version: 0.1
Kernel: 6.2.0-35-generic (x86_64)
------------------------------------
Status: This module version was INACTIVE for this kernel.
depmod....
DKMS: uninstall completed.
------------------------------
Deleting module version: 0.1
completely from the DKMS tree.
------------------------------
Done.
```

We can verify that the status of the drivers is now unknown by dkms because it should not return:

```
$ dkms status | grep helloworld
```

For removing just a specific kernel version, the **-k** parameter can also be used:

```
$ sudo dkms remove -m helloworld -v 0.1 -k `uname -r`
-------- Uninstall Beginning --------
Module: helloworld
Version: 0.1
Kernel: 3.8.0-32-generic (x86_64)
------------------------------------
Status: Before uninstall, this module version was ACTIVE on this kernel.
helloworld.ko:
  - Uninstallation
    - Deleting from: /lib/modules/3.8.0-32-generic/updates/dkms/
  - Original module
    - No original module was found for this module on this kernel.
    - Use the dkms install command to reinstall any previous module
version.

depmod....
DKMS: uninstall completed.
------------------------------
Deleting module version: 0.1
```

```
completely from the DKMS tree.
----------------------------
Done.
```

We have detailed the use of dkms a little more because it is essential professional support that makes the difference when installing a new kernel or when updating a driver; DKMS will ensure that the driver is recompiled so that everything is in phase.

Conclusion

In this chapter, we went into a little more detail on the implementation of an elementary driver, allowing it to manage parameters, dependencies, and know how to compile, load, or unload a driver. This will serve us for the rest of the book.

In the next chapter, we will study the **Linux Device Model (LDM)** in detail, including procfs and sysfs.

Join our book's Discord space

Join the book's Discord Workspace for Latest updates, Offers, Tech happenings around the world, New Release and Sessions with the Authors:

https://discord.bpbonline.com

CHAPTER 4
Linux Device Model

Introduction

After having studied the basics of Linux drivers in the previous chapter, we will see the structure of the **Linux device model** (**LDM**). The GNU / Linux kernel has been standardized to simplify the maintenance and scalability of the kernel and drivers for developers. This chapter will provide a better understanding of these foundations.

Structure

This chapter covers the following topics:

- Linux device model data structure
- The bus model
- The device model
- The driver model
- The classes
- About procfs
- About the DTB device tree

Objectives

The Linux device model is a framework within the Linux kernel that provides a standardized and unified way of representing and managing various hardware devices. It abstracts the details of interacting with different types of devices, allowing the kernel and device drivers to work with a consistent interface. We will investigate all these interfaces one by one to better understand them.

Linux device model data structure

The device model simplifies the task of writing and maintaining device drivers while promoting modularity and ease of device management, such as:

- **Bus model**: Devices are organized into buses, which represent the physical or logical interconnects in the system. Examples of buses include PCI, USB, I2C, and platform buses.

- **Device model**: Devices are represented as objects in the device model, each with a unique identifier and a set of attributes. Devices are organized in a hierarchical structure, reflecting the physical or logical relationships between devices.

- **Device nodes**: Devices are associated with device nodes in the **/sys** filesystem. These nodes provide a user-readable and writable interface for interacting with device attributes. Users and applications can query and configure devices by reading or writing values in the corresponding device nodes. The kernel provides a representation of its model in user space via the sysfs virtual file system. It is typically mounted in the **/sys** directory and contains the following subdirectories:

  - **Block**: All block devices are available in the system (disks, partitions)
  - **Bus**: Bus types to which physical devices are connected (pci, ide, usb)
  - **Class**: Driver classes are available in the system (net, sound, usb)
  - **Devices**: The hierarchical structure of devices is connected to the system
  - **Firmware**: System firmware information (Advanced Configuration and Power Interface)
  - **Fs**: Information about mounted filesystems
  - **Kernel**: Kernel state information (logged-in users, hotplug)
  - **Module**: The list of currently loaded modules
  - **Power**: Information related to the energy management subsystem

- **Class model**: Devices are categorized into classes based on their functionality or type (e.g., block devices, network devices). Each class defines a set of common attributes and behaviors that devices within that class should adhere to.

- **Driver model**: The driver model defines the interface between device drivers and the device model. Drivers register themselves with the model, associating with specific types of devices. When a compatible device is detected, the appropriate driver is bound to that device.

- **Driver binding**: The binding process involves associating a device with an appropriate driver. The kernel matches devices with drivers based on criteria such as device identifiers (e.g., PCI IDs), allowing the correct driver to handle a specific device.

- **Driver core**: The driver core is a fundamental part of the Linux device model. It oversees the process of registering and unregistering drivers and devices. Its primary function is to match devices with appropriate drivers and ensure smooth communication between them.

- **Device tree**: On architectures that use device trees (e.g., ARM), the device tree is a data structure that describes the hardware topology and properties. It is used to instantiate devices and configure the device model during the kernel boot process.

The Linux device model provides a flexible and extensible framework that accommodates a wide range of hardware architectures and devices. It promotes the separation of concerns between hardware-specific details and driver logic, making it easier to develop and maintain drivers for various devices.

Device drivers written for the Linux kernel typically interact with the device model through the driver model interfaces, allowing them to register devices, manage resources, and communicate with the rest of the kernel. The device model is a fundamental aspect of the Linux kernel, enabling it to support a diverse ecosystem of hardware.

Sysfs information is found in files containing some standard attributes represented by files or directories with the same name:

- **Dev**: Major and minor device identifier. It can be used to automatically create entries in the **/dev** directory

- **Device**: A symbolic link to the directory containing devices; It can be used to discover hardware devices that provide a particular service (e.g., ethi PCI card)

- **Driver**: A symbolic link to the driver directory (located in **/sys/bus/*/drivers**)

Examples of several kinds of data structures used with device drivers:

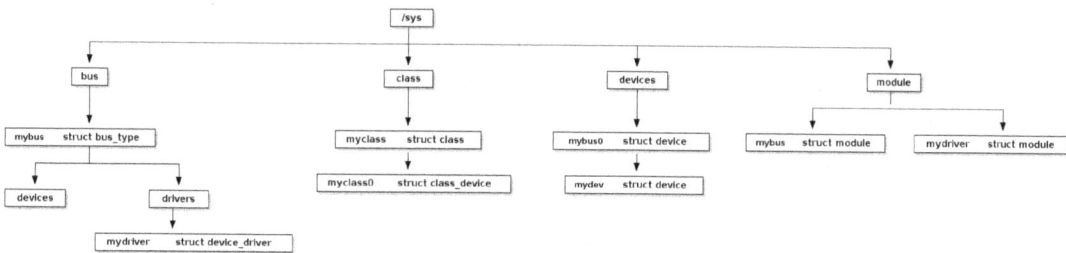

Figure 4.1: *Attributes are available, depending on the bus and driver use*

The **kobject** structure is usually embedded in a larger structure. It integrates a set of features that will be used at a higher abstraction level in the Linux device model hierarchy.

For example, the **cdev** structure has the following definition:

```
struct cdev {
        struct kobject kob;
        struct module *owner;
        const struct file_operations *ops;
        struct list_head list;
        dev_t dev;
        unsigned int count;
};
```

We can notice in this structure the presence of a field of type **kobject**, which in turn has the following definition:

```
struct kobject {
        const char              *name;
        struct list_head        entry;
        struct kobject          *parent;
        struct kset             *kset;
        struct kobj_type        *ktype;
        struct sysfs_dirent     *sd;
        struct kref             kref;
        unsigned int state_initialized:1;
        unsigned int state_in_sysfs:1;
        unsigned int state_add_uevent_sent:1;
        unsigned int state_remove_uevent_sent:1;
        unsigned int uevent_suppress:1;
};
```

kobject structures are, therefore, hierarchical: an object has a parent and contains a **kset** member, which contains objects of the same level.

This structure requires initialization with the **kobject_init()** function. It is also necessary to set the **kobject** structure name in the initialization process, which will appear in **sysfs**, using the **kobject_set_name()** function.

Any operation on a **kobject** is done by incrementing its internal counter using **kobject_get()** or decrementing it if it is no longer used using **kobject_put()**. Thus, a **kobject** will only be released when its internal counter is 0. A notification method is necessary so that resources associated with the device structure that includes the **kobject** structure are released (e.g., **cdev**). The method used is called release and is associated with the object via the **ktype** field (struct **kobj_type**).

The **kobject** structure is the basic structure of the Linux device model. The upper-level structures of the model are struct **bus_type**, struct **device**, and struct **device_driver**.

More help about LDM can be obtained here:

- **https://www.devicetree.org/specifications/**
- **https://docs.kernel.org/**

The bus model

A bus refers to a logical or physical interconnect that connects various hardware devices to the system. The bus model is an abstraction that provides a standardized way to represent and manage different types of buses within the kernel.

This abstraction is crucial for handling the diversity of hardware architectures and the multitude of buses that may exist in a computer system.

The Linux Bus Model is a framework within the Linux kernel that provides a systematic way to represent and manage buses, which are the communication pathways or interconnects between different hardware components and devices. Buses play a crucial role in connecting various hardware elements, such as processors, memory, peripheral devices, and other subsystems, allowing them to communicate and work together.

The features and concepts of the Linux Bus Model include:

- **Bus type**: The bus model defines different bus types, each representing a specific kind of interconnect technology or architecture. Examples of bus types include **Peripheral Component Interconnect (PCI)**, **Universal Serial Bus (USB)**, **Inter-Integrated Circuit (I2C)**, and **Serial Peripheral Interface (SPI)**.

- **Bus subsystem**: Each bus type is implemented as a subsystem within the Linux kernel. The bus subsystem is responsible for managing devices connected to that specific bus type.

- **Bus devices**: Devices that are part of a particular bus are represented as bus devices. Each bus device is associated with a specific bus type and has characteristics that are common to that type of bus.

- **Bus attributes**: Buses have attributes that describe their properties, such as speed, address range, and other relevant information. These attributes are typically exposed in the **/sys** filesystem.

- **Bus registration**: Buses and bus devices register themselves with the kernel, allowing the kernel to discover and manage the hardware connected to these buses dynamically.

- **Bus enumeration**: The kernel enumerates the devices on each bus during the boot process or when a new device is hot-plugged. Enumeration involves discovering the devices present on the bus, initializing them, and making them available to the system.

- **Device attachment**: Devices are attached to buses, and the bus model helps in organizing the hierarchy of devices within the system. The hierarchy reflects the physical or logical connectivity between devices and buses.

- **Hotplug support**: The bus model supports **hotplug** operations, allowing devices to be dynamically added or removed from the system without requiring a reboot. This is particularly important for buses and devices that support **hotplug**, such as USB or PCI devices.

By providing a standardized framework for representing buses and their devices, the Linux Bus Model contributes to the overall modularity, scalability, and flexibility of the Linux kernel. It simplifies the development of device drivers by providing a common infrastructure for handling buses and devices, regardless of the underlying hardware architecture. The **/sys/bus** directory in the **/sys** filesystem is the entry point for accessing bus-related information and configuration in user space.

The Linux device model provides several data structures to ensure the interaction between a hardware device and the device driver. The model is based on the **kobject** structures. Hierarchies are built using the following structures:

- struct bus_type
- struct device
- struct device_driver

The following figure illustrates the hierarchy of data structures within a driver record:

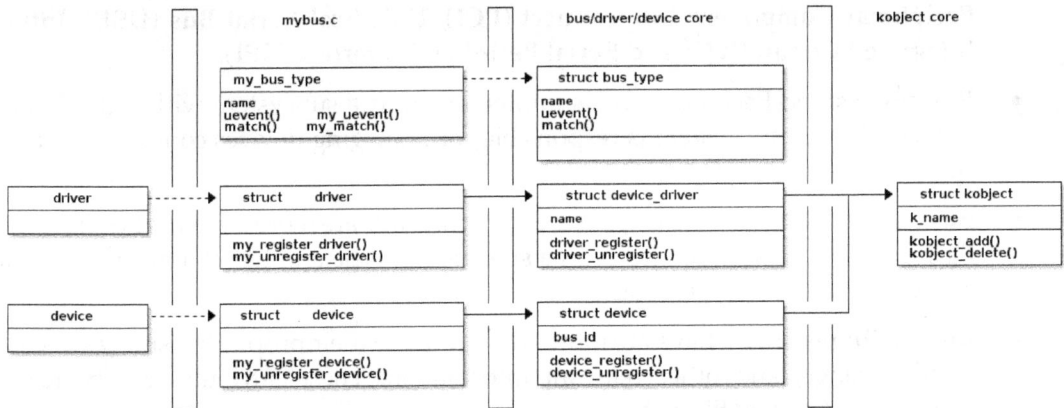

Figure 4.2: Different interactions between layers

The Linux bus model encompasses a variety of buses, each serving a specific purpose. Common bus types include:

- **Peripheral component interconnect**: PCI is used for connecting expansion cards to the motherboard.

- **Universal Serial Bus**: USB is common for connecting peripherals and external devices.

- **Inter-integrated circuit**: I2C is used for communication between integrated circuits on a board.

- **Platform bus**: Represents devices that are integrated into the system board.

The various steps involved in recording a bus include multiple operations, which are as follows:

- **Bus type registration**: Each type of bus is registered with the Linux kernel, indicating that the kernel supports devices connected to that type of bus. The registration process includes providing a set of functions that define how devices on that bus are enumerated and managed.

- **Bus-specific operations**: Bus-specific operations define how devices on a particular bus are discovered, probed, and initialized. These operations are specific to the characteristics of the bus and may include methods for enumerating devices, reading configuration information, and setting up resources.

- **Bus device enumeration**: The bus model assists in enumerating devices on a particular bus. It provides a consistent way to discover and represent devices connected to that bus, allowing the kernel to recognize the hardware configuration.

- **Device relationships**: Devices on a bus are organized in a hierarchical manner to represent their relationships. For example, a PCI bus may have slots, and each slot may contain a device. This hierarchical structure is reflected in the device model.

- **/sys filesystem representation**: The information about buses and their devices is exposed to user space through the **/sys** filesystem. Users and applications can query and configure devices by interacting with the corresponding files and directories within **/sys/bus**.

A bus is a communication channel between the processor and an input/output device. To ensure that the model is generic, all I/O devices are connected to the processor via a bus (even though it can be virtual without physical hardware).

When adding a system bus, it will appear in the **sysfs** file system in **/sys/bus**. As with **kobjects**, buses can be organized into hierarchies and will be represented in **sysfs**.

The Linux device model is, therefore, a bus represented by the structure **struct bus_type**:

```
struct bus_type {
        const char              *name;
        const char              *dev_name;
        struct device           *dev_root;
        struct bus_attribute    *bus_attrs;
        struct device_attribute *dev_attrs;
```

```
        struct driver_attribute *drv_attrs;
        struct subsys_private *p;

        int             (*match)(struct device *dev, struct device_driver
*drv);
        int             (*uevent)(struct device *dev, struct kobj_uevent_
env *env);
        int             (*probe)(struct device *dev);
        int             (*remove)(struct device *dev);
        //...
};
```

Each bus has a name, a list of default attributes, several specific functions, and private driver data. The **uevent** function (formerly **hotplug**) is used with **hotplug** devices.

Bus operations are as follows:

- The record
- Implementing the operations described in the struct **bus_type** structure
- Iteration
- Inspection

Devices connected to the bus

A bus is registered using **bus_register()** and unregistered using **bus_unregister()**.

Example of implementation:

```
#include <linux/device.h>

//bus type
struct bus_type my_bus_type = {
  .name   "= "my"us",
  .match  = my_match,
  .uevent = my_uevent,
};

static int __init my_bus_init(void)
{
  int err;

  //...
```

```
  err = bus_register(&my_bus_type);
  if (err)
    return err;
  //...
}


static void __exit my_bus_exit(void)
{
  //...
  bus_unregister(&my_bus_type);
  //...
}
```

The functions typically initialized within a **bus_type** structure are match and uevent:

```
#include <linux/device.h>
#include <linux/string.h>


// match devices to drivers; just do a simple name test
static int my_match(struct device *dev, struct device_driver *driver)
{
  return !strncmp(dev_name(dev), driver->name, strlen(driver->name));
}


// respond to hotplug user events; add environment variable DEV_NAME
static int my_uevent(struct device *dev, struct kobj_uevent_env *env)
{
  add_uevent_var(env, "DEV_NAME=%s", dev_name(dev));
  return 0;
}
```

The match function is used when a new device or driver is added to the bus. Its role is to make a comparison between the device ID and the driver ID. The uevent function is called before generating a hotplug in user space and has the role of adding environment variables.

Other possible operations on a bus are to browse the drivers or devices connected to it. Although we cannot access them directly (driver and device lists being stored in the driver private data, **subsys_private *p** field), these can be iterated using the **bus_for_each_dev** and **bus_for_each_drv** macros.

The LDM interface allows you to create attributes for related objects. These attributes will have a corresponding file in the **sysfs** bus subdirectory.

The attributes associated with a bus are described by the **bus_attribute** structure:

```
struct bus_attribute {
        struct attribute attr;
        ssize_t (*show)(struct bus_type *, char *buf);
        ssize_t (*store)(struct bus_type *, const char *buf, size_t
count);
};
```

An attribute is defined by the **BUS_ATTR** macro, then the **bus_create_file()** and **bus_remove_file()** functions can be used to add/remove an attribute in the bus structure.

An example of defining an attribute for **my_bus** is shown as follows:

```
#define MY_BUS_DESCR     "BPB my bus"

// export a simple bus attribute
static ssize_t my_show_bus_descr(struct bus_type *bus, char *buf)
{
        return snprintf(buf, PAGE_SIZE, "%s\n", MY_BUS_DESCR);
}


/*
 * define attribute - attribute name is descr;
 * full name is bus_attr_descr;
 * sysfs entry should be /sys/bus/mybus/descr
 */
BUS_ATTR(descr, 0444, my_show_bus_descr, NULL);

// specify attribute - in module init function
static int __init my_bus_init(void)
{
        int err;
        //...
        err = bus_create_file(&my_bus_type, &bus_attr_descr);
        if (err) {
                /* handle error */
        }
        //...
}


static void __exit my_bus_exit(void)
```

```
{
    //...
    bus_remove_file(&my_bus_type, &bus_attr_descr);
    //...
}
```

The bus is the representation of both a **bus_type** object and a device object (the bus is also a device).

The device models

The bus model plays a crucial role in the driver-binding process. It helps match devices on a bus with the appropriate drivers. When a compatible driver is found, it is bound to the device, allowing the driver to manage the device.

On architectures that use device trees (e.g., ARM), the bus model integrates with the device tree to instantiate buses and devices during the kernel boot process.

The Linux bus model is an integral part of the overall device model, providing a foundation for handling different types of buses and the devices connected to them. It ensures a unified approach to managing devices across various hardware architectures and contributes to the kernel's modularity and portability.

The device nodes refer to entries in the **/sys** filesystem that provide a standardized interface for interacting with devices. They serve as a means for users and applications to query and configure devices in the system. The **/sys** filesystem is a virtual filesystem that exposes information about devices, drivers, and other kernel-related entities to user space.

Definition of device nodes in the Linux device model:

- **Filesystem representation**: Device nodes are represented as files and directories within the **/sys** filesystem. Each device and device-related entity (such as device classes) has a corresponding entry in **/sys** that users can navigate and interact with.

- **Device attributes**: Device nodes expose various attributes and parameters associated with the corresponding device. These attributes can include information about the device's state, configuration settings, and other relevant data.

- **Read and write access**: Users and applications can read information from device nodes to retrieve details about the associated device. Additionally, some device nodes support write operations, allowing users to configure or control aspects of the device.

- **Device identification**: The path to a device node often reflects the device's position in the device model hierarchy. For example, devices connected to a specific bus may have device nodes located under the corresponding bus directory in **/sys**.

- **Consistent naming convention**: Device nodes follow a consistent naming convention to make it easier for users to identify and locate devices. The names of device nodes are often based on the device's type or functionality.

- **Device class nodes**: For devices belonging to a particular class (e.g., block devices, network devices), there are class-specific directories containing device nodes for each instance of the class. This hierarchical organization helps users navigate the device model.

- **Dynamic creation and deletion**: Device nodes are dynamically created and deleted based on the devices present in the system. When a new device is detected, the kernel creates the corresponding device node in **/sys**. When a device is removed or becomes inaccessible, the associated device node is typically removed.

- **/sys/class and /sys/devices**: The **/sys/class** directory contains subdirectories for different device classes, each containing device nodes for instances of that class. The **/sys/devices** directory provides a more detailed and complete view of the device model hierarchy, including devices and their relationships.

Device nodes play a crucial role in providing a user-friendly and standardized interface for interacting with devices in the Linux kernel. They facilitate communication between the user space and the kernel, allowing users to query device information, configure settings, and perform other operations related to device management.

The class model refers to a framework that categorizes devices based on their functionality or type. Devices that share common characteristics and behaviors are grouped into classes, and each class defines a set of standard attributes and methods that devices within that class should adhere to. This classification simplifies the management of devices by providing a standardized interface for interacting with devices of a particular type.

Definitions of the class model in the Linux kernel include:

- **Device classes**: Device classes categorize devices based on their functionality or purpose. Examples of device classes include block devices, network devices, graphics devices, input devices, and more. Each class represents a specific type of device.

- **Common attributes and behaviors**: Each device class defines a set of common attributes and behaviors that devices within that class are expected to have. This includes standard methods for device initialization, configuration, and resource management.

- **Device class hierarchy**: Device classes are organized in a hierarchical manner, reflecting relationships between different types of devices. For example, a block device class may have subclasses for specific types of block devices like hard drives, SSDs, or USB drives.

- **/sys Filesystem representation**: Information about device classes and their associated devices is exposed to user space through the **/sys** filesystem. Users and applications can query and configure devices by interacting with the corresponding files and directories within **/sys/class**.

- **Driver binding and matching**: Device drivers typically register themselves with specific classes, indicating their compatibility with devices of that type. During the driver binding process, the kernel matches drivers with devices based on their class, ensuring that the appropriate driver handles a specific type of device.

- **Standardized interfaces**: Device classes provide standardized interfaces for device drivers, making it easier to write drivers that adhere to a common set of conventions. This promotes code reusability and helps maintain a consistent approach to handling devices of a particular class.

- **Dynamic loading of classes**: The Linux kernel supports dynamic loading of classes, allowing new classes to be added or removed during runtime. This flexibility is essential for accommodating a wide range of devices and evolving hardware architectures.

- **Device enumeration**: The class model assists in enumerating devices of a specific class, making it easier for the kernel to discover and manage devices during system initialization.

By organizing devices into classes, the class model provides a high-level abstraction that simplifies the development of device drivers, enhances code modularity, and promotes a consistent and standardized approach to managing devices in the Linux kernel. Each class encapsulates the common characteristics of devices within its category, allowing for more efficient and streamlined device management.

Every device is associated with a struct device structure. Devices are discovered by various kernel methods (hotplug, device drivers, system initialization, etc.) and are registered in the system. Each device present in the kernel has an entry in **/sys/devices**.

At the lowest level, a device in the Linux Device Model is represented by a **struct device** structure:

```
struct device {
        //...
        struct device           *parent;
        struct device_private   *p;
        struct kobject          kobj;

        const char              *init_name; /* initial name of the device
*/
        //...
        struct bus_type         *bus;       /* type of bus device is on */
        struct device_driver    *driver;    /* which driver has allocated
```

```
this

                                         device */
        //...
        void    (*release)(struct device *dev);
};
```

Structure fields include the parent device, which is usually a controller, the associated **kobject**, the bus it is connected to, the device driver, and a function called at free time when the device counter reaches 0.

Here, too, we have the register/unregister functions **device_register()** and **device_unregister()**.

To work with attributes, we have the **struct device_attribute** structure, the **DEVICE_ATTR** macro for definition, and the functions **device_create_file()** and **device_remove_file()** to add/remove the attribute to/from the device.

One important thing to note is that the **struct device** structure is typically not used directly but is embedded within another structure. For example:

```
// my device type
struct my_device {
    char *name;
    struct my_driver *driver;
    struct device dev;
};
```

Typically, a bus driver will provide functions to add or remove such a device, as demonstrated as follows:

```
/* BUS DEVICE (parent) */

// parent device release
static void my_bus_device_release(struct device *dev)
{
}

// parent device
static struct device my_bus_device = {
  .init_name   = "mybus0",
  .release     = my_bus_device_release
};
```

```
/* DEVICE */

/*
 * as we are not using the reference count, we use a no-op
 * release function
 */
static void my_dev_release(struct device *dev)
{
}

int my_register_device(struct my_device *mydev)
{
  mydev->dev.bus = &my_bus_type;
  mydev->dev.parent = &my_bus_device;
  mydev->dev.release = my_dev_release;
  dev_set_name(&mydev->dev, mydev->name);

  return device_register(&mydev->dev);
}

void my_unregister_device(struct my_device *mydev)
{
  device_unregister(&mydev->dev);
}

/* export register/unregister device functions */
EXPORT_SYMBOL(my_register_device);
EXPORT_SYMBOL(my_unregister_device);
```

The **my_register_device()** and **my_unregister_device()** functions are used to add/ remove a device to/from a bus, and are defined in the same file where the bus is defined. The device structures are, therefore, not initialized; they will be initialized when the devices are discovered by the system by **hotplug** or direct registration from the driver, and the **my_register_device** function will then be called to add a device to the bus. To use the bus defined above in the driver implementation, we must define a structure of type **my_device**, initialize it, and register it using the function exported by the bus (**my_register_device**), this is shown as follows:

```
static struct my_device mydev;
char devname[NAME_SIZE];
```

```
//...

//register
int errprintntf(devnam", "myd"v0");
mydev.name = devname;
mydev.driver = &mydriver;
dev_set_drvdata(&mydev.dev, &mydev);
err = my_register_device(&mydev);
if (err < 0) {
  /*handle error */
}

//..

//unregister
my_unregister_device(&mydev);
```

The driver model

The Linux Driver Model helps maintain a clean separation between the core kernel functionality and the various device drivers, making the kernel more modular, scalable, and maintainable.

Description of the Linux Driver Model includes:

- **Device driver registration and initialization**:
  - **struct device_driver**: Each device driver is represented by a **struct device_driver** data structure. This structure contains information about the driver, such as its name, supported devices, and callbacks for initialization and cleanup.
  - **module_driver()**: Macro used for registering a driver with the kernel. It associates the driver with a specific kernel module.
- **Device registration and management**:
  - **struct device**: Each device in the system is represented by a struct device data structure. This structure contains information about the device, such as its name, type, and the associated driver.
  - **device_create()**: Function used to create a device and associate it with a device driver.
  - **device_destroy()**: Function used to destroy a previously created device.

- **Driver and device matching**:
  - ○ **Driver matching**: Drivers are matched with devices based on criteria such as device type, vendor ID, and product ID.
  - ○ **Driver binding**: When a device is detected, the kernel attempts to bind it to the appropriate driver.

- **Driver operations**:
  - ○ **struct file_operations**: A structure containing pointers to various file operations that a driver can implement, such as open, read, write, and release.
  - ○ **struct platform_driver and struct pci_driver**: Specialized driver structures for platform devices and PCI devices, respectively.

- **Kernel object model**: Devices, drivers, and other related entities are represented as kernel objects. They are organized hierarchically and can be accessed through the **/sys** filesystem.

- **Sysfs interface**: The Linux Driver Model exposes a **sysfs** interface in the **/sys** filesystem, allowing user-space tools and applications to query and configure driver and device information.

- **Hotplug and Hotswap support**: The Driver Model supports **hotplug** and **hotswap** operations, enabling devices to be dynamically added or removed from the system without rebooting.

- **Device attributes and properties**: The Linux Driver Model provides a standardized way to represent and query device attributes and properties, making it easier for user-space applications and scripts to interact with devices.

By adopting the Linux Driver Model, developers can create drivers that follow a standardized interface, making it easier to integrate new hardware into the Linux kernel. The modular and extensible nature of the driver model contributes to the overall stability and maintainability of the Linux kernel.

LDM is used to enable a simple association between system devices and drivers. Drivers can export information independently of the physical device.

Within **sysfs**, driver information is not associated with any single subdirectory; They are found in the directory tree in different places: the loaded module is located in **/sys/module**, in **/sys/devices** you will find the driver associated with each device, in **/sys/class** the drivers belonging to a class, in **/sys/bus** the drivers associated with each bus.

A device driver is represented by the **struct device_driver** structure, which is as follows:

```
struct device_driver {
        const char              *name;
```

```
        struct bus_type          *bus;
        struct driver_private     *p;
        struct module             *owner;
        const char                *mod_name;      /* used for built-in
modules */
        int      (*probe)         (struct device *dev);
        int      (*remove)        (struct device *dev);
        void     (*shutdown)      (struct device *dev);
        int      (*suspend)       (struct device *dev, pm_message_t state);
        int      (*resume)        (struct device *dev);
};
```

In the structure fields, we find the name of the driver that appears in **sysfs**, the bus with which the driver works, and the functions called at different times during the operation of a device.

There are also functions similar to what we saw previously **driver_register()** and **driver_unregister()**, to register/unregister a driver. To work with attributes, we have the **struct driver_attribute** structure, the **DRIVER_ATTR** macro for setting, and the **driver_create_file()** and **driver_remove_file()** functions for adding the attribute to the device.

Similar to devices, the **struct device_driver** structure is often integrated into a more specialized structure tailored to a specific bus type, such as PCI or USB. Refer to the following:

```
// my driver type
struct my_driver {
  struct module *module;
  struct device_driver driver;
};

#define to_my_driver(drv) container_of(drv, struct my_driver, driver);

int my_register_driver(struct my_driver *driver)
{
  int err;

  driver->driver.bus = &my_bus_type;
  err= driver_register(&driver->driver);
  if (err)
    return err;
```

```
  return 0;
}


void my_unregister_driver(struct my_driver *driver)
{
  driver_unregister(&driver->driver);
}


/* export register/unregister driver functions */
EXPORT_SYMBOL(my_register_driver);
EXPORT_SYMBOL(my_unregister_driver);
```

Driver registration/unregistration operations are exported for use in other modules. As for the operations for the drivers are defined during bus initialization and are exported for use by the drivers themselves.

When implementing a driver that uses devices connected to a bus, the **my_register_driver** and **my_unregister_driver** functions will be called to associate with the bus.

To utilize the functions within the driver implementation, we need to declare a structure of type **my_driver**, initialize its members, and then register it using a function provided by the bus, shown as follows:

```
static struct my_driver mydriver = {
  .module = THIS_MODULE,
  .driver = {
    .name = "bpbdriver",
  },
};
//...


//register
int err;
err = my_register_driver(&mydriver);
if (err < 0) {
  /*handle error */
}
//..


//unregister
my_unregister_driver(&mydriver);
```

The classes

A class is a high-level view of the Linux device model, which summarizes implementation details. There are drivers for SCSI and ATA drivers, etc., but all belong to the disk class. Classes provide a grouping of devices based on their functionality, not how they are connected or how they work. Classes have a correspondent in **/sys/classes**.

There are two main structures that describe classes: the **"struct class"** and the **"struct device"**. The class structure describes a generic class, while the **struct device** structure describes a class associated with a device. There are several functions to initialize/uninitialize and add attributes for each, described in **include/linux/device.h**.

The advantage of these classes is mainly for the proper functioning of the **udev** binary (in userspace) and which automatically creates devices in the **/dev** directory based on class information.

A generic class is defined by the **class** structure:

```
struct class {
        const char              *name;
        struct module           *owner;
        struct kobject          *dev_kobj;
        struct subsys_private   *p;
        struct class_attribute          *class_attrs;
        struct class_device_attribute   *class_dev_attrs;
        struct device_attribute         *dev_attrs;

        int     (*dev_uevent)(struct device *dev, struct kobj_uevent_env
*env);
        void    (*class_release)(struct class *class);
        void    (*dev_release)(struct device *dev);
        //...
};
```

The **class_register()** and **class_unregister()** functions are used for initializing and deinitializing a class as follows:

```
static struct class my_class = {
        .name = "myclass",
};


static int __init my_init(void)
{
```

```
        int err;
        //…
        err = class_register(&my_class);
        if (err < 0) {
                /* handle error */
        }
        //...
}


static void __exit my_cleanup(void)
{
        //...
        class_unregister(&my_class);
        //...
}
```

The **device_create()** function initializes the structure of the device, and assigns the generic class structure and the device received as a parameter. Additionally, this will create an attribute of the **class**, **dev**, which contains the minor and major of the device (**minor:major**).

The **udev** binary (in userspace) can read the necessary data from this attributes file to create a node in the **/dev** directory by calling **makenod**.

An example of initialization is shown as follows:

```
struct device* my_classdev;
struct cdev cdev;
struct device dev;


//init class for device cdev.dev
my_classdev = device_create(&my_class, NULL, cdev.dev, &dev, "myclass0");


//destroy class for device cdev.dev
device_destroy(&my_class, cdev.dev);
```

When a new device is detected, it is assigned to a specific class, and a corresponding node is created in the **/dev** directory. For instance, in the previous example, the node **/dev/ myclass0** would be generated.

About procfs

Just like its **/sys** counterpart, **/proc** is a filesystem that can allow information to be exchanged with the user space.

```c
#include <linux/kernel.h>
#include <linux/module.h>
#include <linux/proc_fs.h>
#include <linux/sched.h>
#include <linux/uaccess.h>
#include <linux/version.h>
#if LINUX_VERSION_CODE >= KERNEL_VERSION(5, 10, 0)
#include <linux/minmax.h>
#endif

#if LINUX_VERSION_CODE >= KERNEL_VERSION(5, 6, 0)
#define HAVE_PROC_OPS
#endif

#define PROCFS_MAX_SIZE 2048UL
#define PROCFS_ENTRY_FILENAME "buffer"
#define PROCFS_ENTRY_FOLDER   "bpb"

static struct proc_dir_entry *parent;
static struct proc_dir_entry *proc_file;
static char procfs_buffer[PROCFS_MAX_SIZE];
static unsigned long procfs_buffer_size = 0;

static ssize_t procfs_read(struct file *filp, char __user *buffer,
                           size_t length, loff_t *offset)
{
    if (*offset || procfs_buffer_size == 0) {
        pr_debug("procfs_read: END\n");
        *offset = 0;
        return 0;
    }
    procfs_buffer_size = min(procfs_buffer_size, length);
    if (copy_to_user(buffer, procfs_buffer, procfs_buffer_size))
```

```
        return -EFAULT;
    *offset += procfs_buffer_size;

    pr_debug("procfs_read: read %lu bytes\n", procfs_buffer_size);
    return procfs_buffer_size;
}


static int procfs_open(struct inode *inode, struct file *file)
{
    try_module_get(THIS_MODULE);
    return 0;
}
static int procfs_close(struct inode *inode, struct file *file)
{
    module_put(THIS_MODULE);
    return 0;
}


#ifdef HAVE_PROC_OPS
static struct proc_ops file_ops_proc_file = {
    .proc_read    = procfs_read,
    .proc_open    = procfs_open,
    .proc_release = procfs_close,
};
#else
static const struct file_operations file_ops_proc_file = {
    .read    = procfs_read,
    .open    = procfs_open,
    .release = procfs_close,
};
#endif


static int __init procfs_init(void)
{
    parent = proc_mkdir(PROCFS_ENTRY_FOLDER,NULL);
    if( parent == NULL )
    {
```

```
                pr_info("Error creating proc entry");
                goto r_device;
        }


        proc_file = proc_create(PROCFS_ENTRY_FILENAME, 0644, parent,
                                    &file_ops_proc_file);
        if (proc_file == NULL) {
            pr_debug("Error: Could not initialize /proc/%s\n",
                    PROCFS_ENTRY_FILENAME);
            return -ENOMEM;
        }
        proc_set_size(proc_file, 80);
        proc_set_user(proc_file, GLOBAL_ROOT_UID, GLOBAL_ROOT_GID);

        pr_debug("/proc/%s created\n", PROCFS_ENTRY_FILENAME);
        return 0;

r_device:
        return -1;
}

static void __exit procfs_exit(void)
{
        proc_remove(parent); // /proc/bpb
        // or
        //remove_proc_entry("bpb/buffer", parent);

        pr_debug("/proc/%s removed\n", PROCFS_ENTRY_FILENAME);
}

module_init(procfs_init);
module_exit(procfs_exit);

MODULE_LICENSE("GPL");
```

Note: The example code makes the entry in procfs read-only. A read-write version is accessible for download from the GitHub repository linked to this book.

Here is some information about the main useful functions:

- **proc_mkdir()** function is used to create a new directory or sub-directory entry in the **/proc** filesystem. This directory can be used to organize and provide access to specific information or functionalities related to the kernel or kernel modules.

- Prototype: `struct proc_dir_entry *proc_mkdir(const char *name, struct proc_dir_entry *parent);`

- **proc_create()** function is used to create a new entry (file or directory) in the **/proc** filesystem. This function allows kernel developers to expose information or functionality to user-space applications through the virtual **/proc** filesystem.

- Prototype: `struct proc_dir_entry *proc_create(const char *name, umode_t mode, struct proc_dir_entry *parent, const struct file_operations *proc_fops);`

  o **Where:**

    ▪ **name**: The name of the entry to be created.

    ▪ **mode**: The permissions mode for the entry, specifying the access permissions for the owner, group, and others.

    ▪ **parent**: A pointer to the parent directory where the new entry should be created. If a parent is **NULL**, the entry will be created in the root of the **/proc** filesystem.

    ▪ **proc_fops**: A pointer to a structure containing file operations (e.g., open, read, write, release) for the newly created entry.

  o The function returns a pointer to the created **proc_dir_entry** structure, which can be used for further manipulations or to provide additional information. The structure having evolved at a given moment in the evolution of the GNU/Linux kernel, the names of the fields change and must be tested to maintain backward compatibility:

```
#ifdef HAVE_PROC_OPS
static struct proc_ops file_ops_proc_file = {
    .proc_read    = procfs_read,
    .proc_write   = procfs_write,
    .proc_open    = procfs_open,
    .proc_release = procfs_close,
};
#else
static const struct file_operations file_ops_proc_file = {
    .read    = procfs_read,
    .write   = procfs_write,
```

```
        .open    = procfs_open,
        .release = procfs_close,
    };
    #endif
```

- **remove_proc_entry()** is used to remove entries from the **/proc** directory.

  Prototype: **void remove_proc_entry(const char *name, struct proc_dir_entry *parent);**

  Here, **name** is the name of the entry to be removed, and **parent** is a pointer to the parent directory where the entry is located. The function removes the specified entry from the **/proc** directory.

  It is worth noting that the **/proc** filesystem is used to provide information about processes and other system information in a file-like structure. The specific details and functionalities of the **/proc** filesystem can vary between different versions of the Linux kernel. If you are working with this function, it's important to refer to the documentation or source code of the specific kernel version you are using for accurate and up-to-date information.

- **proc_remove()** is used to recursively remove a folder and its children.

- Prototype: **void proc_remove(struct proc_dir_entry *parent);**

To exchange data between the user space and the kernel space, we will use two important functions: **'copy_from_user'** and **'copy_to_user'**. These functions are essential for handling data transfer between the user space applications and the kernel, ensuring proper memory access and security.

The **copy_from_user function()** is used to copy data from the user space to the kernel space.

Prototype: **long copy_from_user(void *to, const void __user *from, unsigned long n);**

Parameters:

- **to**: Destination pointer in the kernel space
- **from**: Source pointer in the user space
- **n**: Number of bytes to copy

Return value: It returns the number of bytes that could not be copied. If the return value is zero, the copy was successful

Example:

```
char buffer[256];
if (copy_from_user(buffer, user_ptr, sizeof(buffer)) != 0) {
```

```
    // Handle error
}
    // Continue processing with the data in 'buffer'
```

The **copy_to_user function()** is used to copy data from the kernel space to the user space.

Prototype: `long copy_to_user(void __user *to, const void *from, unsigned long n);`

Parameters:

- **to**: Destination pointer in the user space
- **from**: Source pointer in the kernel space
- **n**: Number of bytes to copy

Return value:

- It returns the number of bytes that could not be copied. If the return value is zero, the copy was successful

   Example:

```
char kernel_data[256];
// Populate kernel_data
if (copy_to_user(user_ptr, kernel_data, sizeof(kernel_data)) != 0)
{
    // Handle error
}
    // Continue processing or inform the user about the data
```

Those functions are crucial for system calls and various kernel operations where data must be exchanged between the user space and the kernel space. They handle issues such as memory protection and alignment, making sure that data is copied safely and efficiently. It is important to check the return values to handle errors appropriately in the kernel code. We will detail these functions in the next chapter.

To make it work, we will use the **makefile** defined in the previous chapter.

To compile:

```
$ make clean && make
make M=/home/tgayet/Documents/bpb/04-linux-device-model/code_4_procfs -C /
lib/modules/6.2.0-36-generic/build clean
make[1]: Entering directory '/usr/src/linux-headers-6.2.0-36-generic'
make[1]: Leaving directory '/usr/src/linux-headers-6.2.0-36-generic'
make M=/home/tgayet/Documents/bpb/04-linux-device-model/code_4_procfs -C /
```

```
lib/modules/6.2.0-36-generic/build modules
make[1]: Entering directory '/usr/src/linux-headers-6.2.0-36-generic'
warning: the compiler differs from the one used to build the kernel
  The kernel was built by: x86_64-linux-gnu-gcc-11 (Ubuntu
11.4.0-1ubuntu1~22.04) 11.4.0
  You are using:            gcc-11 (Ubuntu 11.4.0-1ubuntu1~22.04) 11.4.0
  CC [M]  /home/tgayet/Documents/bpb/04-linux-device-model/code_4_procfs/
procfs.o
  MODPOST /home/tgayet/Documents/bpb/04-linux-device-model/code_4_procfs/
Module.symvers
  CC [M]  /home/tgayet/Documents/bpb/04-linux-device-model/code_4_procfs/
procfs.mod.o
  LD [M]  /home/tgayet/Documents/bpb/04-linux-device-model/code_4_procfs/
procfs.ko
  BTF [M] /home/tgayet/Documents/bpb/04-linux-device-model/code_4_procfs/
procfs.ko
Skipping BTF generation for /home/tgayet/Documents/bpb/04-linux-device-
model/code_4_procfs/procfs.ko due to unavailability of vmlinux
make[1]: Leaving directory '/usr/src/linux-headers-6.2.0-36-generic'
modinfo ./procfs.ko
filename:        /home/tgayet/Documents/bpb/04-linux-device-model/code_4_
procfs/./procfs.ko
license:         GPL
srcversion:      F3D612AB0B75B392BDD51C5
depends:
retpoline:       Y
name:            procfs
vermagic:        6.2.0-36-generic SMP preempt mod_unload modversions
```

Now, we can load the module and check it is well loaded:

```
$ sudo insmod ./procfs.ko
$ lsmod|grep procfs
procfs                20480  0
```

We can check the existence of the new entry **'bpb/buffer'** within **/proc**:

```
$ tree /proc/bpb
/proc/bpb
└── buffer
$ ls -alh /proc/bpb/buffer
-rw-r--r-- 1 root root 80 nov.  14 20:46 buffer
```

The entry has **rw** rights because we have used the **0644** at its creation. That means the root can read and write, but the other can just read.

In the example code, we will define a buffer that can be initialized with the **/procfs** entry we have defined.

Initially, the buffer is empty:

```
$ cat /proc/bpb/buffer
```

If we try to send a string, it will work only for root:

```
$ sudo echo "hello bpb" > /proc/bpb/buffer
zsh: permission denied: /proc/bpb/buffer


$ sudo su
# id
uid=0(root) gid=0(root) groups=0(root)
```

Now that we are root, we can send a string **othe** the **procfs** entry:

```
# echo "hello bpb" > /proc/bpb/buffer
```

Finally, we can re-read the content of the buffer:

```
# cat /proc/bpb/buffer
hello bpb
```

One of the key benefits that the cloud provides is elasticity, which allows it to use only the required resources and pay for that portion only. A very common use case for certain workloads is that on weekends, offices are closed and there is not much load, hence infrastructure can be reduced to a minimal. Similarly, at the end of every month during payroll processing, the utilization of related infrastructure like databases, servers, and so on, is very high and needs more resources. In such cases, scaling needs to be done very frequently as compared to scenarios where, during the holiday period, infrastructure needs to be scaled up for a few days, once a year, to support sales and business. It is important to continuously analyze the utilization as well as related cost, detect the patterns, and accordingly provide required recommendations or take automated action to both provide the right-sized infrastructure and to optimize the cost.

Along with cost optimization, this analysis also helps in preventing potential security-related issues or threats. For example, on weekends, there is not much connection or usage, but if your data suddenly shows a spike in utilization, this may indicate a security attack. Algorithms can be used to find such anomalies in the data automatically and alert the FinOps teams to these events.

About the DTB device tree

The **Device Tree Blob** (**DTB**) is a binary representation of hardware configuration data used by the Linux kernel on systems that require a dynamic description of their hardware, such as embedded **systems or systems-on-chip** (**SoCs**). It provides a structured way for the kernel to understand the available hardware without needing this information hardcoded in the kernel itself.

The device tree is a data structure for describing hardware. It originated in the PowerPC world but has become widely adopted in embedded systems. It helps to separate hardware-specific details from the operating system or software.

The device tree is written in a human-readable format called the **Device Tree Source** (**DTS**). It is compiled into a binary format called the DTB for use by the Linux kernel.

Purpose

The purpose is explained as follows:

- Describe hardware components and their interconnections (e.g., CPUs, memory, buses, GPIOs, etc.).

- Allow the Linux kernel to operate on a wide range of hardware with minimal modification.

- Provide a mechanism for device-specific data to be passed to the operating system.

A device tree consists of nodes and properties, which are explained as follows:

- **Nodes**: Represent devices or hardware components. Nodes can have child nodes for hierarchical hardware descriptions (e.g., a bus with attached devices).

- **Properties**: Key-value pairs associated with nodes. They describe attributes like memory addresses, IRQs, and compatibility strings.

The following figure shows accessing the device tree from Linux:

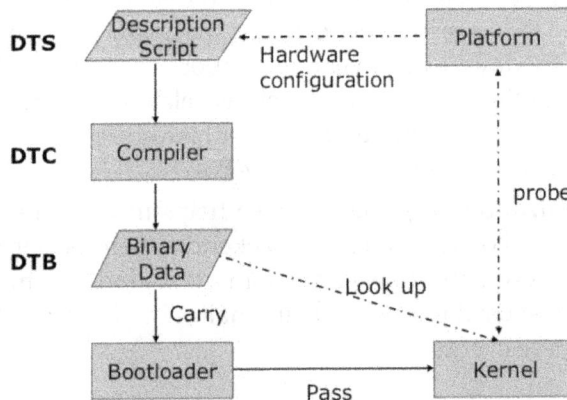

Figure 4.3: Relationships and links between DTS, DTC, and DTB

Figure 4.3 describes a DTS:

```
/dts-v1/;

/ {
    compatible = "my-board,example";
    model = "My Custom Board";

    memory {
        device_type = "memory";
        reg = <0x80000000 0x20000000>; // Start address, size
    };

    soc {
        compatible = "simple-bus";
        ranges;

        uart0: serial@1000 {
            compatible = "ns16550";
            reg = <0x1000 0x100>;
            interrupt-parent = <&intc>;
            interrupts = <5>;
        };

        gpio: gpio@2000 {
            compatible = "gpio-controller";
            reg = <0x2000 0x100>;
            gpio-controller;
            #gpio-cells = <2>;
        };
    };
};
```

The following are the key components:

- **/ (root node)**: The top-level node, describing the system as a whole.
- **compatible**: Strings identifying the device or board. The kernel matches drivers based on this.
- **reg**: Specifies memory-mapped registers for a device.
- **interrupts**: Describes the interrupt lines used by the device.

- **Labels (e.g., uart0)**: Allow referencing nodes elsewhere in the DTS.

To use a device tree, the DTS source is compiled into a binary DTB file using the **Device Tree Compiler (DTC)**.

Compilation command

The following is the compilation command:

```
$ dtc -I dts -O dtb -o my-device-tree.dtb my-device-tree.dts
```

Where:

- **-I dts**: Input format is DTS.
- **-O dtb**: Output format is DTB.
- **-o**: Specifies the output file.

The DTB is then passed to the Linux kernel during boot.

When the Linux kernel boots, it uses the DTB to probe and initialize hardware. Here is the workflow:

- **Bootloader**:
  - The bootloader (e.g., U-Boot) loads the kernel and provides the DTB.
  - The DTB can be embedded in the kernel or loaded separately.

- **Kernel**:
  - The kernel reads the DTB to gather information about the hardware.
  - Drivers are matched to hardware components based on the `compatible` property in the DTB.

- **Dynamic configuration**:
  - The device tree allows dynamic reconfiguration without recompiling the kernel.
  - Overlays (additional DT fragments) can be used to modify the hardware description at runtime (e.g., enabling a new device).

The main advantages of using DTB are:

- **Hardware abstraction**: Kernel developers do not need to hardcode hardware details into the kernel.
- **Portability**: The same kernel binary can run on different boards by simply changing the DTB.
- **Flexibility**: Supports runtime modifications via overlays.

Practical example: Consider a system with a UART and GPIO controller. The DTS would define these devices, and the kernel would use the DTB to initialize them.

Using U-Boot to Load DTB

The following are the steps to use the U-Boot to load DTB:

1. Place the DTB in the boot partition.

2. Update the bootloader configuration:

   ```
   setenv fdtfile my-device-tree.dtb
   saveenv
   ```

3. Boot the kernel:

   ```
   bootz ${kernel_addr} - ${fdt_addr}
   ```

4. When the system fails to boot, or a device is not recognized:

   a. Use the **dtc** tool to decompile the DTB back into a readable DTS:

   ```
   $ dtc -I dtb -O dts -o output.dts my-device-tree.dtb
   ```

   b. Check kernel logs (**dmesg**) for errors related to device initialization.

   c. Ensure the **compatible** strings match the expected values in kernel drivers.

Overlays allow adding or modifying the device tree at runtime. This is useful for modular hardware designs or conditional configurations.

Example:

```
/dts-v1/;
/plugin/;

/ {
    fragment@0 {
        target = <&gpio>;
        __overlay__ {
            new-led {
                compatible = "gpio-led";
                gpios = <&gpio 5 GPIO_ACTIVE_HIGH>;
                label = "user-led";
            };
        };
    };
};
```

This overlay adds an LED device to the GPIO controller.

The DTB is an essential part of the Linux kernel's hardware abstraction mechanism, especially in embedded systems. Understanding its structure, creation, and usage can greatly simplify kernel development and debugging for diverse hardware configurations.

Conclusion

This chapter allowed us to once again enter the world of the GNU/Linux kernel by detailing the foundations developed over the years to simplify its maintainability, but also its development.

Taking into account the elements seen so far, we will address the development of character drivers in the next chapter.

Join our book's Discord space

Join the book's Discord Workspace for Latest updates, Offers, Tech happenings around the world, New Release and Sessions with the Authors:

https://discord.bpbonline.com

CHAPTER 5
Character Device Drivers

Introduction

In this chapter, we will study the character drivers used in many Linux drivers. These drivers allow you to manage a plethora of devices, such as a keyboard, a mouse, and so on. This is one of the simplest driver models, but it can be used for multiple purposes.

Structure

This chapter covers the following topics:

- Types of drivers
- The mknod command
- Communication userspace/kernel
- The udev daemon and the dynamic files
- First readonly character's drivers
- Second readwrite character's drivers
- Third ioctl character's drivers
- Loading a driver at boot

Objectives

The objective of this book is to understand the different types of drivers, the predefined nodes, and the modes of communication between user space and kernel space. Next, we will start by exploring character drivers.

Types of drivers

Linux drivers play a crucial role in enabling the operating system to communicate with and control hardware devices.

There are several types of Linux drivers, each serving specific functions:

- **Character device drivers**: These handle devices that transfer data character by character, such as keyboards, mice, and serial ports.

- **Block device drivers**: They manage devices that store and retrieve data in fixed-size blocks, like hard drives and SSDs.

- **Network device drivers**: These facilitate communication between the Linux kernel and **network interface cards** (**NICs**) or network adapters.

- **Filesystem drivers**: They enable the OS to read and write to different file systems like ext4, NTFS, FAT32, etc., allowing compatibility and data access.

- **USB drivers**: Responsible for managing USB devices like flash drives, keyboards, mice, printers, etc., connected to the system.

- **Graphics drivers**: These control graphical output, enabling the OS to work with graphics cards and displays.

- **Sound drivers**: Manage audio devices and enable sound output and input functionalities.

- **Virtual device drivers**: For virtualization purposes, these drivers handle communication between the guest operating system and the host system in virtual environments.

- **Platform drivers**: These handle hardware that's platform-specific, like drivers for embedded systems or specialized hardware.

- **Firmware drivers**: They interact with the firmware of various devices, assisting in their initialization and operation.

These drivers are essential for the kernel to interact with diverse hardware components effectively. Each type of driver follows specific protocols and interfaces, ensuring seamless interaction between the OS and hardware.

The mknod command

The **mknod** command in Linux serves as a crucial utility for creating device nodes within the **/dev** directory or any desired location in the file system. Its primary function is to generate special files that represent devices, including both block and character devices.

This command allows users to create device nodes manually, specifying the type of device (character or block), major and minor device numbers, and the file name to create.

For character devices, **mknod** enables the creation of special files that handle data characters by characters, like terminals or mice. Block devices, on the other hand, manage data in fixed-size blocks and include devices such as hard drives or SSDs.

The syntax for **mknod** involves specifying the file name to create, its type (c for character or b for block), and the major and minor device numbers. The major number identifies the device driver associated with the device, while the minor number specifies a particular device instance or unit.

This command is typically used by system administrators or developers for device management and configuration, especially when dealing with specialized or custom devices that might not be automatically created during system startup.

However, caution is necessary when using **mknod** as it operates at a low level, and incorrect usage can lead to system instability or security issues. Proper permissions and understanding of device types and numbers are crucial for its safe and accurate usage.

Usage: `mknod [options] <device_name> <type> <major> <minor>`

Here is an explanation of the parameters:

> `<device_name>`: Specifies the name of the device node to be created.
> `<type>`: Indicates the type of device to create:
>> `c`: Character device
>> `b`: Block device
> `<major>`: Represents the major device number, identifying the device driver associated with the device.
> `<minor>`: Indicates the minor device number, specifying a particular device instance or unit.

The **mknod** command does not have an extensive list of options; its primary usage involves specifying the device type (character or block), major and minor device numbers, and the name of the device node to be created.

Here are a few examples showcasing the usage of the mknod command to create device nodes for different types of devices:

- To create a character device node for a terminal:
  ```
  $ sudo mknod /dev/myterminal c 5 1
  ```

This creates a character device node named **myterminal** with major number 5 and minor number 1.

- For instance, to create a block device node for a partition:

```
$ sudo mknod /dev/mydisk b 8 0
```

This creates a block device node named **mydisk** with major number 8 and minor number 0.

- Creating a first-in-first-out pipe (named **pipe**):

```
$ sudo mknod /tmp/myfifo p
```

This creates a FIFO special file (named **pipe**) named **myfifo** in the **/tmp** directory.

- Creating a null device node:

```
$ sudo mknod /dev/null c 1 3
```

This recreates the commonly used **/dev/null** device node with major number 1 and minor number 3, which discards all data written to it.

- Creating a random number generator device node:

```
$ sudo mknod /dev/random c 1 8
```

This creates a device node **/dev/random** that provides random data, with major number 1 and minor number 8.

Remember, using **mknod** requires superuser privileges (**sudo**) as it deals with system-level device node creation. Additionally, creating device nodes manually should be done carefully, ensuring the correct major and minor numbers and understanding the implications of creating or modifying these nodes on system functionality.

Communication userspace/kernel

User space primarily houses user applications and system libraries like the **C standard library** (**libc**). These applications, such as web browsers, text editors, and games, operate within this space, leveraging system libraries for various functionalities.

The kernel space, on the other hand, constitutes the core of the operating system. It handles critical tasks such as managing hardware, memory, and processes and providing essential services to user space.

When a user application needs a service provided by the kernel, it initiates a system call—a request for a specific operation, like I/O operations or process creation. This call triggers a context switch, transitioning the CPU's execution from user space to kernel space.

During this transition, the kernel gains access to both user space and kernel space memory. However, for security and stability reasons, user space processes cannot directly access kernel space memory.

The kernel offers a multitude of services to the user space, encompassing process management, memory management, device drivers, and more. These services are accessed through controlled interfaces like system calls, ensuring proper interaction while maintaining system integrity.

Moreover, interrupts and signals, whether generated by hardware events or software commands, prompt the CPU to switch from executing user-space code to handling these events in the kernel space.

Inter-process communication (**IPC**) mechanisms like pipes, sockets, and shared memory facilitate communication between different processes in user space, with the kernel managing and regulating these communications.

Additionally, file system access by user applications is mediated through system calls managed by the kernel. This provides an interface for reading from and writing to files, directories, and other file system-related operations.

In summary, the interaction between kernel space and user space is governed by controlled interfaces and mechanisms like system calls, interrupts, and IPC, allowing user applications to access kernel-managed services and resources while upholding system security, stability, and functionality.

To exchange data with the Gnu/Linux kernel, the user space will mainly use either:

- Files
- Sockets
- Very specific nodes, which we will see later

Exchanges on those nodes will take place by characters or by blocks: this is what will differentiate the types of drivers.

In Linux, absolutely everything is a file. By convention, the files allowing communications with the drivers will be in the **/dev(ice)** directory:

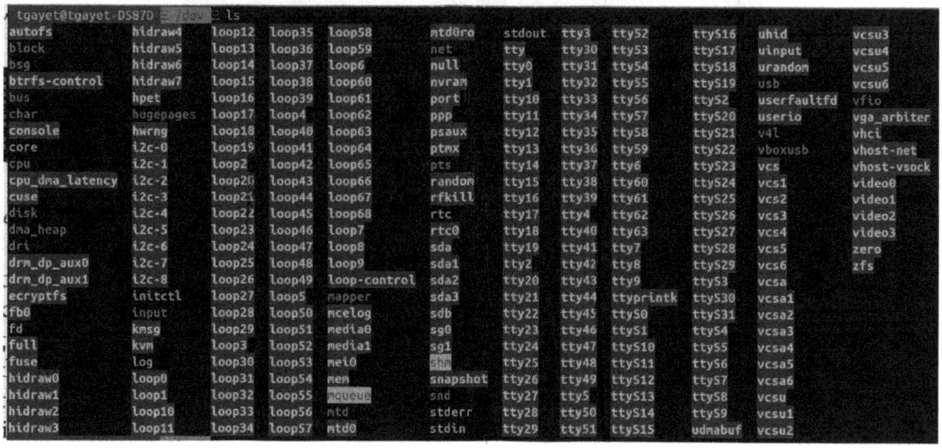

Figure 5.1: Listing of the main files in /dev

The **/dev** directory in Linux serves as a pivotal repository for special device files that act as interfaces to hardware components, peripheral devices, and system resources. This directory, short for *device*, contains files representing various devices within a system, functioning as access points or symbolic links rather than traditional data storage. These device files, often referred to as device nodes, are categorized into different types, such as character devices and block devices. Character devices, like terminals or mice, operate by handling data character by character, while block devices, including hard drives and SSDs, manage data in fixed-size blocks.

Applications and users interact indirectly with physical and virtual devices through these device files housed in **/dev**. For instance, to access a CD-ROM, an application might communicate with the corresponding device file in **/dev**.

During system boot, the **/dev** directory's contents are managed or generated by subsystems like **udev** or **devfs**. This process is crucial for the system to initialize and configure devices properly.

Permissions for these device files are critical in maintaining system security. Typically owned by the root user, these permissions control which users or groups can access and manipulate specific devices. Direct access to certain device files, like **/dev/sda** representing the entire hard drive, grants significant control over the system.

The content within the **/dev** directory can change dynamically as devices are added, removed, or modified during runtime. This dynamic nature reflects the system's current state and the devices connected at any given time.

Ultimately, the **/dev** directory acts as a crucial interface between the kernel and user space, providing a standardized means for applications and users to interact with hardware devices and system resources through these special device files.

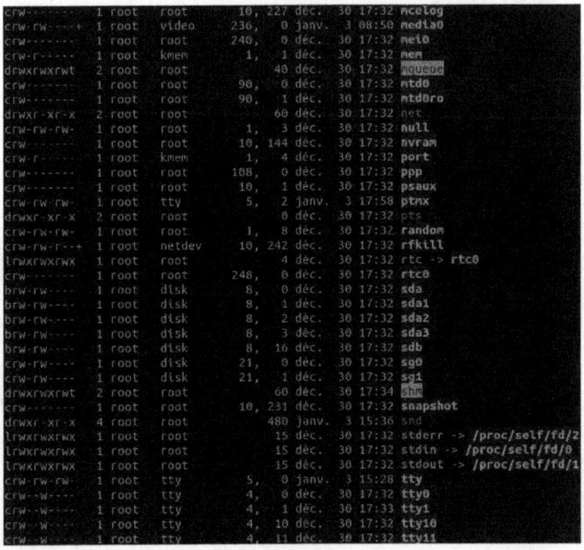

Figure 5.2: Listing of several files that we will describe

In the above listing, the first letter has a different meaning:

- b means a block driver
- c means character driver

These files are used to communicate between kernel space and user space or between kernel space and user space to communicate.

If we refer to the following official documentation, we will see how all these device files are defined:

https://www.kernel.org/doc/Documentation/admin-guide/devices.txt

Here is an example with the major 1-character driver:

```
 1 char       Memory devices
               1 = /dev/mem          Physical memory access
               2 = /dev/kmem         Kernel virtual memory access
               3 = /dev/null         Null device
               4 = /dev/port         I/O port access
               5 = /dev/zero         Null byte source
               6 = /dev/core         OBSOLETE - replaced by /proc/kcore
               7 = /dev/full         Returns ENOSPC on write
               8 = /dev/random   Nondeterministic random number gen.
               9 = /dev/urandom  Faster, less secure random number gen.
              10 = /dev/aio          Asynchronous I/O notification
interface
              11 = /dev/kmsg         Writes to this come out as printk's
              12 = /dev/oldmem   Used by crashdump kernels to access
                                 the memory of the kernel that crashed.
```

As an example, we can check the presence of **/dev/urandom**, which has a major number equal to 1 and a minor number equal to 9:

$ ls -al /dev/urandom

crw-rw-rw- 1 root root 1, 9 déc. 30 17:32 /dev/urandom

As an example, we can check the presence of **/dev/urandom**. This file gives access to a random number generator.

Request random numbers via this device file:

$ hexdump /dex/urandom

```
002a580 558b 4ec6 6225 f686 f7b7 d7df 749a 29be
002a590 871f 5e91 fcf4 362d a39f 9857 3956 9c4a
```

```
002a5a0 2d03 617f 56f4 8246 28ac c966 cc02 c709
002a5b0 d10f 9f3c c23d 6a1f fdaf b124 34cc 144d
002a5c0 1965 6148 0ddd 800b a9fd 88f4 20dd 9685
002a5d0 e2b7 66a7 03ab a808 a2f9 ee6b b368 d6d9^C
```

Let us create a new device file called **alea** in the **/dev** folder:

```
$ sudo mknod /dev/alea c 1 9
```

```
$ ls -al /dev/alea
crw-r--r--. 1 root root 1, 9 Sep 14 13:34 /dev/alea
```

We can now request random numbers via this new device file:

```
$ hexdump /dex/alea
```

```
002a580 558b 4ec6 6225 f686 f7b7 d7df 749a 29be
002a590 871f 5e91 fcf4 362d a39f 9857 3956 9c4a
002a5a0 2d03 617f 56f4 8246 28ac c966 cc02 c709
002a5b0 d10f 9f3c c23d 6a1f fdaf b124 34cc 144d
002a5c0 1965 6148 0ddd 800b a9fd 88f4 20dd 9685
002a5d0 e2b7 66a7 03ab a808 a2f9 ee6b b368 d6d9^C
```

Thus, **/dev/urandom** and **/dev/alea** communicate with the same random number generator of the **gnu/linux** kernel:

The following figure shows two instances having the same major and minor:

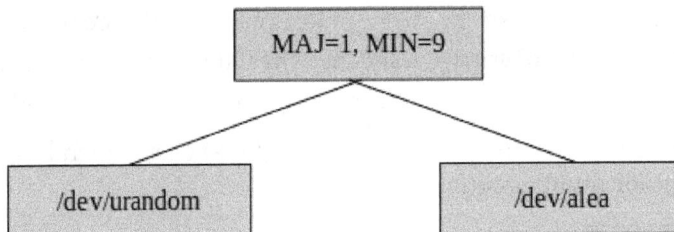

Figure 5.3: Two device files created from the same major/minor pair

Static device files in the **/dev** directory are device nodes that represent hardware devices present in the system. These files are often created during system boot by mechanisms like **udev**, **mdev**, or other device management systems.

Some commonly encountered static device files within the **/dev** directory include the following:

- **tty and pty**: Terminals are represented by files in **/dev/tty** and **/dev/pts**. Pseudo-terminals are represented by **/dev/ptmx**.

- **null, zero, random**: **/dev/null** represents a device that discards all data written to it. **/dev/zero** outputs zeros. **/dev/random** and **/dev/urandom** provide random data.

- **sda, sdb, hda, etc.**: These files represent hard drives or SSDs. For example, **/dev/sda** might represent the first hard drive.

- **loopX**: **/dev/loopX** represents loop devices used for mounting disk image files.

- **console**: **/dev/console** typically represents the system console.

- **fbX**: **/dev/fbX** devices are used for framebuffer devices.

- **dsp**: **/dev/dsp** represents a sound device.

- **lp0, lp1**: Printer devices are represented by these files.

- **eventX**: Event devices for input devices like keyboards and mice are represented by **/dev/input/eventX**.

These static device files provide interfaces for interacting with hardware devices connected to the system. They are utilized by applications and users to access the hardware functionalities of the system.

The udev daemon and the dynamic files

Dynamic device files in the **/dev** directory of Linux are special files that represent devices and are created, removed, or modified dynamically during system runtime. Unlike static device files, these are generated or managed as devices are connected or disconnected from the system.

These dynamic device files can include the following:

- **USB devices**: When USB devices like flash drives, external hard drives, or peripherals are connected, corresponding device nodes such as **/dev/sdb**, **/dev/ttyUSB0**, or **/dev/input/mouse0** can be created dynamically.

- **Hot-plugged devices**: Any device that supports hot-plugging (the ability to connect or disconnect while the system is running) may generate dynamic device nodes. For example, inserting an SD card might create **/dev/mmcblk0**.

- **Virtual devices**: Devices created by virtualization systems like QEMU or VirtualBox often generate dynamic device nodes in **/dev** when virtual devices are added or removed within the virtual environment.

- **Network devices**: Dynamic device files like **/dev/net/tun** are created for network-related functionalities, particularly for virtual network interfaces or VPNs.

- **Temporary and transient devices**: Some devices, like certain types of network interfaces or temporary storage devices, might generate transient device nodes that appear when the device is in use and disappear when it is disconnected or not in use.

These dynamic device files allow the kernel and user space to communicate and manage hardware resources as they are detected, connected, or removed during the system's operation. They offer a flexible and adaptable means of accessing and utilizing various hardware components in real-time.

Udev in Linux is a device manager that dynamically manages device nodes in the **/dev** directory. Its primary role is to handle the creation, deletion, and management of device nodes in response to hardware changes or device events within the system.

The following figure shows the communication of the **udev** module with the kernel:

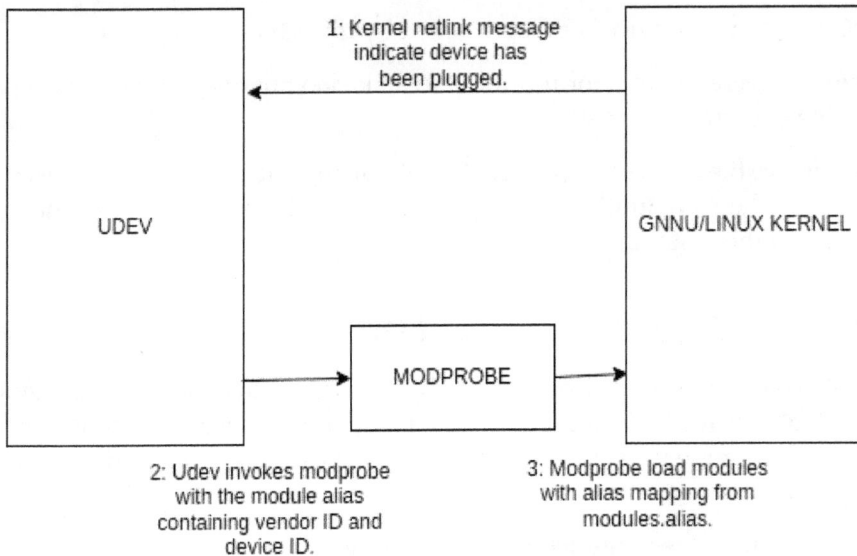

Figure 5.4: Global architecture of udev

Example of **netlink** message:

```
recv(4, // socket id
"add@/class/input/input9/mouse2\0 // message
ACTION=add\0 // action type
DEVPATH=/class/input/input9/mouse2\0 // path in /sys
SUBSYSTEM=input\0 // subsystem (class)
SEQNUM=1064\0 // sequence number
PHYSDEVPATH=/devices/pci0000:00/0000:00:1d.1/usb2/2-2/2-2:1.0\0
// device path in /sys
PHYSDEVBUS=usb\0 // bus
PHYSDEVDRIVER=usbhid\0 // driver
```

```
MAJOR=13\0 // major number
MINOR=34\0", // minor number
2048, // message buffer size
0) // flags
= 221 // actual message size
```

The following is how **udev** works:

- **Kernel events**: When hardware devices are connected, disconnected, or undergo changes, the kernel generates events to notify user space about these modifications. These events can include device detection, driver loading, or hardware configuration changes.

- **Rule-based system**: **udev** operates based on a set of rules defined in configuration files. These rules define how devices should be named, what permissions they should have, and which drivers they should use. Rules are stored **in /etc/udev/ rules.d/** and are processed in order of their file names.

- **Matching devices**: **udev** matches incoming events from the kernel with these rules to determine how to handle the events and how to create or modify device nodes accordingly.

- **Dynamic node creation**: Based on the rules, **udev** dynamically creates or removes device nodes in the **/dev** directory as needed. It assigns appropriate names (like **/ dev/sda** for a hard drive) and sets permissions, ensuring accessibility to users or applications.

- **Persistent naming**: **udev** also provides a way to assign persistent names to devices, ensuring that a device retains the same name across reboots even if its physical location or connection order changes. This is particularly useful for devices like hard drives or network interfaces.

- **Custom rules**: System administrators can create custom **udev** rules to define specific behaviors for certain devices, assign specific names, or trigger specific actions when certain hardware events occur.

- **Real-time response**: **udev** operates dynamically, responding to changes in hardware configurations or device connections in real time. It allows the system to adapt to hardware modifications without requiring manual intervention or system restarts.

In essence, **udev** is integral to the dynamic management of device nodes, ensuring proper recognition, configuration, and consistent naming of devices in a Linux system, providing a flexible and adaptable environment for managing hardware resources.

The following figure details the internal workings of **udev**:

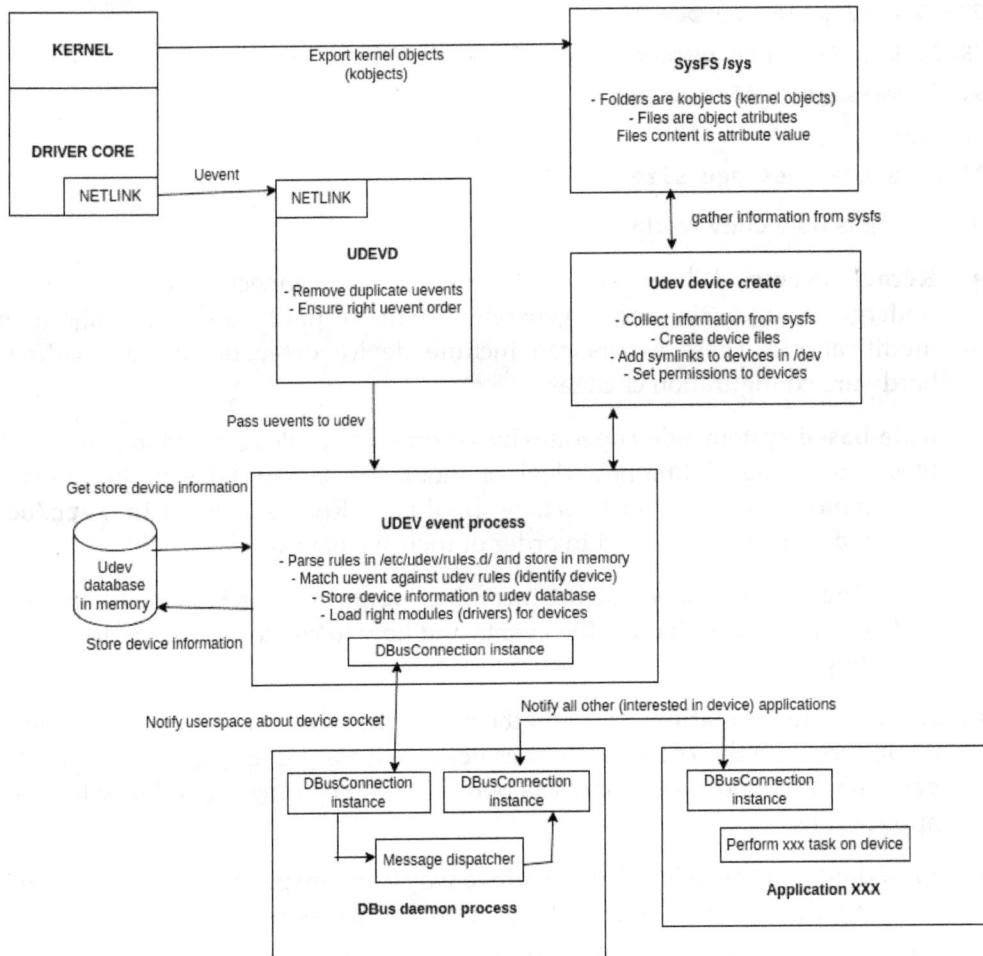

Figure 5.5: Detailed view of the udev process

First readonly character's drivers

Character drivers in Linux serve as essential bridges between the kernel and character-oriented hardware devices, enabling transparent communication and control for devices that transmit or receive data on a character-by-character basis, such as keyboards, mice, sensors, or terminals.

We will discuss a read-only version that will allow you to read information from a device but not write it.

Structure and functionality are as follows:

- **Driver registration**: These drivers register themselves with the kernel, using structures like **struct file_operations** and **struct cdev**, establishing their presence and capabilities within the system.

- **File operations handling**: Character drivers define and manage various file operations through function pointers within **struct file_operations**, including **open**, **close**, **read**, **write**, **ioctl**, and **poll**.

- **User-kernel interaction**: The interaction between user space and character devices occurs through system calls. When invoked, these system calls trigger corresponding functions within the character driver, facilitating data transfer and device control.

A character driver usually handles the following features:

- **File operations implementation**: Developers write specific functions (e.g., **open**, **read**, **write**, **release**) within the driver code to handle corresponding interactions between the kernel and the device.

- **Device initialization and registration**: During initialization, drivers register themselves with the kernel, initializing necessary resources and establishing their functionalities.

- **Synchronization and error handling**: Robust character drivers often incorporate synchronization mechanisms like mutexes or spinlocks to manage concurrent access. Additionally, they implement comprehensive error handling to address various failure scenarios.

Character drivers form a crucial layer in the Linux kernel, providing a standardized interface for user applications to interact with character-oriented hardware devices.

Their well-defined structure and functionalities ensure efficient and reliable communication between the kernel and diverse hardware components, enabling seamless integration and operation within the Linux environment.

The following code shows a read-only character driver. To better understand it, this code can be divided into several parts that I will detail to better understand it:

At the very beginning, we have the necessary Linux kernel headers for the device driver:

- **atomic.h**: For atomic operations (used to prevent race conditions).

- **cdev.h, fs.h**: For managing character devices and file operations.

- **uaccess.h**: For safely copying data between the kernel and the user space.

- **module.h**: For creating kernel modules.

- **device.h**: For device-related utilities.

- **errno.h**: For error codes.

```
#include <linux/atomic.h>
#include <linux/cdev.h>
#include <linux/delay.h>
#include <linux/device.h>
```

```
#include <linux/fs.h>
#include <linux/init.h>
#include <linux/kernel.h> /* for sprintf() */
#include <linux/module.h>
#include <linux/printk.h>
#include <linux/types.h>
#include <linux/uaccess.h> /* for get_user and put_user */
#include <linux/version.h>
#include <asm/errno.h>
```

Then we have some local prototypes of functions for the device's file operations:

- **device_open**: Called when the device file is opened.

- **device_release**: Called when the device file is closed.

- **device_read**: Called when reading data from the device.

- **device_write**: Called when writing data to the device.
  ```
  static int device_open(struct inode *, struct file *);
  static int device_release(struct inode *, struct file *);
  static ssize_t device_read(struct file *, char __user *, size_t,
  loff_t *);
  static ssize_t device_write(struct file *, const char __user *,
  size_t, loff_t *);
  ```

We can define some macros used in the code:

- **SUCCESS**: Represents success status (0).

- **DEVICE_NAME**: The name of the device as it appears in **/dev/**.

- **BUF_LEN**: Maximum length of the message buffer.
  ```
  #define SUCCESS 0
  #define DEVICE_NAME "chardev" /* Dev name as it appears in /proc/
  devices    */
  #define BUF_LEN 80 /* Max length of the message from the device */
  ```

Some global variables of the driver can be defined:

- **major**: The major number assigned to the device.

- **already_open**: An atomic variable to track whether the device is open.

- **msg**: Buffer to store the message to be read from the device.

- **cls**: Pointer to the class for the device (used for /dev entry creation).

```
/* Global variables are declared as static, so are global within the
file. */
static int major; /* major number assigned to our device driver */

enum {
    CDEV_NOT_USED = 0,
    CDEV_EXCLUSIVE_OPEN = 1,
};

/* Is device open? Used to prevent multiple access to device */
static atomic_t already_open = ATOMIC_INIT(CDEV_NOT_USED);

static char msg[BUF_LEN + 1]; /* The msg the device will give when
asked */

static struct class *cls;
```

The file operations supported by the device are important for associating a function to one operation:

- **read**, **write**, **open**, and **release** are function pointers to their respective handlers.

```
static struct file_operations chardev_fops = {
    .read = device_read,
    .write = device_write,
    .open = device_open,
    .release = device_release,
};
```

We can now define the module initialization:

- Registers the character device, assigning a major number dynamically

- Creates a **device** class and **/dev** entry for user access.

- Log success or failure during initialization.

```
static int __init chardev_init(void)
{
    major = register_chrdev(0, DEVICE_NAME, &chardev_fops);

    if (major < 0) {
        pr_alert("Registering char device failed with %d\n", major);
        return major;
```

```
        }

        pr_info("I was assigned major number %d.\n", major);

#if LINUX_VERSION_CODE >= KERNEL_VERSION(6, 4, 0)
        cls = class_create(DEVICE_NAME);
#else
        cls = class_create(THIS_MODULE, DEVICE_NAME);
#endif
        device_create(cls, NULL, MKDEV(major, 0), NULL, DEVICE_NAME);

        pr_info("Device created on /dev/%s\n", DEVICE_NAME);

        return SUCCESS;
    }
```

The module cleanup includes the following:

- Removes the **/dev** entry and class.

- Unregisters the device from the kernel.

```
    static void __exit chardev_exit(void)
    {
        device_destroy(cls, MKDEV(major, 0));
        class_destroy(cls);

        /* Unregister the device */
        unregister_chrdev(major, DEVICE_NAME);
    }
```

Now that it is almost defined, we can implement the open function:

- Prevents multiple processes from opening the device simultaneously.

- Updates a message (**msg**) for reading.

- Increments the module's usage count.

```
    /* Called when a process tries to open the device file, like
     * "sudo cat /dev/chardev"
     */
    static int device_open(struct inode *inode, struct file *file)
    {
```

```
        static int counter = 0;

        if (atomic_cmpxchg(&already_open, CDEV_NOT_USED, CDEV_EXCLUSIVE_
    OPEN))
                return -EBUSY;

        sprintf(msg, "I already told you %d times Hello world!\n",
    counter++);
        try_module_get(THIS_MODULE);

        return SUCCESS;
    }
```

The release function is as follows:

- Marks the device as available for other processes.

- Decrements the module's usage count.

```
    /* Called when a process closes the device file. */
    static int device_release(struct inode *inode, struct file *file)
    {
        /* We're now ready for our next caller */
        atomic_set(&already_open, CDEV_NOT_USED);

        /* Decrement the usage count, or else once you opened the file,
    you will
         * never get rid of the module.
         */
        module_put(THIS_MODULE);

        return SUCCESS;
    }
```

The read function also follows:

- Copies the device's message (**msg**) to the user space buffer.

- Tracks the offset to handle partial reads and EOF.

```
    /* Called when a process, which already opened the dev file, attempts
    to
     * read from it.
     */
```

```
static ssize_t device_read(struct file *filp, /* see include/linux/
fs.h   */
                           char __user *buffer, /* buffer to fill
with data */
                           size_t length, /* length of the buffer
*/
                           loff_t *offset)
{
    /* Number of bytes actually written to the buffer */
    int bytes_read = 0;
    const char *msg_ptr = msg;

    if (!*(msg_ptr + *offset)) { /* we are at the end of message */
        *offset = 0; /* reset the offset */
        return 0; /* signify end of file */
    }

    msg_ptr += *offset;

    /* Actually put the data into the buffer */
    while (length && *msg_ptr) {
        /* The buffer is in the user data segment, not the kernel
         * segment so "*" assignment won't work.  We have to use
         * put_user which copies data from the kernel data segment
to
         * the user data segment.
         */
        put_user(*(msg_ptr++), buffer++);
        length--;
        bytes_read++;
    }

    *offset += bytes_read;

    /* Most read functions return the number of bytes put into the
buffer. */
    return bytes_read;
}
```

For this read-only version, the following function allowing writing will not be used, but it will be for the read-write version. For the moment, we will only display a warning message:

Simply rejects write operations with an error (**-EINVAL**).

```
/* Called when a process writes to dev file: echo "hi" > /dev/hello
*/
static ssize_t device_write(struct file *filp, const char __user
*buff,
                            size_t len, loff_t *off)
{
    pr_alert("Sorry, this operation is not supported.\n");
    return -EINVAL;
}
```

At this point, we only have to register the driver metadata with the GNU/Linux kernel:

- Registers the initialization and cleanup functions.

- Specifies that the module is licensed under GPL.

```
module_init(chardev_init);
module_exit(chardev_exit);
MODULE_LICENSE("GPL");
```

This code defines a basic character device driver that supports open, read, write, and close operations. It creates a device driver called **chardev** with a buffer of 1024 bytes. This example demonstrates how to handle basic operations for a character device driver in the Linux kernel.

Let us break down the important parts of the provided character device driver code:

- **Includes and macros (Lines 1–26):**

    ```
    Lines 1-21: Include headers for various kernel functionalities:
        <linux/atomic.h>: Atomic operations to handle concurrency.
        <linux/cdev.h>: Character device utilities.
        <linux/uaccess.h>: Safe user-kernel data exchange.
        <asm/errno.h>: Error codes like -EINVAL and -EBUSY.
    Lines 23-26: Define constants:
        DEVICE_NAME: Device name appearing in /proc/devices.
        BUF_LEN: Buffer length (80 characters).
    ```

- **Global variables and enums (Lines 28–41):**

    ```
    Line 28: major: Stores the dynamically assigned major number.
    Lines 30-32: CDEV_NOT_USED and CDEV_EXCLUSIVE_OPEN: Flags to
    ```

track device status.

Line 35: already_open: Atomic variable to prevent multiple access to the device.

Line 37: msg: Message buffer for storing output.

Line 39: cls: Holds the class structure for device registration in sysfs.

- **File operations structure (Lines 43–47)**:

    Line 43: chardev_fops defines file operations:

    read: Points to device_read (line 108).

    write: Points to device_write (line 173).

    open: Points to device_open (line 76).

    release: Points to device_release (line 95).

- **Module initialization (Lines 49–66)**:

    chardev_init:

    Lines 51–52: Registers the device with a dynamically allocated major number using register_chrdev.

    Lines 55–56: Creates a device class with class_create (compatible with kernel version checks).

    Line 59: Registers the device (/dev/chardev) with device_create.

    Lines 54, 61: Logs messages about successful initialization.

- **Module exit (Lines 68–74)**:

    chardev_exit:

    Line 69: Removes the /dev/chardev file using device_destroy.

    Line 70: Destroys the class created earlier.

    Line 73: Unregisters the major number, cleaning up resources.

- **Device open (Lines 76–93)**:

    device_open:

    Lines 80–81: Ensures exclusive access by using atomic_cmpxchg. If already open, returns -EBUSY.

    Line 83: Writes a "Hello world" message into the msg buffer, including the open count.

    Line 84: Increments the module's usage count with try_module_get.

- **Device release (Lines 95–106)**:

  ```
  device_release:
  ```
  Line 98: Sets the atomic already_open back to CDEV_NOT_USED, allowing other processes to open the device.

  Line 103: Decrements the module's usage count using module_put.

- **Device read (Lines 108–145)**:

  ```
  device_read:
  ```
  Lines 113–114: Handles the end-of-message scenario. If the read pointer reaches the end, resets offset to 0 and returns 0 (EOF).

  Line 116: Adjusts the pointer to the current offset within the message.

  Lines 119–127: Copies data from the msg buffer (kernel space) to the buffer (user space) using put_user.

  Line 130: Updates the offset to reflect bytes read.

  Line 133: Returns the number of bytes read.

- **Device write (Lines 173–178)**:

  ```
  device_write:
  ```
  Line 175: Logs a message indicating that writing is not supported.

  Line 176: Returns -EINVAL to signify an invalid operation.

- **Module metadata (Lines 180–182)**:

  Lines 180–181: Registers the module's initialization (chardev_init) and cleanup (chardev_exit) functions.

  Line 182: Provides metadata:

  MODULE_LICENSE("GPL"): Indicates an open-source GPL license.

This code implements a read-only character device with the following functionality:

- **Open**: Ensures exclusive access and logs the number of times the device has been accessed.

- **Read**: Copies a message from the kernel buffer to user space.

- **Write**: Denies write operations with an error.

- **Close**: Releases access for other processes and decreases the module's usage count.

Example of the execution: Several examples of character drivers are available on GitHub:

- `code_5_char_driver_readonly`
- `code_5_char_driver_readwrite`
- `code_5_char_driver_ioctl`

Let us start to compile the first driver (**readonly**):

```
$ make
make M=/home/tgayet/Documents/bpb/05-character-device-drivers/code_5_char_
driver -C /lib/modules/6.2.0-39-generic/build modules
make[1]: Entering directory '/usr/src/linux-headers-6.2.0-39-generic'
warning: the compiler differs from the one used to build the kernel
  The kernel was built by: x86_64-linux-gnu-gcc-11 (Ubuntu
11.4.0-1ubuntu1~22.04) 11.4.0
  You are using:           gcc-11 (Ubuntu 11.4.0-1ubuntu1~22.04) 11.4.0
  CC [M]  /home/tgayet/Documents/bpb/05-character-device-drivers/code_5_
char_driver/chardrv.o
  MODPOST /home/tgayet/Documents/bpb/05-character-device-drivers/code_5_
char_driver/Module.symvers
  CC [M]   /home/tgayet/Documents/bpb/05-character-device-drivers/code_5_
char_driver/chardrv.mod.o
  LD [M]   /home/tgayet/Documents/bpb/05-character-device-drivers/code_5_
char_driver/chardrv.ko
  BTF [M] /home/tgayet/Documents/bpb/05-character-device-drivers/code_5_
char_driver/chardrv.ko
Skipping BTF generation for /home/tgayet/Documents/bpb/05-character-device-
drivers/code_5_char_driver/chardrv.ko due to unavailability of vmlinux
make[1]: Leaving directory '/usr/src/linux-headers-6.2.0-39-generic'
modinfo ./chardrv.ko
filename:        /home/tgayet/Documents/bpb/05-character-device-drivers/
code_5_char_driver/./chardrv.ko
license:        GPL
srcversion:     D4620EBD654E39173DAF5D4
depends:
retpoline:      Y
name:           chardrv
vermagic:       6.2.0-39-generic SMP preempt mod_unload modversions
```

Once compiled, we can load it with the GNU/Linux kernel:

```
$  sudo insmod ./chardrv.ko
```

We can check if the driver is well-loaded:

```
$ lsmod |grep chardrv
chardrv                  16384  0
$ cat /proc/modules|grep chardrv
chardrv 16384 0 - Live 0x0000000000000000 (OE)
```

At that time, the character's driver exposed the following data in **sysfs**:

```
$ tree /sys/module/chardrv
/sys/module/chardrv
├── coresize
├── holders
├── initsize
├── initstate
├── notes
├── refcnt
├── sections
│   ├── __mcount_loc
│   └── __patchable_function_entries
├── srcversion
├── taint
└── uevent
```

Three directories, nine files

Modules have generated traces that can be useful for us to know the major number used:

```
$ dmesg
(...)
[423384.382019] I was assigned major number 235.
[423384.382098] Device created on /dev/chardev
```

 Note: The major number obtained is 235.

At that time, the driver cannot communicate with the userspace. With this number, we can now create a virtual device file

Syntax: mknod <device> <b/c> MAJOR MINOR

We will use the following:

- **device**: "/dev/mydriver"
- **type**: "b" as the type of the driver
- **major** : "235" as dynamically provided by the kernel
- **minor**: "0" juste let's start at zero

```
$ sudo mknod /dev/mydriver c 235 0
```

```
$ la -al /dev/mydriver
crw-r--r-- 1 root root 235, 0 janv.   4 15:18 /dev/mydriver
```

Application of rights to device **/dev/mydriver**:

```
$ sudo chmod 777 /dev/mydriver
```

Your driver is now accessible from user space via **/dev/mydriver**.

```
cat /dev/mydriver
I already told you 0 times Hello world!
$ cat /dev/mydriver
I already told you 1 times Hello world!
$ cat /dev/mydriver
I already told you 2 times Hello world!
$ cat /dev/mydriver
I already told you 3 times Hello world!
$ cat /dev/mydriver
I already told you 4 times Hello world!
(...)
```

This first driver is just in **readonly**, if we try to write something, it will fail.

```
$ sudo echo "0" > /dev/mydriver
permission denied: /dev/mydriver
```

Second readwrite character's drivers

We can now move on to the second driver, which will be in *read-write* mode, meaning that it will allow reading, but also writing to a device.

However, before that, let us unload the current driver:

```
$ sudo rmmod ./chardrv.ko
```

Let us switch to the second driver (**readwrite**)

All the above commands are the same, but now we can change the content of the internal buffer:

```
$ make
```

```
$ sudo insmod ./chardrv.ko
```

We can change the internal buffer of the driver:

```
$ sudo echo "hi bpb" > /dev/mydriver
```

Then, we can display its content:

```
$ cat /dev/mydriver
```

Third ioctl character's drivers

This driver is similar to the previous one by adding an **ioctl** support.

At the end of the build, we may have two binaries used for unit testing:

- chardrv_ioctl_userspace
- test_ioctl

```
$ sudo insmod ./chardrv.ko
$ dmesg
[434216.878779] Device created on /dev/char_dev
```

The driver has created a device file by itself; let us add the rights:

```
$ sudo chmod 777 /dev/char_dev
```

A first call can check that the buffer is empty:

```
$ cat /dev/char_dev
$ dmesg
[434254.461111] device_open(000000005b82830e)
[434254.461137] device_release(0000000047783d40,000000005b82830e)
```

Let us fill it:

```
$ echo 'hello bpb' > /dev/char_dev
$ dmesg
[434271.155629] device_open(00000000d75bfae3)
[434271.155641] device_write(00000000d75bfae3,00000000d561ffa7,6)
[434271.155649] device_release(0000000047783d40,00000000d75bfae3)

$ cat /dev/char_dev
hello bpb
$ dmesg
[434276.769177] device_open(00000000ac6f6b22)
[434276.769192] Read 6 bytes, 131066 left
[434276.769208] device_release(0000000047783d40,00000000ac6f6b22)
```

We can also all an **ioctl** call:

```
$ sudo ./chardrv_ioctl_userspace
get_nth_byte message:Message passed by ioctl
get_msg message:Message passed by ioctl
```

The binary sends a string by an **ioctl** syscall.

Loading a driver at boot

Loading GNU/Linux drivers at boot can be achieved in two ways: using **/etc/modules** or **/etc/modules-load.d/**:

Using **/etc/modules**:

- **Open the file** /etc/modules: `$ sudo nano /etc/modules`

- **Add the module name at the end of the file:** `<module_name>` **(Eg: v4l2loopback)**

- Save and exit (*Ctrl+O, Enter, then Ctrl+X*).

Using **/etc/modules-load.d/**:

- **Create a configuration file in** /etc/modules-load.d/: `$ sudo nano /etc/modules-load.d/<module_name>.conf`

- **Add the module name:** `<module_name>` **(Eg: v4l2loopback)**

- Save and exit.

If the driver requires options, add them to **/etc/modprobe.d/**:

- **Create a configuration file in** /etc/modprobe.d/: `$ sudo nano /etc/modprobe.d/<module_name>.conf`

- **Add the options in the following format:** `options <module_name> option1=value1 option2=value2`

- Save and exit.

Conclusion

We have reached the end of this chapter, which showed the use of character drivers in different forms. We also saw the types of drivers and how to communicate with these modules with device files, whether created manually or dynamically.

In the next chapter, we will see the other essential types, namely block drivers, but also filesystems and the VFS abstraction layer.

CHAPTER 6
Block Drivers and Virtual Filesystem

Introduction

In the previous chapter, we saw character drivers with several implementations. This time, we will extend to the block drivers' usage to manage **Integrated Drive Electronics (IDE)** or **Advanced Technology Attachment (ATA)**, **Small Computer System Interface (SCSI)**, **Non-Volatile Memory Express (NVME)** used by **Solid-State Drives (SSD)** devices, **Redundant Array of Independent Disks (RAID)**, Microsoft's hardware virtualization (HYPER-V), **Linux Virtualization Input/Output (VIRTIO)**, and many other kinds of disks.

Furthermore, beyond the block drivers controlling the hardware, we will also see the I/O layer with its scheduler and, finally, the **Virtual File System (VFS)** abstraction layer.

Structure

This chapter covers the following topics:

- The GNU/Linux storage stack
- The I/O layer
- The I/O scheduler
- The block drivers
- The virtual file system layer
- Implement a new filesystem in user/kernel space

Objectives

This chapter aims to provide a comprehensive understanding of block drivers, following the same principles used for character drivers. Additionally, it will explore the overall architecture of storage managers, which is crucial for understanding the role of the I/O scheduler in managing data transfers. The VFS layer serves as an abstraction between the physical hardware and the structured data within a filesystem. Finally, we will examine how to implement a new filesystem, either in kernel space or user space, using the VFS API or libfuse.

The GNU/Linux storage stack

At the heart of the Linux storage stack is the Block Layer, which serves as the primary interface for block devices, abstracting the unique characteristics of different storage hardware. It manages data in fixed-size blocks and coordinates the flow of I/O requests throughout the system.

The following figure provides a schematic representation of the architecture used for disk management or mass storage:

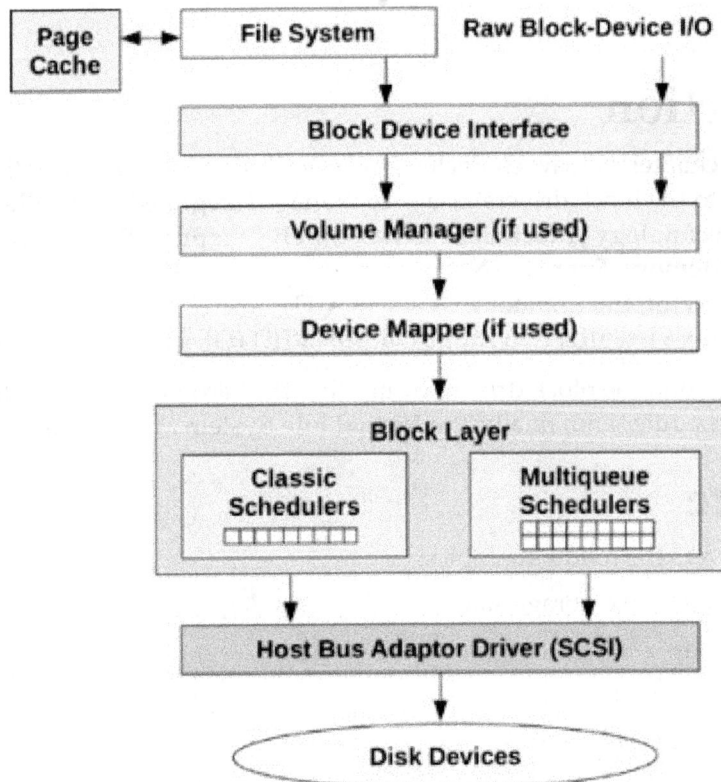

Figure 6.1: Global view of the GNU/Linux storage stack

The device drivers, residing atop the block layer, forge the connection between the kernel and a multitude of storage devices. They facilitate direct communication with hardware components, facilitating low-level interactions and handling diverse I/O operations.

Venturing further, the File System Layer takes center stage. It is here that the intricate dance of data storage, retrieval, and organization unfolds. File systems such as **Ext4**, **XFS**, and **Btrfs reign**, sculpting the binary wilderness of blocks into a structured oasis of files, directories, and metadata.

The VFS artfully abstracts the underlying file systems, providing a unified interface to userspace applications. It allows the seamless interaction of various file systems through a standardized set of system calls, transcending the diversities beneath.

Tweaking the performance knobs, we encounter the I/O Scheduler. This ingenious layer orchestrates the symphony of read and write requests, harmonizing them in a sequence designed to optimize throughput and reduce latency. Different algorithms govern this scheduler, striving to achieve an optimal balance between competing demands.

Not content with mere simplicity, Device Mapper and RAID enter the arena. Here, intricate configurations like software RAID arrays, logical volume management, and encryption schemes are crafted. This layer empowers users to mold storage setups to their precise specifications.

Networking Storage, another facet of this multifaceted construct, extends the storage realm beyond local boundaries. Protocols like **Network File System (NFS)**, **Common Internet File System (CIFS)**, and **Internet Small Computer System Interface (iSCSI)** weave a tapestry of remote storage access over networks, broadening the horizons of data accessibility.

This labyrinthine structure, meticulously crafted and constantly evolving, forms the backbone of Linux storage. Its complexities are the underpinnings of efficient data management, ensuring the integrity, accessibility, and resilience of the ever-expanding digital universe.

The following two-part figure represents the architecture around VFS managing mass storage:

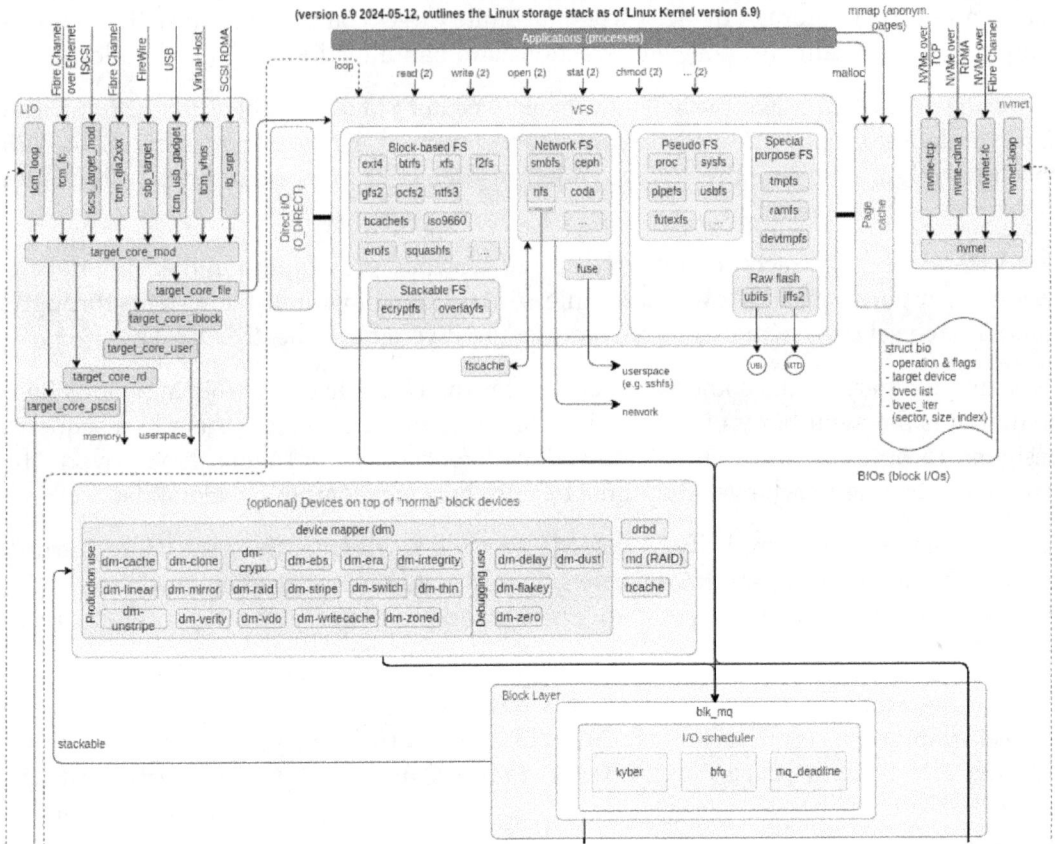

Figure 6.2: *Detailed view of the upper part of the storage architecture*

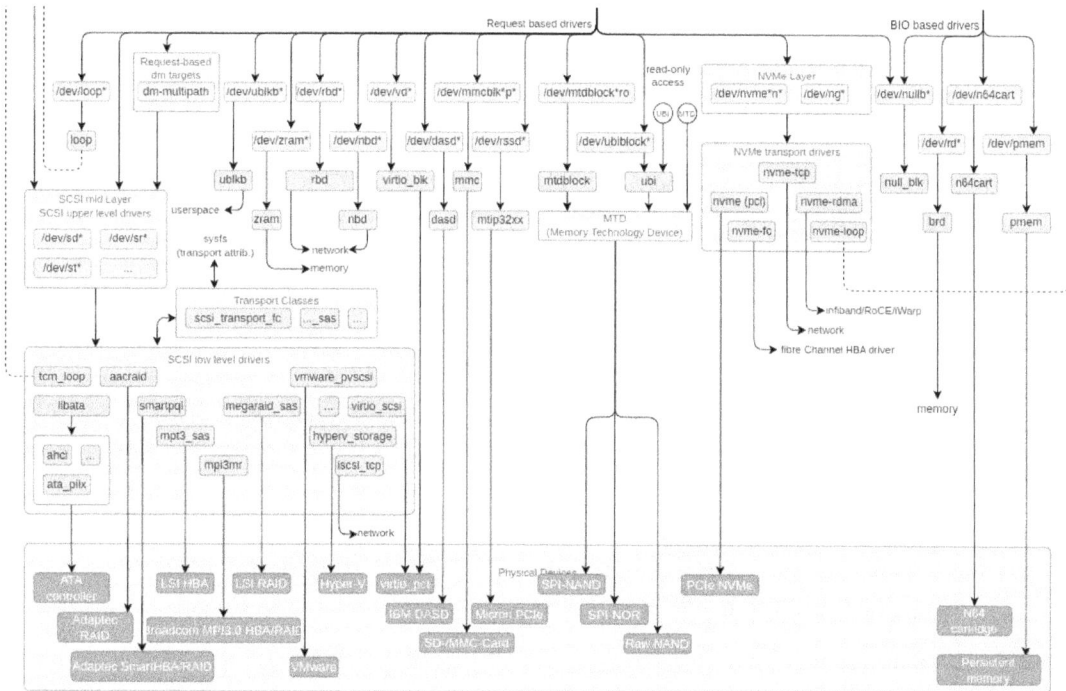

Figure 6.3: *Detailed view of the lower part of the storage architecture*

The I/O layer

In Linux, there are two primary methods of handling **input/output** (**I/O**) operations: Buffered I/O and Direct I/O (often referred to as O_DIRECT). These are discussed in detail as follows:

- **Buffered I/O**: It involves using the kernel's buffer cache to temporarily store data being read from or written to a storage device.

  When an application requests data, the kernel reads it from the storage device into the buffer cache. Subsequent reads of the same data can be satisfied from this cache, reducing the need for repeated disk accesses.

  For write operations, data is initially stored in the buffer cache. The kernel then manages write operations in the background, optimizing disk writes by performing them in larger, more efficient chunks or during idle periods.

  Buffered I/O can improve performance by reducing the number of actual disk accesses and taking advantage of the faster system memory. It allows the kernel to optimize read-ahead and write-behind operations.

- **Direct I/O (O_DIRECT)**: It bypasses the kernel's buffer cache entirely. Instead of caching data in system memory, Direct I/O reads from or writes data directly to the storage device. This approach reduces memory overhead and potentially improves performance, especially for large I/O operations.

This method is beneficial in scenarios where strict control over data caching or minimizing latency is critical, such as in databases, real-time systems, or applications handling large files. However, it may lead to increased disk I/O due to the absence of caching, potentially impacting overall system performance.

Let us examine the several options:

- **Performance and latency**: Direct I/O might offer better performance and reduced latency for certain applications due to its avoidance of caching overhead.

- **Data consistency**: Buffered I/O ensures data consistency by storing data in the buffer cache before committing it to disk, while Direct I/O immediately writes data to the disk.

- **Application-specific needs**: The choice between Buffered and Direct I/O depends on the specific requirements of the application, including performance needs, data consistency, and the trade-offs between cache utilization and direct disk access.

Both Buffered and Direct I/O mechanisms provide flexibility in managing I/O operations in Linux, allowing developers to choose the most suitable method based on their application's needs and performance considerations.

The I/O scheduler

Linux I/O schedulers manage the order in which read and write operations are executed on block devices (such as hard drives or SSDs). Each scheduler aims to optimize I/O performance based on different criteria.

I/O scheduling should generally work with hard drives that have long access times for requests placed far from the current disk head position (this operation is called **seeking**).

To minimize the effect this has on system performance, most I/O schedulers implement a variation of the elevator algorithm that reorders randomly ordered incoming requests so that the associated data can be accessed with minimal head movement.

I/O schedulers can have many goals depending on the objectives; common goals are as follows:

- To minimize time wasted by hard drive searches.

- To prioritize I/O requests for certain processes.

- To give a share of disk bandwidth to each running process.

- Guarantee that certain requests will be issued before a particular deadline.

Overview of Linux I/O schedulers

The overview of Linux I/O Schedulers is as follows:

- **Noop scheduler (noop)**: It is the simplest scheduler used for SSDs and devices with their own I/O scheduling mechanisms. Passes the I/O requests to the underlying hardware without reordering.

  The following figure describes the architecture of a noop type I/O scheduler:

  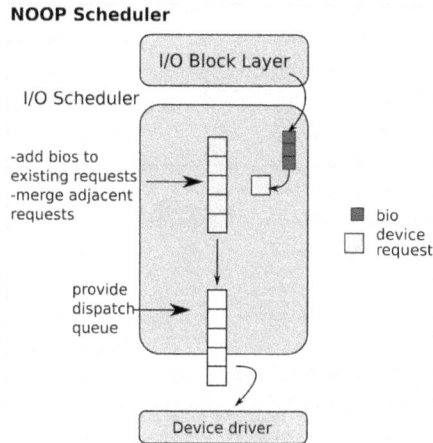

  Figure 6.4: The noop I/O scheduler

- **Deadline scheduler (deadline)**: It focuses on reducing latency for read and write operations. It separates I/O requests into sync (read/write requests that need an immediate response) and async (requests that can be delayed) queues. It ensures fairness by imposing deadlines on requests to avoid starvation.

  The following figure describes the architecture of a deadline type I/O scheduler:

  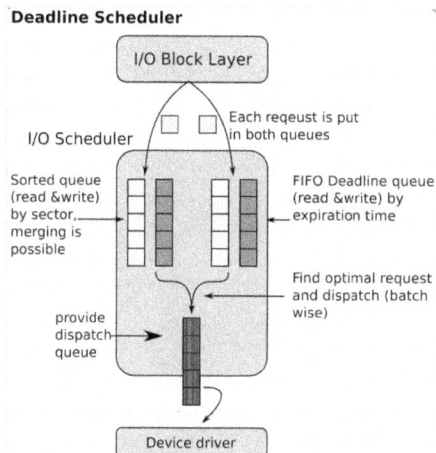

  Figure 6.5: The deadline I/O scheduler

- **mq-deadline**: This indicates the active scheduler. In this example, mq-deadline represents the deadline scheduler with multi-queue support.

- **Completely Fair Queuing (CFQ) scheduler**: It divides I/O requests into per-process queues, aiming for fairness among different processes. Each queue gets a slice of the disk time, ensuring that no single process monopolizes the I/O bandwidth.

The following figure describes the architecture of a CFQ type I/O scheduler:

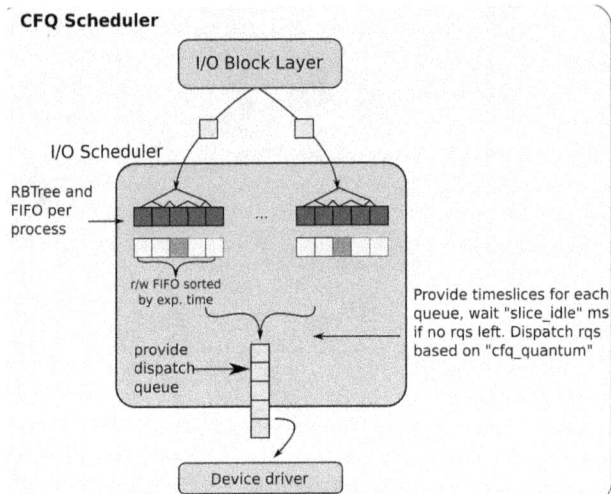

Figure 6.6: *The CFQ I/O scheduler*

- **Budget Fair Queuing (BFQ) scheduler (bfq)**: It enhances CFQ by providing better latency and throughput for interactive workloads. Prioritizes I/O for applications that require low-latency responsiveness.

The following figure describes the architecture of a BFQ type I/O scheduler:

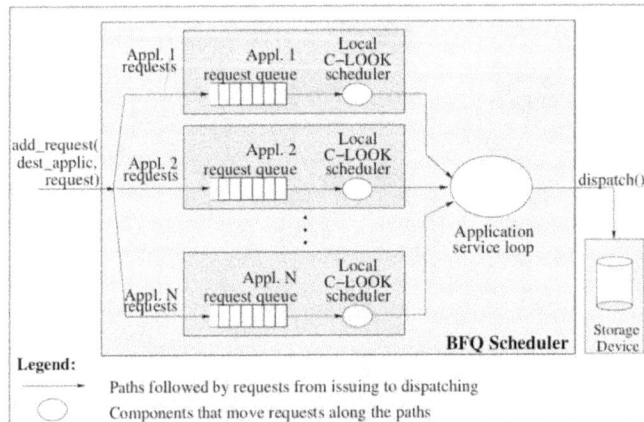

Figure 6.7: *The BFQ I/O scheduler*

- **Kyber scheduler**: It focuses on reducing I/O latency and improving throughput for modern storage devices. Adapts dynamically to different workloads by dynamically adjusting its algorithms.

The following figure describes the architecture of a kyber-type I/O scheduler:

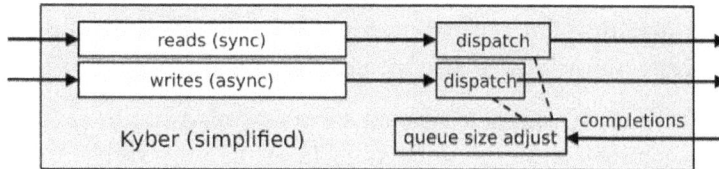

Figure 6.8: The kyber I/O scheduler

Note: This indicates that the device might support multiple scheduling algorithms, but it is not actively using any particular one at the moment.

Beyond the schedulers listed above, the following is a whole usable list:

- **Random scheduling (RSS)**
- **First in, first out (FIFO)**, also known as **first come, first served (FCFS)**
- **Last in, first out (LIFO)**
- Shortest Seek First, also known as Shortest Seek/**Service Time First (SSTF)**
- Elevator algorithm, also known as SCAN (including its variants, C-SCAN, LOOK, and C-LOOK)
- N-Step-SCAN SCAN of N records at a time
- FSCAN, N-Step-SCAN, where N equals the queue size at the start of the SCAN cycle
- **Budget Fair Queueing (BFQ)** scheduler on Linux
- **Completely Fair Queuing (CFQ)** scheduler on Linux
- Anticipatory scheduling
- Noop scheduler
- Deadline scheduler
- mClock scheduler
- Kyber
- NONE (used for NVM Express drives)

- mq-deadline (used for SSD SATA drives)
- cfq bfq, and bfq-mq (used for HDD drives)

Considerations and choosing a scheduler

To choose an I/O scheduler, several criteria must be studied:

- **Performance characteristics**: Each scheduler is optimized for different workloads and storage devices. Some prioritize throughput, others prioritize low latency.

- **Hardware specifics**: The type of storage device (SSD, HDD) and its characteristics (rotational speed, cache size) can impact the effectiveness of different schedulers.

- **Workload types**: Workloads vary in terms of read/write patterns, size of I/O operations, and latency sensitivity. Choosing the right scheduler involves understanding the workload's characteristics.

- **Tuning and customization**: Linux allows users to select schedulers per block device and tweak scheduler parameters, providing opportunities for optimization.

The choice of scheduler can significantly impact I/O performance based on the specific workload and hardware configurations. Linux offers flexibility in scheduler selection and customization to cater to diverse system requirements.

The output you provided indicates that the I/O scheduler currently in use for the **/dev/sda** block device is **mq-deadline**.

```
$ cat /sys/block/sda/queue/scheduler
none [mq-deadline]
```

The command lists all the I/O schedulers available in the current kernel. The scheduler inside the square brackets is the active one. In this case, it is **mq-deadline**. The **mq-deadline** scheduler is an I/O scheduler that implements a multi-queue mechanism with deadlines for each queue. It is designed to improve performance in multi-core systems by optimizing the I/O requests.

If you want to change the I/O scheduler for this block device, you can do so by echoing the desired scheduler into the scheduler file. For example, to change it to **noop**, you could use:

```
$ echo noop > /sys/block/sda/queue/scheduler
```

Note: Changing the I/O scheduler might impact the performance based on the workload and the characteristics of the storage device, so it is essential to consider this before making any changes.

To monitor the I/O scheduling, two commands are useful:

```
$ iostat -c -d -x -t -m /dev/sda 2
```

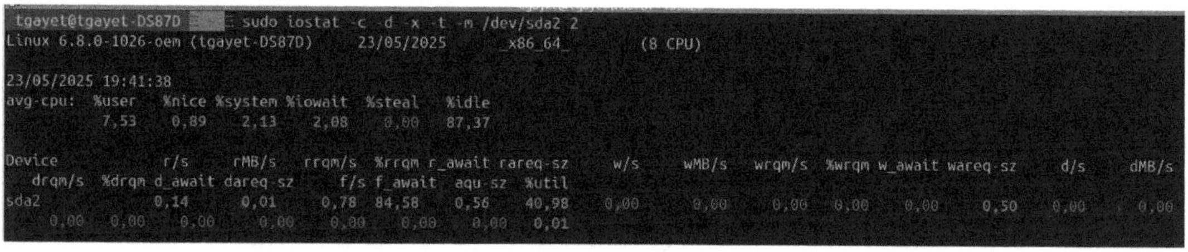

```
tgayet@tgayet-DS87D     sudo iostat -c -d -x -t -m /dev/sda2 2
Linux 6.8.0-1026-oem (tgayet-DS87D)     23/05/2025      _x86_64_        (8 CPU)

23/05/2025 19:41:38
avg-cpu:  %user   %nice %system %iowait  %steal   %idle
           7,53    0,89    2,13    2,08    0,00   87,37

Device            r/s     rMB/s   rrqm/s  %rrqm r_await rareq-sz     w/s     wMB/s   wrqm/s  %wrqm w_await wareq-sz     d/s     dMB/s
   drqm/s  %drqm d_await dareq-sz     f/s f_await  aqu-sz  %util
sda2             0,14      0,01     0,78  84,58    0,56    40,98    0,00      0,00     0,00   0,00    0,00     0,50    0,00      0,00
     0,00   0,00    0,00     0,00    0,00    0,00    0,00   0,01
```

Figure 6.9: iostat in action

```
$ sudo iotop
```

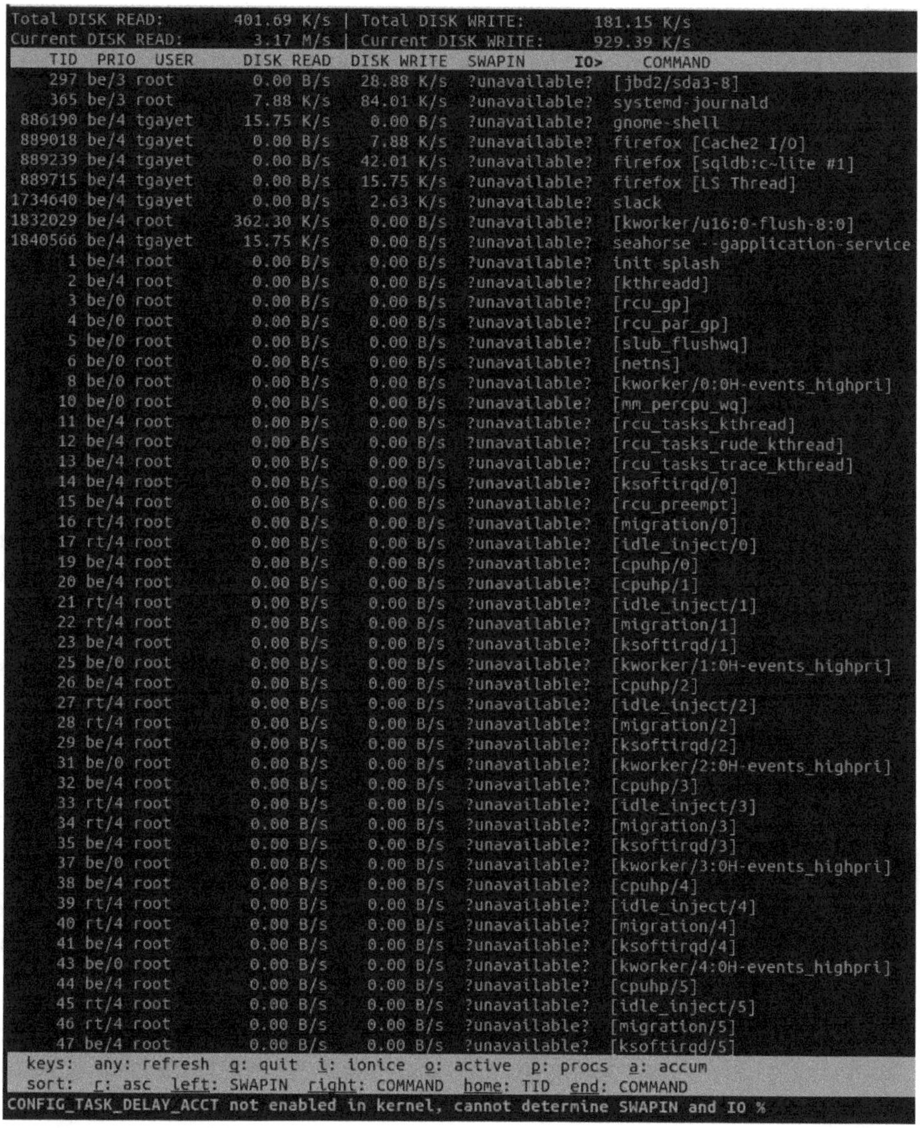

```
Total DISK READ:        401.69 K/s | Total DISK WRITE:        181.15 K/s
Current DISK READ:        3.17 M/s | Current DISK WRITE:      929.39 K/s
    TID  PRIO  USER     DISK READ  DISK WRITE  SWAPIN     IO>    COMMAND
    297 be/3 root        0.00 B/s   28.88 K/s ?unavailable?  [jbd2/sda3-8]
    365 be/3 root        7.88 K/s   84.01 K/s ?unavailable?  systemd-journald
 886190 be/4 tgayet     15.75 K/s    0.00 B/s ?unavailable?  gnome-shell
 889018 be/4 tgayet      0.00 B/s    7.88 K/s ?unavailable?  firefox [Cache2 I/O]
 889239 be/4 tgayet      0.00 B/s   42.01 K/s ?unavailable?  firefox [sqldb:c~lite #1]
 889715 be/4 tgayet      0.00 B/s   15.75 K/s ?unavailable?  firefox [LS Thread]
1734640 be/4 tgayet      0.00 B/s    2.63 K/s ?unavailable?  slack
1832029 be/4 root      362.30 K/s    0.00 B/s ?unavailable?  [kworker/u16:0-flush-8:0]
1840566 be/4 tgayet     15.75 K/s    0.00 B/s ?unavailable?  seahorse --gapplication-service
      1 be/4 root        0.00 B/s    0.00 B/s ?unavailable?  init splash
      2 be/4 root        0.00 B/s    0.00 B/s ?unavailable?  [kthreadd]
      3 be/0 root        0.00 B/s    0.00 B/s ?unavailable?  [rcu_gp]
      4 be/0 root        0.00 B/s    0.00 B/s ?unavailable?  [rcu_par_gp]
      5 be/0 root        0.00 B/s    0.00 B/s ?unavailable?  [slub_flushwq]
      6 be/0 root        0.00 B/s    0.00 B/s ?unavailable?  [netns]
      8 be/0 root        0.00 B/s    0.00 B/s ?unavailable?  [kworker/0:0H-events_highpri]
     10 be/0 root        0.00 B/s    0.00 B/s ?unavailable?  [mm_percpu_wq]
     11 be/4 root        0.00 B/s    0.00 B/s ?unavailable?  [rcu_tasks_kthread]
     12 be/4 root        0.00 B/s    0.00 B/s ?unavailable?  [rcu_tasks_rude_kthread]
     13 be/4 root        0.00 B/s    0.00 B/s ?unavailable?  [rcu_tasks_trace_kthread]
     14 be/4 root        0.00 B/s    0.00 B/s ?unavailable?  [ksoftirqd/0]
     15 be/4 root        0.00 B/s    0.00 B/s ?unavailable?  [rcu_preempt]
     16 rt/4 root        0.00 B/s    0.00 B/s ?unavailable?  [migration/0]
     17 rt/4 root        0.00 B/s    0.00 B/s ?unavailable?  [idle_inject/0]
     19 be/4 root        0.00 B/s    0.00 B/s ?unavailable?  [cpuhp/0]
     20 be/4 root        0.00 B/s    0.00 B/s ?unavailable?  [cpuhp/1]
     21 rt/4 root        0.00 B/s    0.00 B/s ?unavailable?  [idle_inject/1]
     22 rt/4 root        0.00 B/s    0.00 B/s ?unavailable?  [migration/1]
     23 be/4 root        0.00 B/s    0.00 B/s ?unavailable?  [ksoftirqd/1]
     25 be/0 root        0.00 B/s    0.00 B/s ?unavailable?  [kworker/1:0H-events_highpri]
     26 be/4 root        0.00 B/s    0.00 B/s ?unavailable?  [cpuhp/2]
     27 rt/4 root        0.00 B/s    0.00 B/s ?unavailable?  [idle_inject/2]
     28 rt/4 root        0.00 B/s    0.00 B/s ?unavailable?  [migration/2]
     29 be/4 root        0.00 B/s    0.00 B/s ?unavailable?  [ksoftirqd/2]
     31 be/0 root        0.00 B/s    0.00 B/s ?unavailable?  [kworker/2:0H-events_highpri]
     32 be/4 root        0.00 B/s    0.00 B/s ?unavailable?  [cpuhp/3]
     33 rt/4 root        0.00 B/s    0.00 B/s ?unavailable?  [idle_inject/3]
     34 rt/4 root        0.00 B/s    0.00 B/s ?unavailable?  [migration/3]
     35 be/4 root        0.00 B/s    0.00 B/s ?unavailable?  [ksoftirqd/3]
     37 be/0 root        0.00 B/s    0.00 B/s ?unavailable?  [kworker/3:0H-events_highpri]
     38 be/4 root        0.00 B/s    0.00 B/s ?unavailable?  [cpuhp/4]
     39 rt/4 root        0.00 B/s    0.00 B/s ?unavailable?  [idle_inject/4]
     40 rt/4 root        0.00 B/s    0.00 B/s ?unavailable?  [migration/4]
     41 be/4 root        0.00 B/s    0.00 B/s ?unavailable?  [ksoftirqd/4]
     43 be/0 root        0.00 B/s    0.00 B/s ?unavailable?  [kworker/4:0H-events_highpri]
     44 be/4 root        0.00 B/s    0.00 B/s ?unavailable?  [cpuhp/5]
     45 rt/4 root        0.00 B/s    0.00 B/s ?unavailable?  [idle_inject/5]
     46 rt/4 root        0.00 B/s    0.00 B/s ?unavailable?  [migration/5]
     47 be/4 root        0.00 B/s    0.00 B/s ?unavailable?  [ksoftirqd/5]
  keys:  any: refresh  q: quit  i: ionice  o: active  p: procs  a: accum
  sort:  r: asc  left: SWAPIN  right: COMMAND  home: TID  end: COMMAND
CONFIG_TASK_DELAY_ACCT not enabled in kernel, cannot determine SWAPIN and IO %
```

Figure 6.10: The iotop tool

The block drivers

The Linux block layer is a critical component responsible for handling block devices like hard drives, SSDs, and other storage media. It sits between the physical devices and the file systems, providing an abstraction for data access and storage.

A detailed technical overview without enumeration is discussed further.

Block Layer components

The Block Layer components are as follows:

- **Block Device abstraction**: The block layer abstracts physical devices into block devices, each represented by a struct **block_device**. These devices are accessed in fixed-size blocks, typically 512 bytes or more.

- **Request handling**: It manages I/O requests by queuing them into request queues associated with each block device. The requests are in the form of a struct request. The block layer can merge and sort these requests to optimize access to the underlying storage.

- **I/O scheduling**: It includes various I/O schedulers like CFQ, Deadline, and others (selectable via **/sys/block/<device>/queue/scheduler**). These schedulers prioritize, reorder, and dispatch pending requests to optimize disk performance and reduce latency based on different policies.

- **Elevator algorithm**: The block layer uses elevator algorithms (e.g., the **cfq**, **deadline**, **noop** schedulers) to manage the request queue. These algorithms determine the order in which requests are served. For instance, the CFQ scheduler uses a fair queuing mechanism to allocate bandwidth to different processes.

- **Error handling**: It manages error handling and recovery strategies for devices. This includes bad block management, error correction, and handling timeouts or device failures.

- **Device Mapper and RAID**: The block layer provides facilities for device mapping (via dm—Device Mapper) for creating logical volumes and **Redundant Array of Independent Disks** (**RAID**) for disk redundancy and performance.

- **I/O policies and optimization**: The block layer implements various policies to optimize I/O operations, including read-ahead mechanisms, write-back caching, and I/O barriers for ensuring data integrity during writes.

- **Hardware interface**: It interacts with device drivers to communicate with the underlying hardware, managing I/O operations efficiently by issuing commands to the device drivers for read, write, and other operations.

- **File system interaction**: It mediates data transfer between file systems and block devices, providing an interface that allows file systems to read and write data in fixed-size blocks.

Core operations

The following are the core operations:

- **Request submission**: Processes or the kernel submit I/O requests to the block layer, specifying the block device, operation type (read or write), and the data to be transferred.

- **Queue management**: The block layer manages request queues for each block device, optimizing them by reordering or merging adjacent requests.

- **Dispatching requests**: Based on the configured I/O scheduler, requests are dispatched to the device drivers for execution.

- **Completion and notification**: Once the device drivers execute the requests, the block layer is notified of their completion. It then informs the requesting process or the kernel about the status and result of the I/O operation.

The block layer plays a pivotal role in mediating between storage devices and file systems, ensuring efficient, reliable, and optimized data storage and retrieval in the Linux kernel.

The following is a simplified example of a block driver in Linux. This example does not include all error handling and advanced functionalities, but should give you an idea of how a block driver might look.

To start this code, we have a part intended to load the necessary headers to define the constants, variables, and data structures:

```
#include <linux/module.h>
#include <linux/fs.h>
#include <linux/blkdev.h>
#include <linux/genhd.h>

#define BLOCK_SIZE 512
#define NUM_SECTORS 1024

static struct block_device_operations block_ops;

static struct gendisk *block_disk;
static struct request_queue *block_queue;
```

```
static unsigned char *block_memory;

static int block_major = 0;
```

Then, we have a part used to manage data destined for physical mass storage (SSD, SCSI, etc.):

```
static void block_transfer(struct request *req) {
    unsigned long offset = blk_rq_pos(req) * BLOCK_SIZE;
    unsigned long nbytes = blk_rq_bytes(req);

    if ((offset + nbytes) > (NUM_SECTORS * BLOCK_SIZE)) {
        printk(KERN_ERR "Block: Beyond-end write (%ld %ld)\n", offset,
nbytes);
        return;
    }

    if (rq_data_dir(req) == WRITE) {
        memcpy(block_memory + offset, req->buffer, nbytes);
    } else {
        memcpy(req->buffer, block_memory + offset, nbytes);
    }
}

static int block_request(struct request_queue *q) {
    struct request *req;

    req = blk_fetch_request(q);
    while (req != NULL) {
        if (req == NULL || (req->cmd_type != REQ_TYPE_FS)) {
            printk(KERN_NOTICE "Block: Skip non-CMD request\n");
            __blk_end_request_all(req, -EIO);
            continue;
        }

        block_transfer(req);
        if (!__blk_end_request_cur(req, 0)) {
            req = blk_fetch_request(q);
        }
    }
```

```
    return 0;
}
```

Finally, we have the initialization of the two hooks executed on the entry and exit of the driver:

```
static int __init block_init(void) {
    block_memory = kmalloc(NUM_SECTORS * BLOCK_SIZE, GFP_KERNEL);
    if (!block_memory) {
        return -ENOMEM;
    }

    block_queue = blk_init_queue(block_request, NULL);
    if (!block_queue) {
        kfree(block_memory);
        return -ENOMEM;
    }

    block_major = register_blkdev(0, "block");
    if (block_major < 0) {
        printk(KERN_WARNING "Block: Unable to get major number\n");
        return block_major;
    }

    block_disk = alloc_disk(1);
    if (!block_disk) {
        unregister_blkdev(block_major, "block");
        blk_cleanup_queue(block_queue);
        kfree(block_memory);
        return -ENOMEM;
    }

    block_disk->major = block_major;
    block_disk->first_minor = 0;
    block_disk->fops = &block_ops;
    block_disk->queue = block_queue;
    sprintf(block_disk->disk_name, "block");
    set_capacity(block_disk, NUM_SECTORS);
```

```
    add_disk(block_disk);

    return 0;
}

static void __exit block_exit(void) {
    del_gendisk(block_disk);
    put_disk(block_disk);
    unregister_blkdev(block_major, "block");
    blk_cleanup_queue(block_queue);
    kfree(block_memory);
}

module_init(block_init);
module_exit(block_exit);

MODULE_LICENSE("GPL");
MODULE_AUTHOR("bpb");
MODULE_DESCRIPTION("Simple Block Device Driver");
```

This simple block driver creates a block device named **block**. It allocates memory for the block storage, sets up the request queue, and handles **read**/**write** requests to the block device.

This simple block driver sets up a virtual block device that operates in the kernel. The following are the main steps for it:

1. **Initialization**:

    a. **Memory allocation**: Allocates a memory area (**block_memory**) to act as the storage for the block device.

    b. **Queue setup**: Initializes a request queue (**block_queue**) and associates it with the driver's request-handling function (**block_request**).

2. **Device registration**:

    a. **Register block device**: Obtains a major number (**block_major**) or a dynamic one and registers the block device.

    b. **Disk setup**: Allocates and initializes a **gendisk** structure (**block_disk**) that represents the block device.

    c. **Capacity set**: Defines the size of the block device using **set_capacity**.

3. **Request handling**:

   a. **Transfer function**: Implements the **block_transfer** function responsible for handling **read/write** requests by copying data between the device's memory (**block_memory**) and the request buffers.

   b. **Request processing**: Handles incoming block I/O requests (**block_request**) by fetching requests from the queue, transferring data, and ending the requests accordingly.

4. **Module initialization and cleanup**:

   a. **Module init**: The **block_init** function handles all the setup and initialization required for the block device.

   b. **Module exit**: The **block_exit** function cleans up resources and unregisters the block device when the module is unloaded.

Keep in mind that production-grade block drivers are far more complex and require robust error handling and additional functionalities.

As we can see, there are many similarities with character drivers, both with **init** and exit macros, but also with callback structures. In detail, the block drivers are relatively more complex.

The virtual file system layer

The **virtual file system** (**VFS**) layer in the Linux kernel is a crucial component responsible for abstracting various filesystem types, providing a unified interface for user-space applications to interact with files and directories, regardless of the underlying filesystem.

The following figure describes the VFS layer as an abstraction to various file systems:

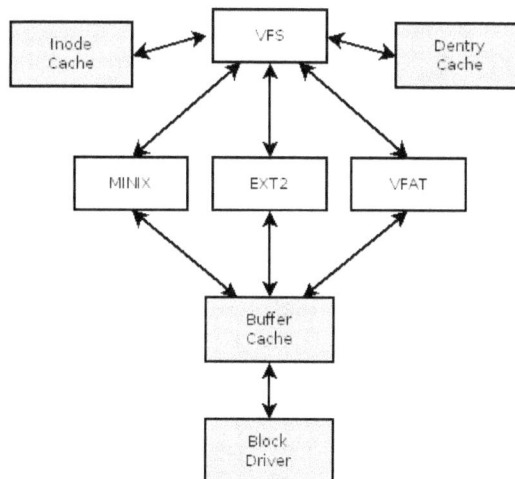

Figure 6.11: *The VFS architecture*

The VFS structure can be described by several functionalities:

- **Abstraction**: VFS abstracts the differences between various filesystems by defining a common interface that all filesystems must adhere to. This interface includes system calls like **open()**, **read()**, **write()**, **close()**, and others that user-space applications use to perform file operations.

- **Inodes and Superblocks**: Inodes represent file metadata (permissions, ownership, timestamps) and are associated with files or directories. Superblocks contain information about mounted filesystems, such as block size, free blocks, and root inodes.

  The following figure details the relationship between important blocks used for indexing files in the file system:

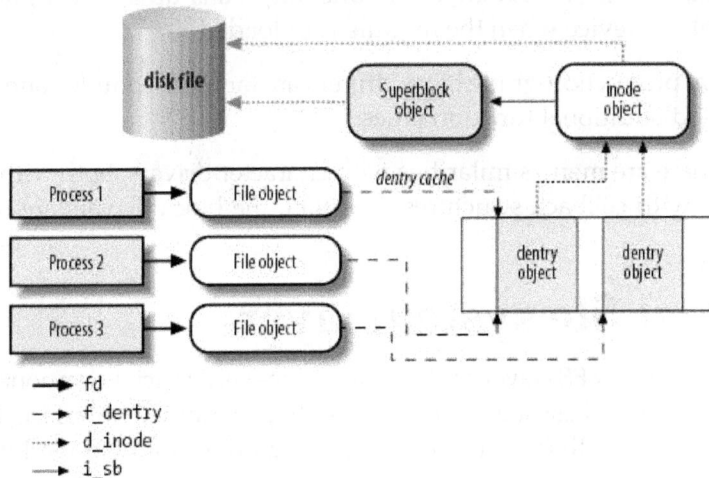

Figure 6.12: Dentry, inode, and superblock

On Linux, a dentry is a directory entry that combines an inode and a file object, but it is not necessarily just a directory; it could represent a file. Dentry enables hard linking, which allows you to create multiple hard links for the same file. So, you can create multiple names for the same file. The Dentry cache is also important for file system performance.

- **VFS data structures**:

  o **struct inode**: Represents a file or directory on disk and contains metadata about the file.

  o **struct dentry**: Represents directory entries and caches the **filename-to-inode mappin gs**.

  o **struct file**: Represents an open file and maintains information like file position, access mode, and a reference to the inode.

The following figure shows us the different data structures used to structure the file system in VFS:

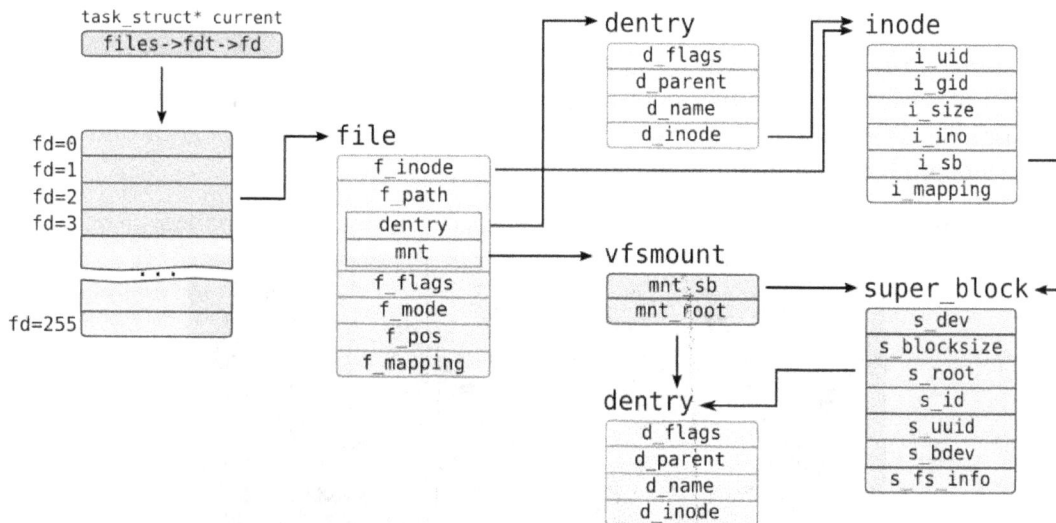

Figure 6.13: *Linux management structures.*

- **Pathname resolution**: When a file is accessed, the VFS translates the pathname to an inode. It starts from the root of the filesystem and traverses the directory tree, following the path components until it reaches the target file or directory.

- **Filesystem mounting and unmounting**: VFS manages the mounting and unmounting of filesystems. When a filesystem is mounted, its superblock is added to the system. The unmounting process involves detaching the superblock and releasing associated resources.

- **Filesystem operations**: VFS provides an interface for filesystem-specific operations by defining function pointers in the struct **file_operations**. These pointers are populated by the filesystem and handle operations like reading, writing, and I/O control.

- **Cache management**: VFS maintains several caches to improve performance, such as the dentry cache, inode cache, and page cache. These caches store frequently accessed directory entries, inodes, and file data, respectively.

- **Filesystem registration**: Each filesystem type registers itself with the VFS during initialization. This registration process includes providing function pointers to handle operations specific to that filesystem type.

- **Interaction with Block layer**: VFS interacts with the block layer to read and write data from and to storage devices. It provides an abstraction that enables different filesystems to access underlying block devices uniformly.

- **Concurrency and locking**: VFS manages concurrency and ensures proper locking mechanisms to maintain consistency and prevent race conditions when multiple processes access the filesystem simultaneously.

In summary, the VFS layer acts as an intermediary between user-space applications and various filesystems. It provides a unified view of the filesystem, allowing applications to perform file operations without needing to know the specific details of each underlying filesystem implementation.

The VFS layer can be understood from the user space via several commands:

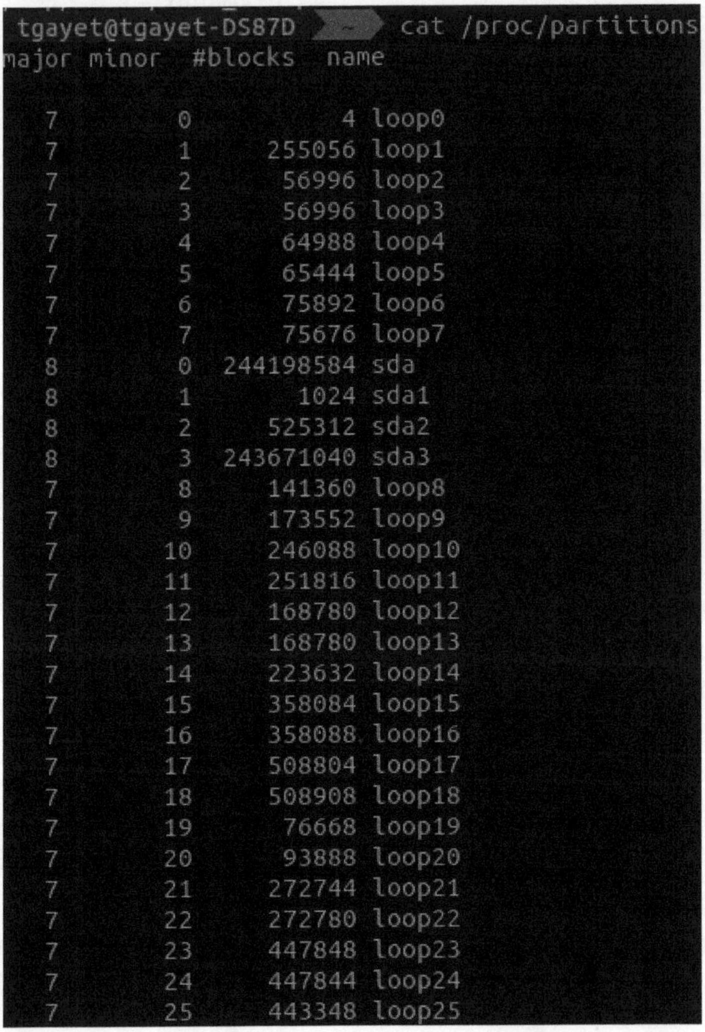

```
tgayet@tgayet-DS87D    ~    cat /proc/partitions
major  minor   #blocks    name
    7      0          4  loop0
    7      1     255056  loop1
    7      2      56996  loop2
    7      3      56996  loop3
    7      4      64988  loop4
    7      5      65444  loop5
    7      6      75892  loop6
    7      7      75676  loop7
    8      0  244198584  sda
    8      1       1024  sda1
    8      2     525312  sda2
    8      3  243671040  sda3
    7      8     141360  loop8
    7      9     173552  loop9
    7     10     246088  loop10
    7     11     251816  loop11
    7     12     168780  loop12
    7     13     168780  loop13
    7     14     223632  loop14
    7     15     358084  loop15
    7     16     358088  loop16
    7     17     508804  loop17
    7     18     508908  loop18
    7     19      76668  loop19
    7     20      93888  loop20
    7     21     272744  loop21
    7     22     272780  loop22
    7     23     447848  loop23
    7     24     447844  loop24
    7     25     443348  loop25
```

Figure 6.14: Enumeration of the partitions

Now that we have listed the active partitions, we can list the filesystem types present on the system. Refer to the following figure:

```
tgayet@tgayet-DS87D  cat /proc/filesystems
nodev   sysfs
nodev   tmpfs
nodev   bdev
nodev   proc
nodev   cgroup
nodev   cgroup2
nodev   cpuset
nodev   devtmpfs
nodev   configfs
nodev   debugfs
nodev   tracefs
nodev   securityfs
nodev   sockfs
nodev   bpf
nodev   pipefs
nodev   ramfs
nodev   hugetlbfs
nodev   devpts
        ext3
        ext2
        ext4
        squashfs
        vfat
nodev   ecryptfs
        fuseblk
nodev   fuse
nodev   fusectl
nodev   mqueue
nodev   pstore
        btrfs
nodev   autofs
nodev   rpc_pipefs
nodev   nfsd
nodev   binfmt_misc
nodev   overlay
```

Figure 6.15: Filesystems available in the GNU/Linux kernel

The above list is a current representation of the filesystem support in the GNU/Linux kernel and can be easily extended via dynamic module loading.

We can also list the mounted partitions. Refer to the following figure:

```
tgayet@tgayet-DS87D  cat /proc/mounts
sysfs /sys sysfs rw,nosuid,nodev,noexec,relatime 0 0
proc /proc proc rw,nosuid,nodev,noexec,relatime 0 0
udev /dev devtmpfs rw,nosuid,relatime,size=8091068k,nr_inodes=2022767,mode=755,inode64 0 0
devpts /dev/pts devpts rw,nosuid,noexec,relatime,gid=5,mode=620,ptmxmode=000 0 0
tmpfs /run tmpfs rw,nosuid,nodev,noexec,relatime,size=1626256k,mode=755,inode64 0 0
/dev/sda3 / ext4 rw,relatime,errors=remount-ro 0 0
securityfs /sys/kernel/security securityfs rw,nosuid,nodev,noexec,relatime 0 0
tmpfs /dev/shm tmpfs rw,nosuid,nodev,inode64 0 0
tmpfs /run/lock tmpfs rw,nosuid,nodev,noexec,relatime,size=5120k,inode64 0 0
cgroup2 /sys/fs/cgroup cgroup2 rw,nosuid,nodev,noexec,relatime,nsdelegate,memory_recursiveprot 0 0
pstore /sys/fs/pstore pstore rw,nosuid,nodev,noexec,relatime 0 0
bpf /sys/fs/bpf bpf rw,nosuid,nodev,noexec,relatime,mode=700 0 0
systemd-1 /proc/sys/fs/binfmt_misc autofs rw,relatime,fd=32,pgrp=1,timeout=0,minproto=5,maxproto=5,direct,pipe_ino=198
mqueue /dev/mqueue mqueue rw,nosuid,nodev,noexec,relatime 0 0
tracefs /sys/kernel/tracing tracefs rw,nosuid,nodev,noexec,relatime 0 0
debugfs /sys/kernel/debug debugfs rw,nosuid,nodev,noexec,relatime 0 0
hugetlbfs /dev/hugepages hugetlbfs rw,nosuid,nodev,relatime,pagesize=2M 0 0
fusectl /sys/fs/fuse/connections fusectl rw,nosuid,nodev,noexec,relatime 0 0
configfs /sys/kernel/config configfs rw,nosuid,nodev,noexec,relatime 0 0
tmpfs /run/qemu tmpfs rw,nosuid,nodev,relatime,mode=755,inode64 0 0
```

Figure 6.16: Enumeration of the mounted partitions

The Linux VFS API is a fundamental interface that allows interaction between the operating system kernel and various filesystems, providing a unified way for user-space applications to perform file-related operations.

The VFS API exposes system calls that applications use to interact with files and directories. Key system calls include the following:

- **open()**: Opens a file and returns a file descriptor.

- **read() and write()**: Reads from or writes to a file.

- **close()**: Closes a file descriptor.

- **mkdir(), rmdir(), unlink()**: Manipulates directories and files.

- **stat(), fstat(), lstat()**: Retrieves file metadata.

- **chown(), chmod()**: Changes ownership and permissions of files.

Implement a new filesystem in user/kernel space

Developing a new file system can be long and complex within the GNU/Linux kernel. Libfuse is often a simpler alternative in terms of development and especially tuning. Indeed, the definition of the VFS API is quite similar to that of the fuse library.

Filesystem in Userspace (FUSE) is a framework that enables the creation of filesystems in user space rather than within the Linux kernel. Here is a technical breakdown of the Linux **libfuse** library:

- FUSE allows developers to create filesystems without writing kernel code, providing a user-friendly interface for implementing custom filesystems.

- It separates the filesystem implementation from the kernel, enabling user-space programs to define their filesystem behavior.

- FUSE Kernel Module facilitates communication between the kernel and user space. It handles filesystem requests forwarded from the kernel to user space and vice versa.

- FUSE library (**libfuse**) provides an API for creating FUSE-based filesystems. It offers a set of functions and structures that filesystem developers use to interact with the kernel module.

- The **fuse.h** header contains structures and functions needed to interact with FUSE.

The following are the main functions used within fuse:

- **init()**: Initializes the filesystem.

- **getattr(), read(), write()**: Functions handling file metadata retrieval, reading, and writing operations.

- **Readdir()**: Lists directory contents.

- **open(), release()** : Opening and closing files.

- Various other callbacks handling filesystem-specific operations.

The kernel forwards filesystem requests (e.g., file reads, writes, attribute changes) to the FUSE kernel module.

The FUSE kernel module passes these requests to the corresponding user-space process using a communication channel.

libfuse in user space handles these requests by invoking the appropriate callback functions provided by the filesystem developer.

Communication

Uses a simple communication protocol (implemented via a character device or sockets) between the kernel module and user space.

The communication protocol exchanges serialized data structures containing filesystem operation details.

Developers create a FUSE-based filesystem by implementing the callback functions provided by **libfuse**.

These functions define how the filesystem handles operations like file creation, deletion, read/write, metadata access, etc.

FUSE provides error-handling mechanisms for gracefully managing errors occurring during filesystem operations.

Security measures, like privilege checks, are handled by the kernel module to prevent unauthorized access to filesystem operations.

User-space filesystems via FUSE may have slightly higher latency compared to kernel-based filesystems due to user-kernel context switching and additional data copying.

FUSE is widely used for various purposes such as creating virtual filesystems, allowing access to custom storage systems, implementing encryption layers, etc.

In summary, **libfuse** enables the development of custom filesystems in user space by providing an API that interfaces with the FUSE kernel module, allowing developers to define filesystem behavior without kernel-level programming.

The following figure illustrates the architecture utilized by Fuse:

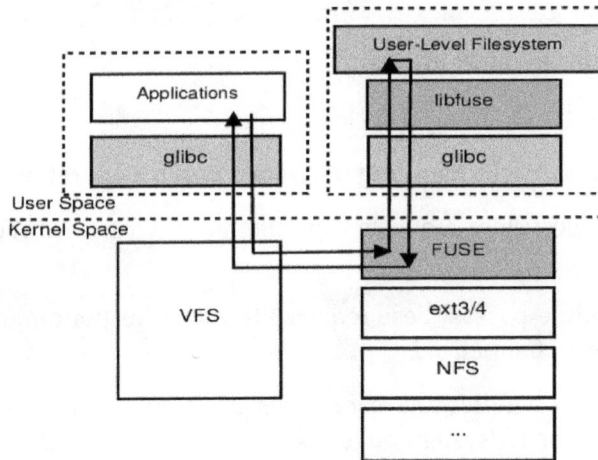

Figure 6.17: Architecture of the libfuse

The following is a simple example of a FUSE-based filesystem using the **libfuse** library in C. This example creates a virtual filesystem with a single file named **"hello.txt"** that contains a fixed string:

```c
#define FUSE_USE_VERSION 31
#include <fuse.h>
#include <stdio.h>
#include <string.h>
#include <errno.h>

static const char *hello_str = "Hello, bpb!\n";
static const char *file_path = "/hello.txt";

static int my_getattr(const char *path, struct stat *stbuf) {
    int res = 0;

    memset(stbuf, 0, sizeof(struct stat));
    if (strcmp(path, "/") == 0) {
        stbuf->st_mode = S_IFDIR | 0755;
        stbuf->st_nlink = 2;
    } else if (strcmp(path, file_path) == 0) {
        stbuf->st_mode = S_IFREG | 0444;
        stbuf->st_nlink = 1;
        stbuf->st_size = strlen(hello_str);
```

```c
    } else {
        res = -ENOENT;
    }

    return res;
}

static int my_read(const char *path, char *buf, size_t size, off_t offset,
struct fuse_file_info *fi) {
    size_t len;
    (void) fi;
    if (strcmp(path, file_path) != 0)
        return -ENOENT;

    len = strlen(hello_str);
    if (offset < len) {
        if (offset + size > len)
            size = len - offset;
        memcpy(buf, hello_str + offset, size);
    } else {
        size = 0;
    }

    return size;
}

static struct fuse_operations my_operations = {
    .getattr = my_getattr,
    .read = my_read,
};

int main(int argc, char *argv[]) {
    return fuse_main(argc, argv, &my_operations, NULL);
}
```

This example defines a simple filesystem with two functions:

- **my_getattr**: Implements the **getattr** callback and provides information about the attributes (like size and permissions) of the file system objects (in this case, the **root** directory and the **"hello.txt"** file).

- **my_read**: Implements the read callback to read the contents of the **"hello.txt"** file.

To compile this code, you will need to link it with the **libfuse** library. Assuming you saved this code in a file named **simplefs.c**, you can compile it with:

```
$ gcc simplehellofs.c `pkg-config fuse --cflags –libs` -o  simplehellofs
```

This would create an executable named **simplefs**. To mount the filesystem, run it with a mount point:

```
$ mkdir -p ~/hello
$ ./simplehellofs ~/hello
```

Then, you can access the mounted directory (**/path/to/mountpoint**) and find a file named **hello.txt** containing the string **"Hello, bpb !"** when read.

Conclusion

In this chapter, we saw the different layers related to storage management, whether, at a low level with block drivers, the I/O layer optimizing transfers, and finally, VFS, which allows data to be structured via a filesystem.

In the next chapter, we will discuss the management of drivers controlling USB-type devices.

Join our book's Discord space

Join the book's Discord Workspace for Latest updates, Offers, Tech happenings around the world, New Release and Sessions with the Authors:

https://discord.bpbonline.com

CHAPTER 7
USB Drivers and libusb

Introduction

In this chapter, we will study the USB stack of the Linux kernel, from the lower parts close to the hardware to the development of a driver in the upper parts, as well as the development of a userspace module based on the use of libusb.

Structures

This chapter covers the following topics:

- USB architecture
- Linux USB subsystem
- Linux USB data struct
- Enumeration
- Class drivers
- Gadget drivers
- Write a USB driver in userspace using the libusb

Objectives

By the end of this chapter, you will be able to understand how USB devices work through the Linux kernel and also write a driver in userspace or in the kernel itself.

USB architecture

The USB or universal serial bus protocol was developed and first launched by *Ajay V. Bhatt* of *Intel* in 1996. This USB replaces different types of serial and parallel ports for transferring data between a computer as well as different peripherals like scanners, printers, keyboards, game controllers, digital cameras, mass storages, and so on.

USB is a common interface used to enable communication between different devices, such as mice, digital cameras, printers, keyboards, multimedia devices, scanners, USB sticks, and external hard drives, as well as a host controller like a smartphone or PC.

A universal serial bus is intended to enable hot swapping and improve plug-and-play. Plug-and-play allows the operating system to spontaneously configure and discover a new device without starting the computer, while hot-swap removes and replaces a device without restarting.

There are different types of USB connectors available in the market, with types A and B being the most commonly used. Currently, the old connectors are being replaced by Mini-USB, Micro-USB, and USB-C cables.

The USB protocol architecture is shown below. Once the various I/O devices are connected via USB to the computer, they are all structured like a tree. In this USB structure, each I/O device will establish a point-to-point connection to transmit data via a serial transmission format.

In this architecture, I/O devices are connected to the computer via USB, called a **hub**. The Hub within the architecture is the connection point between the I/O devices and the computer. The root hub of this architecture is used to connect the entire structure to the hosting computer. The I/O devices in this architecture are keyboard, mouse, speaker, camera, etc.

The following figure illustrates the enumeration of currencies on a USB-type bus, represented in the form of a tree structure:

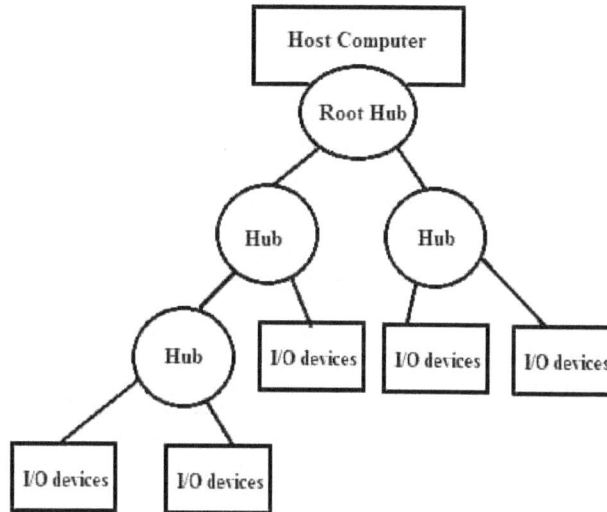

Figure 7.1: *USB protocol architecture*

The USB protocol simply works on the principle of polling because, during polling, the processor continuously checks whether the input/output device is ready to transmit data or not. So, I/O devices do not need to update the processor regarding their status as it is the primary responsibility of the processor to constantly check. So, this will make USB simple and inexpensive.

Each time a new device is associated with the hub, it is addressed as 0. During a normal period, the host computer polls the hubs for their status, which lets the host know that the system's I/O devices are attached or detached from the system.

Once the host becomes responsive to the new device, it knows the capabilities of the device by reading the data available in the particular memory of the device's USB interface. The host uses a suitable driver to communicate with the devices. After that, the host assigns an address to the new device, which is written to the device register. With this device, USB provides plug-and-play functionality.

This feature simply allows the host to automatically identify the new available I/O device once the device is connected. Device I/O capabilities will be determined by the host software.

Another feature of the USB protocol is *hot-pluggable*, which means that the I/O device is plugged into or removed from the host system without performing a shutdown or reboot. This ensures that your system runs continuously when the I/O device is connected or disconnected.

The USB protocol can also support isochronous traffic, where data is transmitted at a predefined time interval. Isochronous data transmission is very fast compared to synchronous and asynchronous data transfer.

To maintain isochronous traffic, the root hub transmits a series of bits over USB that specifies the start of isochronous data, and the actual data can be transmitted after this series of bits.

The following figure shows the electronic details of a USB-type connection:

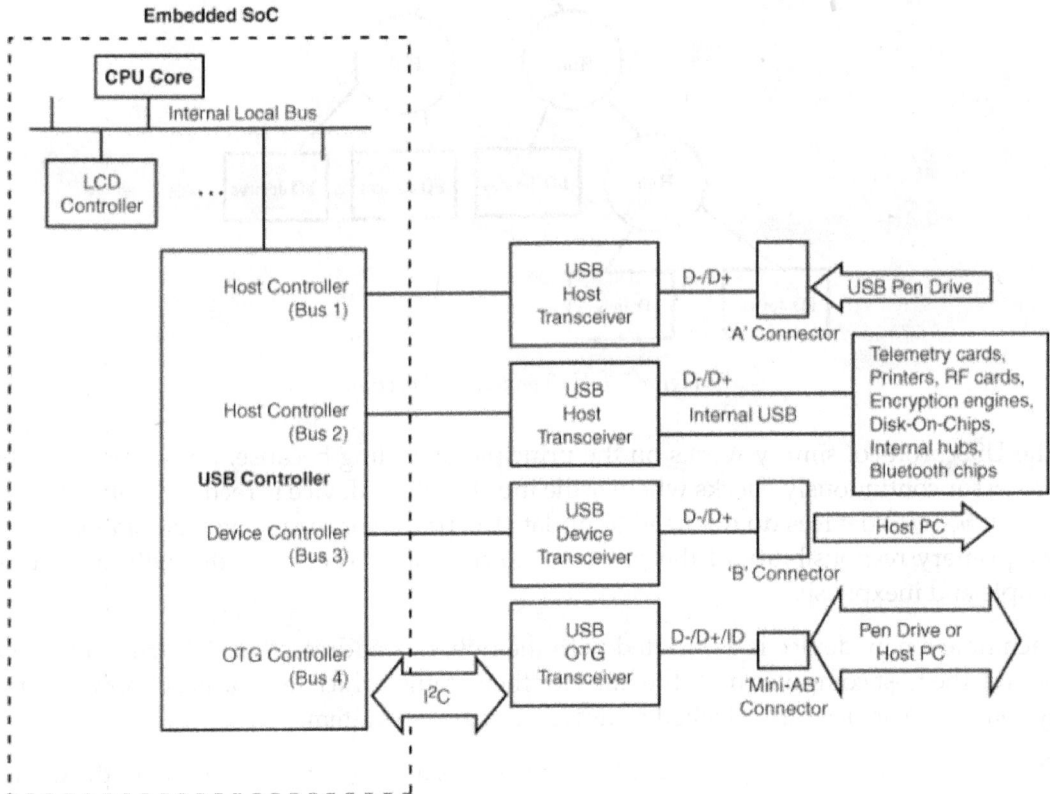

Figure 7.2: Detail of a USB hardware architecture

Only one host can exist in the system, and communication with devices is done from the host's perspective. A host is an upstream component, while a device is a downstream component.

Data moved from the host to the device is an OUT transfer. Data moved to the host from the device is an IN transfer.

The host, specifically the host controller, controls all traffic and sends commands to devices.

There are three common types of USB host controllers:

- **Universal Host Controller Interface (UHCI)**: Produced by *Intel* for USB 1.0 and USB 1.1. The use of UHCI requires a license from *Intel*. This controller supports both low-speed and full-speed.

- **Open Host Controller Interface (OHCI)**: Produced for USB 1.0 and 1.1 by *Compaq*, *Microsoft*, and *National Semiconductor*. Supports low speeds and full speeds and tends to be more efficient than UHCI in performing more functionality in hardware.

- **Extended Host Controller Interface (EHCI)**: Created for USB 2.0 after the USB-IF required that only one host controller specification be created. EHCI is used for high-speed transactions and delegates low-speed and full-speed transactions to a sister OHCI or UHCI controller.

The bus interface layer provides the physical connection, electrical signaling, and packet connectivity. This is the layer that is managed by a device's hardware. This is accomplished with the physical interface external to the device.

The device layer is the view that USB system software has to perform USB operations, such as sending and receiving information. This is accomplished through a serial interface engine, also internal to the device.

Finally, the functions layer is the software side of things. This is the part of a USB device that does something with the information it receives or does something to collect data to transfer to the host.

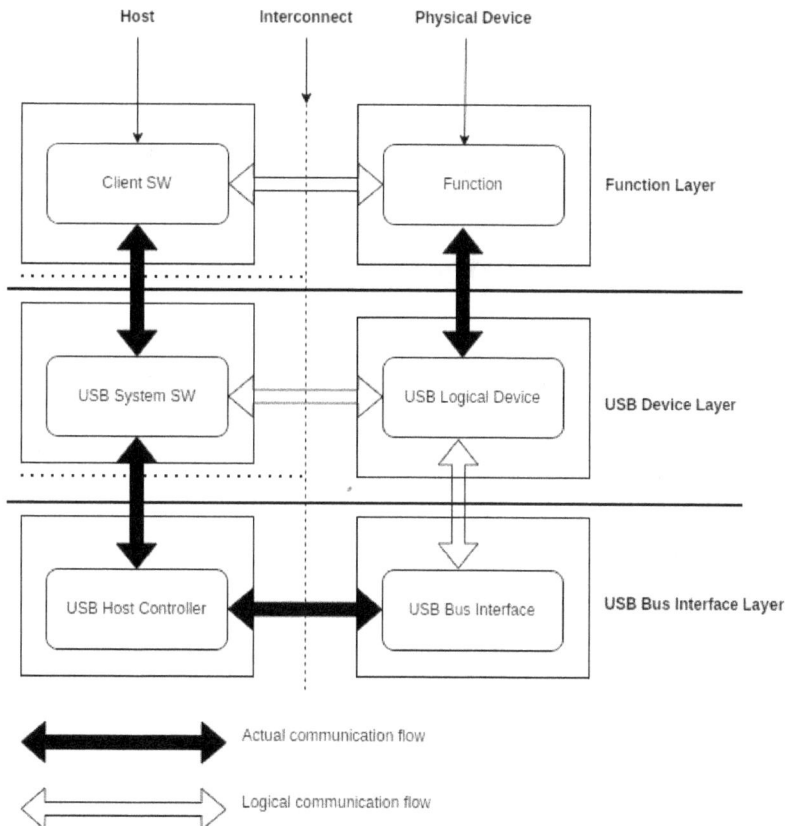

Figure 7.3: Three-layer representation of the management of a USB interface

USB features

There are several USB features, some of which are mentioned as follows:

- The maximum speed of USB 2.0 can reach 480 Mbps.

- An individual USB length can reach up to 40 meters with a hub and up to five meters without a hub.

- USB is a plug-and-play device.

- It can be powered by a computer or its own power supply.

- Using a single USB host controller, more than 100 devices can be connected.

- The power used by a USB device can reach 5 V and deliver up to 500 mA.

- Once a computer enters power-saving mode, some types of USB drives automatically convert to sleep mode.

- A USB port has two wires; one wire is used for power, and another is used to carry data.

- At 5 V, the computer can supply up to 500 mA of power over the power wires.

- Low-power devices can draw power directly from USB.

- Two-way communication is possible using a USB port between the computer and peripherals.

USB standards and specifications

USB standards and specifications are discussed as follows:

- USB specifications will change as USB standards evolve over time.

- USB supports three speed types, namely low speed -1.5 Mbps, full speed -12 Mbps, and high speed - 480 Mbps.

USB 2.0 standard

USB 2.0 standards are as follows:

- This is a high-speed USB port with a maximum data transfer speed of 480 Mbps. This USB supports all connectors.

- The maximum cable length is 5 meters.

- Its maximum charging power can reach 15W.

USB 3.2 standard

USB 3.2 standards are as follows:

- USB 3.2 (Generation 1) is a super-fast USB with a maximum data transfer speed of 5 Gbps.

- It supports different connectors like USB 3 USB-A, USB 3 USB-B and USB-C.

- The maximum cable length for this USB is 3 meters.

- Its maximum charging power can reach 15W.

USB 3.2 generation 2

USB 3.2 standards generation 2 are as follows:

- USB 3.2 (Generation 2) is also a super-fast USB with a maximum data transfer speed of 10 Gbps.

- The maximum cable length for this USB is 1 meter.

- It also supports different connectors like USB 3 USB-A, USB 3 USB-B and USB-C.

- Its maximum charging power can reach 100W.

USB 3.2 generation 2x2

USB 3.2 standards generation 2x2 are as follows:

- USB 3.2 generation 2x2 is a super-fast USB with a maximum data transfer speed of 20 Gbps.

- The maximum cable length for this USB is 1 meter.

- It also supports a USB connector.

- Its maximum charging power can reach 100W.

Thunderbolt 3 standard

USB 3 standards, alias Thunderbolt, are as follows:

- This USB drive is also called Thunderbolt and includes up to 40 Gbps of maximum data transfer speed.

- The maximum cable length for this USB is 2 meters for active cables and 0.8 meters for passive cables.

- It supports a USB connector.

- Its maximum charging power can reach 100W.

USB 4 standard

USB 4 standards are as follows:

- This USB flash drive is also known as Thunderbolt 4, with a maximum data transfer speed of 40 Gbps.

- The maximum cable length for this USB is 2m for active cables and 0.8m for passive cables.

- It supports a USB connector.

- Its maximum charging power can reach 100W.

The USB protocol timeline is shown here and is mainly used in engineering to explain the ON/OFF values of USB wires along a timeline.

If you see a 1, it indicates no charge, and a 0 indicates active. As time passes, you can observe the on/off progression. The following system shows **Non-Return to Zero Invert** (**NRZI**) encoding, which is a more efficient method of transmitting data:

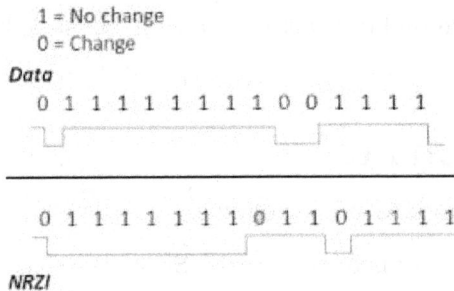

Figure 7.4: USB timing diagram

In *Figure 7.4*, bit stuffing occurs, which means that logical 1s are added to enable synchronization. If the data includes multiple 1s, the USB flash drive cannot synchronize the data. So, in this way, the hardware notices an extra bit and ignores it. It includes overhead to USB but also ensures consistent transfer.

In the USB protocol, master devices are called **USB hosts** which initiate all communications taking place over the USB bus. Here, a computer, if not another controller, is usually considered the master device, so if they request information, they only respond to other devices. The slave device or peripheral is simply connected to the host device, which is programmed to provide the host device with the information it needs to operate. Generally, slave or peripheral devices mainly include keyboards, computer mice, USB drives, cameras, etc.

It is essential that host devices communicate effectively with each other. Once the device is connected to the computer via USB, the computer will notice what type of device it is and automatically load a driver that will allow the device to work.

The small amount of data transmitted between the two devices are called **packets**, where one unit of digital information is transferred with each packet.

USB protocol data is transmitted in least-significant bit (In a binary number, the LSB is the least weighted bit in the number) packets first. There are mainly four types of USB packets: token, data, handshake, and start of frame. Each packet is designed from different field types, which are illustrated in the following message format:

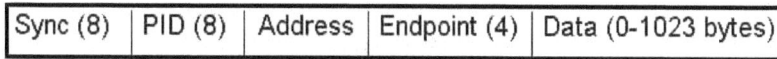

Sync (8)	PID (8)	Address	Endpoint (4)	Data (0-1023 bytes)

Figure 7.5: *Message format diagram of USB*

The following figure shows us the details of a USB frame:

- **SYNC**: In the USB protocol, each USB packet will start with a SYNC field, which is normally used to synchronize the transmitter and receiver to transmit data accurately. In a slow or fast USB system, the field like SYNC includes 3 KJ pairs, which are followed by 2 K to bracket 8 bits of data.

  In a high-speed USB system, synchronization requires 15 KJ pairs followed by 2 K to span 32 bits of data. This field is long with 8 bits at high and low speed, otherwise 32 bits for maximum speed and it is used to synchronize the CLK of the transmitter and receiver. The last 2 bits will indicate where the PID field begins.

- **Packet identification field (PID)**: The packet identification field in the USB protocol is mainly used to recognize the type of packet transmitted and therefore the format of the packet data. The length of this field is 8 bits, with the upper 4 bits recognizing the packet type and the lower 4 bits being the bitwise complement of the upper 4 bits.

- **Address field**: The USB protocol address field indicates which packet device is primarily intended for. The 7-bit length simply allows support for 127 devices. Address zero is invalid because any device that does not yet have an address must react to packets transmitted to address zero.

- **Endpoint field**: The USB protocol endpoint field is 4 bits long and allows additional flexibility in addressing. Usually these are split for data in/out. The 0 endpoint is a special case called the CONTROL endpoint, and every device includes a 0 endpoint.

- **Data field**: The length of the data field is not fixed, so it varies from 0 to 8192 bits and is always an integral part of the byte count.

- **CRC field**: Cyclic Redundancy Checks (CRC) are performed on the packet payload data, where all token packets include a 5-bit CRC and data packets include a 16-bit CRC. The CRC-5 is five bits long and is used by the token packet as well as the start of the frame packet.

- **EOP field**: Each packet ends with an **End of the Packet (EOP)** field, which includes an SE0 or an asymmetric zero for durations of 2 bits, followed by the J for a duration of 1 bit.

Commonly encountered synchronization issues within the USB protocol include the following. Whenever USB devices are developed, USB developers usually face many synchronization issues, also known as USB communication errors. Some of these errors will cause system crashes.

The following are some of the problems that can occur with the USB bus:

- Incorrect packet data and sequencing of USB data.
- USB transmissions or retransmissions.
- Power or VBUS-based issues.
- Problems through enumeration.
- High-speed trading issues.

Advantages and disadvantages of USB

The advantages of USB are as follows:

- Easy to use
- For multiple devices, only one interface is used
- Its size is compact
- Its connection system is robust
- These are not expensive
- It is available in different sizes with different connectors
- Automatic configuration
- Its expansion is easy
- It has great speed
- Reliable and inexpensive
- Energy consumption is low
- Compatible and durable

The disadvantages of USB are as follows:

- Some manufacturers design low-quality USB drives at a lower cost
- Its capacity is limited
- Compared to other systems, its data transfer is not fast

- USB does not offer a broadcast function, so individual messages are only communicated between the host and the device

At present, most of the peripherals are connected via USB to the system, such as mice, printers, scanners, joysticks, modems, webcams, keyboards, digital cameras, storage devices, storage devices, flight controllers, network adapters, and data acquisition devices in the scientific field.

Linux USB subsystem

The Linux USB subsystem is part of the Linux kernel responsible for managing **Universal Serial Bus** (**USB**) devices and their interactions with the system.

It provides the infrastructure and drivers needed to support USB devices on a wide range of hardware architectures.

Here is an introduction to the Linux USB subsystem:

- **USB device classes**:
  - USB device classes are standardized specifications that define how certain types of USB devices should communicate with hosts.
  - Examples of USB classes include:
    - **Human Interface Device** (**HID**): Keyboards, mice, game controllers.
    - **Mass Storage Class** (**MSC**): USB flash drives, external hard drives.
    - **Communication Device Class** (**CDC**): Modems, network adapters, serial ports.
    - **Audio class**: Sound cards, microphones, speakers.
    - **Video class**: Webcams, video cameras.
- **USB class drivers**:
  - Linux provides USB class drivers as kernel modules that implement the protocols defined by USB classes.
  - These drivers abstract the low-level details of USB communication, making it easier for developers to work with specific types of USB devices.
- **Class-specific protocols**:
  - Each USB class has its own set of protocols and specifications that govern communication between the device and the host.
  - Class drivers implement these protocols, ensuring compatibility with the standard and enabling interoperability with USB hosts and other devices.

- **Kernel configuration**:
  - When building the Linux kernel, users can configure which USB classes to support by enabling or disabling corresponding kernel options.
  - The configuration can be done using tools like **make menuconfig** or by directly editing the kernel configuration files.

- **Device recognition**:
  - When a USB device is connected to a Linux system, the USB core automatically recognizes the device class and loads the appropriate class driver if available.
  - This recognition is based on the device's class, subclass, and protocol identifiers provided in its USB descriptors.

- **Composite devices**:
  - USB devices can support multiple functions simultaneously, and class drivers often work together in composite devices.
  - Composite devices combine multiple USB classes to provide a range of functionalities. For example, a single USB device might simultaneously act as a mass storage device and an audio device.

- **User space interaction**:
  - User space applications can interact with USB class devices through standard interfaces and APIs provided by the kernel.
  - For example, file operations for USB mass storage devices are accessible in a manner similar to other block devices.

- **Examples of USB class drivers**:
  - **usb-storage**: Implements the MSC for USB storage devices.
  - **usbhid**: Supports the HID class for input devices.
  - **cdc-acm**: Implements the CDC for serial port communication.

Using USB class drivers in the Linux kernel simplifies the development of USB devices by providing a standardized interface and handling many of the underlying details. It also ensures compatibility with USB hosts that support the same USB classes. Developers can focus on implementing the higher-level functionality of their devices while relying on the USB class drivers to manage the USB communication.

A USB tree can be compared between a logical and physical topology. Physics is reality, and logic is an abstraction allowing us to better understand the separation of host devices by omitting the intermediate hubs. This is shwn in the following figure:

Physical   Logical

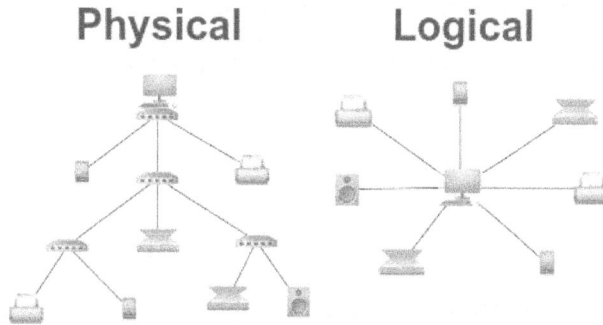

Figure 7.6: *Logical vs. Physical*

A USB device is a hardware peripheral that connects to a computer or other host device via a USB interface. USB devices come in various forms and serve different purposes, ranging from simple input/output devices like keyboards and mice to complex storage devices, network adapters, audio interfaces, and more.

The following figure shows us the relationships between endpoints and interfaces:

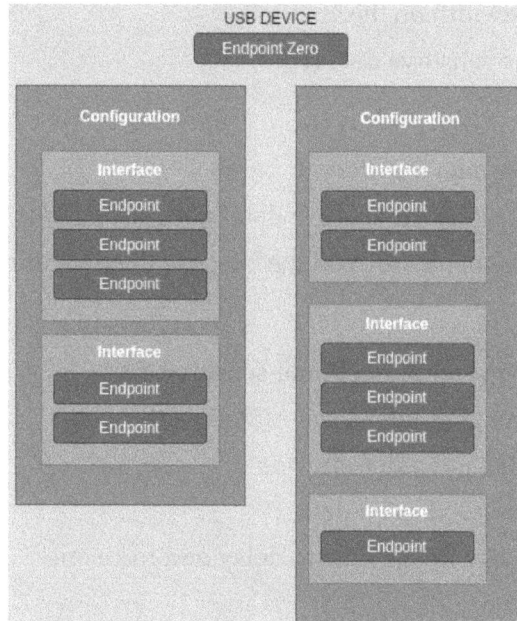

Figure 7.7: *Definition of a USB device*

An *endpoint route* typically refers to the path or route that data takes within a USB communication endpoint. In USB terminology, an *endpoint* represents a specific buffer or destination within a USB device where data is sent or received. Endpoints are identified by unique addresses and can be either *IN* endpoints for data coming into the device or *OUT* endpoints for data going out of the device.

- Endpoint 0 can transfer data in both directions
- All other endpoints can transfer data in one direction:
  - **IN**: Transfer data from device to host
  - **OUT**: Transfer data from host to device

Types of endpoint

Endpoints may have several types:

- **Control**:
  - Two-way endpoint
  - Used for enumeration
  - It can be used for an application

- **Interrupt**:
  - Transfers a small amount of data at low latency
  - Reserve bandwidth on the bus
  - Used for time-sensitive data (HID)

- **Bulk**:
  - Used for large data transfers
  - Used for large, time-insensitive data (network packets, mass storage, etc.).
  - Do not reserve bandwidth on the bus; use the remaining time

- **Isochronous**:
  - Transfers a large amount of time-sensitive data
  - Delivery is not guaranteed (no ACK is sent)
  - Used for audio and video streams
  - Late data is as good as no data
  - Better to drop an image than to delay and force one
  - Retransmission

- **USB is a host-controlled bus:**
  - Nothing on the bus happens without the host first initiating it.
  - Devices cannot initiate any communication.
  - The USB is a Polled Bus.
  - The Host polls each device, requesting data or sending data.

USB transport (IN) algorithm:

USB transport (IN) is as follows:

- The host sends an IN token
- **IF** the device has data, **THEN**:
  - o The device sends data
  - o The host sends an ACK

- **ELSE**:
  - o Device sends NAK
  - o The host will retry until the timeout

The following figure details the sequence diagram of an input transfer on a USB bus:

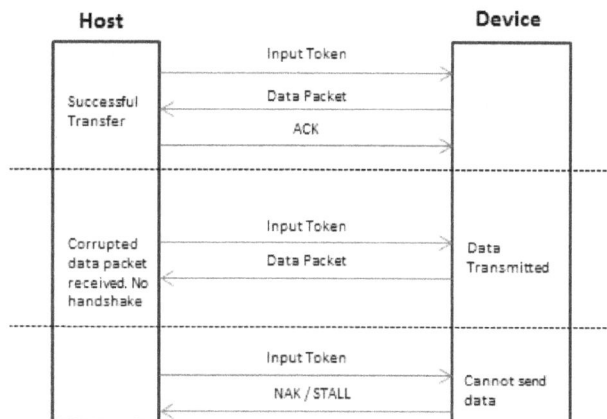

Figure 7.8: *IN transfer sequence diagram*

USB transport (OUT) algorithm

USB transport (OUT) is as follows:

- The host sends an OUT token
- The host sends the data (one packet)
- **IF** the device accepts data transfer, **THEN**:
  - o The device sends an ACK

- **ELSE**:
  - o The device sends an NAK
  - o The host will retry until success or timeout

The following figure details the sequence diagram of an output transfer on a USB bus:

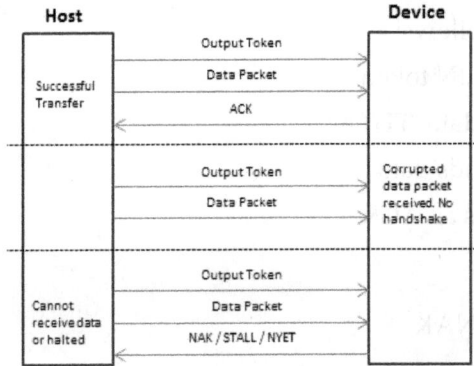

Figure 7.9: OUT *transfer sequence diagram*

The USB standard has many standard connectors that can communicate with each other:

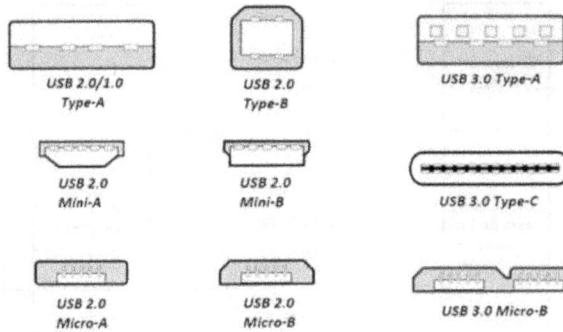

Figure 7.10: *Types of USB connectors as per the USB standard*

Figure 7.11: *Connection matrix between the different connectors*

USB On-The-Go (**USB OTG**) is a specification that allows USB devices to act as either hosts or peripherals dynamically. This means that devices equipped with USB OTG support can function as both USB hosts (like computers) and USB peripherals (like keyboards or flash drives), depending on the situation.

Here are the key aspects of USB On-The-Go:

- **Host or peripheral role switching**: USB OTG enables devices to switch between the roles of USB host and USB peripheral. For example, a smartphone with USB OTG support can act as a USB host when connecting a USB flash drive for data transfer and as a USB peripheral when connected to a computer for data synchronization.

- **Micro-USB and USB-C connectors**: USB OTG is commonly implemented using Micro-USB and USB-C connectors, which feature additional pins compared to standard USB connectors. These additional pins allow for the negotiation of host or peripheral roles between devices.

- **OTG cable or adapter**: To use USB OTG functionality, devices often require an OTG cable or adapter. This cable or adapter includes the necessary wiring and circuitry to enable role switching between the devices.

- **ID pin detection**: USB OTG devices use the ID (identification) pin in the USB connector to detect whether they should act as a host or a peripheral. When the ID pin is grounded, indicating that it is connected to the device's ground, the device acts as a host. When the ID pin is not grounded, the device acts as a peripheral.

- **Dual-role device** (**DRD**): Devices that support USB OTG are referred to as DRDs because they can assume either the host or peripheral role as needed. DRDs must be capable of switching between the roles quickly and efficiently to support seamless operation.

- **Application scenarios**: USB OTG is commonly used in mobile devices such as smartphones and tablets to enable connectivity with USB peripherals like keyboards, mice, game controllers, and storage devices. It allows users to expand the functionality of their devices and transfer data easily without requiring a computer.

- **USB OTG protocols**: USB OTG devices must comply with the USB OTG protocol, which defines the rules and procedures for role negotiation, power management, and data transfer between devices.

The following figure shows the difference between a standard USB cable and an OTG-compatible cable:

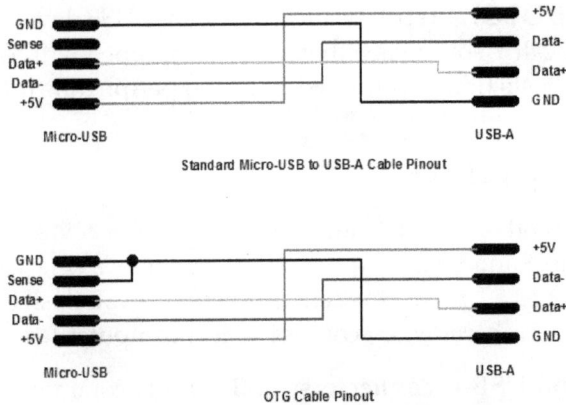

Figure 7.12: *Detail of the wiring between a normal USB cable and OTG*

Detecting a low or high-speed connection depends on the wiring:

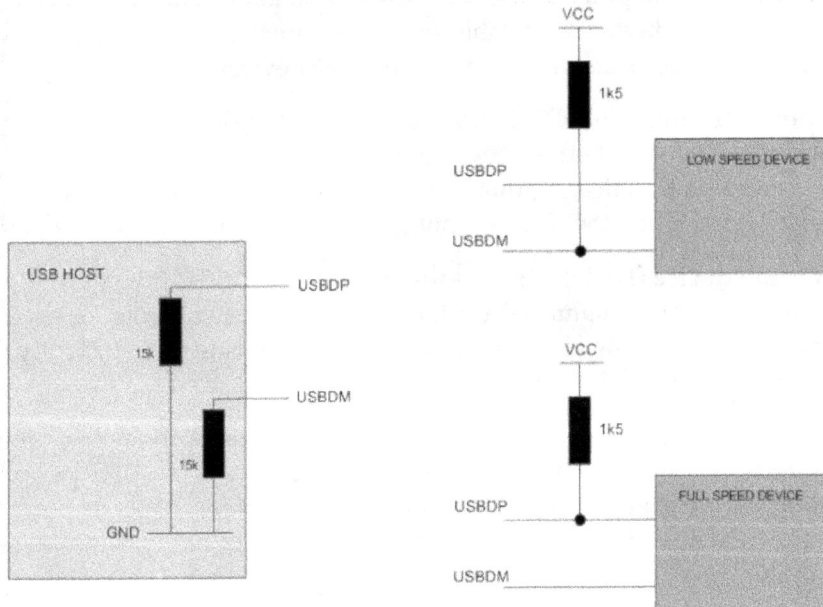

Figure 7.13: *Detecting a USB device connection*

Linux USB data struct

USB data structures are used to represent various components and configurations of USB devices, endpoints, descriptors, and transactions.

These data structures help the kernel manage USB devices, handle communication with USB peripherals, and maintain information about USB configurations.

Here are some commonly used USB data structures in the Linux kernel:

- **usb_device**: Represents a USB device connected to the system. This structure contains information such as the device's vendor ID, product ID, device class, configurations, and endpoints:

```
struct usb_device {
  int devnum;
  char devpath[16];
  u32 route;
  enum usb_device_state state;
  enum usb_device_speed speed;
  struct usb_tt * tt;
  int ttport;
  unsigned int toggle[2];
  struct usb_device * parent;
  struct usb_bus * bus;
  struct usb_host_endpoint ep0;
  struct device dev;
  struct usb_device_descriptor descriptor;
  struct usb_host_config * config;
  struct usb_host_config * actconfig;
  struct usb_host_endpoint * ep_in[16];
  struct usb_host_endpoint * ep_out[16];
  char ** rawdescriptors;
  unsigned short bus_mA;
  u8 portnum;
  u8 level;
  unsigned can_submit:1;
  unsigned persist_enabled:1;
  unsigned have_langid:1;
  unsigned authorized:1;
  unsigned authenticated:1;
  unsigned wusb:1;
  int string_langid;
  char * product;
  char * manufacturer;
  char * serial;
  struct list_head filelist;
```

```
#ifdef CONFIG_USB_DEVICE_CLASS
  struct device * usb_classdev;
#endif
#ifdef CONFIG_USB_DEVICEFS
  struct dentry * usbfs_dentry;
#endif
  int maxchild;
  struct usb_device * children[USB_MAXCHILDREN];
  u32 quirks;
  atomic_t urbnum;
  unsigned long active_duration;
#ifdef CONFIG_PM
  unsigned long connect_time;
  unsigned do_remote_wakeup:1;
  unsigned reset_resume:1;
#endif
  struct wusb_dev * wusb_dev;
  int slot_id;
};
```

- **usb_interface**: Represents an interface of a USB device. Each USB device can have multiple interfaces, each serving a specific function. The **usb_interface** structure contains information about the interface's endpoints, descriptors, and associated USB driver.

```
struct usb_interface {
  struct usb_host_interface *altsetting;
  struct usb_host_interface *cur_altsetting;
  unsigned num_altsetting;
  struct usb_interface_assoc_descriptor *intf_assoc;
  int minor;
  enum usb_interface_condition condition;
  unsigned sysfs_files_created:1;
  unsigned ep_devs_created:1;
  unsigned unregistering:1;
  unsigned needs_remote_wakeup:1;
  unsigned needs_altsetting0:1;
  unsigned needs_binding:1;
  unsigned resetting_device:1;
```

```
      unsigned authorized:1;
      struct device dev;
      struct device *usb_dev;
      struct work_struct reset_ws;
};
```

- **usb_device_descriptor**: Describes an endpoint of a USB device. This structure contains information such as the endpoint address, transfer type (e.g., control, bulk, interrupt, isochronous), maximum packet size, polling interval, and other endpoint-specific attributes.

```
struct usb_device_descriptor {
        __u8  bLength;
        __u8  bDescriptorType;

        __le16 bcdUSB;
        __u8  bDeviceClass;
        __u8  bDeviceSubClass;
        __u8  bDeviceProtocol;
        __u8  bMaxPacketSize0;
        __le16 idVendor;
        __le16 idProduct;
        __le16 bcdDevice;
        __u8  iManufacturer;
        __u8  iProduct;
        __u8  iSerialNumber;
        __u8  bNumConfigurations;
} __attribute__ ((packed));
```

- **usb_host_endpoint**: Represents a host-side endpoint of a USB device. This structure is used by the USB host controller driver to manage communication with endpoints on the USB device.

```
struct usb_host_endpoint {
  struct usb_endpoint_descriptor desc;
  struct usb_ss_ep_comp_descriptor ss_ep_comp;
  struct usb_ssp_isoc_ep_comp_descriptor ssp_isoc_ep_comp;
  struct list_head urb_list;
  void * hcpriv;
  struct ep_device * ep_dev;
  unsigned char * extra;
```

```
    int extralen;
    int enabled;
    int streams;
};
```

- **usb_request**: Represents a USB data transfer request. This structure contains information about the data buffer, transfer type, endpoint address, transfer length, and other parameters required for initiating a USB data transfer.

```
struct usb_request {
  void *buf;
  unsigned length;
  dma_addr_t dma;
  struct scatterlist      *sg;
  unsigned num_sgs;
  unsigned num_mapped_sgs;
  unsigned stream_id:16;
  unsigned no_interrupt:1;
  unsigned zero:1;
  unsigned short_not_ok:1;
  unsigned dma_mapped:1;
  void (*complete)(struct usb_ep *ep, struct usb_request *req);
  void *context;
  struct list_head        list;
  unsigned frame_number;
  int status;
  unsigned actual;
};
```

- **usb_ctrlrequest**: Represents a USB control request. This structure is used for sending control messages to USB devices, such as requests for device descriptors, configuration settings, or feature controls.

```
struct usb_ctrlrequest {
  __u8 bRequestType;
  __u8 bRequest;
  __le16 wValue;
  __le16 wIndex;
  __le16 wLength;
};
```

- **usb_driver**: Represents a USB device driver registered with the USB subsystem.

This structure contains function pointers for handling USB device initialization, attachment, detachment, and data transfer operations.

```
struct usb_driver {
  const char * name;
  int (* probe) (struct usb_interface *intf,const struct usb_device_
id *id);
  void (* disconnect) (struct usb_interface *intf);
  int (* unlocked_ioctl) (struct usb_interface *intf, unsigned int
code,void *buf);
  int (* suspend) (struct usb_interface *intf, pm_message_t
message);
  int (* resume) (struct usb_interface *intf);
  int (* reset_resume) (struct usb_interface *intf);
  int (* pre_reset) (struct usb_interface *intf);
  int (* post_reset) (struct usb_interface *intf);
  const struct usb_device_id * id_table;
  struct usb_dynids dynids;
  struct usbdrv_wrap drvwrap;
  unsigned int no_dynamic_id:1;
  unsigned int supports_autosuspend:1;
  unsigned int disable_hub_initiated_lpm:1;
  unsigned int soft_unbind:1;
};
```

- **usb_device_id**: Defines a USB device ID match entry used by USB device drivers to identify supported devices. This structure contains the vendor ID, product ID, device class, subclass, protocol, and other attributes used for device matching.

```
struct usb_device_id {
    __u16 match_flags;
    // Used for product-specific matches
    __u16 idVendor;     // Vendor ID
    __u16 idProduct;    // Product ID
    // Used for device class matches
    __u8 bDeviceClass;    // Class code
    __u8 bDeviceSubClass; // Subclass code
    __u8 bDeviceProtocol; // Protocol code
    // Used for interface class matches
    __u8 bInterfaceClass;    // Interface class code
```

```
    __u8 bInterfaceSubClass; // Interface subclass code
    __u8 bInterfaceProtocol; // Interface protocol code
    // Not matched against, used by the driver
    kernel_ulong_t driver_info; // Data specific to the driver
};
```

Enumeration

When enumerating a USB device, the main steps involve the initialization of the USB subsystem, detection of connected USB devices, parsing of device descriptors, configuration of the device, and loading of appropriate device drivers.

These steps are discussed further:

1. **USB subsystem initialization**:

   a. The USB subsystem in the operating system initializes during system boot or when the USB driver is loaded.

   b. Initialization involves setting up data structures, registering USB host controllers, and initializing other necessary components.

2. **Host controller detection**:

   a. The USB subsystem detects and initializes USB host controllers present in the system.

   b. Host controllers manage USB communication and provide the physical interface for connecting USB devices.

3. **Device connection detection**:

   a. The USB subsystem detects when a USB device is connected to the system.

   b. This detection may involve hardware interrupts, polling, or other mechanisms depending on the system's USB hardware and configuration.

4. **Device enumeration**:

   a. Upon detecting a connected USB device, the USB subsystem begins the enumeration process.

   b. Enumeration involves sending control requests to the device to retrieve its descriptors and configuration information.

5. **Descriptor parsing**:

   a. The USB subsystem parses the descriptors provided by the device to determine its capabilities, configurations, interfaces, and endpoints.

b. Descriptors contain information such as vendor ID, product ID, device class, endpoint addresses, and transfer types.

6. **Configuration selection**:

a. Based on the device descriptors, the USB subsystem selects an appropriate configuration for the device.

b. USB devices can have multiple configurations, each with different sets of interfaces and endpoints.

7. **Interface initialization**:

a. For each interface in the selected configuration, the USB subsystem initializes the corresponding USB driver.

b. Interface initialization involves loading the appropriate driver module, registering the interface with the driver, and setting up endpoints for data transfer.

8. **Driver binding**:

a. The USB subsystem binds the initialized interfaces to device drivers based on matching criteria defined in driver configuration or device descriptors.

b. If a suitable driver is found, it is bound to the interface, allowing the device to be fully operational.

9. **Device registration**:

a. The USB subsystem registers the device and its interfaces with the operating system, making them accessible to user space applications.

b. Registered devices may appear as device nodes in the file system or be exposed through system APIs for device access.

10. **Device configuration**:

a. Once enumeration and initialization are complete, the USB device is configured and ready for operation.

b. Applications or device drivers can now communicate with the device, send control requests, and perform data transfers as needed.

The following is a summary of the steps we just discussed:

1. Plug in the device
2. Detect connection
3. Get basic info
4. Set the address

5. Get more details

6. Choose a driver

7. Choose configuration

8. Use it

Class drivers

USB class drivers refer to the kernel modules responsible for supporting specific USB device classes. USB classes define standardized protocols for communication between USB devices and hosts.

Linux provides class drivers to facilitate the implementation of these standard protocols.

- **USB device classes**:
  - USB device classes are standardized specifications that define how certain types of USB devices should communicate with hosts.
  - Examples of USB classes include:
    - **HID**: Keyboards, mice, game controllers.
    - **MSC**: USB flash drives, external hard drives.
    - **CDC**: Modems, network adapters, serial ports.
    - **Audio class**: Sound cards, microphones, speakers.
    - **Video class**: Webcams, video cameras.

- **USB class drivers**:
  - Linux provides USB class drivers as kernel modules that implement the protocols defined by USB classes.
  - These drivers abstract the low-level details of USB communication, making it easier for developers to work with specific types of USB devices.

- **Class-specific protocols**:
  - Each USB class has its own set of protocols and specifications that govern communication between the device and the host.
  - Class drivers implement these protocols, ensuring compatibility with the standard and enabling interoperability with USB hosts and other devices.

- **Kernel configuration**:
  - When building the Linux kernel, users can configure which USB classes to support by enabling or disabling corresponding kernel options.

- o The configuration can be done using tools like **make menuconfig** or by directly editing the kernel configuration files.

- **Device recognition**:

  - o When a USB device is connected to a Linux system, the USB core automatically recognizes the device class and loads the appropriate class driver if available.

  - o This recognition is based on the device's class, subclass, and protocol identifiers provided in its USB descriptors.

- **Composite devices**:

  - o USB devices can support multiple functions simultaneously, and class drivers often work together in composite devices.

  - o Composite devices combine multiple USB classes to provide a range of functionalities. For example, a single USB device might simultaneously act as a mass storage device and an audio device.

- **User space interaction**:

  - o User space applications can interact with USB class devices through standard interfaces and APIs provided by the kernel.

  - o For example, file operations for USB mass storage devices are accessible in a manner similar to other block devices

- **Examples of USB class drivers**:

  - o **usb-storage**: Implements the MSC for USB storage devices.

  - o **usbhid**: Supports the HID class for input devices.

  - o **cdc-acm**: Implements the CDC for serial port communication.

Using USB class drivers in the Linux kernel simplifies the development of USB devices by providing a standardized interface and handling many of the underlying details.

It also ensures compatibility with USB hosts that support the same USB classes.

Host		Peripheral	
Target Product (example)	USB F/W	USB F/W	Target Product (example)
	Mass Storage Class Driver (HMSC)	Mass Storage Class Driver (PMSC)	USB Thumb Drive
	Communication Class Driver (HCDC)	Communication Class Driver (PCDC)	RS232C-USB Conversion
	HID Device Class Driver (HHID)	HID Device Class Driver (PHID)	Mouse, Keyboard
	USB Basic Firmware (USB-BASIC-F/W)	USB Basic Firmware (USB-BASIC-F/W)	Specialized product (Vendor original communication)

USB Device Class Firmware   USB Basic Firmware

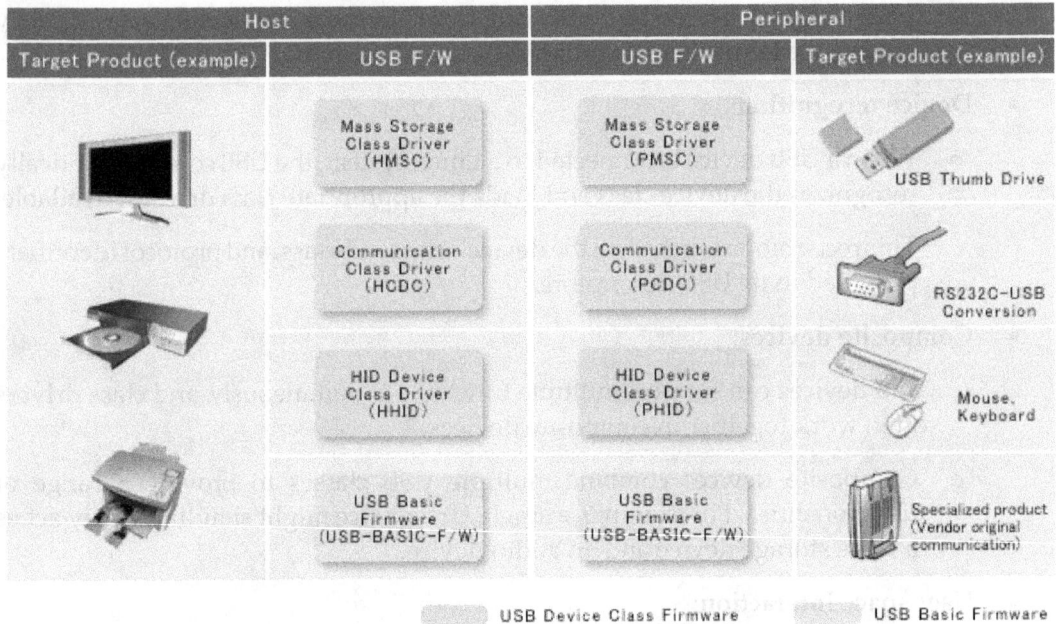

Figure 7.14: USB class summary

Developers can focus on implementing the higher-level functionality of their devices while relying on the USB class drivers to manage the USB communication.

Gadget drivers

USB Gadget drivers refer to the kernel modules responsible for implementing USB device functionality.

Unlike USB host controllers that manage USB peripherals (e.g., keyboards, mice, storage devices), Gadget drivers allow a Linux device to act as a USB peripheral itself.

Here is an introduction to USB Gadget drivers in the Linux kernel:

- **USB Gadget framework:**
  - The USB Gadget framework is a part of the Linux kernel that enables a device to function as a USB peripheral.
  - It provides a set of APIs and infrastructure for implementing various USB Gadget functionalities.
- **Types of USB Gadgets**: Linux supports a variety of USB Gadget types, each representing a different USB device class. Common Gadget types include Mass Storage Gadget (for emulating USB storage devices), Ethernet Gadget (for emulating USB network adapters), and Serial Gadget (for emulating USB serial ports).

- **Gadget drivers:**

    o Gadget drivers are kernel modules that implement specific Gadget functionalities.

    o These drivers define the behavior of the Gadget when it is connected to a USB host. For example, a Mass Storage Gadget driver would define how the Gadget exposes storage to the host.

- **Kernel configuration:** To use USB Gadget functionality, the Linux kernel must be configured with the appropriate options. This involves enabling the USB Gadget Framework and selecting specific Gadget drivers.

- **ConfigFS (Configuration filesystem):**

    o ConfigFS is a virtual filesystem used to configure USB Gadgets dynamically.

    o It allows userspace tools to create, configure, and manage USB Gadget configurations at runtime.

- **Gadget Composite devices:**

    o A single Gadget can support multiple functions simultaneously. For example, a Gadget could emulate both a Mass Storage device and an Ethernet device simultaneously.

    o This is achieved through composite Gadgets, where multiple Gadget drivers work together to provide different USB functions.

- **USB device classes:**

    o Gadget drivers often correspond to specific USB device classes, such as CDC or MSC.

    o Each USB Gadget driver implements the protocol and behavior required for a particular USB device class.

- **User space interaction:**

    o User space applications can interact with USB Gadgets through ConfigFS or by using higher-level libraries and tools.

    o For example, the Gadgetfs interface allows user space to interact with the USB Gadget as if it were a regular filesystem.

Using USB Gadget drivers, Linux devices can provide a wide range of USB functionalities, making them versatile in scenarios where the device needs to act as a USB peripheral.

Whether emulating a USB storage device, network adapter, or serial port, USB Gadget drivers play a crucial role in enabling diverse USB capabilities on Linux-based systems

The following example gives an example of a USB driver based on a Gadget that handles a USB panic button:

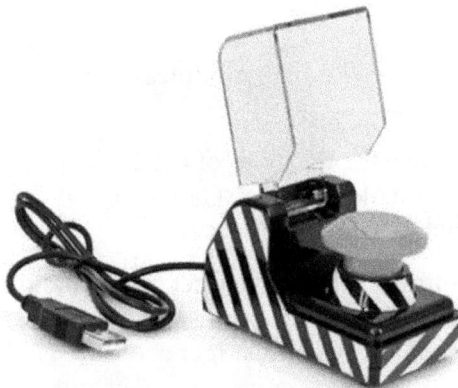

Figure 7.15: *View of a USB panic button*

It includes a Linux driver based on a character driver skeleton and a program that communicates with it from user space:

- **panicb.c**: The Linux USB driver
- **panic_test.c**: the program in userspace
- Makefile for managing (building, (un)loading, etc.) the kernel module

Here is an overview of the Makefile:

```
obj-m := panicb.o
KDIR := /lib/modules/$(shell uname -r)/build
all:
        make M=$(shell pwd) -C $(KDIR) modules
        modinfo ./panicb.ko
        gcc panicb_test.c -o panicb_test
info:
        modinfo ./panicb.ko
load:
        insmod ./panicb.ko
        dmesg
unload:
        rmmod ./panicb.ko
        dmesg
install:
        make M=$(shell pwd) -C $(KDIR) modules_install
        /sbin/panicb -a
clean:
        make M=$(shell pwd) -C $(KDIR) clean
```

Source code of the GNU/Linux kernel driver used to illustrate a USB driver:

```
#include <linux/kernel.h>
#include <linux/errno.h>
#include <linux/init.h>
#include <linux/slab.h>
#include <linux/module.h>
#include <linux/usb.h>
#include <asm/uaccess.h>


MODULE_AUTHOR("BPB");
MODULE_DESCRIPTION("Panic Button driver: no URB + char device");
MODULE_LICENSE("GPL");


#define VENDOR_ID        0x1130
#define PRODUCT_ID    0x0202


// Private structure
struct usb_panicb {
      struct usb_device * udev;
      unsigned int        button;
};


// Forward declaration
static struct usb_driver panicb_driver;


/* Table of devices that work with this driver */
static struct usb_device_id id_table [] = {
      { USB_DEVICE(VENDOR_ID, PRODUCT_ID) },
      { },
};
MODULE_DEVICE_TABLE (usb, id_table);


/* Ask panic button for button status */
static int get_panicb_button_status (struct usb_panicb *panicb_dev)
{
  char *buf;
  int ret = 0;
```

```
  printk (KERN_INFO "get_panicb_button_status\n");

  // Allocate msg buffer
  if (!(buf = kmalloc(8, GFP_KERNEL))) {
    printk(KERN_WARNING "panicb: can't alloc buf\n");
    return -1;
  }

  memset (buf, 0, 8);
  ret = usb_control_msg (panicb_dev->udev, usb_rcvctrlpipe (panicb_dev-
>udev, 0), 0x01, 0xA1, 0x300, 0x00, buf, 8, 2 * HZ);
  if (ret < 0)
    printk (KERN_WARNING "panicb: IN, ret = %d\n", ret);
  else
    panicb_dev->button = *buf;


  kfree (buf);

  return 0;
}

// Char device functions
static int panicb_open (struct inode *inode, struct file *file)
{
  struct usb_panicb *dev;
  struct usb_interface *interface;
  int minor;
  minor = iminor(inode);

  // Get interface for device
  interface = usb_find_interface (&panicb_driver, minor);
  if (!interface)
    return -ENODEV;

  // Get private data from interface
```

```
  dev = usb_get_intfdata (interface);
  if (dev == NULL) {
      printk (KERN_WARNING "panicb: can't find device for minor %d\n",
minor);
      return -ENODEV;
  }

  // Set to file structure
  file->private_data = (void *)dev;

  return 0;
}

static int panicb_release (struct inode *inode, struct file *file)
{
  return 0;
}

static int panicb_ioctl (struct inode *inode, struct file *file, unsigned int
cmd, unsigned long arg)
{
  struct usb_panicb *dev;
  printk(KERN_DEBUG "panicb_ioctl\n");

  /* get the dev object */
  dev = file->private_data;
  if (dev == NULL)
    return -ENODEV;

  switch (cmd) {
    case 0 :
      printk(KERN_INFO "panicb_ioctl\n");
      if (get_panicb_button_status (dev) == 0) {
       if (copy_to_user((void*)arg, &(dev->button), sizeof(int*))) {
         printk (KERN_WARNING "panicb: copy_to_user error\n");
         return -EFAULT;
       }
      }
```

```
      break;

    default :
      printk(KERN_WARNING "panicb_ioctl(): unsupported command %d\n", cmd);

      return -EINVAL;
  }
  return 0;
}

static struct file_operations panicb_fops = {
  .open    = panicb_open,
  .release = panicb_release,
  .ioctl   = panicb_ioctl
};

// USB driver functions
static struct usb_class_driver panicb_class_driver = {
  .name = "usb/panicb",
  .fops = &panicb_fops,
  .minor_base = 0
};

static int panicb_probe (struct usb_interface *interface, const struct usb_
device_id *id)
{
  struct usb_device *udev = interface_to_usbdev (interface);
  struct usb_panicb *panicb_dev;
  int ret;
  printk (KERN_INFO "panicb_probe: starting\n");
  ret = usb_register_dev(interface, &panicb_class_driver);
  if (ret < 0) {
    printk (KERN_WARNING "panicb: usb_register_dev() error\n");
    return ret;
  }

  panicb_dev = kmalloc (sizeof(struct usb_panicb), GFP_KERNEL);
```

```
  if (panicb_dev == NULL) {
    dev_err (&interface->dev, "Out of memory\n");
    return -ENOMEM;
  }


  // Fill private structure and save it with usb_set_intfdata
  memset (panicb_dev, 0x00, sizeof (*panicb_dev));
  panicb_dev->udev = usb_get_dev(udev);
  panicb_dev->button = 0;
  usb_set_intfdata (interface, panicb_dev);
  dev_info(&interface->dev, "USB Panic Button device now attached\n");
  return 0;
}

static void panicb_disconnect(struct usb_interface *interface)
{
  struct usb_panicb *dev;
  dev = usb_get_intfdata (interface);
  usb_deregister_dev (interface, &panicb_class_driver);
  usb_set_intfdata (interface, NULL);
  kfree(dev);
  dev_info(&interface->dev, "USB Panic Button now disconnected\n");
}

static struct usb_driver panicb_driver = {
        .name        ="panicb",
        .probe       =panicb_probe,
        .disconnect  =panicb_disconnect,
        .id_table    =id_table,
};

// Init & exit
static int __init usb_panicb_init(void)
{
  int retval = 0;
  retval = usb_register(&panicb_driver);
  if (retval)
```

```
    printk(KERN_WARNING "usb_register failed. Error number %d", retval);
  return retval;
}


static void __exit usb_panicb_exit(void)
{
  usb_deregister(&panicb_driver);
}


module_init (usb_panicb_init);
module_exit (usb_panicb_exit);
```

Let us detail the main lines of the source code:

- **The header includes the following**: Includes necessary header files for kernel programming, USB support, memory allocation, and user-space access:

  ```
  #include <linux/kernel.h>
  #include <linux/errno.h>
  #include <linux/init.h>
  #include <linux/slab.h>
  #include <linux/module.h>
  #include <linux/usb.h>
  #include <asm/uaccess.h>
  ```

- **Module information**: The following code defines the module's metadata, including its author, description, and license:

  ```
  MODULE_AUTHOR("BPB");
  MODULE_DESCRIPTION("Panic Button driver: no URB + char device");
  MODULE_LICENSE("GPL");
  ```

- **Device identification**: The following code associates the driver with the specified **Vendor_ID** and **Product_ID**:

  ```
  #define VENDOR_ID              0x1130
  #define PRODUCT_ID   0x0202
  ```

  On the one hand, this allows the module to be loaded automatically when this ID pair is detected, for example, through UDEV rules.

- **Private structure**: Defines a private structure, **usb_panicb** to hold device-specific data:

  ```
  struct usb_panicb {
  ```

```
        struct usb_device * udev;
        unsigned int        button;
};
```

- **Forward declaration**: Forward declaration of the USB driver structure:

```
static struct usb_driver panicb_driver;
```

- **USB device ID table**: Defines a table of USB device IDs compatible with the driver and registers it with the kernel:

```
static struct usb_device_id id_table [] = {
    { USB_DEVICE(VENDOR_ID, PRODUCT_ID) },
    { },
};
MODULE_DEVICE_TABLE (usb, id_table);
```

- **Panic button status retrieval**: Implements a function to retrieve the button status from the Panic Button device using USB control messages:

```
static int get_panicb_button_status(struct usb_panicb *panicb_dev) {
```

- **Character device functions**: Implements character device functions for opening, releasing, and performing IOCTL operations on the Panic Button device:

```
static int panicb_open(struct inode *inode, struct file *file)
static int panicb_release(struct inode *inode, struct file *file)
static int panicb_ioctl(struct inode *inode, struct file *file,
unsigned int cmd, unsigned long arg)
```

- **File operations structure**: Initializes a file operations structure with pointers to the character device functions:

```
static struct file_operations panicb_fops = {
  .open    = panicb_open,
  .release = panicb_release,
  .ioctl   = panicb_ioctl
};
```

- **USB class driver initialization**: Initializes a USB class driver structure to handle the character device file operations:

```
static struct usb_class_driver panicb_class_driver = {
  .name = "usb/panicb",
  .fops = &panicb_fops,
  .minor_base = 0
};
```

- **USB probe and disconnect functions**: Implements **probe** and **disconnect** functions called when a compatible USB device is detected or removed:

```
static int panicb_probe(struct usb_interface *interface, const
struct usb_device_id *id)
```

```
static void panicb_disconnect(struct usb_interface *interface)
```

- **USB driver structure**: Defines the USB driver structure with **probe**, **disconnect**, and ID table information:

```
static struct usb_driver panicb_driver = {
        .name      ="panicb",
        .probe     =panicb_probe,
        .disconnect =panicb_disconnect,
        .id_table  =id_table,
};
```

- **Module initialization and exit**: Implements module initialization and **exit** functions and registers them with the kernel:

```
static int __init usb_panicb_init(void)
static void __exit usb_panicb_exit(void)
module_init (usb_panicb_init);
module_exit (usb_panicb_exit);
```

This code defines a Linux kernel module that serves as a driver for a Panic Button device connected via USB.

It includes functionality for probing and disconnecting from the device, handling character device operations, and retrieving button status.

Now, we can study the source code of the tiny program in userspace:

```
#include <stdlib.h>
#include <stdio.h>
#include <unistd.h>
#include <fcntl.h>
#include <errno.h>
#include <string.h>
#include <sys/ioctl.h>
#include <limits.h>

int main (int argc, char **argv)
{
  int b, fd = open(argv[1], O_RDONLY);
```

```
if (fd < 0) {
  perror("open()");
  return EXIT_FAILURE;
}
if (ioctl(fd, 0, &b)) {
  perror("ioctl");
  close(fd);
  return EXIT_FAILURE;
}
printf("button= %d\n", b);
close(fd);
return EXIT_SUCCESS;
}
```

Execution:

$ ./panic_test "/dev/usbpanic"

Replace the **usbpanic** with the right name used with the **mknod** !

Once the program has opened an **ioctl** connection, the driver will give us the button's status and then display it.

Write a USB driver in userspace using the libusb

libusb is a powerful and flexible library that provides a standardized way for user-space applications to communicate with USB devices on various operating systems. At its core, libusb abstracts the low-level details of USB communication, allowing developers to interact with USB devices without dealing with the intricacies of different platforms.

libusb operates by providing a set of APIs that enable applications to perform USB-related tasks, such as device discovery, configuration, and data transfer. It abstracts the USB protocol layers and provides a unified interface, making it easier for developers to work with USB devices across different platforms like Windows, Linux, and macOS.

Key features of libusb include the following:

- **Device discovery**: libusb allows applications to discover connected USB devices, retrieve information about them, and identify their capabilities.

- **Configuration and interface management**: It provides functions to configure USB devices and manage multiple interfaces on a single device. This is crucial for devices with multiple functions or modes.

- **Data transfer**: Libusb facilitates data transfer between the application and the USB device. It supports various transfer types, such as control transfers, bulk transfers, interrupt transfers, and isochronous transfers.

- **Asynchronous operations**: Developers can perform asynchronous operations, enabling non-blocking communication with USB devices. This is particularly useful for applications that require responsiveness without getting blocked during data transfers.

- **Platform independence**: Libusb abstracts the underlying operating system details, allowing developers to write USB applications that work across different platforms without major modifications.

- **Hotplug events**: libusb supports hotplug events, allowing applications to be notified when USB devices are connected or disconnected dynamically.

- **Driver interaction**: It provides mechanisms for interacting with USB device drivers and attaching/detaching kernel drivers from USB devices when needed.

The libusb empowers developers to work with USB devices in a platform-agnostic manner, abstracting the complexities of USB communication. Its comprehensive set of APIs enables a wide range of USB-related tasks, making it a valuable tool for applications requiring USB device interaction.

On a Linux system, the libusb provides a C API that allows developers to interact with USB devices.

The following is an overview of the key components and functions in the libusb API:

- **Initialization and exit functions:**

  o **libusb_init**: Initializes the **libusb** library. This function must be called before any other libusb functions.

  o **libusb_exit**: Deinitializes the **libusb** library when you are done using it.

    Example of usage:

    ```c
    #include <libusb.h>

    int main() {
        libusb_init(NULL); // Initialize Libusb

        // ... (perform USB operations)

        libusb_exit(NULL); // Deinitialize Libusb
        return 0;
    }
    ```

- **USB device discovery functions**:

  o **libusb_get_device_list**: Retrieves a list of USB devices currently connected to the system.

  o **libusb_free_device_list**: Frees the list of devices obtained from **libusb_get_device_list**.

  Example of usage:
  ```
  libusb_device **list;
  ssize_t count = libusb_get_device_list(NULL, &list);
  for (ssize_t i = 0; i < count; ++i) {
      // Access each device in the list
      libusb_device *device = list[i];
      // ... (handle device information)
  }
  libusb_free_device_list(list, 1); // Free the list when done
  ```

- **Functions to obtain information about USB devices**:

  o **libusb_get_device_descriptor**: Retrieves the USB device descriptor, providing information like vendor ID, product ID, etc.

  Example of usage:
  ```
  struct libusb_device_descriptor desc;
  libusb_get_device_descriptor(device, &desc);
  // Access information in the 'desc' structure
  ```

- **Functions allowing the configuration of a device and its interfaces**:

  o **libusb_get_config_descriptor**: Retrieves the configuration descriptor for a device.

  o **libusb_set_configuration**: Sets the active configuration for a device.

  o **libusb_claim_interface**: Claims an interface on a device for use by the application.

  Example of usage:
  ```
  libusb_config_descriptor *config;
  libusb_get_config_descriptor(device, 0, &config); // 0 for the first
  configuration
  // Access information in the 'config' structure
  (...)
  libusb_set_configuration(handle, config->bConfigurationValue);
  libusb_claim_interface(handle, interface_number);
  ```

- **Functions for transferring data:**

  o **libusb_bulk_transfer**: Performs a bulk transfer between the application and a USB device.

    Example of usage:
    ```
    unsigned char buffer[64];
    int transferred;
    libusb_bulk_transfer(handle, endpoint, buffer, sizeof(buffer),
    &transferred, timeout);
    // Access data in the 'buffer' after the transfer
    ```

- **Functions allowing asynchronous data transfer:**

  o **libusb_submit_transfer**: Submits an asynchronous transfer request.

    Example of usage:
    ```
    libusb_transfer *transfer = libusb_alloc_transfer(0);
    // Initialize transfer parameters
    libusb_submit_transfer(transfer);
    // Wait for the transfer to complete or handle it asynchronously
    libusb_free_transfer(transfer);
    ```

- **Functions for error handling:**

  o **libusb_strerror**: Converts a **libusb** error code to a human-readable string.

    Example of usage:
    ```
    int result = libusb_bulk_transfer(handle, endpoint, buffer,
    sizeof(buffer), &transferred, timeout);
    if (result < 0) {
        fprintf(stderr, "Error: %s\n", libusb_strerror(result));
    }
    ```

Interacting with a USB device, such as a push button, as shown in the following figure, through libusb involves understanding the communication protocol of the device:

The exact implementation will vary based on the specifications of your USB device. The following is a simplified example, assuming a hypothetical USB device that sends a signal when a push button is pressed or released.

This example sets up an interrupt transfer on an input endpoint (assumed to be 0x81). It continuously polls the USB device for changes in the button state.

You would need to adapt this code to your specific USB device's communication protocol.

Please refer to your USB device's documentation or specifications for information on the endpoint, communication protocol, and data format. Additionally, ensure that you have the necessary permissions to access the USB device (e.g., by running the program as a user with the appropriate privileges).

Remember to link your program with the **libusb** library during compilation, typically using the **-lusb-1.0** flag. Additionally, make sure your application has the necessary permissions to access USB devices (e.g., by running it with appropriate user privileges or setting up **udev** rules).

To obtain the **VENDOR_ID**, **PRODUCT_ID**, and **ENDPOINT_IN** values for your specific USB device, you typically need to refer to the device's documentation, datasheet, or specifications provided by the manufacturer.

These values are unique to each USB device and are used to identify the device and its communication endpoints.

Here are general steps to find this information:

1. **Check the device documentation**:

   a. Look for the user manual, datasheet, or any documentation that came with your USB device.

   b. Search for information related to the USB interface, vendor ID, product ID, and endpoint configuration.

2. **Use system tools**:

   a. On Linux, you can use tools like **lsusb** and USB-devices to list connected USB devices and view their details.

   b. Open a terminal and run the **lsusb** command. This will display a list of connected USB devices with their vendor and product IDs.

   c. The **dmesg** command may also help.

3. **Check device properties in udev**:

   a. You can also check device properties in the **udev** system. Run the following command to see detailed information about USB devices:

   ```
   $ udevadm info --attribute-walk --name=/dev/your_device
   ```

   ```
   Replace /dev/your_device with the appropriate device
   path.
   ```

4. **Inspect USB traffic**:

   a. Use tools like **Wireshark** or **usbmon** to capture USB traffic and inspect the communication between the device and the system.

b. This can help you identify endpoint addresses, data formats, and other communication details.

5. **Contact the manufacturer**: If you cannot find the required information in the documentation or through system tools, consider reaching out to the manufacturer's support or checking their official website.

Once you have identified the correct values for **VENDOR_ID**, **PRODUCT_ID**, and **ENDPOINT_ IN**, you can use them in your libusb application to interact with the USB device. The **lsusb** command is particularly useful for getting a quick overview of connected USB devices and their IDs.

The following is an example of a simple **CMakeLists.txt** file for a project that uses **libusb** with **pkg-config**. This assumes you have a source file named **main.c** in the same directory.

The following listing details the **CMakeLists.txt** for building the project:

```
cmake_minimum_required(VERSION 3.5)
project(libusbExample)


find_package(PkgConfig REQUIRED)
pkg_check_modules(LIBUSB REQUIRED libusb-1.0)


add_executable(myusbprogram main.c)
```

Here is a brief explanation of each part:

- **Line 4: find_package(PkgConfig REQUIRED)**
  - This line makes sure that **CMake** can find and use **pkg-config**.
- **Line 5: pkg_check_modules(LIBUSB REQUIRED libusb-1.0)**
  - This line uses **pkg-config** to find the necessary information about the **libusb** library, including include directories and libraries.
- **Line 7: add_executable(myusbprogram main.c)**
  - This line tells **CMake** to build an executable named **myusbprogram** from the source file **main.c**.
- **Line 9: target_include_directories(myusbprogram PRIVATE ${LIBUSB_ INCLUDE_DIRS})**
  - This line includes the **libusb** include directories for the target **myusbprogram**.
- **Line 10: target_link_libraries(myusbprogram PRIVATE ${LIBUSB_ LIBRARIES})**:
  - This line links the **libusb** libraries to the **myusbprogram** executable.

Save this content in a file named **CMakeLists.txt** in the same directory as your **main.c**. Then, you can use the following commands to build your project:

```
$ mkdir build && cd build
$ cmake ..
$ make
```

This assumes you have **CMake** installed on your system (**sudo apt-get** install **cmake** on Debian/Ubuntu systems). Adjust the **main.c** and project structure as needed.

Conclusion

In this chapter, we explained how to use USB type devices after a review of its architecture. Then, we detailed how to implement a driver that can control such devices.

In the next chapter, we will see an important part relating to the network stack.

Join our book's Discord space

Join the book's Discord Workspace for Latest updates, Offers, Tech happenings around the world, New Release and Sessions with the Authors:

https://discord.bpbonline.com

CHAPTER 8
Network Drivers

Introduction

In this chapter, we will see one of the most important building blocks of the Linux kernel, namely the network stack. We will see its composition from the network card to its meanders. In addition, we will also see how to make it efficient.

Structure

The chapter covers the following topics:

- History of the network stack
- Network architecture
- Protocols layer
- Network module
- Network driver loading
- The sk_buff
- Performance and tuning
- The DPDK project

Objectives

By the end of this chapter, you will be able to understand how the network stack works, and also develop a driver for a network card, improve the operation of the network stack, or secure its operation.

To be able to manage significant throughputs of the order of gigabits, we will see the structure of the DPDK open-source project.

History of the network stack

The development of the network layer in the Linux kernel was orchestrated by several independent programmers. The goal is to implement a system that is at least as efficient as the others while remaining in the domain of free software.

Above all, it is the TCP/IP protocol that was developed with basic primitives by *Ross Biro*. *Orest Zborowski* produced the first BSD socket interface for the GNU Linux kernel.

The code was then taken over by *Alan Cox* of Red Hat.

The following figure gives a timeline of the development of the network stack under Linux:

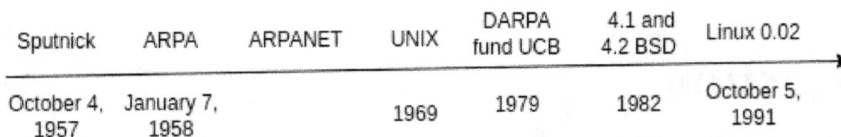

Sputnick	ARPA	ARPANET	UNIX	DARPA fund UCB	4.1 and 4.2 BSD	Linux 0.02
October 4, 1957	January 7, 1958		1969	1979	1982	October 5, 1991

Figure 8.1: The origin of the GNU/Linux network stack

Important stages in developing the network stack under GNU/Linux are as follows:

- **Early networking support (1991-1995):**
  - Linux initially lacked built-in networking support when it was created by *Linus Torvalds* in 1991. However, it quickly gained networking capabilities with the release of version 0.01 in September 1991.
  - The initial networking support in Linux was rudimentary, offering basic functionalities like TCP/IP networking and Ethernet support.

- **Kernel versions 1.x and 2.x (1996-2000):**
  - Throughout the mid to late 1990s, Linux networking capabilities expanded significantly with each kernel release.
  - Kernel version 2.0, released in June 1996, introduced major enhancements to the networking stack, including support for more network protocols, improved performance, and better scalability.

o Kernel version 2.2, released in January 1999, introduced features such as IPv6 support, enhanced routing capabilities, and improved network device drivers.

- **Kernel versions 2.4 and 2.6 (2001-2006):**

o Kernel version 2.4, released in January 2001, marked a significant milestone in Linux networking. It introduced the Netfilter framework, which enabled powerful packet filtering and manipulation capabilities through tools like iptables.

o Kernel version 2.6, released in December 2003, brought further enhancements to the networking stack, including improved scalability, better support for network namespaces, and the introduction of features like TCP/IP stack improvements and the epoll system call for efficient event notification.

- **Kernel versions 3.x and 4.x (2011-2019):**

o Kernel version 3.0, released in July 2011, did not introduce major networking changes but continued to refine and optimize existing features.

o Kernel version 3.10, released in June 2013, introduced the TCP Fast Open feature, aimed at reducing connection setup times for TCP connections.

o Kernel version 4.4, released in January 2016, brought improvements to the network stack's performance and scalability, as well as enhancements to networking protocols and security features.

o Kernel version 4.15, released in January 2018, introduced the Retpoline Spectre mitigation technique, addressing security vulnerabilities in the network stack and other parts of the kernel.

- **Recent developments (2020-present):**

o Recent kernel releases have focused on improving security, performance, and support for emerging networking technologies such as 5G, IoT, and **software-defined networking (SDN)**.

o Ongoing efforts include optimizing the network stack for low-latency applications, enhancing support for network virtualization technologies like VXLAN and Geneve, and improving network protocol implementations for better performance and security.

Network architecture

The Linux network stack is a complex system within the Linux kernel responsible for handling all aspects of networking, including packet processing, protocol implementations, device drivers, and network configuration.

Here is a detailed technical overview of the GNU/Linux network stack:

- **Packet processing:**
  - o Incoming network packets are received by network interfaces, which are represented by device drivers in the kernel.
  - o Upon reception, network packets are encapsulated into data structures known as **socket buffers (sk_buff)**, which contain metadata about the packet, such as protocol type, source and destination addresses, and pointers to the packet data.
  - o The kernel's networking stack processes incoming packets through a series of protocol layers, including link layer (e.g., Ethernet, Wi-Fi), network layer (e.g., IP), transport layer (e.g., TCP, UDP), and application layer (e.g., sockets).

- **Protocol implementations:**
  - o The Linux kernel includes implementations of various network protocols, such as TCP/IP, UDP, ICMP, IPv4, and IPv6.
  - o Each protocol is implemented as a set of functions responsible for packet processing, protocol-specific operations, error handling, and state management.
  - o Protocol implementations interact with each other through well-defined interfaces and data structures, allowing for modular and extensible networking functionality.

- **Device drivers:**
  - o Network interfaces in Linux are represented by device drivers, which are responsible for controlling physical or virtual network devices.
  - o Device drivers interact with the hardware, handling tasks such as packet transmission and reception, interrupt handling, and device initialization.
  - o The kernel's networking subsystem provides a uniform interface for device drivers, allowing them to be easily integrated into the network stack.

- **Socket layer:**
  - o The socket layer in Linux provides an interface for applications to communicate over the network using sockets.
  - o Sockets are communication endpoints identified by an IP address, port number, and protocol type (e.g., TCP, UDP).
  - o Applications interact with sockets through system calls such as **socket()**, **bind()**, **listen()**, **connect()**, **send()**, and **recv()**, which are implemented by the kernel's socket layer.

- **Routing and forwarding:**
  - o The Linux kernel maintains routing tables that determine how network packets are forwarded to their destinations.

- o Routing decisions are based on destination IP addresses and routing policies configured in the kernel.

- o The kernel's routing subsystem also supports advanced routing features such as policy-based routing, source-based routing, and **network address translation (NAT)**.

- **Packet filtering and firewalling:**

  - o Linux includes the Netfilter framework, which provides packet filtering and firewalling capabilities.

  - o Netfilter allows administrators to define rules for filtering, modifying, and forwarding network packets based on criteria such as source and destination addresses, port numbers, and packet content.

  - o Tools like iptables and nftables provide user-space interfaces for configuring Netfilter rules and managing firewall policies.

- **Performance and scalability:**

  - o The Linux network stack is designed for performance and scalability, with optimizations for multi-core processors, high-speed networking, and efficient packet processing.

  - o Techniques such as kernel bypass, zero-copy networking, and interrupt moderation are used to minimize overhead and improve throughput.

  - o The kernel's networking subsystem is continuously optimized and tuned to meet the performance requirements of modern networking applications.

The processing of a frame just received or to be transmitted in the IP stack can be divided into several layers, as shown in the following figure:

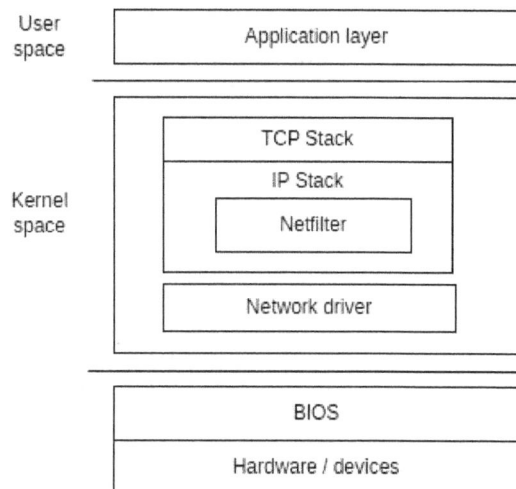

Figure 8.2: Representation of the several layers from the network card to the userspace

This IP treatment has four main phases:

- **Frame reception**: Entry point into the IP layer for frames received on network interfaces.

- **Routing**: Choice of the route to follow by the packet retransmission on another interface/network or local destination.

- **Forwarding**: Control of the TTL and MTU before moving to the retransmission phase.

- **Transmission**: Packets to be transmitted or retransmitted go through this stage. Just before leaving the IP layer, the Ethernet header is completed.

The following figure details the hooks that Netfilter can use on the network stack:

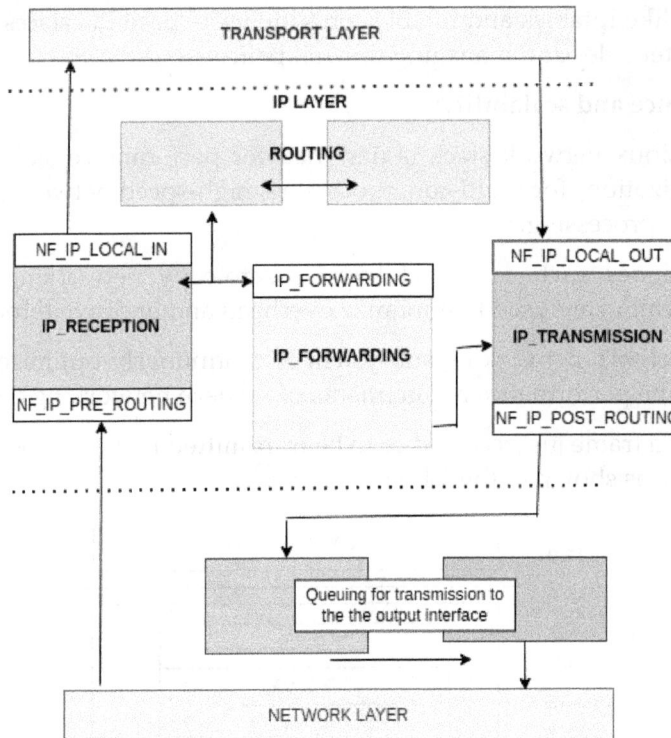

Figure 8.3: Global view of the GNU/Linux network stack

Netfilter is a framework within the Linux kernel that provides facilities for packet filtering, **network address translation** (**NAT**), and packet mangling. It consists of a set of hooks (entry points) in the networking stack where kernel modules, known as Netfilter hooks, can intercept and process network packets.

It is commonly used for implementing firewalls, NAT gateways, packet filtering, and traffic shaping in Linux-based systems, where each hook is an entry point within the

Linux kernel's networking stack, where kernel modules can register callback functions to intercept network packets.

There are five main Netfilter hooks, each corresponding to a specific point in the packet processing path:

- **NF_INET_PRE_ROUTING**: Hook called just before a packet undergoes routing. Useful for packet filtering and NAT operations.

- **NF_INET_LOCAL_IN**: Hook called when a packet is destined for the local system. Useful for local packet filtering and traffic monitoring.

- **NF_INET_FORWARD**: Hook called when a packet is being forwarded to another host. Useful for filtering packets being forwarded by the system.

- **NF_INET_LOCAL_OUT**: Hook called when a packet is being sent from the local system. Useful for filtering outgoing packets and performing NAT.

- **NF_INET_POST_ROUTING**: Hook called just after a packet has been routed. Useful for performing NAT operations on outgoing packets.

Netfilter hooks provide flexibility and granularity for implementing packet filtering and manipulation based on the packet's position in the network stack.

Kernel modules register callback functions, known as hook functions, with Netfilter hooks to intercept and process network packets. Each hook function is called with a pointer to the **sk_buff** structure representing the intercepted packet and other relevant information.

Hook functions can examine packet headers, perform packet filtering based on configurable rules, modify packet contents, and take appropriate actions such as accepting, dropping, or forwarding packets.

In addition to hooks and hook functions, the Netfilter subsystem includes other components such as the Netfilter core, which manages hook registration and packet traversal, and various kernel modules that implement specific packet filtering and NAT functionalities.

Common Netfilter modules include iptables for packet filtering and firewalling, ip6tables for IPv6 packet filtering, ebtables for Ethernet frame filtering, and conntrack for connection tracking and NAT. Netfilter provides a flexible and extensible framework for building complex packet filtering and firewalling solutions in Linux-based systems.

Packet routing in the different layers of the GNU Linux kernel network stack is shown in the following figure:

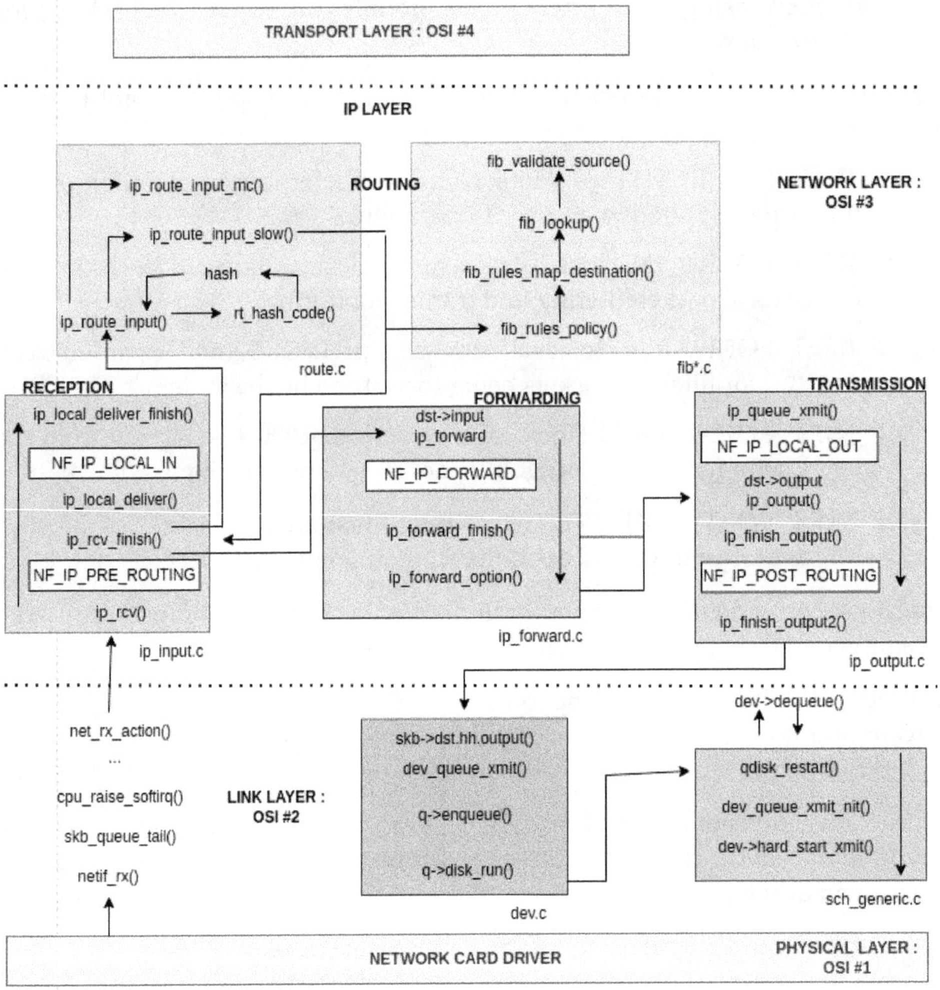

Figure 8.4: Very deep the GNU/Linux netword stack

A network card uses two lists to manage packets, namely incoming packets (**rx_ring**) and outgoing packets (**tx_ring**) of the network interfaces. We can thus distinguish the transmission procedure from the reception procedure. For very old kernels such as 2.2 and below, frame processing was different (e.g., we cannot find the **tx** and **rx** files).

Netfilter framework in the Linux kernel to intercept packets at the **PRE_ROUTING** hook and manipulate them accordingly.

Here is an explanation of the main components and functions useful for that purpose:

- **hook_func_tunnel_in function:**
  - This function serves as the callback for the Netfilter hook **NF_IP_PRE_ROUTING**, which intercepts packets before routing decisions are made.

- o It receives parameters including the hook number, a pointer to the **sk_buff** structure, input and output network devices, and a function pointer for invoking the next hook function.

- o The function first retrieves the **sk_buff** structure and extracts the IP header.

- o It then checks if the packet is received from a specific input network device (**"eth0"**) and if the destination IP address matches a predefined value (**ip1**).

- o If the conditions are met, the function performs tunneling by modifying the packet's MAC header, adjusting the packet length, and enqueuing the packet for transmission on another network device (**"eth1"**).

- o Finally, the function returns **NF_STOLEN** to indicate that it has taken ownership of the packet.

- **init_module function:**

  - o This function serves as the entry point for initializing the Netfilter module.

  - o It sets up a Netfilter hook object (**nfho_tunnel_in**) with the specified hook function (**hook_func_tunnel_in**), hook number (**NF_IP_PRE_ROUTING**), protocol family (**PF_INET**), and priority (**NF_IP_PRI_FIRST**).

  - o The **nf_register_hook** function registers the hook object with the Netfilter framework, allowing it to intercept packets at the specified hook point.

- **cleanup_module function:**

  - o This function serves as the exit point for cleaning up the Netfilter module.

  - o It unregisters the previously registered hook object (**nfho_tunnel_in**) using the **nf_unregister_hook** function.

To build and install this Netfilter kernel module, follow these steps:

1. Save the provided code into a file, e.g., **nf_hook.c**.

2. Set up a Linux kernel development environment on your system.

3. Compile the module using the appropriate kernel build tools (**gcc**, **make**, etc.).

4. Load the module into the kernel using **insmod**.

5. Verify that the module is loaded and functioning as expected using **lsmod** and appropriate logging mechanisms (**dmesg**, **journalctl**, etc.).

The following Linux kernel module implements a Netfilter hook to intercept and redirect IPv4 packets. It captures packets on **eth0** with a specific destination IP, modifies their MAC headers, and forwards them to **eth1** via the queuing discipline. The module uses **NF_STOLEN** to handle packet ownership, ensuring efficient in-kernel tunneling:

```
#include <linux/module.h>
#include <linux/kernel.h>
#include <linux/netfilter.h>
#include <linux/netfilter_ipv4.h>
#include <linux/skbuff.h>
#include <linux/ip.h>
#include <linux/netdevice.h>


static unsigned int hook_func_tunnel_in(unsigned int hooknum,
                                         struct sk_buff *skb,
                                         const struct net_device *in,
                                         const struct net_device *out,
                                         int (*okfn)(struct sk_buff *)) {
    struct iphdr *ip_header;
    struct net_device *dev;
    struct Qdisc *q;
    int len;

    // Check if the packet has IP header
    if (!skb || !skb_network_header(skb))
        return NF_ACCEPT;


    ip_header = ip_hdr(skb);

    // Check if the packet is IPv4
    if (ip_header->version != 4)
        return NF_ACCEPT;


    // Check if the packet is received from eth0 and destination IP is ip1
    if (in && strcmp(in->name, "eth0") == 0 && ip_header->daddr ==
htonl(ip1)) {
        len = skb->len;

        // Perform tunneling
        skb_push(skb, ETH_HLEN);
        skb_reset_mac_header(skb);
        memcpy(skb->data, hd_mac2, ETH_ALEN * 2);
```

```
        // Enqueue the packet for transmission on eth1
        dev = dev_get_by_name("eth1");
        if (!dev)
            return NF_ACCEPT;

        q = dev->qdisc;
        spin_lock_bh(&dev->queue_lock);
        q->enqueue(skb, q);
        qdisc_run(dev);
        spin_unlock_bh(&dev->queue_lock);

        return NF_STOLEN; // Indicate that we have taken ownership of the
packet
    }

    return NF_ACCEPT; // Allow the packet to proceed normally
}

// Netfilter hook structure
static struct nf_hook_ops nfho_tunnel_in = {
    .hook = hook_func_tunnel_in,
    .hooknum = NF_INET_PRE_ROUTING, // Use NF_INET_PRE_ROUTING for IPv4
    .pf = NFPROTO_IPV4, // Use NFPROTO_IPV4 for IPv4
    .priority = NF_IP_PRI_FIRST,
};

// Module initialization function
static int __init nf_hook_init(void) {
    int ret;

    // Register the Netfilter hook
    ret = nf_register_hook(&nfho_tunnel_in);
    if (ret < 0) {
        printk(KERN_ERR "Failed to register Netfilter hook\n");
        return ret;
    }
```

```
    printk(KERN_INFO "NF_HOOK: Module installed\n");
    return 0;
}


// Module cleanup function
static void __exit nf_hook_exit(void) {
    // Unregister the Netfilter hook
    nf_unregister_hook(&nfho_tunnel_in);

    printk(KERN_INFO "NF_HOOK: Module removed\n");
}


module_init(nf_hook_init);
module_exit(nf_hook_exit);


MODULE_LICENSE("GPL");
MODULE_AUTHOR("BPB");
MODULE_DESCRIPTION("Netfilter hook example");
```

Here are the main lines of the above code:

- **Lines 1/7**: Header inclusion: Added necessary header files for Netfilter, skb, IP header, and netdevice.

- **Line 20**: Function parameter checks: Added checks to ensure that function parameters (skb, in) are not NULL before accessing their members.

- **Line 26**: IPv4 check: Added a check to ensure that the packet is IPv4 before accessing its IP header.

- **Line 30**: Endian conversion: Used **htonl()** to convert the destination IP address to network byte order before comparing it with ip1.

- **Line 52**: Return values: Changed return value from **NF_STOLEN** to **NF_ACCEPT** for packets that are not modified to avoid unnecessary processing.

- **Lines 63 and 86**: Module initialization: Renamed **init_module()** to **nf_hook_init()** for clarity and consistency. Also, added error handling for registering the Netfilter hook.

- **Line 79 and 87**: Module cleanup: Renamed **cleanup_module()** to **nf_hook_exit()** for clarity and consistency.

- **Lines 89/91**: Module information: Added module metadata such as license, author, and description.

To build and install this Netfilter kernel module:

1. Compile the module using appropriate kernel build tools (**make**, **gcc**, etc.)

2. Load the module into the kernel using **insmod**

3. Verify that the module is loaded and functioning as expected using appropriate logging mechanisms (**dmesg ...**)

Note about the ARP protocol: On transmission, only packets of type ETH_P_ALL can be captured. It is important to note that, as with the path followed by frames in the kernel, the functions used in packet handling can change depending on the version of the kernel used.

To retrieve ARP frames, simply register a **packet_type** structure in one of the **ptype** lists (**ptype_base or ptype_all**) with the **dev_add_pack()** callback function (defined in **linux/netdevice.h**).

As with **netfilter** hooks, this hook (packet handling) must be removed when the module is removed from the kernel. This is done using the **dev_remove_pack()** function (**linux/ netdevice.h**).

By registering a function for **ETH_P_ALL** our packet type will be found in the **ptype_all** list. We will thus recover all the frames arriving (or destined) from the network card driver.

When we retrieve a **sk_buffer** with this type of hook, it is, in fact, a copy of the captured **sk_buffer** on which we will work. The copy must be destroyed at the end of the function with the **kfree_skb()** function.

This type of hook is therefore not intended to modify the captured packet.

Protocols layer

The Linux network stack and networking protocols are organized into several layers, following the **Open Systems Interconnection (OSI)** model or the TCP/IP model.

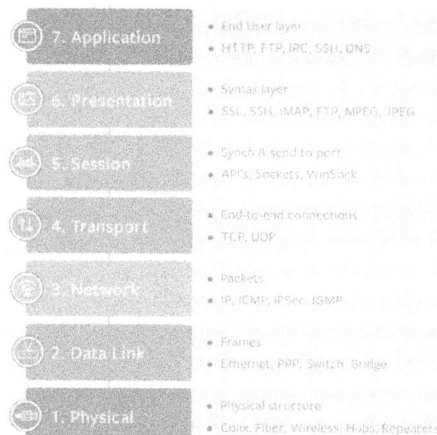

Figure 8.5: The OSI network stack architecture

These layers facilitate the exchange of data between devices over a network and provide a structured framework for implementing network communication. Here is an introduction to each layer within the Linux network stack:

- **Link layer (Layer 2):**

  o The link layer is responsible for transmitting data frames between directly connected devices over a physical or logical link.

  o In Linux, the link layer is implemented by device drivers and includes protocols such as Ethernet, Wi-Fi (802.11), and **Point-to-Point Protocol (PPP)**.

  o Device drivers handle tasks such as frame encapsulation and de-encapsulation, error detection and correction, and **Media Access Control (MAC)** address resolution.

  o Examples of Linux device drivers include e1000 for Intel Ethernet cards and ath9k for Atheros Wi-Fi adapters.

- **Network layer (Layer 3):**

  o The network layer is responsible for routing packets between different networks and ensuring end-to-end delivery of data.

  o In Linux, the network layer is primarily implemented by the IP (Internet Protocol) suite, including IPv4 and IPv6.

  o IP handles tasks such as addressing, packet fragmentation and reassembly, routing, and error reporting.

  o The Linux kernel includes protocol implementations such as ipv4 and ipv6 for IPv4 and IPv6, respectively, as well as support for advanced routing features and network namespaces.

- **Transport layer (Layer 4):**

  o The transport layer is responsible for providing end-to-end communication between applications running on different hosts.

  o In Linux, the transport layer includes protocols such as **Transmission Control Protocol (TCP)** and **User Datagram Protocol (UDP)**.

  o TCP provides reliable, connection-oriented communication with features such as flow control, congestion control, and error recovery.

  o UDP provides unreliable, connectionless communication with minimal overhead, making it suitable for real-time applications such as streaming media and online gaming.

  o The Linux kernel includes protocol implementations such as **tcp** and **udp** for TCP and UDP, respectively, as well as support for socket-based communication through system calls like **socket()**, **bind()**, **connect()**, **send()**, and **recv()**.

- **Application layer (Layer 5-7):**

  o The application layer encompasses various protocols and services that enable specific network applications and services.

  o In Linux, the application layer includes protocols such as **Hypertext Transfer Protocol (HTTP)**, **File Transfer Protocol (FTP)**, **Simple Mail Transfer Protocol (SMTP)**, and **Domain Name System (DNS)**.

  o Applications running on Linux utilize these protocols through libraries and APIs provided by the operating system or third-party software.

  o Examples of application layer services in Linux include the Apache HTTP Server for serving web pages, the Postfix mail server for sending and receiving email, and the BIND DNS server for resolving domain names.

The following table lists the evolution of network protocol implementation over time:

Kernel release	Protocol support
1.x (Early)	Basic TCP/IP networking (IPV4, TCP, UDP, ICMP)
2.0 (1996)	IPV4, TCP, UDP, ICMP, ETHERNET, PPP, SLIP
2.2 (1999)	IPV4 (with enhancements), ARP, RARP, IP forwarding and routing, Ethenrt, PPP, SLIP, DHCP, BOOTP, VLAN tagging
2.4 (2001)	IPV4 (with improvements), IPV6 (early support), IPSEC, ARP, RARP, IP forwarding and routing, Ethernet, PPP
2.6 (2003)	IPV4, IPV6, ARP, RARP, IP forwarding and routing, Ethernet, PPP, VLAN tagging, IGMP, Multicast
3.x (2011)	IPV4, IPV6 (with refinements), ARP, RARP, IP forwarding and routing, Ethernet, PPP, VLAN tagging, IGMP, Multicast
4.x (2015)	IPV4, IPV6, ARP, RARP, IP forwarding and routing, Ethernet, PPP, VLAN tagging, IGMP, Multicast

Table 8.1: Evolution of the protocols by GNU/Linux release

Network module

A network driver in the context of GNU/Linux is a software component responsible for enabling communication between the Linux kernel and network hardware devices.

These drivers are essential for the functioning of **network interface cards** (**NICs**), wireless adapters, and other network devices. Let us take a closer look at the key components and features of a GNU/Linux network driver:

- **Device driver interface:**

  o Network drivers in Linux are typically implemented as kernel modules or built directly into the kernel.

- o They interact with the Linux kernel through the **Network Device Interface Specification** (**NDIS**), which provides a standardized interface for network drivers to register themselves, handle network device operations, and communicate with higher layers of the networking stack.

- **Hardware abstraction:**

  - o Network drivers abstract the details of the underlying network hardware, providing a uniform interface to the Linux kernel and network stack.

  - o They manage hardware-specific tasks such as initializing the device, configuring hardware parameters (e.g., MAC address, MTU), handling interrupts, and transmitting and receiving network packets.

- **Packet processing:**

  - o Network drivers are responsible for transmitting outgoing network packets from the kernel to the network device and receiving incoming packets from the device to the kernel.

  - o They implement packet transmission and reception logic, including buffer management, packet queuing, and **Direct Memory Access** (**DMA**) operations for efficient data transfer between system memory and the network device.

- **Interrupt handling:**

  - o Network drivers handle interrupts generated by the network device to signal the arrival of incoming packets, completion of transmission operations, or occurrence of hardware events.

  - o They register interrupt handlers with the Linux kernel to respond to interrupt signals, process incoming packets, and perform necessary operations to maintain network connectivity and performance.

- **Error handling and recovery:**

  - o Network drivers implement error detection and recovery mechanisms to handle hardware errors, network failures, and other exceptional conditions.

  - o They monitor the status of the network device, detect errors or anomalies, and take appropriate actions such as resetting the device, retrying failed operations, or reporting errors to the kernel for further processing.

- **Configuration and management:**

  - o Network drivers expose configuration parameters and statistics through the Linux `sysfs` interface, allowing administrators to query and adjust driver settings dynamically.

  - o They support features such as link aggregation, VLAN tagging, promiscuous mode, and offloading capabilities (e.g., checksum offload, segmentation offload) to optimize network performance and functionality.

Network drivers in GNU/Linux include the e1000e driver for Intel Gigabit Ethernet controllers, the ath9k driver for Atheros wireless LAN adapters, and the ixgbe driver for Intel 10 Gigabit Ethernet adapters.

A network driver is the third category of Linux drivers after block drivers and characters.

The operation of a network interface within the system is quite similar to a driver of blocks. A block driver is used by the core to transmit or receive blocks of data. From a similar point of view, a network driver registers with the kernel to be able to exchange packets of data with the outside world.

There is, however, a difference with the block driver, which consists of not having an entry point in the dedicated directory to devices **/dev**. It is therefore not possible to apply the rule that says that under Unix/GNU Linux, everything is considered a file.

The most important difference between these two types of drivers is that the block driver is only used when the driver calls on it, while a network driver receives packets from the network outside asynchronously.

Thus, while a block driver requires before sending something be sent to the kernel, the network driver asks to push data.

The following figure shows a breakdown of the different categories of GNU/Linux kernel drivers:

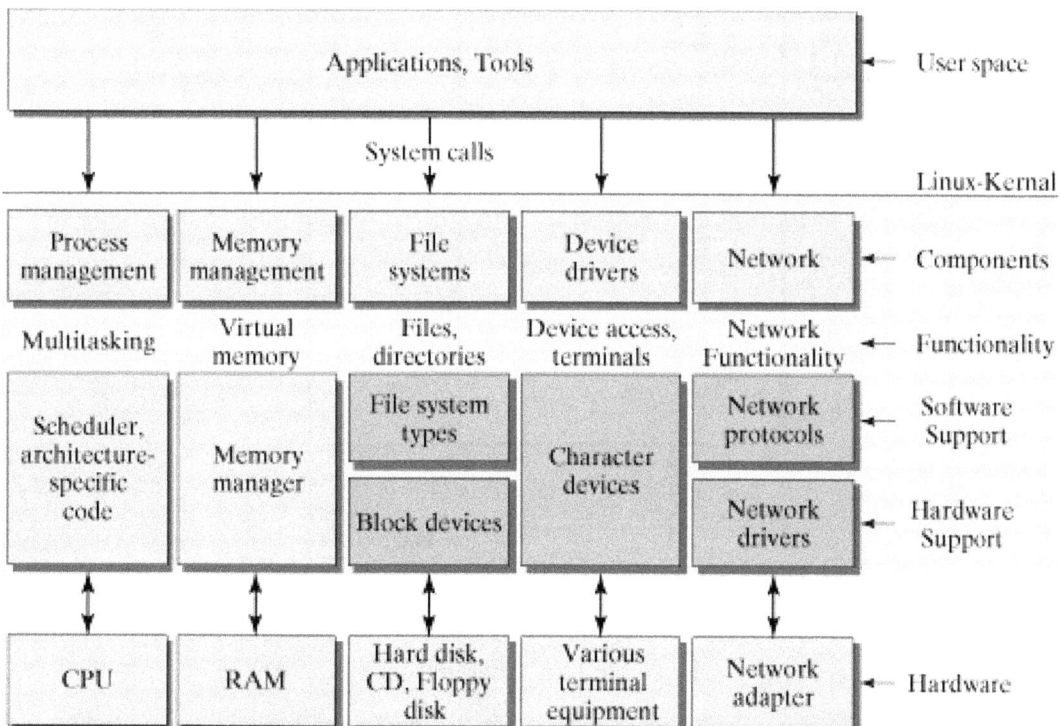

Figure 8.6: Category of drivers under GNU/Linux.

The network architecture allows the Linux kernel to connect to other systems over the network.

There is a significant number of hardware and a significant number of supported protocols.

Each network object is represented via a socket. Sockets are associated with processes in the same sense that i-nodes in a file system can be associated.

A socket can be shared by several processes.

The network architecture uses the Linux kernel process scheduler **schedule()** to suspend or resume a process in a state waiting for data (managed by a control and data flow management system).

In addition, the VFS layer provides a logical file system (as in the case of NFS; there are possibilities in user mode via **libfuse**).

The following figure shows details of the different blocks interacting with both VFS and the network stack:

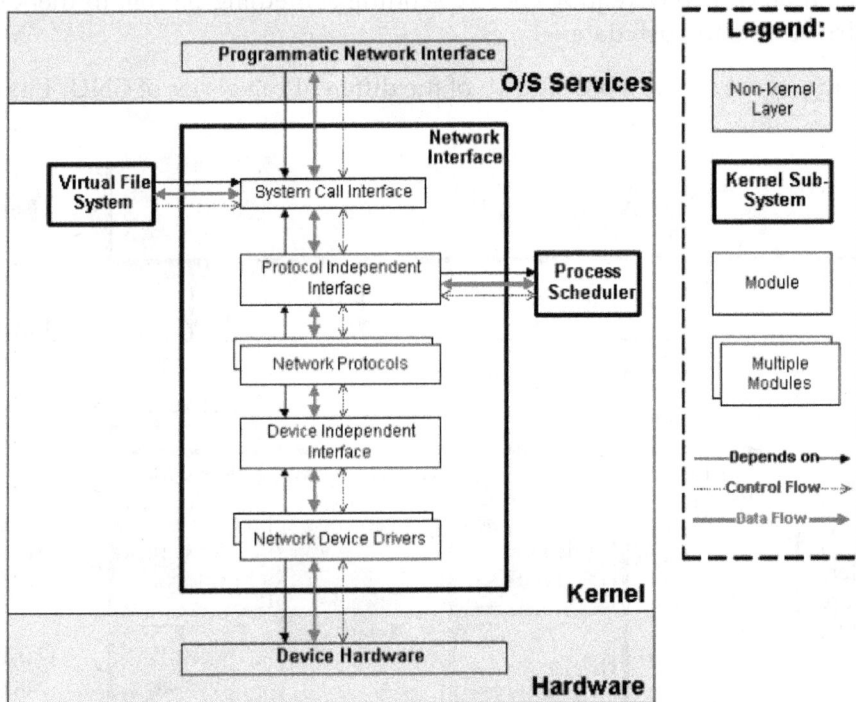

Figure 8.7: Modular or layered division of the network stack under GNU/Linux

All cards can interact with the kernel in two different ways:

- **Polling**: The kernel checks the status of the device at regular intervals to see if there is anything to do.

- **Interrupts**: The card sends a signal to the kernel in the form of an interrupt to tell it that there is something to do:

  - ○ **Hardware**: It accepts incoming packets from network interfaces and positions them directly in the input queue.

  - ○ **Software (NET_RX_SOFTIRQ)**: Executes the receive packet handle. It is responsible for managing protocols. Incoming packets are handled by this interrupt and placed in a queue. The packets to be forwarded are placed in the output queue of the output interface.

Example of code from the source code of the network drivers (**drivers/net/3c59x.c**) intended for Kernel 2.2.14. There are a significant number of **#ifdef MODULEs** and **#if defined (MODULE)**:

```
#if defined(MODULE) && LINUX_VERSION_CODE > 0x20115
MODULE_AUTHOR("Donald Becker <becker@cesdis.gsfc.nasa.gov>");
MODULE_DESCRIPTION("3Com 3c590/3c900 series Vortex/Boomerang driver");
MODULE_PARM(debug, "i");
...
#endif
...
#ifdef MODULE
int init_module(void)
{
...
}
#else
int tc59x_probe(struct device *dev)
{
...
}
#endif /* not MODULE */
```

This is quite representative of the old way of programming which defined the operation of a dynamic module based on how it was compiled as a static module within a kernel image.

```
...
static int vortex_scan(struct device *dev, struct pci_id_info pci_tbl[])
{
...
#if defined(CONFIG_PCI) || (defined(MODULE) && !defined(NO_PCI))
```

```
...
#ifdef MODULE
if (compaq_ioaddr) {
vortex_probe1(0, 0, dev, compaq_ioaddr, compaq_irq,
compaq_device_id, cards_found++);
dev = 0;
}
#endif
return cards_found ? 0 : -ENODEV;
}
...
#ifdef MODULE
void cleanup_module(void)
{
... ... ...
}
#endif
```

In this new version, pre-processing directives are no longer necessary, which removes all **#ifdef** and **#endif**. This makes it easier to read for driver developers through the use of a set of macros (**_ _init, _ _exit, and _ _devinitdata**):

```
static char version[] _ _devinitdata = DRV_NAME " ... ";
static struct vortex_chip_info {
...
}

vortex_info_tbl[] _ _devinitdata = {
{"3c590 Vortex 10Mbps",
... ... ...
}

static int _ _init vortex_init (void)
{
...
}

static void _ _exit vortex_cleanup (void)
{
...
```

```
}

module_init(vortex_init);
module_exit(vortex_cleanup);
```

Here is a sample of code that can manage a network card:

```c
#include <linux/module.h>
#include <linux/pci.h>
#include <linux/netdevice.h>
#include <linux/etherdevice.h>

#define DRIVER_NAME "my_ethernet_driver"

struct my_priv_data {
    struct net_device *netdev;
    struct pci_dev *pdev;
    // Add any driver-specific data here
};

static int my_probe(struct pci_dev *pdev, const struct pci_device_id *ent)
{
    struct my_priv_data *priv;
    struct net_device *netdev;

    // Allocate memory for driver private data
    priv = kzalloc(sizeof(struct my_priv_data), GFP_KERNEL);
    if (!priv)
        return -ENOMEM;

    // Initialize PCI device
    if (pci_enable_device(pdev))
        goto err_free_priv;

    // Enable bus mastering and set up other PCI configuration
    pci_set_master(pdev);

    // Allocate and initialize network device structure
    netdev = alloc_etherdev(sizeof(struct my_priv_data));
```

```
    if (!netdev)
        goto err_disable_dev;

    priv->netdev = netdev;
    priv->pdev = pdev;

    // Set up device-specific parameters (e.g., MAC address, MTU)
    // Example: ether_setup(netdev);

    // Set up driver-specific data and functions
    // Example: netdev->netdev_ops = &my_netdev_ops;

    // Register network device with kernel
    if (register_netdev(netdev))
        goto err_free_netdev;

    // Add device-specific initialization code here

    return 0;

err_free_netdev:
    free_netdev(netdev);
err_disable_dev:
    pci_disable_device(pdev);
err_free_priv:
    kfree(priv);
    return -ENODEV;
}

static void my_remove(struct pci_dev *pdev)
{
    struct my_priv_data *priv = pci_get_drvdata(pdev);
    struct net_device *netdev = priv->netdev;

    // Unregister network device
    unregister_netdev(netdev);
```

```
    // Free network device structure
    free_netdev(netdev);

    // Disable PCI device
    pci_disable_device(pdev);

    // Free driver private data
    kfree(priv);
}

// PCI device ID table
static const struct pci_device_id my_pci_tbl[] = {
    { PCI_DEVICE(0x1234, 0x5678) }, // Vendor and device IDs
    { 0, },
};
MODULE_DEVICE_TABLE(pci, my_pci_tbl);

// PCI driver structure
static struct pci_driver my_driver = {
    .name = DRIVER_NAME,
    .id_table = my_pci_tbl,
    .probe = my_probe,
    .remove = my_remove,
};

// Module initialization
static int __init my_init(void)
{
    return pci_register_driver(&my_driver);
}

// Module cleanup
static void __exit my_exit(void)
{
    pci_unregister_driver(&my_driver);
}
```

```
module_init(my_init);
module_exit(my_exit);

MODULE_LICENSE("GPL");
MODULE_AUTHOR("BPB");
MODULE_DESCRIPTION("My Ethernet Driver");
```

Now, let us explain the main technical aspects of this code:

- **Includes and definitions:**
  - This code includes necessary headers for Linux kernel module development (`<linux/module.h>`, `<linux/pci.h>`, `<linux/netdevice.h>`, `<linux/etherdevice.h>`).
  - It defines a macro for the driver name (**DRIVER_NAME**).

- **Driver data structures:**
  - **struct my_priv_data**: This structure holds driver-specific data, such as pointers to the network device (**netdev**) and PCI device (**pdev**).

- **Probe function (my_probe):**
  - This function is called when the driver is loaded and a matching PCI device is detected.
  - It initializes the PCI device, allocates memory for the driver's private data, sets up the network device, and registers the device with the kernel.

- **Remove function (my_remove):**
  - This function is called when the driver is unloaded, or the associated PCI device is removed.
  - It unregisters the network device, frees allocated resources, and disables the PCI device.

- **PCI device ID table:**
  - **my_pci_tbl**: This table lists the PCI device IDs supported by the driver.

- **PCI driver structure:**
  - **my_driver**: This structure defines the PCI driver, including its name, supported device IDs, probe function, and remove function.

- **Module initialization and cleanup:**
  - **my_init**: This function is called when the module is loaded into the kernel. It registers the PCI driver with the kernel.

- ○ **my_exit**: This function is called when the module is unloaded from the kernel. It unregisters the PCI driver.

- **Module information**: `MODULE_LICENSE`, `MODULE_AUTHOR`, and `MODULE_DESCRIPTION` macros provide information about the module, such as its license, author, and description.

Network driver loading

When dynamically loading a network driver into the kernel, Kmod is the mechanism responsible for modules in the GNU/Linux kernel. Loading initializes the name of the module (**argv[0]**) to load. If instead of using **insmod**, **modprobe** is used, **kmod** will examine the **/etc/modprobe.conf** configuration to see if there are any dependencies.

The following figure shows the dynamic loading of a network driver:

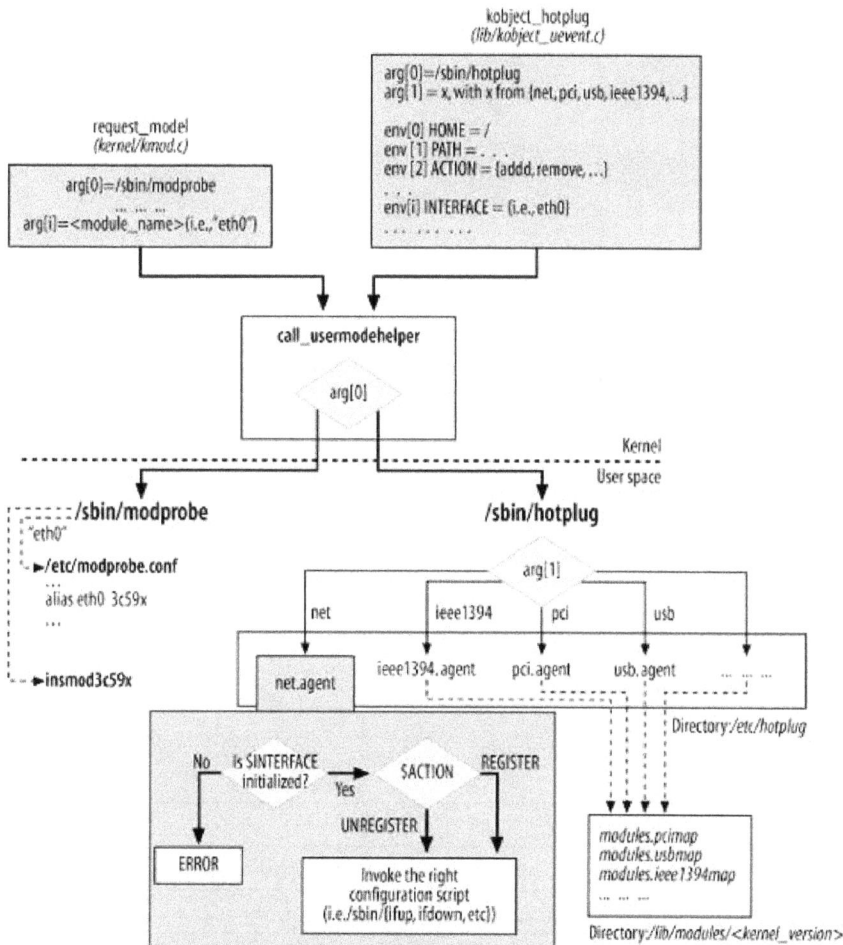

Figure 8.8: The dynamic module loading

List of memory sections that can be initialized by macros in network drivers:

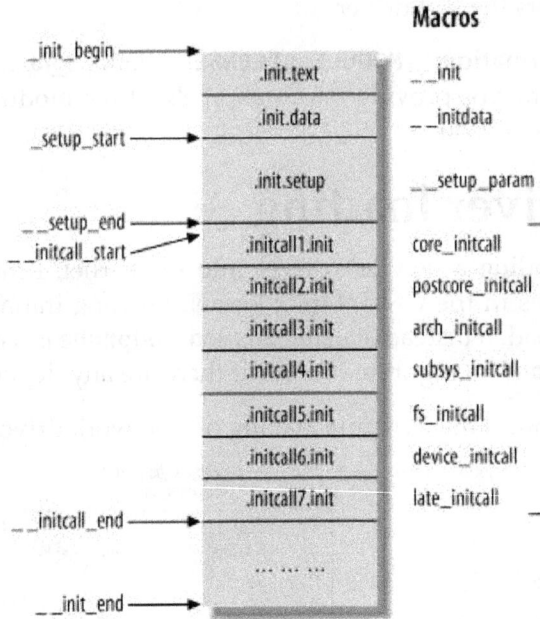

Figure 8.9: Useful macros

Most of these macros are defined in the **include/linux/init.h** header:

Macro	Description
__init	Initialization routine during the boot sequence.
__exit	Called when the kernel component is unloaded from the kernel.
core_initcall, postcore_ initcall, arch_initcall, subsys_initcall, fs_initcall, device_initcall, late_initcall	Set of routines to change the order of priority in the virtualization routines executed during the BOOT sequence.
__initcall	Obsolete macro.
__exitcall	Formerly called by the driver exit routine when unloading it.
_initdata	Initializes a structure to the BOOT sequence.
_exitdata	Initializes a structure to the BOOT sequence.

Table 8.2: Details of some macros

The following figure describes the state machine for registering a network device:

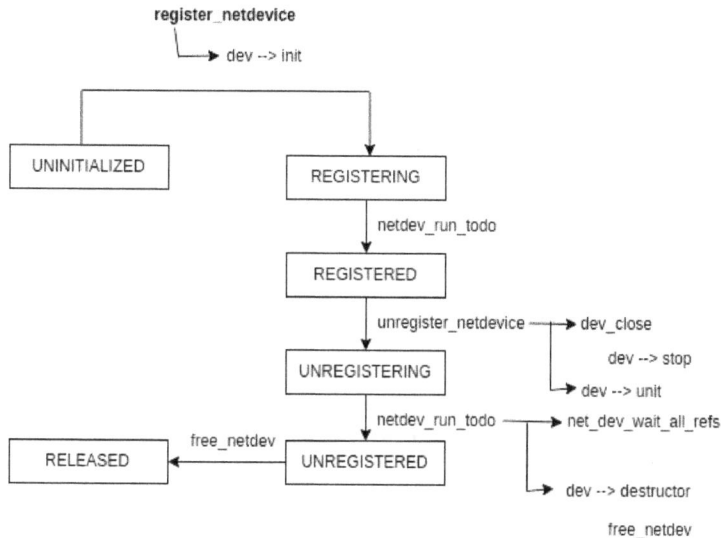

Figure 8.10: Network driver loading

When a network driver loads into the Linux kernel, several stages occur to initialize the driver and make it operational. Here are the main steps involved:

- **Detection and initialization:**
  - When the Linux kernel boots, it scans the system's hardware to detect network devices.
  - If a network device is detected, the kernel loads the appropriate driver module or firmware to initialize the device.
  - This detection process can occur through various mechanisms, such as PCI bus enumeration, USB device detection, or platform-specific probes.

- **Driver registration:**
  - Once a network device is detected and the appropriate driver module is loaded, the driver registers itself with the Linux kernel.
  - Registration involves providing callbacks and data structures to the kernel that define how the driver interacts with the networking subsystem.
  - The driver registers itself with the kernel's network device interface, which manages network devices and their associated drivers.

- **Initialization of data structures:**
  - Upon registration, the driver initializes internal data structures and resources required for packet processing and device management.

- o This includes allocating memory buffers for packet transmission and reception, setting up DMA operations, and initializing hardware registers.

- **Device configuration:**

  - o The driver configures the network device according to its capabilities and the system's network configuration.

  - o This may involve setting parameters such as the device's MAC address, **maximum transmission unit (MTU)**, operating mode (e.g., promiscuous mode), and interrupt handling settings.

- **Interrupt handling setup:**

  - o If the network device generates interrupts to signal events such as packet reception or transmission completion, the driver sets up interrupt handling.

  - o This typically involves registering interrupt handlers with the kernel to handle interrupts generated by the network device.

  - o Interrupt handling routines are responsible for processing incoming packets, managing packet queues, and coordinating packet transmission.

- **Device activation:**

  - o Once initialized and configured, the network device is activated and ready to send and receive network packets.

  - o The driver may enable the device's transmit and receive queues, start DMA operations, and put the device into an operational state.

- **Kernel notification:**

  - o After the network driver completes its initialization process, it may notify the kernel or other system components that the device is ready for use.

  - o This notification may involve sending system log messages, emitting events via the kernel's event subsystem, or updating system status indicators.

The sk_buff

When a packet must be sent or received by the network card, a **sk_buff** is created. A packet inserted in the network stack will never be copied until it passes into the **userspace** part or a possible deletion.

This control structure consists in particular:

- Structures representing the Ethernet, network, and transport layers

- Pointers for managing the **sk_buffer** in the list of **sk_buffers**

- Information about input/output devices
- Information on the type of packet (broadcast, multicast, etc.)
- Of the buffer containing the packet itself

Description of a memory block associated with a **sk_buffer**, one empty and the other initialized with a memory block initialized with a packet.

This header used by the doubly linked list allows efficient management of packets in the Network stack. The left half of the following figure shows a memory block not initialized, and the right figure is a memory block initialized:

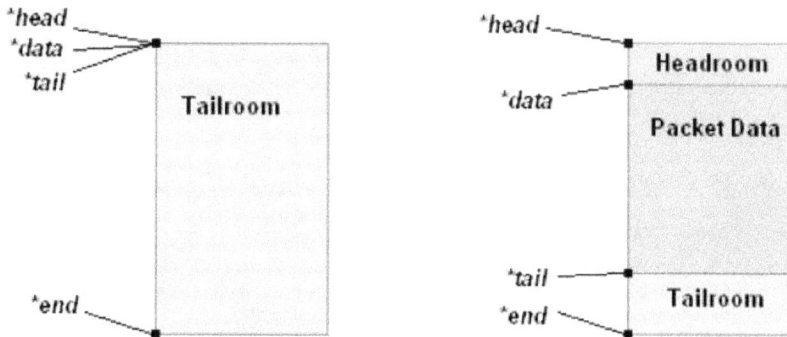

Figure 8.11: Detail of the sk_buf head

A description of how single or double chain lists are used will be discussed in a further chapter.

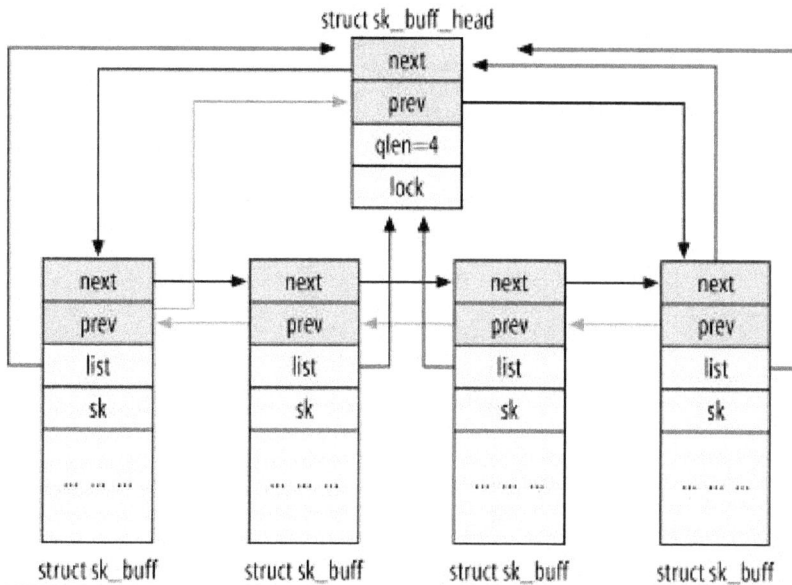

Figure 8.12: Double-chained list of network stack packets

The head is defined by the following data struct:

```
struct sk_buff_head {
    /* These two members must be first. */
    struct sk_buff  *next;
    struct sk_buff  *prev;

    __u32       qlen;
    spinlock_t  lock;
};
```

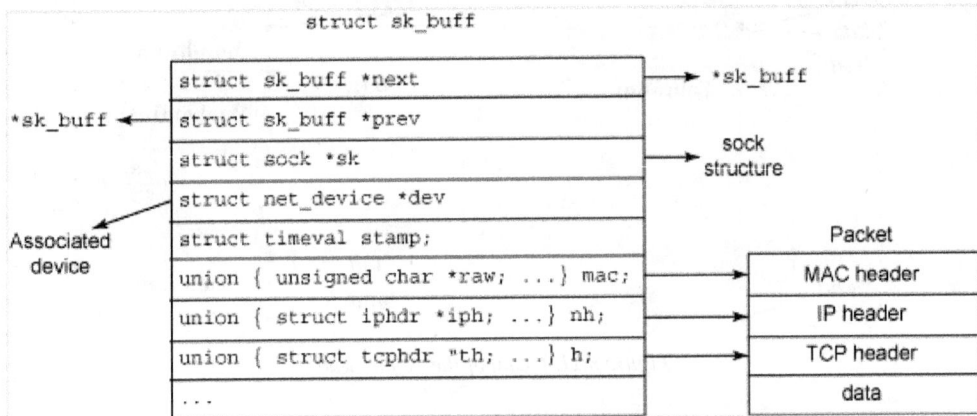

Figure 8.13: Detail of the head sk_buff

Its initialization is quite simple:

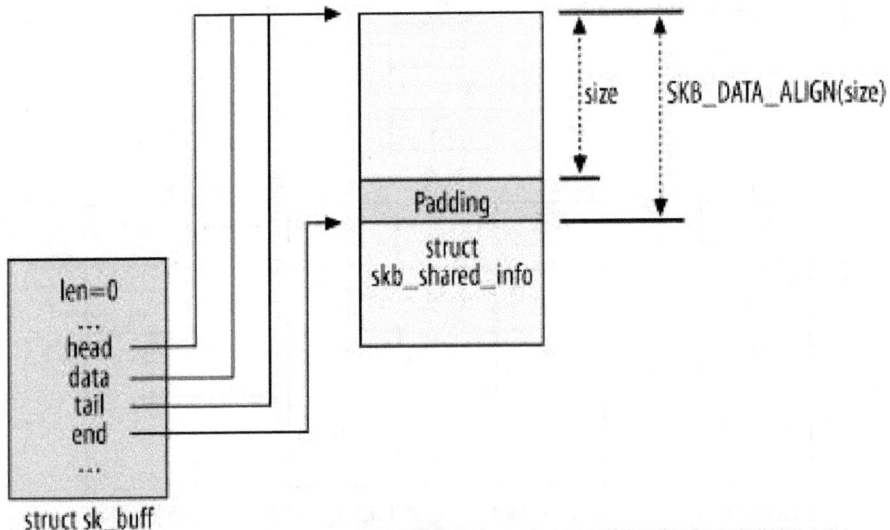

Figure 8.14: Initialization of the sk_buff double chained list

Here are some of the main macros and functions used to work with **sk_buff** structures:

- **Macro: skb_alloc(size, priority, fclone)**: Allocates a new **sk_buff** structure with the specified size.
    - **size**: Size of the data buffer to allocate.
    - **priority**: Priority level for the allocation.
    - **fclone**: Flag indicating whether to allocate a full clone (deep copy) of the buffer.
    - **Example**: `skb_alloc(1500, GFP_KERNEL, 0)`

- **Macro: skb_clone(skb, priority)**: Creates a shallow copy of an existing **sk_buff** structure.
    - **skb**: Pointer to the original **sk_buff** structure.
    - **priority**: Priority level for the allocation.
    - **Example**: `skb_clone(skb_orig, GFP_KERNEL)`

- **Function: skb_put(skb, len)**: Adjusts the tail pointer of an **sk_buff** structure to make space for additional data.
    - **skb**: Pointer to the **sk_buff** structure.
    - **len**: Number of bytes to add to the buffer.
    - Returns a pointer to the start of the added space.
    - **Example**: `skb_put(skb, 100)`

- **Function: skb_pull(skb, len)**: Removes data from the start of an **sk_buff** structure.
    - **skb**: Pointer to the **sk_buff** structure.
    - **len**: Number of bytes to remove from the buffer.
    - **Example**: `skb_pull(skb, 50)`

- **Function: skb_reserve(skb, len)**: Reserves space at the head of an **sk_buff** structure for additional headers.
    - **skb**: Pointer to the **sk_buff** structure.
    - **len**: Number of bytes to reserve.
    - **Example**: `skb_reserve(skb, 32)`

- **Function: skb_copy_expand(skb, new_len, headroom, tailroom)**: Copies the contents of an **sk_buff** structure to a new buffer with an expanded size and additional **headroom**/**tailroom**.
    - **skb**: Pointer to the original **sk_buff** structure.
    - **new_len**: New size of the buffer.

- o **headroom**: Additional headroom to reserve.

- o **tailroom**: Additional `tailroom` to reserve.

- o Returns a pointer to the new **sk_buff** structure.

- o **Example: `skb_copy_expand(skb_orig, new_len, 16, 16)`**

- **Function: skb_clone_sk(skb)**: Creates a deep copy of an **sk_buff** structure, including associated socket and transport headers.

  - o **skb**: Pointer to the original **sk_buff** structure.

  - o Returns a pointer to the cloned **sk_buff** structure.

  - o **Example: `skb_clone_sk(skb_orig)`**

Performance and tuning

Tuning the GNU/Linux network stack involves adjusting various parameters to optimize network performance, throughput, latency, and resource utilization for specific workloads and environments.

Here is a wide and comprehensive set of parameters commonly used for tuning the GNU/Linux network stack:

- **TCP/IP parameters:**

  - o **net.ipv4.tcp_mem**: Defines the minimum, initial, and maximum amount of memory allocated for TCP buffers.

  - o **net.ipv4.tcp_window_scaling**: Enables TCP window scaling to support large bandwidth-delay products.

  - o **net.ipv4.tcp_timestamps**: Enables TCP timestamps for round-trip time measurements and congestion control.

  - o **net.ipv4.tcp_sack**: Enables **Selective Acknowledgment (SACK)** for more efficient retransmission of lost packets.

  - o **net.ipv4.tcp_syncookies**: Enables TCP SYN cookies to mitigate SYN flooding attacks.

  - o **net.ipv4.tcp_tw_reuse** and **net.ipv4.tcp_tw_recycle**: Controls TCP TIME-WAIT socket reuse and recycling behavior.

  - o **net.core.rmem_default** and **net.core.wmem_default**: Defines the default receive and send socket buffer sizes.

  - o **net.core.rmem_max and net.core.wmem_max**: Defines the maximum receive and send socket buffer sizes.

  - o **net.ipv4.tcp_keepalive_time**, **net.ipv4.tcp_keepalive_intvl**, **net.ipv4.tcp_keepalive_probes**: Configure TCP keepalive settings.

- **Network interface parameters:**

  o **net.core.netdev_max_backlog**: Sets the maximum length of the receive packet queue for network interfaces.

  o **net.core.dev_weight**: Adjusts the weight of network interfaces for load balancing.

  o **net.ipv4.tcp_mtu_probing**: Enables TCP **Maximum Transmission Unit (MTU)** probing for path MTU discovery.

  o **net.ipv4.tcp_congestion_control**: Specifies the TCP congestion control algorithm (e.g., `cubic`, `reno`, `bbr`).

- **Buffer and memory management parameters:**

  o **net.core.optmem_max**: Defines the maximum amount of memory that can be allocated for network-related buffers.

  o **net.ipv4.tcp_mem**: Specifies the minimum, initial, and maximum amount of memory allocated for TCP buffers.

  o **net.ipv4.udp_mem**: Specifies the minimum, initial, and maximum amount of memory allocated for UDP buffers.

  o **vm.dirty_background_bytes and vm.dirty_bytes**: Control the amount of dirty memory before triggering background and synchronous writes, respectively.

- **Packet processing parameters:**

  o **net.core.busy_poll**: Enables busy polling mode for reducing network latency.

  o **net.core.dev_weight**: Sets the weight of network interfaces for load balancing.

  o **net.core.somaxconn**: Specifies the maximum number of pending connections in the listen queue.

  o **net.ipv4.tcp_fastopen**: Enables TCP Fast Open for reducing connection establishment latency.

  o **net.ipv4.tcp_fin_timeout**: Specifies the timeout for closing inactive TCP connections.

- **Security and firewall parameters:**

  o **net.ipv4.conf.all.accept_redirects** and **net.ipv4.conf.all.secure_redirects**: Controls IPv4 ICMP redirect acceptance and secure redirect settings.

  o **net.ipv4.conf.default.rp_filter**: Sets the default **Reverse Path Filtering (RPFilter)** mode.

  o **net.ipv4.conf.all.accept_source_route**: Controls IPv4 source routing acceptance.

  o **net.ipv4.conf.all.log_martians**: Logs suspicious IPv4 packets (martians).

- **IPv6 parameters:**

  o Parameters similar to IPv4 counterparts for tuning IPv6 behavior.

  o **net.ipv6.conf.all.disable_ipv6**: Disables IPv6 on all interfaces.

- **Firewall parameters (iptables/nftables):**

  o Various parameters for configuring packet filtering, NAT, and connection tracking rules.

  o **netfilter** and **nft** commands can be used to manage firewall rules and settings.

All these parameters can be modified via the **sysctl** command. **sysctl** is a command-line utility in Linux used to view, set, and manage kernel parameters dynamically at runtime.

It allows administrators to configure various aspects of the kernel's behavior and performance, such as network settings, virtual memory management, and security options.

With **sysctl**, users can query the current values of kernel parameters, modify them temporarily, or persist changes across reboots by editing configuration files.

The **sysctl** command is commonly used for tasks such as adjusting network buffer sizes, enabling/disabling IP forwarding, tuning TCP parameters, and controlling process scheduling.

Administrators can explore available kernel parameters and their current values by using **sysctl -a**, while specific parameters can be modified using **sysctl -w**.

Configuration changes made with **sysctl** take effect immediately, affecting the behavior of the running system without requiring a reboot. However, to make changes persistent across reboots, administrators should update the appropriate configuration files, such as **/etc/sysctl.conf** or files in the **/etc/sysctl.d/** directory.

It is important to exercise caution when modifying kernel parameters with **sysctl**, as incorrect settings can potentially affect system stability, performance, and security.

The **sysctl** utility provides a powerful mechanism for fine-tuning the Linux kernel to suit specific workloads, hardware configurations, and security requirements.

Overall, **sysctl** is a versatile tool for system administrators to optimize and customize the behavior of the Linux kernel according to their needs.

Here is a study aimed at estimating the cost (time and memory consumption) of copying packets into the network stack: estimation of memory copies of a network packet from the network card to the BSD socket:

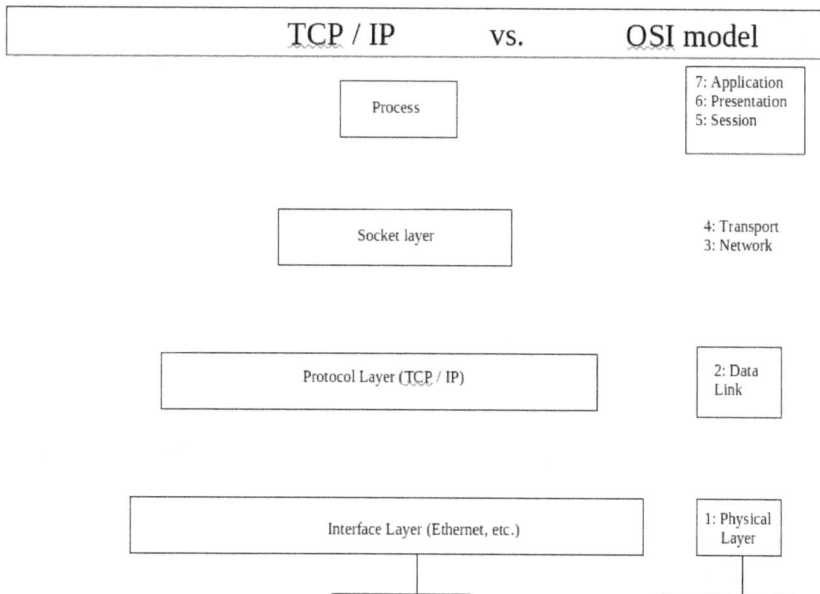

Figure 8.15: High-level view of the network stack used for the study

Zero-copy (or zero-copy networking) is an important concept in the design of network stacks, including Linux's network stack. It refers to a technique where data is transferred from one memory buffer to another without intermediate copying by the CPU.

Instead of copying data between kernel and user space or between different kernel buffers, zero-copy mechanisms allow data to be transferred directly from the source buffer to the destination buffer, typically through mechanisms like DMA.

Zero-copy networking is important for several reasons:

- **Reduced CPU overhead**: By eliminating the need for intermediate copying of data, zero-copy networking reduces CPU overhead associated with memory copies. This can lead to significant performance improvements, especially for high-speed networking applications that handle large volumes of data.

- **Lower latency**: Copying data between buffers involves CPU processing and memory access, which can introduce latency in packet processing. Zero-copy mechanisms minimize latency by bypassing these intermediate steps, allowing data to be transmitted more quickly through the network stack.

- **Improved throughput**: By reducing CPU overhead and latency, zero-copy networking can improve overall network throughput, enabling higher data transfer rates and better scalability for network-bound applications.

- **Better resource utilization**: Zero-copy networking can help optimize system resource utilization by reducing the amount of CPU time and memory bandwidth consumed by data copying operations. This can lead to more efficient use of available system resources and improved performance for multitasking and multi-threaded applications.

- **Energy efficiency**: By reducing CPU usage and memory accesses, zero-copy networking can contribute to improved energy efficiency in networked systems, particularly in power-constrained environments such as mobile devices and data centers.

In Linux, various mechanisms and APIs support zero-copy networking, including:

- **Socket Buffers (sk_buff)**: Linux's **sk_buff** data structure provides support for zero-copy networking by allowing network packets to be processed without intermediate copying between kernel and user space.

- **Direct I/O (DIO)**: Linux provides DIO interfaces such as **sendfile()** and **splice()** that support zero-copy data transfers between file descriptors and network sockets.

- **Memory-mapped I/O (mmap)**: Linux supports memory-mapped I/O (**mmap**) operations, allowing user space processes to access kernel buffers directly without copying data.

Overall, zero-copy networking is an essential optimization technique that helps improve the performance, efficiency, and scalability of networked systems, making it a valuable feature in modern network stacks like Linux.

Let us go into a little detail:

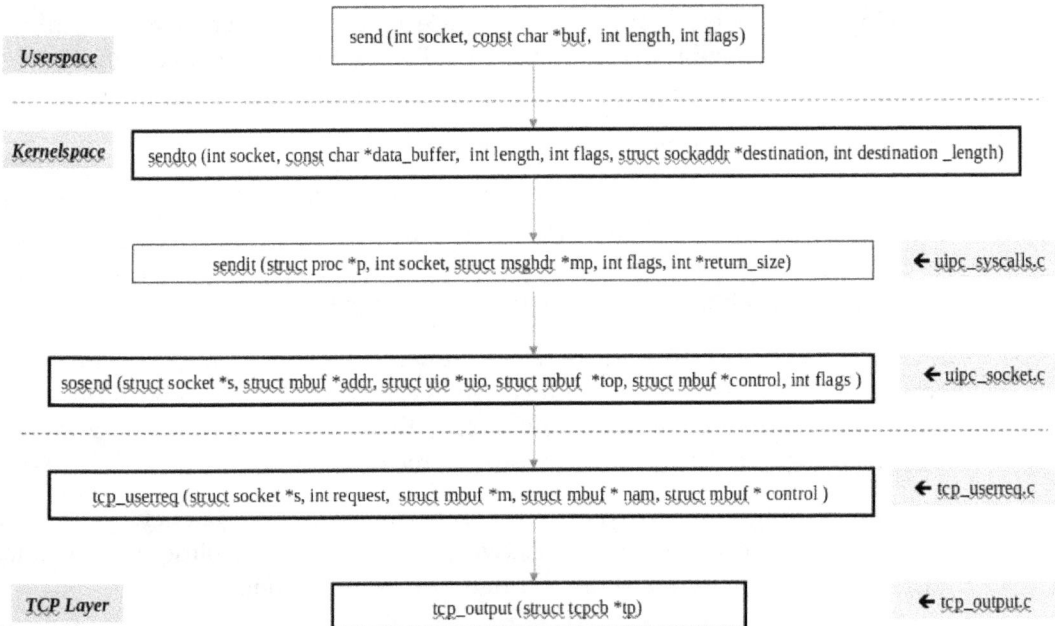

Figure 8.16: Workflow within the network stack

The reception of packets revolves around the buffer ring:

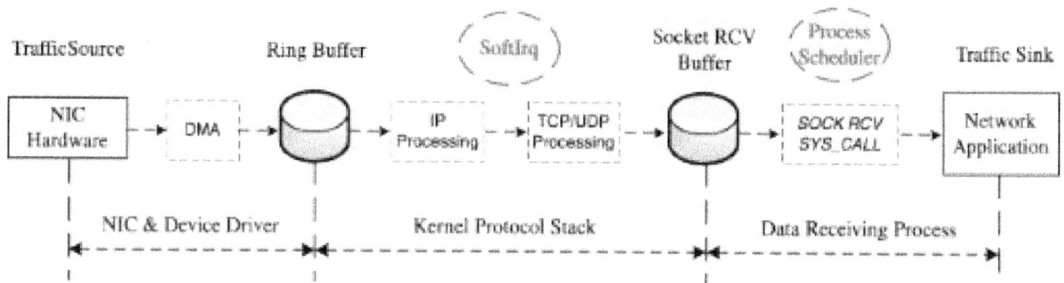

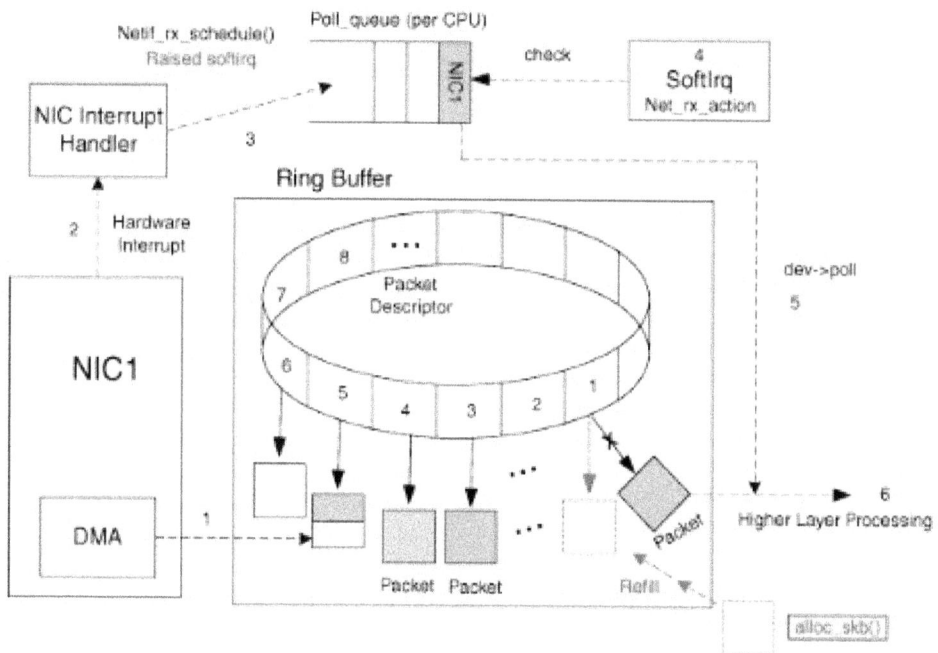

Figure 8.17: The Rx processing

The following figure details the transmission stack flow:

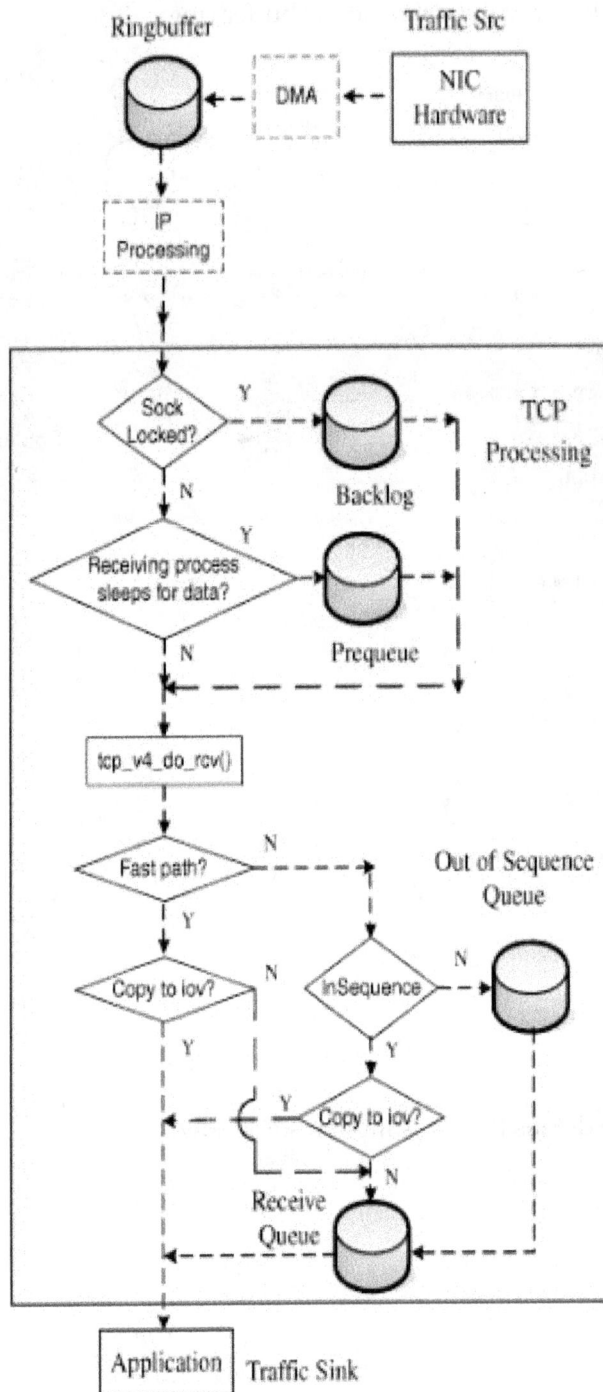

Figure 8.18: *The Tx processing*

The ring can be managed using the **ethtool** utility:

```
tgayet@tgayet-DS87D    ~   ifconfig enp3s0
enp3s0: flags=4163<UP,BROADCAST,RUNNING,MULTICAST>  mtu 1500
        inet 172.16.0.27  netmask 255.255.255.0  broadcast 172.16.0.255
        inet6 fe80::b5dc:1bac:ed:a4d4  prefixlen 64  scopeid 0x20<link>
        ether 80:ee:73:b0:3f:cf  txqueuelen 1000  (Ethernet)
        RX packets 1166275  bytes 1087095858 (1.0 GB)
        RX errors 0  dropped 0  overruns 0  frame 0
        TX packets 733356  bytes 288676057 (288.6 MB)
        TX errors 0  dropped 0 overruns 0  carrier 0  collisions 0

tgayet@tgayet-DS87D    ~   ethtool -g enp3s0
Ring parameters for enp3s0:
Pre-set maximums:
RX:             256
RX Mini:        n/a
RX Jumbo:       n/a
TX:             256
Current hardware settings:
RX:             256
RX Mini:        n/a
RX Jumbo:       n/a
TX:             256
```

Figure 8.19: Using ethtool to interact with input and output buffers

If possible, this is possible to change the ring buffer's size in Tx and Rx:

```
$ sudo ethtool enp3s0 -G tx 256 rx 256
```

Studying the latency of the TCP/IP network stack layers on sending a 1024-byte packet in UDP and TCP every second shows the following results:

- Overall, the copy time for 1024 bytes is 1 μs, the call to the BSD socket system primitive is around 2 μs, and the checksum time in UDP is also 2 μs.

- The use of DMA for data transfer between the device and memory is a real advantage from a performance point of view.

- The transmission time by the network driver of a network packet is below 2 μs, but it increases to around 4 μs in reception due to the inherent complexity of the driver in its reception mode. In addition, this last mode has a non-negligible memory copy.

- **UDP**: The transmission time for 1024 bytes in UDP when the checksum is required is 18.9 μs, while receiving this Request is 35 μs. The maximum sending capacity in UDP is therefore 433 Mbits/s while the reception rate is 234 Mbps.

- **TCP**: With the TCP protocol, sending a 1024-byte packet takes 22.5 μs and 36 μs to receive. The maximum speed in Transmission is 364Mbits/s, while reception is 228Mbits/s.

When the recipient/sender is local (localhost) the maximum capacity is approximately 150 Mbit/s.

The overall time required in the GNU Linux kernel for memory copies, checksums, and system calls is 22% for the transmission part in TCP and 16.7% for the reception part with the same protocol. Same for UDP.

The DPDK project

DPDK, which stands for Data Plane Development Kit, is an open-source project that provides a set of libraries and drivers for accelerating packet processing tasks in software-based network data planes. Developed primarily by Intel, DPDK aims to optimize packet processing performance on commodity hardware, particularly for networking applications requiring high throughput, low latency, and scalability.

DPDK is a revolutionary software brick enabling speeds of up to several gigabits to be achieved, which is true technological performance. This is why DPDK is often used with very specific network cards such as the NVIDIA CONNECTX-6 DX card housing two SFP cages for optical fibers.

The following is the official website **https://www.dpdk.org**

Here is an introduction to the key features and components of the DPDK project:

- **Packet processing acceleration:**
  - DPDK offers a framework for building high-performance packet processing applications by bypassing the Linux kernel networking stack and interacting directly with network interfaces and hardware.
  - By leveraging techniques such as polling, zero-copy packet I/O, and lockless data structures, DPDK achieves significant performance improvements compared to traditional kernel-based networking approaches.

- **User-space networking stack:**
  - DPDK provides a user-space networking stack, including libraries for packet I/O, memory management, buffer pools, and protocol processing.
  - Applications developed with DPDK can perform packet processing entirely in user space, bypassing the overhead of kernel context switches and memory copies, resulting in lower latency and higher throughput.

- **Supported hardware:**
  - DPDK supports a wide range of **network interface controllers** (**NICs**) and hardware platforms, including Intel Ethernet controllers, Mellanox InfiniBand adapters, and various virtualized network interfaces.

- o DPDK leverages hardware features such as Intel's DPDK, which provides optimized drivers and libraries for Intel Ethernet controllers, enhancing performance and scalability.

- **Packet processing libraries:**

  - o DPDK includes a collection of packet processing libraries that provide optimized implementations of common networking tasks, such as packet classification, filtering, forwarding, and traffic management.

  - o These libraries offer APIs for building custom packet processing pipelines and applications, enabling developers to achieve fine-grained control over network traffic and performance.

- **Integration with other software:**

  - o DPDK can be integrated with other software frameworks and projects to accelerate network functions and applications, such as **software-defined networking** (**SDN**) controllers, **virtual network functions** (**VNFs**), and network monitoring tools.

  - o DPDK is often used in conjunction with projects like **Open vSwitch** (**OVS**), FD.io (Vector Packet Processing, VPP), and **Programming Protocol-Independent Packet Processors** (**P4**) to enhance packet processing performance and scalability in software-defined networking environments.

- **Community and ecosystem:**

  - o DPDK has a vibrant open-source community and ecosystem, with contributions from various companies, organizations, and individuals.

  - o The DPDK community actively develops and maintains the project, providing regular updates, bug fixes, and new features to improve performance, functionality, and compatibility with a wide range of hardware platforms and software environments.

Overall, DPDK is a powerful and widely used framework for accelerating packet processing tasks in software-based network data planes, offering performance, flexibility, and scalability for a variety of networking applications and use cases.

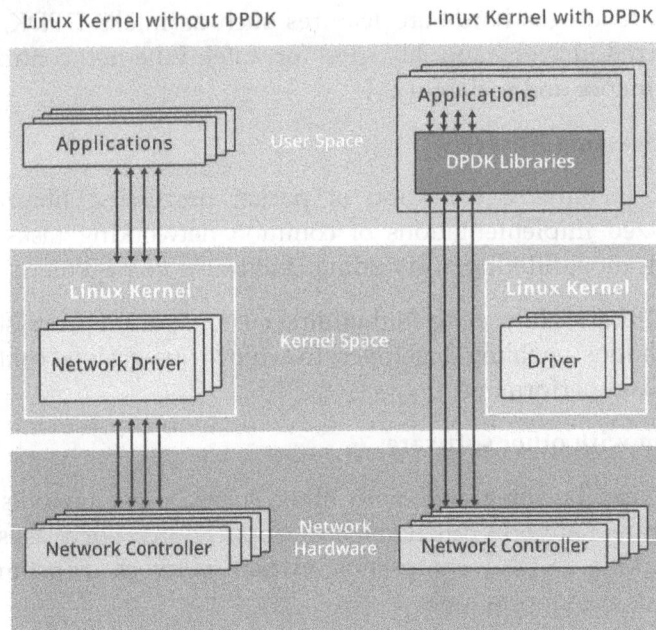

Figure 8.20: The DPDK architecture

The following is a simplified example of how to implement packet processing using DPDK. This example demonstrates basic packet reception, packet processing, and packet transmission using DPDK's APIs.

Note that this example assumes familiarity with C programming and basic networking concepts:

```
#include <linux/module.h>
#include <linux/pci.h>
#include <linux/netdevice.h>
#include <linux/etherdevice.h>

#define DRIVER_NAME "my_ethernet_driver"

struct my_priv_data {
    struct net_device *netdev;
    struct pci_dev *pdev;
    // Add any driver-specific data here
};

static int my_probe(struct pci_dev *pdev, const struct pci_device_id *ent)
```

```
{
    struct my_priv_data *priv;
    struct net_device *netdev;

    // Allocate memory for driver private data
    priv = kzalloc(sizeof(struct my_priv_data), GFP_KERNEL);
    if (!priv)
        return -ENOMEM;

    // Initialize PCI device
    if (pci_enable_device(pdev))
        goto err_free_priv;

    // Enable bus mastering and set up other PCI configuration
    pci_set_master(pdev);

    // Allocate and initialize network device structure
    netdev = alloc_etherdev(sizeof(struct my_priv_data));
    if (!netdev)
        goto err_disable_dev;

    priv->netdev = netdev;
    priv->pdev = pdev;

    // Set up device-specific parameters (e.g., MAC address, MTU)
    // Example: ether_setup(netdev);

    // Set up driver-specific data and functions
    // Example: netdev->netdev_ops = &my_netdev_ops;

    // Register network device with kernel
    if (register_netdev(netdev))
        goto err_free_netdev;

    // Add device-specific initialization code here

    return 0;
```

```
err_free_netdev:
    free_netdev(netdev);
err_disable_dev:
    pci_disable_device(pdev);
err_free_priv:
    kfree(priv);
    return -ENODEV;
}

static void my_remove(struct pci_dev *pdev)
{
    struct my_priv_data *priv = pci_get_drvdata(pdev);
    struct net_device *netdev = priv->netdev;

    // Unregister network device
    unregister_netdev(netdev);

    // Free network device structure
    free_netdev(netdev);

    // Disable PCI device
    pci_disable_device(pdev);

    // Free driver private data
    kfree(priv);
}

// PCI device ID table
static const struct pci_device_id my_pci_tbl[] = {
    { PCI_DEVICE(0x1234, 0x5678) }, // Vendor and device IDs
    { 0, },
};
MODULE_DEVICE_TABLE(pci, my_pci_tbl);

// PCI driver structure
static struct pci_driver my_driver = {
```

```
    .name = DRIVER_NAME,
    .id_table = my_pci_tbl,
    .probe = my_probe,
    .remove = my_remove,
};

// Module initialization
static int __init my_init(void)
{
    return pci_register_driver(&my_driver);
}

// Module cleanup
static void __exit my_exit(void)
{
    pci_unregister_driver(&my_driver);
}

module_init(my_init);
module_exit(my_exit);

MODULE_LICENSE("GPL");
MODULE_AUTHOR("BPB");
MODULE_DESCRIPTION("My Ethernet Driver");
```

Here are some details in the example above:

- We initialize the DPDK environment using **rte_eal_init()** and create a memory pool for packet buffers using **rte_pktmbuf_pool_create()**.

- We configure and initialize each network port for RX and TX operations using **rte_eth_dev_configure()**, **rte_eth_rx_queue_setup()**, **rte_eth_tx_queue_setup()**, and **rte_eth_dev_start()**.

- In the main packet processing loop, we continuously receive packets from the first network port (**rte_eth_rx_burst()**) and forward them to the second network port (**rte_eth_tx_burst()**).

- The packet processing loop runs indefinitely until the program is terminated.

This example demonstrates a basic packet forwarding application using DPDK's APIs for network port configuration, packet buffer management, and packet I/O operations.

Actual DPDK applications may include additional features such as packet filtering, packet inspection, and protocol processing, depending on the specific requirements of the application.

To build the DPDK example provided, you will need to set up your development environment and compile the code. Here are the general steps to build the example:

1. Ensure you have DPDK installed on your system. You can download DPDK from the official website (**https://www.dpdk.org/**).

2. Follow the DPDK installation instructions to set up your development environment, including setting environment variables (**RTE_SDK** and **RTE_TARGET**) and configuring hugepages.

3. Create a new C file and copy the DPDK example code provided in the previous response into the file.

4. Use the DPDK-provided build system to compile the example code. Typically, you will use the make command with the appropriate parameters to build DPDK applications.

5. Create a Makefile to build the example. The Makefile should include the necessary DPDK library and header file paths and specify the target architecture (**RTE_ TARGET**).

6. Run the make command to compile the example code. This will generate an executable file for the DPDK application.

7. Once the example is compiled successfully, you can run the executable file to execute the DPDK application. Ensure that you have the appropriate permissions and configurations to access the network interfaces.

Here is a simplified example of a Makefile for building the DPDK example:

```
# Makefile for DPDK example

CC := gcc
CFLAGS := -O3 -std=gnu99 -Wall

# DPDK configuration
RTE_SDK := /path/to/dpdk
RTE_TARGET := x86_64-native-linuxapp-gcc

# Include DPDK build system
include $(RTE_SDK)/mk/rte.vars.mk

# Application build options
```

```
APP := dpdk_example
SRCS := dpdk_example.c
OBJS := $(SRCS:.c=.o)

# compile rule
$(APP):$(OBJS)
        $(CC) $(LDFLAGS) $(OBJS) -o $@ $(LDLIBS)

# Dependency rule
%.o:%c
        $(CC) $(CFLAGS) $(EXTRA_CFLAGS) -c $< -o $0

# Clean rule
clean:
        rm -f $(OBJS) $(APP)
```

Note: Replace /path/to/dpdk with the actual path to your DPDK installation directory.

If the compilation is successful, you should have an executable file named **dpdk_example**, which you can run to execute the DPDK application. Make sure to set up your system environment and network interfaces appropriately for DPDK applications to access and process network packets.

Conclusion

In this chapter, we explained how the network stack of the GNU/Linux kernel works in detail, including the development of drivers for a network card, its tuning, but also its security. Finally, the latest advances in terms of significant flow management oriented around the DPDK open-source project were discussed.

In the next chapter, we will learn more about securing the Linux kernel.

Join our book's Discord space

Join the book's Discord Workspace for Latest updates, Offers, Tech happenings around the world, New Release and Sessions with the Authors:

https://discord.bpbonline.com

## CHAPTER 9

Linux Security Modules

Introduction

In this chapter, we will see how the **Linux Security Modules** (**LSMs**) work, which are responsible for the advanced security of the entire system. Several currently exist, such as SELinux, AppArmor, Smack, and Tomoyo. We will finally see how we can implement ours.

Structure

This chapter covers the following topics:

- Mandatory access control
- Anatomy of the usual Linux Security Modules
- Architecture of a Linux Security Module
- Develop a custom Linux Security Module

Objectives

By the end of this chapter, we will be able to understand the intricacies of the existing mechanisms used to secure the GNU/Linux system. We will be able to implement ours. Access control models are important because they regulate which users, applications, and devices can view, edit, add, and delete resources in an organization's environment. Controlling access is one of the key practices to protect sensitive data from theft, misuse, abuse, and other threats. There are two levels of access control: physical and logical.

Mandatory access control

Mandatory access control (MAC) is a security model used in IT systems to restrict and control access to resources based on predefined security policies defined by system administrators or security architects.

Unlike **discretionary access control (DAC)**, where access control decisions are typically made by resource owners, MAC imposes access restrictions based on rules defined by the system itself, often independently of user actions or permissions.

In a MAC system:

- **Access decisions**: Access decisions are made based on security labels attached to both subjects (e.g., processes, users) and objects (e.g., files, devices). These labels denote the sensitivity or classification of the subject and the sensitivity or classification of the object, respectively.

- **Enforcement**: The MAC system enforces access control policies regardless of the preferences or actions of users. This means that even privileged users cannot bypass the access controls defined by the system.

- **Centralized control**: MAC policies are typically centrally defined and administered, often by system administrators or security professionals. This ensures consistent enforcement of security policies across the system.

- **Fine-grained control**: MAC systems often provide fine-grained control over access permissions, allowing administrators to specify detailed rules governing who can access what resources under what conditions.

- **Isolation and segregation**: MAC can be used to enforce strict isolation and segregation of resources, ensuring that sensitive data or critical system components are accessed only by authorized entities.

- **High assurance**: MAC systems are often preferred in high-security environments where strong guarantees of confidentiality, integrity, and availability are required. They provide a higher level of assurance compared to discretionary access control mechanisms.

Examples of MAC implementations include **Security-Enhanced Linux (SELinux)**, AppArmor, IMA/EVM, LoadPin, Yama, **Simplified Mandatory Access Control Kernel (Smack)**, and TOMOYO. These systems enforce mandatory access controls by assigning security labels to subjects and objects and enforcing access decisions based on predefined security policies.

The following figure shows the differences between several MACs usable under GNU/ Linux:

Feature	SELinux	AppArmor	Yama	TOMOYO Linux	Smack
Purpose	Mandatory Access Control (MAC)	Profile-based Access Control	Process-related security	Lightweight, pathname-based Access Control	Lightweight, labeling-based Access Control
Development	National Security Agency (NSA)	Open-source community	Community-driven	Community-driven	Community-driven
Default Inclusion	Mainstream RHEL-based distributions (e.g., CentOS)	Mainstream Ubuntu-based distributions	Some mainstream distributions (e.g., Fedora)	Not included by default	Not included by default
Access Control Approach	MAC - Flexible and fine-grained access controls	Profile-based - pre-configured profiles for apps	Process-related - Attach/trace restrictions	Pathname-based - Path-based access control	Labeling-based - Security labels for processes/files
Complexity	Higher complexity due to fine-grained control	Moderate complexity with pre-configured profiles	Simpler process-related restrictions	Moderate complexity with pathname-based policies	Simpler labeling-based access control
Usage	Commonly used in RHEL-based enterprise systems	Commonly used in Ubuntu-based distributions	Limited usage, primarily process-related security	Limited usage, specific distributions and use cases	Limited usage, specific distributions and use cases
Integration	Requires specific kernel build with SELinux support	Included by default in Ubuntu and some distributions	Included in some mainstream distributions	Requires specific kernel build with TOMOYO support	Requires specific kernel build with Smack support

Figure 9.1: Comparison of several LSM

MAC is an access control model where the operating system provides users with access based on data privacy and user permission levels. In this model, access is granted on a need-to-know basis: users must demonstrate a need for information before accessing it. MAC is also called the **non-discretionary control model**, which means that control is not obtained at the discretion of the user or owner of the file. MAC implements zero trust principles with its control mechanisms. MAC is considered the most secure of all access control models. Access rules in this model are manually set by the system administrators and strictly enforced by the operating system or security core. Regular users cannot change security attributes even for data they created.

The most important principles of a MAC are the following:

- The highest confidentiality and privacy of organizational information resources are essential. No one has default privileges for accessing or modifying someone's data.

- Provision of access is centrally administered.

- Each individual and resource in the system has security labels with their ranking and category.

The following figure shows the different interactions between the components of a MAC:

Figure 9.2: *Architecture of a MAC*

With MAC, the access process looks like this:

- The administrator configures access policies and defines security attributes: privacy levels, access permissions, different projects, and types of resources.

- The administrator assigns to each subject (user or resource who accesses data) and object (file, database, port, etc.) a set of attributes.

- When a subject attempts to access an object, the operating system examines the subject's security attributes and decides whether access can be granted.

- To get access to the object, the user provides them with credentials.

In addition to checking privacy and permission levels (classification matches between subject and object), operating systems pay attention to category matches between subjects and objects. Having a *top secret* classification does not automatically mean giving a user full access to a file if it does not belong to the category required for the object.

Let us take the example of mandatory access control again. Implementation. Suppose an organization has data that carries *top secret* and *engineered project* confidentiality security level. It is accessible to a set of users having both the *top* authorization (classification) *secret* and authorization of access to engineering documents (category). These users may also access information requiring a lower permission level. However, employees with lower permission levels or without technical access rights documents cannot access this information. MAC brings many benefits to a cybersecurity system. But this has several drawbacks to consider.

Let us look at the disadvantages and advantages of mandatory access control:

- **Pros**:

  o **High level of data protection**: An administrator defines access to objects, and users can not alter that access.

  o **Granularity**: An administrator sets user access rights and object access parameters manually.

  o **Immunity to Trojan Horse attacks**: Users cannot declassify data or share access to classified data.

  o **Fewer errors**: Strict and constantly controlled policies help reduce system errors that lead to over-privileged users.

  o **Strict division**: Admins divide users into subsets and limit resource exposure for these subsets using security attributes.

- **Cons:**

  o **Maintainability**: Manual configuration of security levels and clearances requires constant attention from administrators.

  o **Scalability**: MAC does not scale automatically. New users and pieces of data demand constant updates in objects and account configurations.

  o **Interference with users' work**: Users have to request access to each new piece of data; they cannot configure access.

  o Parameters for their own data.

This access control model is mainly used by government, organizations, military, and law enforcement institutions. For better data protection and compliance in the insurance and banking industries, organizations use MAC to control access to customer account data. This non-discretionary access control model can also protect access to a database, where procedures, tables, views, and other elements will be the objects. It is reasonable to use MAC in organizations that value data security more than operational flexibility and costs. Implementation of MAC in a private organization is rare due to the complexity and rigidity of such a system.

A pure MAC model provides a high, granular level of security. On the other hand, it is difficult to set up and maintain. This is why it is common to combine MAC with other access control models. For example, combining it with the role-based model speeds up the configuration of user profiles. Instead of setting access rights for each user, an administrator can create user roles. Every organization has users with similar roles and access rights: employees in the same position, third-party vendors, and so on. An administrator can configure roles for these groups instead of setting up individual user profiles from scratch.

The following figure details the different interests in acquiring a resource:

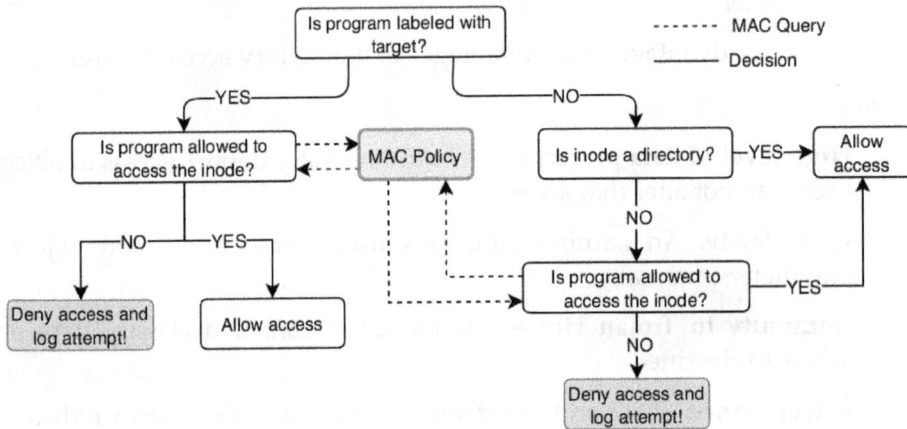

Figure 9.3: Resource access request

Another popular combination is MAC and the **discretionary access control (DAC)**, model. MAC can be used to secure sensitive data, while DAC allows colleagues to share information within a corporate file system.

Anatomy of the usual Linux Security Modules

Linux Security Modules (LSM) drivers are a crucial aspect of the Linux kernel security architecture. LSM provides a framework for various security modules to be integrated into the kernel, allowing the enforcement of access control policies and other security mechanisms. LSM allows the implementation of different security models without modifying the kernel itself, thus ensuring flexibility and maintainability.

LSM drivers are essentially kernel modules that integrate with the Linux kernel security infrastructure. These drivers intercept security-related system calls and other kernel operations to enforce security policies. Examples of LSM drivers include. **Security-Enhanced Linux (SELinux)**, AppArmor, Smack, TOMOYO, and others. Here is a brief overview of some prominent LSM drivers:

- **Security-Enhanced Linux (SELinux):**

  o Developed originally by the United States **National Security Agency (NSA)** and later open-sourced.

  o Provides a fine-grained MAC system.

  o Uses security labels attached to files, processes, and other objects to enforce access control policies.

o Enforces access controls based on security labels, providing powerful isolation and protection against privilege escalation.

o Requires a specific kernel build with SELinux support, and policies can be complex to configure and manage.

o **Documentation**:

▪ **https://selinuxproject.org/page/User_Resources**

▪ **https://www.kernel.org/doc/html/v4.15/admin-guide/LSM/SELinux.html**

The following figure details the different components of the SELINUX architecture:

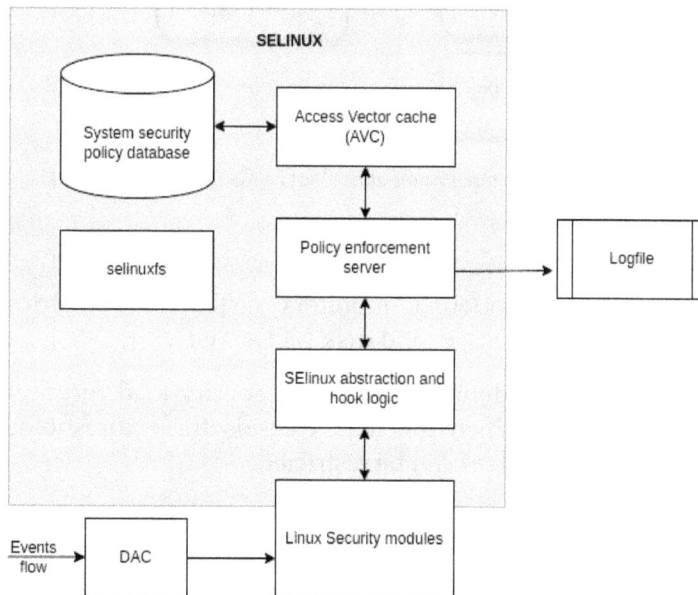

Figure 9.4: *SELinux architecture*

• **Yama**:

o Yama focuses on process-related security features, allowing fine-grained restrictions on process operations.

o It enables administrators to limit process tracing, prevent process attachment, and restrict process capabilities.

o Available in some mainstream distributions, such as Fedora, Yama provides additional process-level security controls.

o **Documentation**:

▪ **https://www.kernel.org/doc/html/v4.15/admin-guide/LSM/Yama.html**

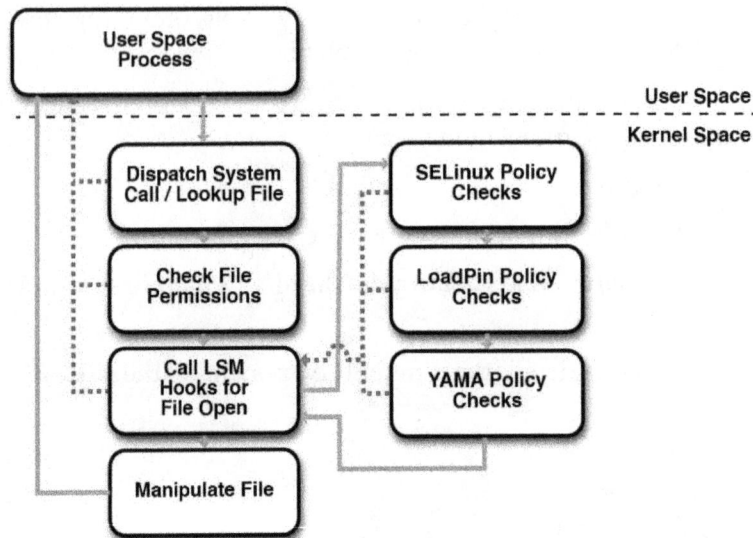

Figure 9.5: Yama integration with other LSMs (Loadpin, selinux)

- **LoadPin:**

    o LoadPin LSM continuously monitors system load metrics such as CPU utilization, memory usage, and disk I/O activity.

    o Administrators can define policies that specify load thresholds for different system resources. When the load exceeds these thresholds, access to the corresponding resources can be restricted.

    o LoadPin LSM can help protect critical system resources from being overwhelmed by excessive load. For example, it can prevent new processes from being spawned or restrict access to certain files or directories if the system load is too high.

    o LoadPin LSM allows administrators to dynamically adjust load thresholds and access control policies based on changing system conditions. This flexibility enables fine-tuning of resource protection mechanisms to suit specific workload patterns.

    o LoadPin LSM can be used in conjunction with other LSMs, such as SELinux or AppArmor, to provide comprehensive security enforcement.

    o **Documentation:**

        ▪ **https://www.kernel.org/doc/html/v4.15/admin-guide/LSM/LoadPin.html**

        ▪ **https://github.com/torvalds/linux/blob/master/security/loadpin/loadpin.c**

- **AppArmor**:
  - Originally developed by Immunix, acquired by Novell, and later integrated into the mainline Linux kernel.

  - Focuses on confining individual programs rather than users.

  - Uses path-based profiles to specify allowed and denied access for applications.

  - AppArmor is integrated into mainstream Ubuntu-based distributions and provides profile-based access control.

  - Offers pre-configured profiles for commonly used applications, simplifying the setup and management of security policies.

  - Uses path-based access control to restrict access to files and resources, enhancing application-level security.

  - Provides a balance between security and usability, making it more approachable for many users.

  - **Documentation**:
    - **https://apparmor.net/**
    - **https://www.kernel.org/doc/html/v4.15/admin-guide/LSM/apparmor.html**

The following figure details the different components of the APPARMOR architecture:

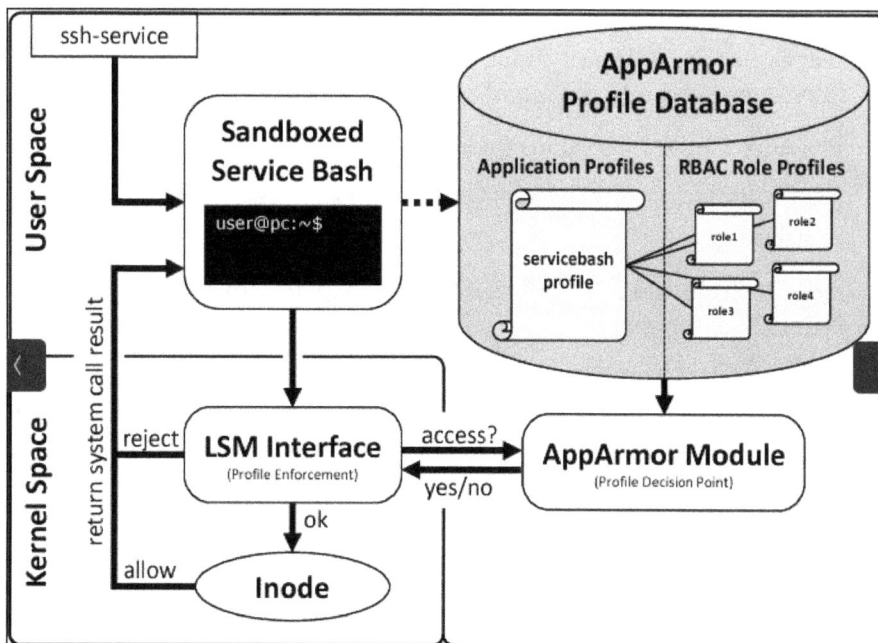

Figure 9.6: *AppArmor architecture*

- **Simplified Mandatory Access Control Kernel (Smack):**

  o Developed by Casey Schaufler at Immunix and later integrated into the mainline Linux kernel.

  o Implements a simpler MAC system compared to SELinux.

  o Uses labels attached to processes and files to enforce access control.

  o Smack, a lightweight labeling-based access control LSM, focuses on simplicity and flexibility.

  o Uses security labels assigned to processes and files to enforce access control policies.

  o Smack's labeling approach enables fine-grained access control, enhancing security in a lightweight manner.

  o It is not included by default in mainstream distributions but can be enabled with a specific kernel build.

  o **Documentation:**

    ▪ **http://schaufler-ca.com/**

    ▪ **https://www.kernel.org/doc/html/v4.18/admin-guide/LSM/Smack.html**

- **TOMOYO:**

  o Developed by **Nippon Telegraph and Telephone Corporation (NTT)** and later integrated into the mainline Linux kernel.

  o Provides a policy-based access control mechanism.

  o Uses path-based policy specification and learning mode to generate security policies.

  o Administrators define policies based on paths, executables, and attributes, reducing complexity.

  o Offers a white-listing approach to security, allowing only explicitly permitted operations and enhancing security through simplicity.

  o Limited usage compared to SELinux and AppArmor, typically found in specific distributions and niche use cases.

  o **Documentation:**

    ▪ **https://tomoyo.sourceforge.net/**

    ▪ **https://www.kernel.org/doc/html/v4.15/admin-guide/LSM/tomoyo.html**

Each LSM driver has its own approach to access control and security policy enforcement, catering to different use cases and security requirements.

LSM drivers are an integral part of the Linux kernel's security infrastructure, contributing significantly to the overall security and integrity of Linux-based systems. They enable administrators to enforce access control policies, mitigate security threats, and protect sensitive resources effectively.

Architecture of a Linux Security Module

At the GNU/Linux kernel submission of 2001, several security projects were proposed for the kernel. These different approaches were often incompatible. Un the guidance of Linux Torvald, a group was formed to create the Linux Security Modules framework, which follows the principles:

- The GNU/Linux kernel still does its normal security checks.

- When the kernel needs to decide if access should be granted, it also asks a security module whether the action is okay.

- An administrator should pick the security module they want.

The LSM framework was designed so that almost all of its hooks would be restrictive.

- An **authoritative hook** makes the absolute final decision: if the hook says a request should be granted, then it is granted no matter what.

- A **restrictive hook** can only add additional restrictions; it cannot grant new permissions.

So, several components have been added to the kernel:

- An interface of security functions:

  o The **security.h** has a **security_operations** structure, which defines security functions as function pointers.

  o It defines a global variable:

    ▪ **extern struct security_operation_security_ops;**

  o The **security.h** defines a set of static functions that correspond to each security call

  o For each static function **x**, it executes **security_ops→x();**. Thus, the kernel calls **x,** and **x** calls the registered function pointer.

- Insert calls to security functions at various points within the kernel code:

  o LSM inserts calls to security functions at critical points within the kernel code to perform access control:

- **fork.c**: task creation
- **namei.c**: virtual file system creation

  o LSM inserts calls to security functions at critical points in the kernel code to manage the security fields:

  - inode.c: `security_inode_alloc()`
  - inode.c: `security_inode_free()`
  - fork.c: `security_task_alloc()`
  - fork.c: `security_tasl_free()`

- Adding security fields to kernel objects:

  o Security fields (**void*** security) added to various kernel objects

  o The settings of security fields are handled by security modules

  o These fields are used by security modules for labeling

The following table shows the impact of an **lsm** in terms of kernel objects:

Task struct	Task (process)
linux_binprm	Program
Super_block	File system
inode	Pipe, file or socket
sk_buff	Network buffer
net_device	Network device
kern_ipc_perm	Semaphore, shared memory, segment or message queue

Table 9.1: Kernel object impacted

- Providing functions and allowing kernel modules to register and unregister themselves as security modules:

  o The primary security module must register itself using the **register_security** function in **security.c** file.

  o It only registers one module as a primary module.

  o The decision of module stacking is left to the primary module:

  - If the secondary module fails to register using **register_security()**, it needs to call **mod_reg_security**, which calls the primary function in order to decide about stacking.

- Move capabilities logic into an optional security module:

  o The name **capabilities** comes from the defunct **POSIX 1003.1e**

o   These capabilities are a partitioning of the powerful root privileges

o   A process has three sets of bitmaps called the inheritable(I), permitted(P), and effective(E) capabilities.

o   Each capability is implemented as a bit in each of the three bitmaps, which is either set or unset.

o   The kernel will check the appropriate bit in the effective set of the process for privileged operation.

The following table details the different capabilities associated with a process:

CAP_AUDIT_WRITE	Allox to generate audit messages by writing in netlink sockets
CAP_AUDIT_ CONTROL	Allow to control kernel auditing activities by means of netlink sockets
CAP_CHOWN	Ignore restrictions on file user and group ownership changes
CAP_DAC_ OVERRIDE	Ignore file access permissions
CAP_DAC_READ_ SEARCH	Ignore file/directory ready and search permissions
CAP_FOWNER	Generally ignore permission checks on file ownership
CAP_FSETID	Ignore restrictions on setting the setuid and setgid flags for files
CAP_KILL	Bypass permission checks when generating signal
CAP_SETGID	Ignore restrictions on groups process credentials manipulations
CAP_SETPCAP	Allow capability manipulations on other processes
CAP_SETUID	Ignore restrictions on user's process cedentials manipulations
CAP_SYS_ADMIN	Allow general system administration
CAP_SYS_BOOT	Allow use of reboot()
CAP_SYS_CHROOT	Allow use of chroot()
CAP_SYS_PTRACE	Allow use of ptrace() on every process
CAP_SYS_ RESOURCE	Allow resource limits to be increase
CAP_SYS_TIME	Allow manipulation of system clock and real-time clock

Table 9.2: Subset of capabilities

The authoritative model is more flexible, but it requires many radical changes to the Linux kernel.

The following figure details the modular design of the different elements of an LSM:

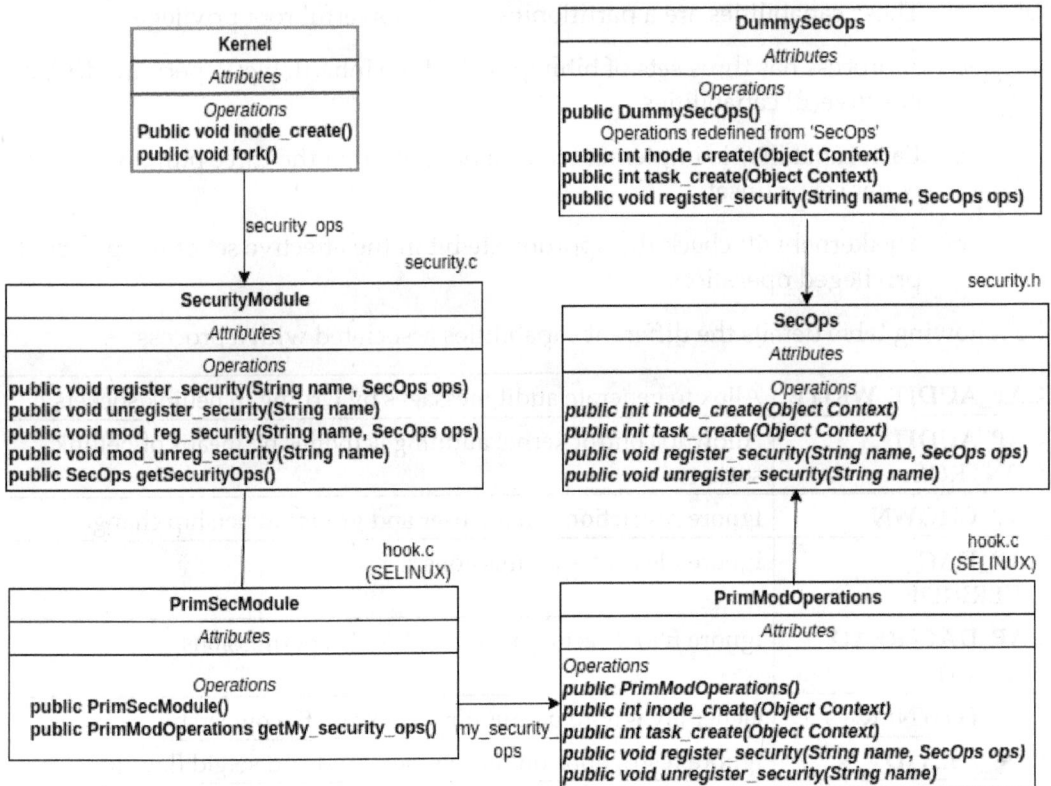

Figure 9.7: LSM UML diagram

Security is a chronic and growing problem, as more systems come online, motivated attacks are increasing, and Linux is not immune to this threat:

- Linux systems experience a large number of software vulnerabilities.

An important way to mitigate software vulnerabilities is to use access controls effectively.

LSM seeks to solve this problem by providing a framework for security policy modules.

For a DAC, there are only two categories of users: the administrator and the users. It avoids privilege escalations.

Uid=0, we are root, and gid=0 is the root group. If uid=0, the kernel bypasses the permission cheks. When a process is created, it always inherits the credentials of its parents. Effective credentials can be modified using system calls:

- `setuid()`
- `setresuitd()`
- `setfsuid()`
- `setreuid()`

The following table lists the different identifiers used within an LSM:

uid,gid	User and group real identifiers
fuid,egid	User and group effective identifiers
fsuid,fsgid	User and group effective identifiers for file access
groups	Supplemental group identifiers
suid,sgid	User and group saved identifiers

Table 9.3: Credentials associated with each process

The LSM framework provides hooks—specific points in the Linux kernel where security decisions can be made, or security checks can be enforced.

These hooks allow LSM modules to intercept various kernel operations and apply security policies based on the module's specific security model.

The following figure shows the exchanges of an LSM between kernel space and user space:

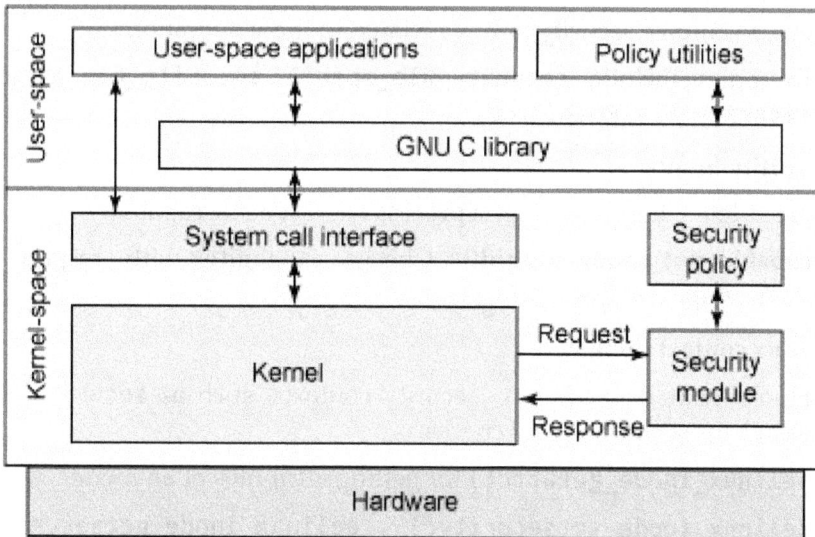

Figure 9.8: LSM architecture between user and kernel space

Here are some of the key hooks used by LSM modules:

- **Filesystem hooks**:
  - **inode_permission()**: Checks permissions when accessing a file or directory.
  - **inode_create()**: Controls file creation.
  - **inode_unlink()**: Controls file deletion.
  - **inode_mkdir(), inode_rmdir()**: Controls directory creation and deletion.

- **Process hooks**:
  - **task_create()**: Controls the creation of new processes.
  - **cred_alloc_blank()**, **cred_prepare()**: Manages the initialization of process credentials.
  - **bprm_check_security()**: Controls the execution of binary programs.

- **Network hooks**:
  - **socket_create()**, **socket_bind()**, **socket_connect()**: Controls network socket operations.
  - **skb_send_security()**, **skb_recv_security()**: Manages security checks on network packets.
  - **inet_conn_request()**: Handles incoming network connections.

- **System call hooks**:
  - Hooks into specific system calls such as `open()`, `read()`, `write()`, `execve()`, etc., to enforce security policies related to these operations.
  - Examples include `security_file_open()`, `security_file_permission()`, `security_file_mmap()`, etc.

- **Capability hooks**:
  - **capable()**: Checks whether a process has a specific capability.
  - **capable_wrt_inode_uidgid()**: Checks capability with respect to inode ownership.

- **SELinux context hooks**:
  - Hooks related to SELinux security contexts, such as `security_sock_rcv_skb()` for socket security checks.
  - `selinux_inode_getattr()` for getting attributes of an inode.
  - `selinux_inode_setsecurity()`, `selinux_inode_getsecurity()` for setting and getting security contexts of inodes.

- **Audit hooks**:
  - **inode_post_setxattr()**, **inode_post_removexattr()**: Hooks for auditing extended attribute changes on inodes.

- **Mount hooks**:
  - `sb_mount()` and `sb_umount()` hooks for mounting and unmounting filesystems.
  - **sb_alloc_security()**, **sb_free_security()**: Hooks for managing security context allocation and deallocation for mounted filesystems.

These hooks represent only a subset of the hooks available in the LSM framework. LSM modules can choose to implement any subset of these hooks depending on their specific security model and requirements.

The following figure details the different stages of validation of a resource by an LSM:

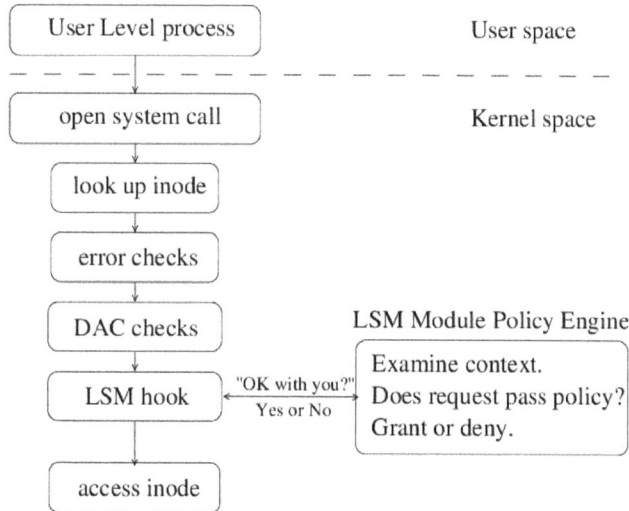

Figure 9.9: Kernel detail to an inode access

By intercepting these hooks, LSM modules can enforce security policies, perform access control checks, manage security contexts, and provide fine-grained security enforcement in the Linux kernel.

Develop a custom Linux Security Module

Creating a fully complete LSM that implements all hooks is a significant effort, as it involves implementing features for a wide range of kernel operations and ensuring that security policies are correctly enforced on the different components of the system.

The following **c** details an excerpt of the function pointer data structure for hooks usable within **lsm**:

```
struct security_operations {
    int (*ptrace_access_check)(struct task_struct *child, unsigned int
mode);
    int (*ptrace_traceme)(struct task_struct *parent);
    int (*capget)(struct task_struct *target, kernel_cap_t *effective,
                kernel_cap_t *inheritable, kernel_cap_t *permitted);
    int (*capset)(struct cred *new, const struct cred *old,
                const kernel_cap_t *effective, const kernel_cap_t
```

```
*inheritable,
                const kernel_cap_t *permitted);
    int (*bprm_check_security)(struct linux_binprm *bprm);
    int (*inode_alloc_security)(struct inode *inode);
    int (*inode_free_security)(struct inode *inode);
    int (*inode_permission)(struct inode *inode, int mask);
    int (*file_open)(struct file *file);
    int (*file_permission)(struct file *file, int mask);
    // Many more hooks...
};
```

As we can see, there are many hooks to implement.

The following is a simplified example of a Linux LSM module implementing several hooks related to filesystem access control:

```
#include <linux/kernel.h>
#include <linux/init.h>
#include <linux/module.h>
#include <linux/security.h>
#include <linux/fs.h>


// Hook function for file permissions
static int my_lsm_inode_permission(struct inode *inode, int mask) {
    // Check if the current process has permission to access the file
    if (!security_task_is_allowed(current, mask)) {
        printk(KERN_INFO "LSM: Access denied for PID %d to inode %lu\n",
            current->pid, inode->i_ino);
        return -EACCES; // Access denied
    }
    return 0; // Access granted
}


// Hook function for file creation
static int my_lsm_inode_create(struct inode *dir, struct dentry *dentry,
umode_t mode, bool excl) {
    // Check if the current process is allowed to create a file in the
directory
    if (!security_task_is_allowed(current, MAY_WRITE)) {
        printk(KERN_INFO "LSM: Creation of file denied for PID %d in
```

```
directory %lu\n",
                current->pid, dir->i_ino);
        return -EACCES; // Creation denied
    }
    return 0; // Creation allowed
}


// Hook function for file deletion
static int my_lsm_inode_unlink(struct inode *dir, struct dentry *dentry) {
    // Check if the current process is allowed to delete the file
    if (!security_task_is_allowed(current, MAY_WRITE)) {
        printk(KERN_INFO "LSM: Deletion of file denied for PID %d in
directory %lu\n",
                current->pid, dir->i_ino);
        return -EACCES; // Deletion denied
    }
    return 0; // Deletion allowed
}


// Hook functions registration
static struct security_hook_list my_lsm_hooks[] = {
    LSM_HOOK_INIT(inode_permission, my_lsm_inode_permission),
    LSM_HOOK_INIT(inode_create, my_lsm_inode_create),
    LSM_HOOK_INIT(inode_unlink, my_lsm_inode_unlink),
    // Add more hooks as needed
};


// LSM initialization
static int __init my_lsm_init(void) {
    printk(KERN_INFO "LSM: Initializing LSM\n");
    // Register the LSM hooks
    security_add_hooks(my_lsm_hooks, ARRAY_SIZE(my_lsm_hooks));
    return 0;
}


// LSM cleanup
static void __exit my_lsm_exit(void) {
```

```
    printk(KERN_INFO "LSM: Cleaning up LSM\n");
}

module_init(my_lsm_init);
module_exit(my_lsm_exit);

MODULE_LICENSE("GPL");
MODULE_AUTHOR("BPB");
MODULE_DESCRIPTION("A simple Linux Security Module");
```

Here are some explanations:

- **Line #1-5**: These lines include necessary header files for kernel development, including headers for kernel logging (**kernel.h**), module initialization (**init.h**), module development (**module.h**), security framework (**security.h**), and filesystem operations (**fs.h**).

- **Line #8**: This line defines a static function named **my_lsm_inode_permission**, which is a hook function for the **inode_permission** hook. This hook is triggered whenever a process attempts to perform an operation on a file. The function takes two arguments: a pointer to the **inode** structure representing the file and an integer **mask** indicating the requested operation.

- **Line #10**: This line checks whether the current process is allowed to perform the requested operation (**mask**) on the file (**inode**). It calls the **security_task_is_allowed** function provided by the LSM framework, passing the current process (**current**) and the operation mask.

- **Line #11**: If access is denied, this line logs a message indicating that access was denied for the current process (**current->pid**) to the specified inode (**inode→i_ino**).

- **Line #13**: If access is denied, this line returns **-EACCES** to indicate that the operation should be denied.

- **Line #15**: If access is granted, this line returns **0** to indicate that the operation should proceed

- **Line #19 and #30**: The **my_lsm_inode_create** and **my_lsm_inode_unlink** functions are similar to **my_lsm_inode_permission** but handle file creation and deletion operations, respectively.

- **Line #40-46**: This block initializes an array **my_lsm_hooks** containing instances of **struct security_hook_list**. Each instance pairs a hook name with its corresponding **hook** function.

- **Line #49**: This line defines the initialization function for the LSM module.

- **Line #50**: This line logs a message indicating that the LSM module is being initialized.

- **line #52**: This line registers the LSM hooks defined in the **my_lsm_hooks** array with the LSM framework.

- **Line #53**: This line returns **0** to indicate that the initialization was successful.

- **Line #57**: This line defines the cleanup function for the LSM module.

- **Line #58**: This line logs a message indicating that the LSM module is being cleaned up.

- **Line #61-66**: These lines specify the initialization and cleanup functions for the LSM module, as well as module metadata such as the license, author, and description.

As a summary, here is a list of the features of the above source code:

- **Access control hooks**:

  - The LSM driver intercepts several access control-related hooks, including **inode_permission**, **inode_create**, and **inode_unlink**. These hooks are essential for enforcing access control policies on filesystem objects.

  - **inode_permission**: Controls permissions when accessing a file or directory. The hook function **my_lsm_inode_permission** checks if the current process has permission to perform the requested operation on the specified inode.

  - **inode_create**: Manages file creation operations. The hook function **my_lsm_inode_create** ensures that the current process is allowed to create files in the specified directory.

  - **inode_unlink**: Handles file deletion operations. The hook function **my_lsm_inode_unlink** verifies that the current process is authorized to delete files.

- **Permission checking**:

  - The hook functions utilize the **security_task_is_allowed** function provided by the LSM framework to check whether the current process is permitted to perform the requested operation. This function takes the current process and the operation mask as arguments.

  - If access is denied, the hook functions log a message indicating the denial and return an appropriate error code (e.g., **-EACCES**).

- **Initialization and cleanup**:

  - The LSM driver defines initialization and cleanup functions (**my_lsm_init** and **my_lsm_exit**, respectively) to manage the lifecycle of the LSM module.

- o During initialization (**my_lsm_init**), the driver registers its hooks (**my_lsm_hooks**) with the LSM framework using **security_add_hooks**.

- o During cleanup (**my_lsm_exit**), the driver performs any necessary cleanup tasks.

- **Module metadata**: The LSM module provides metadata such as the license, author, and description using module macros (**MODULE_LICENSE**, **MODULE_AUTHOR**, **MODULE_DESCRIPTION**).

- **Logging**: The driver logs messages using **printk** to provide informational output about access control decisions and module initialization/cleanup.

- **Error handling**: The driver returns appropriate error codes (e.g., **-EACCES**) when access is denied, ensuring that the caller is notified of the failure.

- **Extensibility**: The driver can be extended to include additional hooks as needed to enforce a broader range of security policies. For example, hooks related to network operations, process creation, or system calls could be added to enhance the LSM's functionality.

Conclusion

This is the chapter finished; we hope you were able to understand a little more about the mechanisms used to secure the system. These mechanisms are optional and are not always implemented on the one hand because of their complexity, but also because this adds an overhead to the consumption of CPU/memory resources. However, it is a must-have to have an ultra-secure server or workstation, and this is also the challenge of the Android system using SELinux or Tomoyo.

In the next chapter we will see memory management via the GNU/Linux kernel.

Join our book's Discord space

Join the book's Discord Workspace for Latest updates, Offers, Tech happenings around the world, New Release and Sessions with the Authors:

https://discord.bpbonline.com

CHAPTER 10
Kernel Memory and DMA

Introduction

This chapter of the book will explain how memory works in the GNU/Linux system. You will look at how virtual memory and allocations work in the drivers. Finally, you will see the use of DMA.

A GNU/Linux system is based on several concepts used in memory management:

- **Physical memory**: This is the actual **random access memory (RAM)** hardware installed in the system.

- **Virtual memory**: An abstraction layer that allows each process to use a large, contiguous address space (or the illusion of it), which may be non-contiguous in physical memory.

- **Paging**: A method of fetching data from the physical memory by using a storage area called the **swap** space on the hard disk as an overflow area for when the RAM is full.

- **Memory pages**: These are blocks of a fixed size that the memory is divided into to manage the swapping of data between the RAM and disk space.

Structure

The chapter covers the following topics:

- From physical to virtual memory
- Userspace commands
- Accessing memory using a DMA

Objectives

By the end of this chapter, you will be able to understand how memory works under GNU/Linux. You will understand the purpose of virtual memory, the operation of the translation table, and the allocation modes in the Linux kernel through direct access via the DMA.

Memory management is a core component of any operating system's architecture. It allows efficient use of the physical memory among processes, optimizes the **Control Processing Unit (CPU)** caching, and manages necessary disk space for virtual memory.

GNU/Linux, a robust multi-user, multitasking operating system, uses several innovative and traditional techniques to manage memory on the x86_32 and x86_64 architectures.

From physical to virtual memory

Physical memory management in Linux, whether for 32-bit (x86_32) or 64-bit (x86_64) architectures, is an intricate process involving multiple strategies and mechanisms.

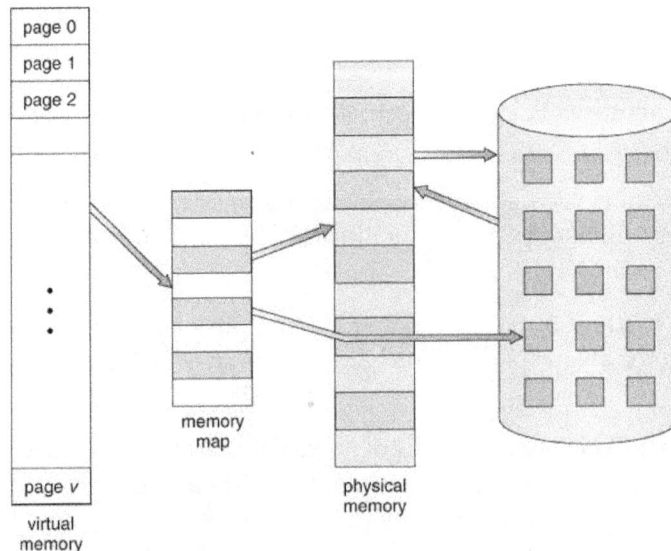

Figure 10.1: Virtual memory is a mapping between the address you request to the memory you really have

To create this map, the operating system (kernel) divides the program's memory into pages (the left stack). The program considers the memory as a single unit and uses it as if it were accessing physical memory.

The hardware has a built-in device called a **Memory Management Unit** (**MMU**) that takes the address the program wants and then looks for it in the memory card. The entry in the memory map then provides a replacement address, which is then used to access physical memory.

Now, if the kernel did not have enough physical memory available to fit everything into the map, the entry in the memory map would show as `missing`. In this case, the kernel takes over and looks at *why it is missing*. In many cases, the reference contains a location on disk, which means the data is stored in a paging file or partition on disk. The kernel can then load the page into physical memory, update the memory map, and tell the hardware to continue. In this case, the program, although delayed, continues as if nothing had happened.

Sometimes, the kernel has to *free space* before it can load the page. In this case, it examines various memory cards for several running programs and selects a page that has not been used for some time. This page would then be written to an unused page in the paging file, have the corresponding entry in the memory card where it is used to say `on disk`, then the page would become free and would be used for an entry in a memory map.

Sometimes the entry in the map says `unauthorized`, in which case the kernel recognizes that the running program is doing something wrong. In this case, abort the program and free all pages allocated to the program's memory card.

The advantage is being able to make disk storage slow and usable as if it were physical memory (by swapping pages), allowing a program to appear to have a much larger amount of physical memory.

It also allows multiple programs to run at the same time, *all* with the ability to run as if they had more physical memory than might exist.

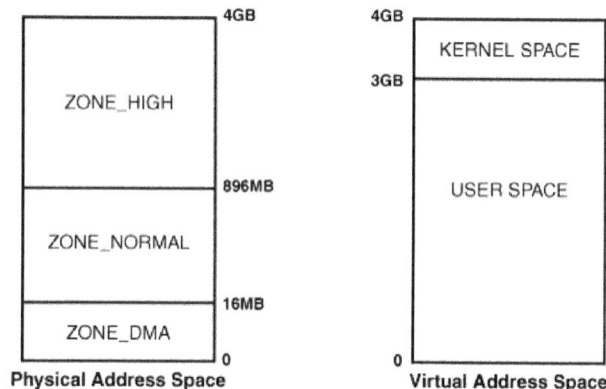

Figure 10.2: Physical vs. virtual memory

The page table indicating all the addresses inside the 3G virtual space is located in the kernel, as shown in the following figure:

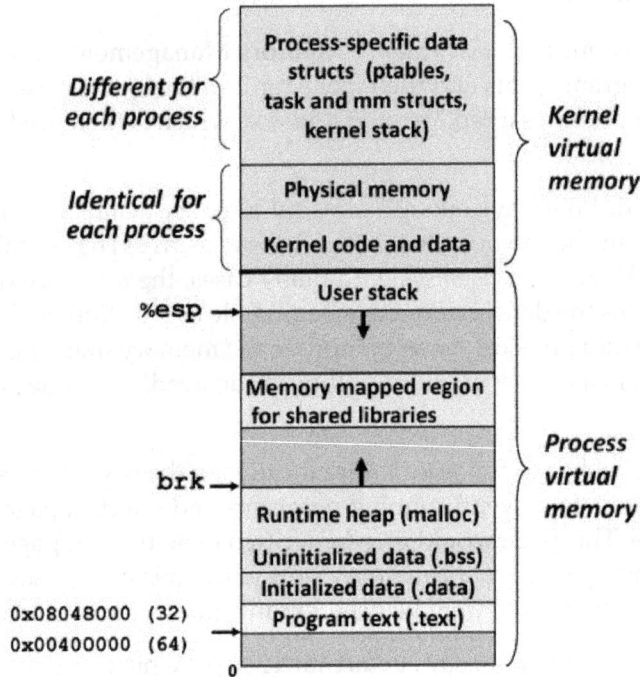

Figure 10.3: Kernel and user memory mapping

Within the kernel **virtual memory** (**VM**), there is a lower part called identity mapping, which is mapped identically for all processes, and there is another part for HIGHMEM elements that specify different elements specific to processes or kernel modules.

So, in short, DMA or NORMAL memory is identity mapping, and the preceding, different sets of page tables are needed for different linear (non-identity mapped) addresses. If you have 16GB or 32GB of physical memory, it is still possible to map anywhere, provided the page table sizes can be accommodated.

On an x86_32 platform, physical memory management is based on the following concepts:

- **Addressing:**

  o By default, the 32-bit architecture supports up to 4 GB of physical memory, directly addressing each byte with a 32-bit address.

  o **Physical Address Extension** (**PAE**) is a memory management feature provided by *Intel* that extends the addressability of physical memory from 32 bits to 36 bits, thereby increasing the maximum addressable memory size from 4 GB to 64 GB. This is achieved by adding an additional layer to the page table structure.

- **Paging:**

    ○ Without PAE, the GNU/Linux system uses standard paging with a two-level page table system. The first level is the page directory, and the second level is the page table, with each table capable of addressing 4 MB and 4 KB of memory, respectively.

    ○ When PAE is enabled, the Linux system uses the paging model in a three-level structure, which includes an additional **Page Directory Pointer Table (PDPT)**, thereby improving the addressable memory range.

- **Limits:**

    ○ The Linux kernel often has to manage a distribution between high memory and low memory. *Low memory* is directly mapped into the kernel address space and is easily accessible, while *high memory* is not directly accessible and requires special mappings.

The following is the differences under GNU/Linux x86_64:

- **Addressing:**

    ○ The x86_64 architecture greatly expands the addressable memory space. Theoretically, it can be extended up to 16 exabytes, although practical system limitations and current technology make this unfeasible.

    ○ A GNU/Linux system on x86_64 typically manages a 48-bit linear address space, which is expandable to 56 bits in newer architectures, partitioned into user and kernel space.

- **Paging:**

    ○ Under x86_64, GNU/Linux uses a more complex paging system than under x86_32. It involves four levels of page tables: **Page Global Directory (PGD)**, **Page Upper Directory (PUD)**, **Page Middle Directory (PMD)**, and **Page Table (PT)**.

    ○ It supports large pages more extensively, using 2MB or 1GB pages, which reduces the overhead of page table entries and can improve the performance of large applications.

- **Effective use:**

    ○ Features such as **memory remapping (MTRR)** can be used to optimize the use of memory and hardware caches, thereby improving performance in memory-intensive operations.

    ○ The x86_64 architecture is often offered in multiprocessor configurations where memory access speeds differ depending on the physical location of the memory relative to each processor. Linux supports **non-uniform memory**

access (**NUMA**), which allows it to optimize application performance by intelligently allocating memory and scheduling processes based on memory access speeds.

Non-uniform memory access

Modern microprocessors contain integrated memory controllers connected via channels to memory. Memory access can be organized in two ways:

- **Uniform memory access (UMA)**
- **Non-uniform memory access (NUMA)**

Unlike UMA, which provides a centralized memory pool (and therefore does not scale after a certain number of processors), a NUMA architecture divides memory into local and remote memory relative to the microprocessor.

Local memory is directly connected to the processor's integrated memory controller. Memory connected to the memory controller of another microprocessor (multi-socket systems) is considered remote memory. If a memory controller accesses remote memory, it must cross the interconnect and connect to the remote memory controller.

Thus, accessing remote memory adds additional latency overhead to accessing local memory. Due to different memory locations, a NUMA system experiences non-uniform memory access time. As a result, the best performance is achieved by keeping memory access local.

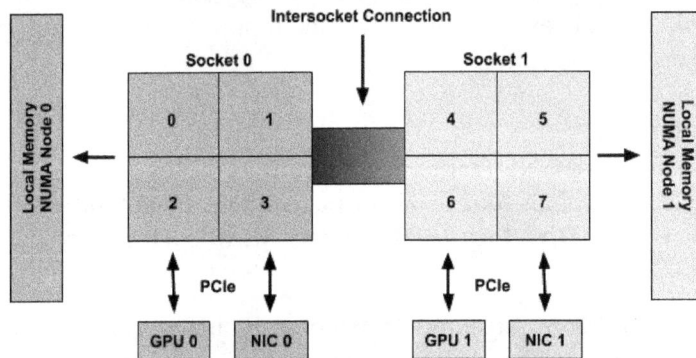

Figure 10.4: NUMA overview

The goal of virtual memory in computing, including in Linux operating systems across architectures like x86_32 and x86_64, is to decouple the physical memory (RAM) from the memory that applications and the operating system use. Virtual memory serves several crucial purposes that enhance the computing environment, both for system administrators and users.

One of the primary purposes of virtual memory is to provide an *illusion* of having more memory in the system than the actual physical memory that exists. This is achieved by using disk file space as additional memory, which allows programs to run with a combined memory limit of the RAM and designated disk space (swap space or paging file). This allows systems to run larger applications or more concurrent applications than the available physical memory would normally permit.

Virtual memory provides a strong isolation mechanism between processes, ensuring that each process runs in its own sandbox-like environment with a private virtual address space. Each process is prevented from accessing the memory addresses used by other processes without explicit permissions. This isolation helps enhance the security and stability of the operating system, as it minimizes the risk of one process affecting the operation of another, either maliciously or accidentally.

Virtual memory allows operating systems to use physical memory more efficiently. By swapping portions (pages) of programs from physical memory to disk and back, the system can prioritize memory access to those pages that are needed frequently, while less-used pages can be stored on disk. This leads to optimized use of the RAM, as only actively used data occupies precious primary memory space.

Virtual memory enables various memory-protection schemes to be implemented, such as marking certain areas of memory as read-only or executable only. This is crucial for preventing programs from inadvertently or maliciously altering their executable code. It protects the integrity of the operating system and user applications by ensuring that actions such as writing to memory are performed only where permitted.

For application developers, virtual memory abstracts the complexity of the underlying physical memory management. Applications can request memory as needed without regard for the amount of physical memory available. Developers can focus on the logic of their applications without needing to manage memory allocation manually, which can be particularly challenging in large or complex applications.

By using techniques like demand paging, where only the required memory pages are loaded into RAM, virtual memory systems can reduce the startup time of applications and make the execution of large programs feasible even on systems with limited RAM. This enables more efficient program execution and can improve system responsiveness.

Linux and other modern operating systems with virtual memory capabilities allow for overcommitting memory, that is, letting processes allocate more memory than is available in physical RAM and swap space combined. This can be useful for programs that allocate a lot of memory but do not use it all simultaneously, allowing for more efficient use of system resources. The details are as follows:

- **Memory allocation**: GNU/Linux uses the following strategies for memory allocation:

  - **Buddy system**: This method is used for allocating memory in contiguous blocks that are powers of two. It helps minimize fragmentation in the physical memory.

o **Slab allocation**: It is used for kernel objects like process descriptors and file objects. It groups objects of similar sizes into caches to minimize the time taken to allocate and deallocate them, thus optimizing kernel operations.

o **Zone allocator**: Linux divides physical memory into zones based on the range of addresses they can handle. The most commonly used zones are DMA, Normal, and HIGHMEM.

- **Paging**: Paging is essential for virtual memory management. It helps decouple the user's view of memory from the physical memory, which allows Linux to use disk space as overflow memory, effectively increasing the amount of usable memory. This is done through the following:

  o **Page tables**: Linux uses a multi-level page table structure. In x86_32 systems, it can be either two-level (with and without PAE) or three-level (with PAE). x86_64 systems typically use a four-level page table structure.

  o **Page replacement algorithm**: When a page needs to be swapped in from disk, Linux decides which existing page to swap out using algorithms like **Least Recently Used** (LRU), which tracks page usage over time to make an informed decision.

  o **Swap space**: This is the disk area used to store pages that are not currently held in the RAM. The size of the swap space can affect the performance of the system, especially if the system frequently runs out of memory.

- **Advanced memory management features**

  o **Transparent Huge Pages** (THP): This feature automatically manages the allocation of large pages (usually about 2 MB in size, but up to 1 GB in certain configurations), reducing the overhead of managing multiple small pages.

  o **Kernel Same-page Merging** (KSM): KSM reduces memory usage by identifying duplicate pages among different processes and merging them into a single page that is marked read-only. If any process needs to modify the page, a new copy is made just for that process (Copy on Write).

  o **Memory overcommit**: This allows the system to allocate more memory to applications than the total available physical memory and swap space. This is useful for applications that reserve more RAM than they actually use, but can lead to system instability if not managed carefully.

The x86 MMU has a segmentation unit and a paging unit. The segmentation unit can be used to define segments of logical memory defined by a logical start address (virtual), a base linear address (mapped), and a size.

A segment can also restrict access based on the type of access (read, execute, or write) or the privilege level (certain segments can be defined so that they are accessible only by the kernel, for example).

When the processor performs a memory access, it uses the segmentation unit to translate the logical address into a linear address based on the information contained in the segment descriptor.

If paging is enabled, the linear address will then be transformed into a physical address using information from the page tables. Note that the segmentation unit cannot be disabled, so if the MMU has been enabled, segmentation will still be used.

Userspace commands

The following is the list of the most useful Linux commands to inspect memory usage:

Command	Description
free	Displays the amount of free and used memory in the system, including physical and swap memory.
cat /proc/ meminfo	Displays detailed information about memory usage, including total, free, and available memory, as well as memory-related kernel parameters.
vmstat	Reports virtual memory statistics, including memory usage, paging, and block I/O activity.
ps	Lists information about active processes, including memory usage.
pmap	Displays memory map of a process, showing the memory regions allocated by the process.
pidstat	Reports statistics for processes, including memory usage, CPU usage, and I/O activity.
slabtop	Displays real-time kernel slab cache information, showing memory usage by kernel data structures.
smem	Reports memory usage per process, user, or group, providing detailed information about memory consumption.
sar	System activity reporter that collects and reports system performance metrics, including memory usage.
numastat	Reports memory usage and statistics for NUMA nodes.
lshw	Displays detailed hardware information, including memory configuration and attributes.
dmidecode	Reports information about the system's hardware components, including memory configuration.
dmesg	Displays kernel messages, including information about memory initialization and errors.
exmap	External tool for memory mapping analysis.

Table 10.1: Memory command listing

For instance, you can dump the memory mapping used by a userspace's process. As an example, the **cron** binary located in **/usr/bin/cron** has been used.

The second column defines the access rights to the memory area:

- **r--p**: This is the code of the binary.

- **r-xp**: It is the pointer on the context used by the process's scheduler.

- **rw-p**: This is the data block associated with the code.

The following is a result from the Linux proc filesystem (**procfs**)

```
$ sudo cat /proc/1519/maps
59cd5b45d000-59cd5b460000 r--p 00000000 08:03 10231771                   /
usr/sbin/cron
59cd5b460000-59cd5b467000 r-xp 00003000 08:03 10231771                   /
usr/sbin/cron
59cd5b467000-59cd5b469000 r--p 0000a000 08:03 10231771                   /
usr/sbin/cron
59cd5b469000-59cd5b46a000 r--p 0000b000 08:03 10231771                   /
usr/sbin/cron
59cd5b46a000-59cd5b46b000 rw-p 0000c000 08:03 10231771                   /
usr/sbin/cron
59cd5b822000-59cd5b843000 rw-p 00000000 00:00 0
[heap]
75fa26a00000-75fa26f74000 r--p 00000000 08:03 10230064                   /
usr/lib/locale/locale-archive (deleted)
75fa27169000-75fa2716b000 r--p 00000000 08:03 10229260                   /
usr/lib/x86_64-linux-gnu/libpcre2-8.so.0.10.4
75fa2716b000-75fa271d6000 r-xp 00002000 08:03 10229260                   /
usr/lib/x86_64-linux-gnu/libpcre2-8.so.0.10.4
75fa271d6000-75fa271fe000 r--p 0006d000 08:03 10229260                   /
usr/lib/x86_64-linux-gnu/libpcre2-8.so.0.10.4
75fa271fe000-75fa271ff000 r--p 00094000 08:03 10229260                   /
usr/lib/x86_64-linux-gnu/libpcre2-8.so.0.10.4
75fa271ff000-75fa27200000 rw-p 00095000 08:03 10229260                   /
usr/lib/x86_64-linux-gnu/libpcre2-8.so.0.10.4
75fa27200000-75fa27228000 r--p 00000000 08:03 10225772                   /
usr/lib/x86_64-linux-gnu/libc.so.6 (deleted)
75fa27228000-75fa273bd000 r-xp 00028000 08:03 10225772                   /
usr/lib/x86_64-linux-gnu/libc.so.6 (deleted)
75fa273bd000-75fa27415000 r--p 001bd000 08:03 10225772                   /
usr/lib/x86_64-linux-gnu/libc.so.6 (deleted)
```

```
75fa27415000-75fa27416000 ---p 00215000 08:03 10225772          /
usr/lib/x86_64-linux-gnu/libc.so.6 (deleted)
75fa27416000-75fa2741a000 r--p 00215000 08:03 10225772          /
usr/lib/x86_64-linux-gnu/libc.so.6 (deleted)
75fa2741a000-75fa2741c000 rw-p 00219000 08:03 10225772          /
usr/lib/x86_64-linux-gnu/libc.so.6 (deleted)
75fa2741c000-75fa27429000 rw-p 00000000 00:00 0
75fa27433000-75fa27436000 rw-p 00000000 00:00 0
75fa27436000-75fa27438000 r--p 00000000 08:03
(...)


75fa274ab000-75fa274ac000 rw-p 00010000 08:03 10223699          /
usr/lib/x86_64-linux-gnu/libpam.so.0.85.1
75fa274db000-75fa274e2000 r--s 00000000 08:03 10910710          /
usr/lib/x86_64-linux-gnu/gconv/gconv-modules.cache (deleted)
75fa274e2000-75fa274e4000 rw-p 00000000 00:00 0
75fa274e4000-75fa274e6000 r--p 00000000 08:03 10225756          /
usr/lib/x86_64-linux-gnu/ld-linux-x86-64.so.2 (deleted)
75fa274e6000-75fa27510000 r-xp 00002000 08:03 10225756          /
usr/lib/x86_64-linux-gnu/ld-linux-x86-64.so.2 (deleted)
75fa27510000-75fa2751b000 r--p 0002c000 08:03 10225756          /
usr/lib/x86_64-linux-gnu/ld-linux-x86-64.so.2 (deleted)
75fa2751c000-75fa2751e000 r--p 00037000 08:03 10225756          /
usr/lib/x86_64-linux-gnu/ld-linux-x86-64.so.2 (deleted)
75fa2751e000-75fa27520000 rw-p 00039000 08:03 10225756          /
usr/lib/x86_64-linux-gnu/ld-linux-x86-64.so.2 (deleted)
7ffd46b72000-7ffd46b93000 rw-p 00000000 00:00 0
[stack]
7ffd46baa000-7ffd46bae000 r--p 00000000 00:00 0
[vvar]
7ffd46bae000-7ffd46bb0000 r-xp 00000000 00:00 0
[vdso]
ffffffffff600000-ffffffffff601000 --xp 00000000 00:00 0
[vsyscall]
```

Each dynamic library has its code shared in the whole operating system (in memory), but it has a separate data and context memory area.

The following is the same result as the preceding one, but it uses the **pmap** command:

```
$ sudo pmap -X 1519
1519:   /usr/sbin/cron -f -P
```

```
          Address Perm    Offset Device    Inode Size Rss Pss Pss_Dirty
Referenced Anonymous LazyFree ShmemPmdMapped FilePmdMapped Shared_Hugetlb
Private_Hugetlb Swap SwapPss Locked THPeligible Mapping
     59cd5b45d000 r--p 00000000 08:03 10231771   12   0   0         0
0          0         0             0                0                0
0     0         0         0       0 cron
     59cd5b460000 r-xp 00003000 08:03 10231771   28  16  16         0
16         0         0             0                0                0
0     0         0         0       0 cron
     59cd5b467000 r--p 0000a000 08:03 10231771    8   4   4         0
4          0         0             0                0                0
0     0         0         0       0 cron
     59cd5b469000 r--p 0000b000 08:03 10231771    4   4   4         4
4          4         0             0                0                0
0     0         0         0       0 cron
     59cd5b46a000 rw-p 0000c000 08:03 10231771    4   4   4         4
4          4         0             0                0                0
0     0         0         0       0 cron
     59cd5b822000 rw-p 00000000 00:00        0  132  36  36        36
36         36        0             0                0                0
0     48        48        0       0 [heap]
     75fa26a00000 r--p 00000000 08:03 10230064 5584   0   0         0
0          0         0             0                0                0
0     0         0         0       0 locale-archive (deleted)
     75fa27169000 r--p 00000000 08:03 10229260    8   0   0         0
0          0         0             0                0                0
0     0         0         0       0 libpcre2-8.so.0.10.4
     75fa2716b000 r-xp 00002000 08:03 10229260  428   0   0         0
0          0         0             0                0                0
0     0         0         0       0 libpcre2-8.so.0.10.4
     75fa271d6000 r--p 0006d000 08:03 10229260  160   0   0         0
0          0         0             0                0                0
0     0         0         0       0 libpcre2-8.so.0.10.4
     75fa271fe000 r--p 00094000 08:03 10229260    4   0   0         0
0          0         0             0                0                0
0     4         4         0       0 libpcre2-8.so.0.10.4
     75fa271ff000 rw-p 00095000 08:03 10229260    4   0   0         0
0          0         0             0                0                0
0     4         4         0       0 libpcre2-8.so.0.10.4
     75fa27200000 r--p 00000000 08:03 10225772  160   0   0         0
0          0         0             0                0                0
```

```
0      0       0       0          0 libc.so.6 (deleted)
    75fa27228000 r-xp 00028000  08:03 10225772 1620 516  10        0
400         0       0            0            0            0
0      0       0       0          0 libc.so.6 (deleted)
    75fa273bd000 r--p 001bd000  08:03 10225772  352 68   0         0
68          0       0            0            0            0
0      0       0       0          0 libc.so.6 (deleted)
    75fa27415000 ---p 00215000  08:03 10225772    4   0   0         0
0           0       0            0            0            0
0      0       0       0          0 libc.so.6 (deleted)
    75fa27416000 r--p 00215000  08:03 10225772   16  12  12        12
12         12       0            0            0            0
0      4       4       0          0 libc.so.6 (deleted)
    75fa2741a000 rw-p 00219000  08:03 10225772    8   8   8         8
8           8       0            0            0            0
0      0       0       0          0 libc.so.6 (deleted)
    75fa2741c000 rw-p 00000000  00:00          0   52  12  12        12
12         12       0            0            0            0
0     12      12       0          0
    75fa27433000 rw-p 00000000  00:00          0   12   8   8         8
8           8       0            0            0            0
0      0       0       0          0
    75fa27436000 r--p 00000000  08:03 10230156    8   0   0         0
0           0       0            0            0            0

(…)
0               0       0       0          0          0 gconv-modules.cache
(deleted)
    75fa274e2000 rw-p 00000000  00:00          0    8   0   0         0
0           0       0            0            0            0
0      8       8       0          0
    75fa274e4000 r--p 00000000  08:03 10225756    8   0   0         0
0           0       0            0            0            0
0      0       0       0          0 ld-linux-x86-64.so.2 (deleted)
    75fa274e6000 r-xp 00002000  08:03 10225756  168   0   0         0
0           0       0            0            0            0
0      0       0       0          0 ld-linux-x86-64.so.2 (deleted)
    75fa27510000 r--p 0002c000  08:03 10225756   44   0   0         0
0           0       0            0            0            0
0      0       0       0          0 ld-linux-x86-64.so.2 (deleted)
    75fa2751c000 r--p 00037000  08:03 10225756    8   4   4         4
```

```
4         4         0                   0               0                     0
0    4         4         0              0 ld-linux-x86-64.so.2 (deleted)
     75fa2751e000 rw-p 00039000   08:03 10225756       8   0   0             0
0         0         0                   0               0                     0
0    8         8         0              0 ld-linux-x86-64.so.2 (deleted)
     7ffd46b72000 rw-p 00000000   00:00        0   132  16  16            16
16        16        0                   0               0                     0
0    20        20        0              0 [stack]
     7ffd46baa000 r--p 00000000   00:00        0    16   0   0             0
0         0         0                   0               0                     0
0    0         0         0              0 [vvar]
     7ffd46bae000 r-xp 00000000   00:00        0     8   4   0             0
4         0         0                   0               0                     0
0    0         0         0              0 [vdso]
ffffffffff600000 --xp 00000000   00:00        0     4   0   0             0
0         0         0                   0               0                     0
0    0         0         0              0 [vsyscall]
                                               ==== === === =========
========== ========= ======== ============== ============ ==============
============== ==== ======= ====== ==========
                                            9504 712 134           104
596       104       0                   0               0                     0
0    152       152       0              0 KB
```

The following figure illustrates the different memory sections used by a program running on Linux:

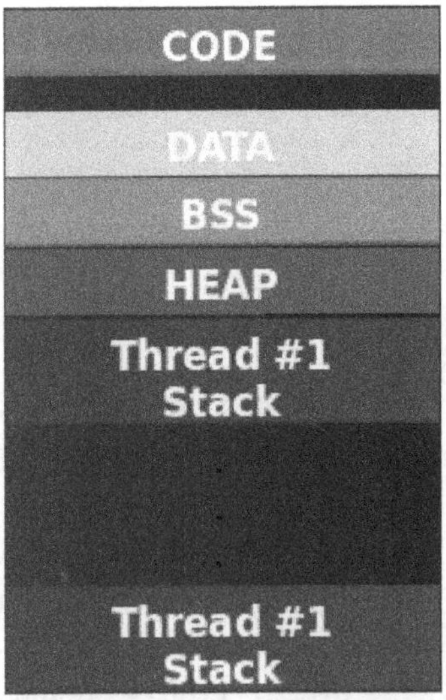

Figure 10.5: Memory stack of a user's process

A binary is, therefore, mainly composed of a memory area for its code, its data, its **Block Started by Symbol** (**BSS**) section, and its heap.

For each dynamic library, there is a code area (shared between processes), a data area, and an area for saving its context. Finally, each thread has an area for its stack.

Allocation within a driver: In Linux kernel programming, there are several ways to allocate memory within a driver based on its usage.

Methods of memory allocation

The following is an overview of the main memory allocation methods available:

- **kmalloc**: This function allocates physically contiguous memory in the kernel's address space. It is suitable for allocating relatively small amounts of memory, typically up to a few kilobytes. The allocated memory is not guaranteed to be physically contiguous across page boundaries.

  ```
  void *kmalloc(size_t size, gfp_t flags);
  ```

  o **Size limitation**: It is suitable for small memory allocations.

  o **Contiguity**: Memory may not be contiguous across page boundaries.

  o **Fragmentation**: It is susceptible to memory fragmentation.

  o **Usage**: It is typically used for small buffers, data structures, and control blocks.

Option	Description
GFP_KERNEL	Requests memory that can be put under memory pressure and is eligible for swapping. This is the most common option for kernel memory allocations.
GFP_ATOMIC	Requests memory that must be allocated atomically, without sleeping. Suitable for use in interrupt context or other contexts where sleeping is not allowed.
GFP_DMA	Requests memory suitable for DMA (Direct Memory Access) transfers. Ensures that the allocated memory is physically contiguous and can be accessed by DMA-capable devices.
GFP_NOWAIT	Requests memory without waiting for it to become available. If memory is not immediately available, NULL is returned instead of blocking.
GFP_NOIO	Requests memory that is not eligible for I/O operations. Suitable for use in contexts where I/O operations should not trigger additional memory allocations.
GFP_NOFS	Requests memory that is not eligible for file system operations. Suitable for use in contexts where file system operations should not trigger additional memory allocations.

Option	Description
GFP_USER	Requests memory that can be accessed by user-space processes. Suitable for allocating memory on behalf of user-space applications.
GFP_HIGHUSER	Requests memory from the high memory area, suitable for large user-space allocations. Often used in combination with GFP_USER.
__GFP_ZERO	Requests that the allocated memory is zero-initialized. Can be combined with other flags to zero-initialize the memory.

Table 10.2: Details of the flags that can be used with kmalloc

These flags can be combined using the bitwise OR (|) operator to specify multiple options. For example, **GFP_KERNEL | __GFP_ZERO** requests kernel memory that is zero-initialized.

- **kzalloc**: It is similar to **kmalloc**, but the allocated memory is zero-initialized.

  void *kzalloc(size_t size, gfp_t flags);

  o **Initialization**: The memory is zero-initialized.

  o **Size-limitation**: It is the same as **kmalloc**.

  o **Contiguity**: Same as **kmalloc**.

  o **Usage**: When zero-initialized memory is required, such as for data structures or buffers.

- **vmalloc**: This function allocates virtually contiguous memory, which may span multiple non-contiguous physical pages. It is suitable for larger memory allocations that do not require physically contiguous memory.

  void *vmalloc(unsigned long size);

  o **Size-limitation**: It is suitable for larger memory allocations.

  o **Contiguity**: It is not guaranteed to be physically contiguous.

  o **Usage**: Typically used for large buffers, device drivers, and data structures that do not require physically contiguous memory.

- **kmalloc_array and kzalloc_array**: These are similar to **kmalloc** and **kzalloc**, but for allocating arrays.

  void *kmalloc_array(size_t n, size_t size, gfp_t flags);

  void *kzalloc_array(size_t n, size_t size, gfp_t flags);

  o **Array allocation**: These are convenient for allocating arrays of a specific size.

  o **Size-limitation**: Same as **kmalloc** and **kzalloc**.

  o **Contiguity**: Same as **kmalloc** and **kzalloc**.

  o **Usage**: Used when allocating arrays of a fixed size.

- **dma_alloc_coherent**: The **dma_alloc_coherent** function allocates memory that is suitable for DMA operations. It ensures that the allocated memory is both physically contiguous and suitable for DMA transfers by mapping it into the DMA address space.

  ```
  void *dma_alloc_coherent(struct device *dev, size_t size, dma_addr_t
  *dma_handle, gfp_t flag);
  ```

  o **DMA use**: It is suitable for DMA buffers.

  o **Contiguity**: It guarantees physical contiguity.

  o **Usage**: It is essential for DMA buffers in device drivers.

- **dma_alloc_attrs**: It is similar to **dma_alloc_coherent**, but allows specifying additional allocation attributes.

  ```
  void *dma_alloc_attrs(struct device *dev, size_t size, dma_addr_t
  *dma_handle, gfp_t flag, struct dma_attrs *attrs);
  ```

  o **Additional attributes**: It allows specifying additional allocation attributes.

  o **Usage**: It is used when additional allocation attributes are required.

- **alloc_pages**: The **alloc_pages** function allocates a specified number of physically contiguous pages. It returns a pointer to the allocated memory as a **struct page** *, which can be converted to a kernel virtual address using the **page_address** macro.

  ```
  struct page *alloc_pages(gfp_t flags, unsigned int order);
  ```

  o **Size flexibility**: It allows allocation of a variable number of contiguous pages.

  o **Contiguity**: It guarantees physical contiguity within the allocated pages.

  o **Usage**: It is suitable for larger memory allocations that require physical contiguity, such as buffers for DMA transfers or kernel data structures.

- **get_free_pages**: It is similar to **alloc_pages** but allows specifying the number of pages directly instead of the order (log base 2 of the number of pages).

  ```
  unsigned long get_free_pages(gfp_t flags, unsigned int order);
  ```

  o **Size flexibility**: It allows allocation of a variable number of contiguous pages.

  o **Contiguity**: It guarantees physical contiguity within the allocated pages.

  o **Usage**: It is the same as **alloc_pages**, but with a different interface.

- **dma_pool**: The **dma_pool** mechanism manages a pool of memory buffers suitable for DMA transfers. It provides efficient allocation and deallocation of DMA-safe memory blocks, which are pre-allocated during pool initialization.

```
struct dma_pool *dma_pool_create(const char *name, struct device *dev,
size_t size, size_t align, size_t allocation);
void *dma_pool_alloc(struct dma_pool *pool, gfp_t flags, dma_addr_t
*dma_handle);
void dma_pool_free(struct dma_pool *pool, void *vaddr, dma_addr_t dma_
handle);
```

o **Efficiency**: It pre-allocates memory during pool initialization for efficient allocation and deallocation.

o **Contiguity**: It guarantees physical contiguity of memory blocks within the pool.

o **Usage**: It is commonly used for managing pools of DMA buffers in device drivers to minimize overhead and fragmentation.

Functions for memory-level operations

There are several functions that can be used for memory-level operations. The following list mentions them:

- **memset**: It sets the first **n** bytes of the memory area pointed to by **s** to the specified value **c**.

  ```
  void *memset(void *s, int c, size_t n);
  ```

  o **Purpose**: It sets the first **n** bytes of the memory area pointed to by **s** to the specified value **c**.

  o **Usage**: It is often used to initialize memory buffers or reset memory regions to a specific value.

- **memcpy**: It copies **n** bytes from the memory area **src** to the memory area **dest**.

  ```
  void *memcpy(void *dest, const void *src, size_t n);
  ```

  o **Purpose**: It copies **n** bytes from the memory area **src** to the memory area **dest**. The memory areas must not overlap. Use **memmove** with overlapping areas.

  o **Usage**: It is used for copying data from one memory location to another.

- **memmove**: It is similar to **memcpy**, but it handles overlapping memory regions correctly by performing a temporary buffer-based copy.

  ```
  void *memmove(void *dest, const void *src, size_t n);
  ```

  o **Purpose**: It is similar to **memcpy**, but it handles overlapping memory regions correctly by performing a temporary buffer-based copy.

  o **Usage**: It is used when the memory areas may overlap.

- **memcmp**: It compares the first **n** bytes of the memory areas **s1** and **s2**.

  `int memcmp(const void *s1, const void *s2, size_t n);`

  - **Purpose**: It compares the first **n** bytes of the memory areas **s1** and **s2**. It returns an integer less than, equal to, or greater than zero if **s1** is found, respectively, to be less than, to match, or to be greater than **s2**.

  - **Usage**: It is used for comparing memory regions, such as in sorting algorithms.

- **memscan**: It searches memory for a sequence of bytes, returning the address of the first occurrence.

  `void *memscan(void *addr, int c, size_t size);`

  - **Purpose**: It searches memory for a sequence of bytes, returning the address of the first occurrence.

  - **Usage**: It is often used for pattern matching or scanning memory for specific data structures.

- **memcpy_fromio**: It copies **n** bytes from an I/O memory area **src**, to the memory area **dest**.

  `void *memcpy_fromio(void *dest, const volatile void __iomem *src, size_t n);`

  - **Purpose**: It copies **n** bytes from an I/O memory area **src** to the memory area **dest**.

  - **Usage**: It is used for copying data from I/O memory regions to system memory.

- **memcpy_toio**: It copies **n** bytes from the memory area **src** to an I/O memory area **dest**.

  `void *memcpy_toio(volatile void __iomem *dest, const void *src, size_t n);`

  - **Purpose**: It copies **n** bytes from the memory area **src** to an I/O memory area **dest**.

  - **Usage**: It is used for copying data from system memory to I/O memory regions.

- **memset_io**: It sets count bytes in an I/O memory area **dst**, to the specified value **val**.

  `void *memset_io(volatile void __iomem *dst, unsigned long val, size_t count);`

o **Purpose**: It sets count bytes in an I/O memory area, **dst**, to the specified value **val**.

o **Usage**: It is used for initializing I/O memory regions to a specific value.

These functions provide powerful tools for manipulating memory in kernel space efficiently, allowing developers to perform tasks such as initialization, copying, comparison, and search operations on memory regions.

Many functions equivalent to those of **glibc** are defined in **include/linux/string.h**.

There are two functions allowing the transfer of data between the user space and the kernel and vice versa:

- **copy_from_user**: It is used to copy data from user space to kernel space.

  ```
  unsigned long copy_from_user(void *to, const void __user *from,
  unsigned long n);
  ```

  Parameters:

  o **to**: Pointer to the destination buffer in kernel space.

  o **from**: Pointer to the source buffer in user space.

  o **n**: Number of bytes to copy.

  o **Return value**: It returns the number of bytes that could not be copied. If the return value is zero, the copy is successful.

- **copy_to_user**: It is used to copy data from kernel space to user space.

  ```
  unsigned long copy_to_user(void __user *to, const void *from, unsigned
  long n);
  ```

  Parameters:

  o **to**: Pointer to the destination buffer in **user** space.

  o **from**: Pointer to the source buffer in **kernel** space.

  o **n**: Number of bytes to copy.

  o **Return value**: It returns the number of bytes that could not be copied. If the return value is zero, the copy is successful.

The following is an example of a Linux driver that uses each memory allocation method except for DMA:

```
#include <linux/module.h>
#include <linux/kernel.h>
#include <linux/init.h>
#include <linux/slab.h>
#include <linux/mm.h>
```

```
#define DRIVER_NAME "memory_allocation_driver"

struct mem_alloc_driver {
    void *kmalloc_buffer;
    void *vmalloc_buffer;
    struct page *alloc_pages_buffer;
    unsigned long get_free_pages_buffer;
    struct dma_pool *dma_pool_buffer; // We'll declare this but won't use
it since it's not part of this example
};

static int __init mem_alloc_init(void)
{
    struct mem_alloc_driver *drv;

    drv = kmalloc(sizeof(struct mem_alloc_driver), GFP_KERNEL);
    if (!drv)
        return -ENOMEM;

    drv->kmalloc_buffer = kmalloc(1024, GFP_KERNEL);
    if (!drv->kmalloc_buffer)
        goto fail;

    drv->vmalloc_buffer = vmalloc(4096);
    if (!drv->vmalloc_buffer)
        goto fail_kmalloc;

    drv->alloc_pages_buffer = alloc_pages(GFP_KERNEL, 2); // Allocate 2
pages (8KB)
    if (!drv->alloc_pages_buffer)
        goto fail_vmalloc;

    drv->get_free_pages_buffer = __get_free_pages(GFP_KERNEL, 2); //
Allocate 2 pages (8KB)
    if (!drv->get_free_pages_buffer)
        goto fail_alloc_pages;
```

```
    // DMA pool initialization (not used in this example)
    // drv->dma_pool_buffer = dma_pool_create("example_pool", NULL, 4096,
32, 0);

    pr_info("Memory allocation example driver loaded successfully\n");
    return 0;

fail_alloc_pages:
    __free_pages(drv->alloc_pages_buffer, 2);
fail_vmalloc:
    vfree(drv->vmalloc_buffer);
fail_kmalloc:
    kfree(drv->kmalloc_buffer);
fail:
    kfree(drv);
    return -ENOMEM;
}

static void __exit mem_alloc_exit(void)
{
    struct mem_alloc_driver *drv = NULL;

    // Cleanup resources
    // DMA pool cleanup (not used in this example)
    // if (drv->dma_pool_buffer)
    //     dma_pool_destroy(drv->dma_pool_buffer);

    // Free resources
    if (drv) {
        __free_pages(drv->alloc_pages_buffer, 2);
        vfree(drv->vmalloc_buffer);
        kfree(drv->kmalloc_buffer);
        kfree(drv);
    }

    pr_info("Memory allocation example driver unloaded\n");
}
```

```
module_init(mem_alloc_init);
module_exit(mem_alloc_exit);

MODULE_LICENSE("GPL");
MODULE_AUTHOR("BPB");
MODULE_DESCRIPTION("Memory Allocation Example Driver");
```

In the preceding example:

- **kmalloc** is used to allocate a 1KB buffer.

- **vmalloc** is used to allocate a 4KB buffer.

- **alloc_pages** is used to allocate two contiguous physical pages (8KB total).

- **get_free_pages** is used to allocate two contiguous physical pages (8KB total).

Note: DMA pool initialization and cleanup are included in the example, but not utilized, as the focus is on other memory allocation methods.

Accessing memory using a DMA

DMA is a mechanism that allows peripheral devices to transfer data to and from memory without involving the CPU. In Linux, DMA is commonly used in device drivers to optimize data transfer performance. This section will delve into the intricacies of implementing DMA in a Linux driver, focusing on its usage and considerations.

For any DMA transfer, the first issue to consider is that the user may request a large transfer (from KB to MB) to a given buffer. However, due to the way in which virtual memory is managed, this area, contiguous in virtual space, can be composed of a sequence of pages fragmented throughout the physical memory. Linux expects that any transfer exceeding a page size (4 KB on an x86 system) must be described by a **scatter/gather list (SG list)**. Usually, these lists are constructed by the **Block I/O (BIO)** layer. A key task of the device driver is to set the BIO layer to divide I/O into SG list items.

Nearly all devices optimized for high-volume data transfers are designed to handle these transfers using a **scatter-gather (SG)** list. While the specific format of this list may vary from the one provided by the kernel, adapting it to the device's requirements is typically straightforward.

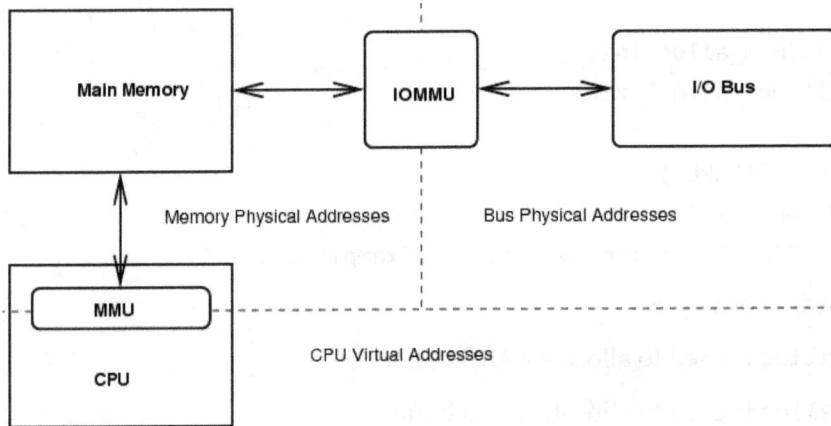

Figure 10.6: *Address domains in DMA*

An IOMMU is a memory management unit that connects the I/O bus (or bus hierarchy) and main memory. This MMU is distinct from the IOMMU integrated into the CPU. To perform a transfer from the device to the main memory, the IOMMU must be programmed with the address translations for the transfer in almost exactly the same way that the CPU's MMU would be programmed. One advantage of doing this is that an SG list generated by the BIO layer can be programmed into the IOMMU such that the memory region again appears contiguous to the device on the bus.

A **Graphics Address Remapping Table (GART)** is basically like a simple **Input-Output Memory Management Unit (IOMMU)**. It consists of a window in physical memory and a list of pages. Its job is to remap the physical addresses in the window to the physical pages in the list. The window is generally narrow, only about 128 MB or so, and any access to physical memory outside of this window is not remapped. This inadequacy reveals a weakness in the way the Linux kernel currently handles DMA, as none of the DMA APIs have failure feedback if the memory mapping fails. However, a GART has a limited amount of remapping space, and once that space is exhausted, nothing can be mapped until some I/O completes and frees up mapping space.

Sometimes, like a GART, an IOMMU can be programmed to not perform address remapping between the I/O bus and memory in certain windows. This is called **bypass mode** and may not be possible for all types of IOMMU. Bypass mode is sometimes desirable because the act of remapping adds a performance hit to the transfer, so removing the IOMMU may help increase throughput.

The BIO layer, however, assumes that if an IOMMU is present, it is used and calculates the space needed for the SG list of devices accordingly. Currently, there is no way to inform the BIO layer that the device wants to bypass the IOMMU. A problem occurs if the BIO layer assumes the presence of an IOMMU; this also assumes that SG entries are grouped by the IOMMU. So, if the device driver decides to bypass the IOMMU, it may end up with more SG entries than the device allows.

Both issues are being fixed in kernel 2.6. A fix for the IOMMU bypass is already under consideration and will be invisible to driver writers because the platform code will choose when to perform the bypass. The solution to not being able to map will likely be to make the mapping APIs return a failure. Since this fix affects all DMA drivers on the system, the implementation is going to be slow.

To communicate the maximum addressing width, each generic device has a parameter, called a DMA mask, which contains a map of set bits corresponding to the accessible address lines that must be configured by the device driver. DMA width has two distinct meanings depending on whether an IOMMU is used or not. If there is an IOMMU, the DMA mask simply represents a limitation of the bus addresses that can be mapped, but thanks to the IOMMU, the device is able to reach every part of physical memory. If there is no IOMMU, the DMA mask represents a fundamental limitation of the device. It is impossible for the device to transfer to a region of physical memory outside of this mask.

The block layer uses the DMA mask when creating an SG list to determine if the page should be returned. Bounce is the block layer that takes a page from a region of the DMA mask and copies all the data from the out-of-range page to it. After the DMA completes, the block layer copies it again to the out-of-range page and releases the bounce page. This copy is inefficient, which is why most manufacturers try to ensure that the devices their server-style machines ship with do not have DMA mask limitations.

DMA occurs without using the CPU, so the kernel must provide an API to synchronize the CPU caches with the memory modified by the DMA. One thing to remember is that the DMA API updates CPU caches only with respect to kernel virtual addresses. A separate API must be used, as described in my article, *Understanding Caching*, to update caches against user space.

Sometimes, high-end bus chips also have caching circuits. The underlying concept is that CPU writes to the chipset are fast, whereas writes to the bus are relatively slow. To optimize performance, the bus controller may cache writes transparently. If a memory-based read is performed on any part of the device's memory region, all previously cached writes are guaranteed to be flushed to the bus before the read operation begins.

No API is available to help with posting, so driver writers need to remember to obey the bus posting rules when reading and writing a device's memory region. A good trick to remember is that if you really cannot think of a necessary read to flush the pending writes, simply read a piece of information from the device's bus configuration space.

The API is documented thoroughly in the kernel documentation directory (**Documentation/DMA-API.txt**). The generic DMA API also has a counterpart that applies only to **Peripheral Component Interconnect**. (**PCI**) devices and is described in **Documentation/DMA-mapping.txt**. The intent of this section is to provide a high-level overview of all the steps necessary to get DMA working correctly. For detailed instructions, you should also read the preceding documentation mentioned.

To begin, when the device driver is initialized, the DMA mask must be set:

```
int dma_set_mask(struct device *dev, mask u64);
```

In the preceding command, **dev** is the generic device, and **mask** is the mask you are trying to set. The function returns **true** if the mask was accepted and **false** otherwise. The mask may be rejected if the actual width of the system is narrower; that is, a 32-bit system may reject a 64-bit mask. So, if your device is capable of addressing all 64 bits, you should try a 64-bit mask first and fall back to a 32-bit mask if setting the 64-bit mask fails.

Next, you need to allocate and initialize the queue. This process is somewhat beyond the scope of this chapter, but it is documented in Documentation/block/. Once you have a queue, two essential settings need to be adjusted. First, allow the largest size of your SG table (or tell it to accept an arbitrarily large one) with:

```
empty blk_queue_max_hw_segments(request_queue_t *q,          max_
unsigned short segments);
```

Second, if you need it, set the overall maximum size in the following manner:

```
empty blk_queue_max_sectors(request_queue_t *q, unsigned short max_sectors);
```

Finally, the DMA mask must be programmed into the queue:

```
empty blk_queue_bounce_limit(request_queue_t *q, u64 max_address);
```

Usually you set **max_address** to the DMA mask. However, if an IOMMU is used, **max_address** must be set to **BLK_BOUNCE_ANY** to instruct the block layer not to perform a bounce.

To make a device work, it must have a query function (see the BIO documentation) whose job is to loop through and extract requests from the device's queue using the command:

```
structure request *elv_next_request(request_queue_t *q);
```

The number of mapping entries required by the query can be found in **req->nr_phys_segments**. You need to allocate an intermediate table of this size in units of **sizeof(struct scatterlist)**. Then, do the intermediate mapping with the following:

```
int blk_rq_map_sg(request_queue_t *q, structure query *req, struct scatterlist *sglist);
```

This returns the number of SG list entries used.

The following command provides the provisional table provided by the block layer, which is finally mapped using:

```
int dma_map_sg(struct device *dev,
               struct scatterlist *sglist, int number,
               enum dma_data_direction dir);
```

In the preceding, **count** is the returned value, and **sglist** is the same list passed into the **blk_rq_map_sg** function. The return value is the number of actual SG list entries needed for the query.

The SG list is reused and populated with the actual inputs that need to be programmed into the device's SG inputs. The directory provides guidance on how to properly manage cache coherence.

It can have three values:

- **DMA_TO_DEVICE**: Data is being transferred from memory to the device.
- **DMA_FROM_DEVICE**: The device transfers data only to the main memory.
- **DMA_BIDIRECTIONAL**: No indication is given about the direction of the transfer.

Two macros must be used when traversing the SG list to program the device SG table in the following manner:

```
dma_addr_t sg_dma_address(struct scatterlist *sglist_entry);
```

Additionally add:

```
int sg_dma_len(struct scatterlist *sglist_entry);
```

The preceding macros return the physical address of the bus and the length of the segments of each input, respectively.

The reason for this two-step query mapping is that the BIO layer is designed to be a generic code and has no direct interaction with the platform layer, which knows how to program the IOMMU. So, the only thing the BIO layer can calculate is the number of SG segments created by the IOMMU for the request. The BIO layer does not know the bus addresses that the IOMMU assigns to these segments, so it must transmit a list of physical memory addresses of all pages that need to be mapped. It is the **dma_map_sg** function that communicates with the platform layer, programs the IOMMU, and retrieves the physical list of bus addresses. This is also why the number of elements the BIO layer needs for its list may be longer than the number returned by the DMA API.

Once the DMA is complete, the DMA transaction should be deleted with the following command:

```
int dma_unmap_sg(struct device *dev,
            struct scatterlist *sglist,
            int hwcount,
            enum dma_data_direction dir);
```

In the preceding command, all parameters are the same as those passed in **dma_map_sg** except for **hwcount**, which should be the value returned by this function.

Usually, the device driver operates without touching any of the data it is transferring. Occasionally, however, the device driver may need to modify or inspect the data before handing it back to the block layer. To do this, the CPU caches must be made coherent with the data by using the following:

```
int
dma_sync_sg(struct device *dev,
            struct scatterlist *sglist,
            int hwcount,
            enum dma_data_direction dir);
```

In the preceding command, the arguments are identical to **dma_unmap_sg**.

The most important factor in accessing data is when you do it.

The rules for accessing depend on **dir**:

- **DMA_TO_DEVICE**: The API must be called after modifying the data but before sending it to the device.

- **DMA_FROM_DEVICE**: The API must be called after the device has returned the data but before the driver attempts to read it.

- **DMA_BIDIRECTIONAL**: The API may need to be called twice, after modifying the data but before sending it to the device, and after the device finishes with it but before the driver accesses it again.

Most devices use mailbox-type regions of memory for communication between the device and the driver. The usual characteristic of this mailbox region is that it is never used beyond the device driver. Managing the coherency of the mailbox using the previous API would be quite a chore, so the kernel provides a method for allocating a region of memory guaranteed to be coherent at all times between the device and the CPU:

```
void *dma_alloc_coherent(struct device *dev, size_tsize,
                    dma_addr_t *physaddr, int flag);
```

This returns the virtual address of a coherent region of size that also has a bus physical address (**physaddr**) to the device. The flag is used to specify the allocation type, **GFP_KERNEL** to indicate the allocation may sleep to obtain the memory, and **GFP_ATOMIC** to indicate the allocation may not sleep; it may return **NULL** if it cannot obtain the memory. All memory allocated by this API is also guaranteed to be contiguous both in virtual and physical memory. There is an absolute requirement that the size be less than 128 KB.

As part of driver removal, the coherent region of memory must be freed with the following:

```
void dma_free_coherent(struct device *dev, size_tsize,
                    void *virtaddr,
                    dma_addr_t *physaddr);
```

In the preceding command, the **size** is the size of the coherent region, and **virtaddr** and **physaddr** are the CPU virtual and bus physical addresses, respectively, returned for the coherent region.

DMA enables efficient data transfers by offloading the data movement tasks from the CPU to dedicated DMA controllers. This is particularly useful for high-speed I/O devices such as network interfaces, storage controllers, and graphics cards. By utilizing DMA, the CPU can focus on other tasks while data transfers occur independently.

In the Linux kernel, DMA is managed through the DMA Engine framework, which provides a unified interface for device drivers to interact with DMA controllers. This framework abstracts the hardware-specific details, making it easier to develop portable drivers across different architectures.

DMA allows a hardware device to access system memory without any assistance from the CPU. By doing so, a device can transfer data to and from memory much faster than via the processor. Think about a case where you need to move large amounts of data, such as storage devices, network cards, etc. You can see in the following diagram an example of using DMA:

DMA is a protocol (like TCP/UDP in computer networks), which has the following players: the CPU, the device, the DMA controller, and the main memory. The controller has different registers to manage DMA operations and transmit information to and from the CPU. There are also three main programming modes that a controller can support: **Burst Mode**, **Cycle Flight Mode**, and **Transport Mode**.

The following figure illustrates how DMA memory works in detail:

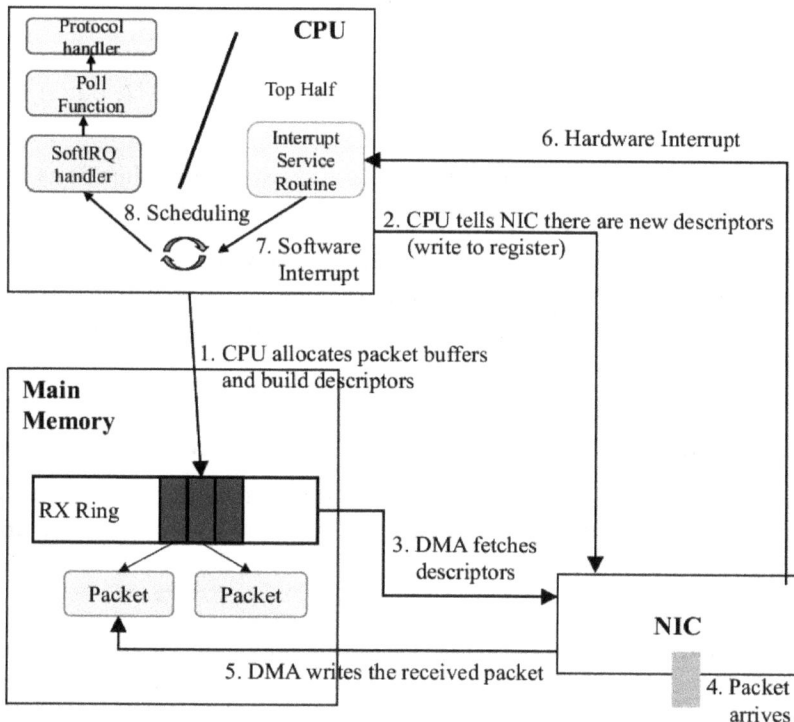

Figure 10.7: *Example of a DMA with a NIC*

To illustrate how DMA is implemented in a Linux driver, consider a hypothetical scenario of developing a driver for a PCIe-based **network interface card (NIC)**.

- **Device initialization**: The driver initializes the NIC and the associated DMA controller during system boot-up. This involves probing the PCIe bus, identifying the NIC device, and configuring the DMA controller.

- **DMA buffer allocation**: The driver allocates memory buffers for DMA transfers. These buffers need to be contiguous physical memory regions accessible by both the DMA controller and the NIC.

- **Descriptor setup**: DMA transfers are typically controlled by descriptors, which contain information such as the source and destination addresses, transfer size, and transfer direction. The driver sets up these descriptors to initiate DMA transfers between the NIC and the allocated memory buffers.

- **DMA transfer operations**: When data needs to be transmitted or received, the driver programs the DMA controller with the appropriate descriptors to start the transfer. The DMA controller then autonomously moves the data between the NIC and memory without CPU intervention.

- **Interrupt handling**: Once the DMA transfer completes or encounters an error, the DMA controller generates an interrupt to notify the driver. The driver handles these interrupts by processing the completed transfers, updating buffer status, and potentially initiating new transfers.

- **Buffer management**: After data transfer completion, the driver may need to process or transmit the received data further. It manages the DMA buffers accordingly, recycling or deallocating them as needed.

When implementing DMA in a Linux driver, the following considerations and practices should be followed to ensure optimal performance and reliability:

- **Buffer alignment**: DMA transfers often require buffer alignment constraints dictated by the hardware. It is essential to align the buffer addresses according to these requirements to avoid performance penalties or data corruption.

- **Cache management**: Cache coherence issues may arise when DMA involves memory regions cached by the CPU. Proper cache management techniques, such as cache flushing and invalidation, should be employed to maintain data integrity.

- **Error handling**: DMA transfers can encounter errors due to various factors such as bus contention, buffer overflows, or hardware malfunctions. The driver should implement robust error-handling mechanisms to detect and recover from these situations gracefully.

- **Synchronization**: Proper synchronization mechanisms, such as DMA completion callbacks or synchronization primitives like semaphores or spinlocks, should be used to coordinate access to shared resources between the driver and DMA controller.

The following is a simplified example of a Linux driver that utilizes DMA for data transfer. This example focuses on a fictitious NIC driver that transfers data between the NIC and memory buffers using DMA.

The following code illustrates the use of memory management via DMA:

```c
#include <linux/module.h>
#include <linux/kernel.h>
#include <linux/init.h>
#include <linux/pci.h>
#include <linux/netdevice.h>
#include <linux/slab.h>
#include <linux/dma-mapping.h>

#define DRIVER_NAME "dma_nic_driver"

struct dma_nic_device {
    struct pci_dev *pdev;
    struct net_device *netdev;
    void *tx_buffer;
    dma_addr_t tx_buffer_dma_addr;
};

static int dma_nic_probe(struct pci_dev *pdev, const struct pci_device_id
*ent)
{
    struct dma_nic_device *dev;
    int err = 0;

    dev = kzalloc(sizeof(struct dma_nic_device), GFP_KERNEL);
    if (!dev)
        return -ENOMEM;

    dev->pdev = pdev;

    // Enable the device
    err = pci_enable_device(pdev);
    if (err) {
        dev_err(&pdev->dev, "Failed to enable PCI device\n");
        goto err_free_dev;
    }
```

```c
    // Allocate memory buffer for DMA transfer
    dev->tx_buffer = dma_alloc_coherent(&pdev->dev, TX_BUFFER_SIZE, &dev-
>tx_buffer_dma_addr, GFP_KERNEL);
    if (!dev->tx_buffer) {
        dev_err(&pdev->dev, "Failed to allocate DMA buffer\n");
        err = -ENOMEM;
        goto err_disable_device;
    }

    // Initialize network device
    dev->netdev = alloc_etherdev(sizeof(struct dma_nic_device));
    if (!dev->netdev) {
        err = -ENOMEM;
        goto err_free_dma_buffer;
    }

    // Set up DMA descriptors, initialize NIC, etc. (not shown for brevity)

    return 0;

err_free_dma_buffer:
    dma_free_coherent(&pdev->dev, TX_BUFFER_SIZE, dev->tx_buffer, dev->tx_
buffer_dma_addr);
err_disable_device:
    pci_disable_device(pdev);
err_free_dev:
    kfree(dev);
    return err;
}

static void dma_nic_remove(struct pci_dev *pdev)
{
    struct dma_nic_device *dev = pci_get_drvdata(pdev);

    // Clean up resources
    if (dev) {
        if (dev->netdev)
            free_netdev(dev->netdev);
```

```
        if (dev->tx_buffer)
            dma_free_coherent(&pdev->dev, TX_BUFFER_SIZE, dev->tx_buffer,
dev->tx_buffer_dma_addr);

        pci_disable_device(pdev);
        kfree(dev);
    }
}

static struct pci_device_id dma_nic_id_table[] = {
    { PCI_DEVICE(0x1234, 0x5678) }, // Example PCI vendor and device IDs
    { 0, }
};

MODULE_DEVICE_TABLE(pci, dma_nic_id_table);

static struct pci_driver dma_nic_driver = {
    .name = DRIVER_NAME,
    .id_table = dma_nic_id_table,
    .probe = dma_nic_probe,
    .remove = dma_nic_remove,
};

static int __init dma_nic_init(void)
{
    return pci_register_driver(&dma_nic_driver);
}

static void __exit dma_nic_exit(void)
{
    pci_unregister_driver(&dma_nic_driver);
}

module_init(dma_nic_init);
module_exit(dma_nic_exit);

MODULE_LICENSE("GPL");
MODULE_AUTHOR("BPB");
MODULE_DESCRIPTION("Example DMA NIC Driver");
```

The explanation for some of the terms in the preceding example is as follows:

- The **dma_nic_probe** function is called when the driver is loaded and initializes the NIC and DMA buffers. It allocates memory for DMA transfers using **dma_alloc_coherent**.

- The **dma_nic_remove** function is called when the driver is unloaded and cleans up the resources allocated during the probe.

- The **pci_driver** structure defines the driver's characteristics, including its name, probe and remove functions, and the PCI device ID table.

- The **MODULE_DEVICE_TABLE(pci, dma_nic_id_table)** macro defines the PCI device ID table used by the driver to match with supported devices.

- The **dma_nic_init** and **dma_nic_exit** functions are module initialization and cleanup routines, respectively.

Please note that this example is simplified and does not include all the necessary details for a complete driver implementation, such as DMA descriptor setup, interrupt handling, and actual data transfer logic.

Additionally, the **TX_BUFFER_SIZE** constant should be defined appropriately based on the size of the DMA buffer required by the hardware.

Conclusion

In this chapter, you learned how memory works under a Linux system and how to manage it within allocations in the drivers or via DMA.

In the next chapter, you will learn more about the different communication interfaces (i2c, spi, serial, etc.).

Join our book's Discord space

Join the book's Discord Workspace for Latest updates, Offers, Tech happenings around the world, New Release and Sessions with the Authors:

https://discord.bpbonline.com

## CHAPTER 11

Navigating Linux Communication Interfaces

Introduction

This chapter will explain how the different hardware communication elements are structured in the GNU/Linux kernel. It complements *Chapter 7, USB Drivers and libusb*, dealing with the USB protocol. We would start by studying the software foundations of each means of communication before proposing an example of use adapted to recent Linux kernels.

Structure

The chapter covers the following topics:

- 2-Wire interface architecture
- Serial Peripheral Interface architecture
- Serial architecture
- Peripheral Component Interconnect architecture

Objectives

By the end of this chapter, you will be able to understand and implement different communication protocols such as I2C, SPI, SERIAL, and PCI, as well as understand RTC clocks. Indeed, there are several types of buses allowing communication with different hardware modules, this is what we will see in this chapter.

2-Wire interface architecture

2-Wire interface (I2C) is a serial protocol for a two-wire interface for connecting low-speed devices such as microcontrollers, EEPROMs, A/D and D/A converters, I/O interfaces, and other similar peripherals in embedded systems.

The I2C terminologies are as follows:

- **Transmitter**: Device that transmits data to the bus

- **Receiver**: Device that receives data from the bus

- **Master**: Device that generates a clock, starts communication, sends I2C commands, and stops communication

- **Slave**: Device that listens to the bus and is addressed by the master

- **Multi-master**: I2C can have more than one master, and each can send commands

- **Arbitration**: A process to determine which of the masters on the bus can use it when more masters need to use the bus

- **Synchronization**: Process to synchronize the clocks of two or more devices

It was invented by Philips and is now used by almost all major integrated circuit manufacturers. Every I2C slave device needs an address, which should always be obtained from NXP (formerly Philips Semiconductors).

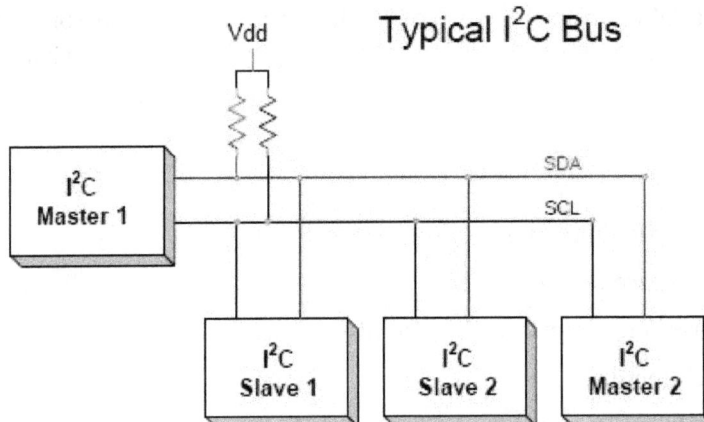

Figure 11.1: Diagram of an I2C bus between a master and slaves

The I2C bus is popular because it is simple to use, there can be more than one master, only the top speed of the bus is set, and only two wires with pull-up resistors are needed to connect an almost unlimited number of I2C devices.

I2C can use even slower microcontrollers with general-purpose I/O pins since they only need to generate correct start and stop conditions in addition to the read and write functions of one byte.

Each slave device has a unique address. Transfer to and from the master device occurs serially and is divided into 8-bit packets. All these simple requirements make it very simple to implement the I2C interface, even with cheap microcontrollers that do not have a special I2C hardware controller. You only need 2 free I/O pins and some simple I2C routines to send and receive commands.

The I2C bus specification describes four operating speed categories for bidirectional data transfer:

Standard-mode (Sm)	A bit rate up to 100 kbit/s
Fast-mode (Fm)	A bit rate up to 400 kbit/s
Fast-mode plus (Fm+)	A bit rate up to 1 Mbit/s
High-speed mode (Hs-mode)	A bit rate up to 3.4 Mbit/s
Ultra-fast mode (UFm)	A bit rate up to 5 Mbit/s

Table 11.1: Data transfer speed by mode

I2C only uses two wires:

- SCL (serial clock)
- SDA (serial data)

Both must be raised with resistance to +Vdd. There are also I2C level shifters that can be used to connect to two I2C buses with different voltages.

Basic I2C communication uses 8-bit or byte transfers. Each I2C slave device has a 7-bit address that must be unique on the bus (*Figure 11.2*). Some devices have fixed I2C addresses, while others have a few address lines that determine the lower bits of the I2C address. This makes it very easy to have all I2C devices on the bus with a single I2C address. There are also devices with a 10-bit address, as the specification allows.

The 7-bit address represents bits 7 to 1, while bit 0 is used to signal reading or writing to the device. If bit 0 (in the address byte) is set to 1, the master device will read from the slave I2C device.

The master device does not need any addresses since it generates the clock (via SCL) and addresses the individual I2C slave devices.

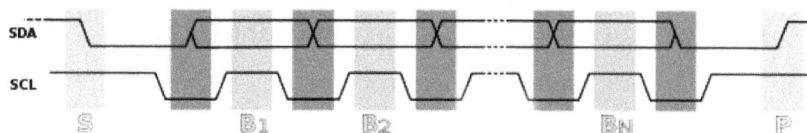

Figure 11.2: Example of a frame used on an I2C bus

In a normal state, both lines (SCL and SDA) are high. Communication is initiated by the master device. It generates the start condition (S) followed by the address of the slave device (B1). If bit 0 of the address byte is set to 0, the master device will write to the slave device (B2). Otherwise, the next byte will be read from the slave device. Once all bytes are read or written (Bn), the master device generates a stop condition (P). This signals other devices on the bus that communication is complete, and another device can use the bus.

Most I2C devices support repeated boot conditions. This means that before the communication ends with a stop condition, the master device can repeat the start condition with the address byte and change the mode from write to read.

Usage

The kernel has divided the I2C subsystem (*Figure 11.3*) into buses and peripherals. Buses are again divided into algorithms and adapters. Devices are again divided into drivers and clients.

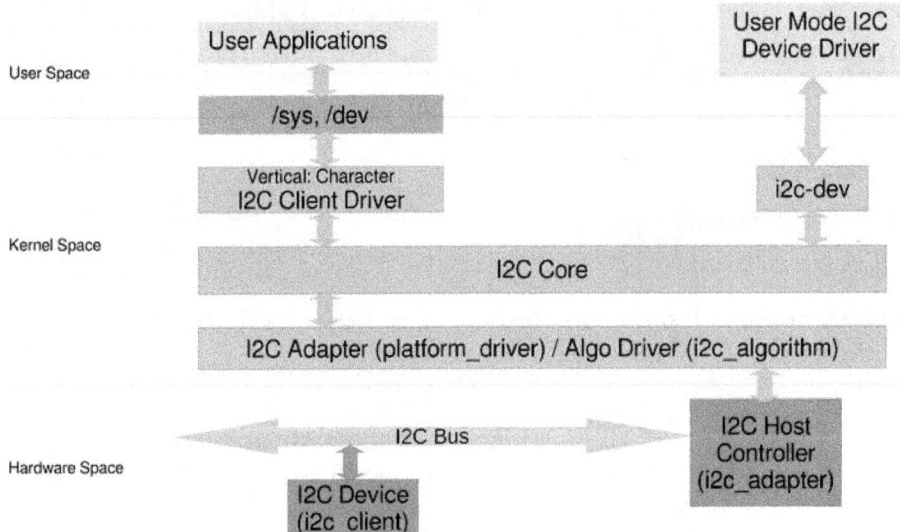

Figure 11.3: *GNU/Linux I2C subsystem*

The Linux I2C subsystem is the interface through which the system running Linux can interact with devices connected to the system's I2C bus. It is designed in such a way that the system running Linux is always the I2C master. It includes the following subsections.

There can be multiple I2C buses on the board, so each system bus is represented on Linux using the **i2c_adapter** structure (defined in **include/linux/i2c.h**).

Here are the important fields present in this structure:

- **bus number**: Each bus in the system is assigned a number present in the structure of the I2C adapter, which represents it.

- **I2C algorithm**: Each I2C bus works with a certain communication protocol between devices. The algorithm used by the bus is defined by this field. There are currently three algorithms for the I2C bus, namely **pca**, **pcf**, and **bitbanging**. These algorithms are used to communicate with devices when the driver requests to write or read data from the device.

- **I2C client**: Each device connected to the I2C bus on the system is represented using the **i2c_client** structure (defined in **include/linux/i2c.h**). Here are the important fields present in this structure.

- **Address**: This field consists of the address of the device on the bus. This address is used by the driver to communicate with the device.

- **Name**: This field is the device name used to match the driver with the device. Interrupt number: This is the device interrupt line number. I2C adapter: This is the **i2c_adapter** struct, which represents the bus on which this device is connected. Whenever the driver makes write or read requests to the bus, this field is used to identify which bus this transaction should be performed on and also what algorithm should be used to communicate with the device.

- **I2C driver**: For each device in the system, there must be a driver that controls it. For the I2C device, the corresponding driver is represented by struct **i2c_driver** (defined in **include/linux/i2c.h**). Here are the important fields defined in this structure.

- **Probe**: This is the function pointer to the driver probe routine, which is called when both the device and the driver are found on the system by the Linux device driver subsystem.

Usually, you will implement a single driver structure and instantiate all clients from it. Remember that a driver structure contains general access routines and must be initialized to zero, except for fields containing the data you provide. A client structure contains device-specific information, such as the driver model's device node and its I2C address.

```
static struct i2c_device_id foo_idtable[] = {
        { "foo", my_id_for_foo },
        { "bar", my_id_for_bar },
        { }
};


MODULE_DEVICE_TABLE(i2c, foo_idtable);


static struct i2c_driver foo_driver = {
        .driver = {
                .name   = "foo",
```

```
        .pm       = &foo_pm_ops,  /* optional */
    },

    .id_table      = foo_idtable,
    .probe_new     = foo_probe,
    .remove        = foo_remove,
    /* if device autodetection is needed: */
    .class         = I2C_CLASS_SOMETHING,
    .detect        = foo_detect,
    .address_list  = normal_i2c,

    .shutdown      = foo_shutdown, /* optional */
    .command       = foo_command,  /* optional, deprecated */
}
```

The name field is the name of the driver and must not contain spaces. It must match the module name (if the driver can be compiled as a module), although you can use **MODULE_ ALIAS** (passing "foo" in this example) to add another name for the module. If the driver name does not match the module name, the module will not be automatically loaded (**hotplug/coldplug**).

All other fields are for callback functions, which will be explained as follows.

Each client structure has a special data field that can point to any structure. You should use it to maintain device-specific data:

```
/* store the value */
void i2c_set_clientdata(struct i2c_client *client, void *data);


/* retrieve the value */
void *i2c_get_clientdata(const struct i2c_client *client);
```

Note that starting with kernel 2.6.34, you no longer need to set the data field to NULL in **Remove()** or if **probe()** fails. The **i2c** core does this automatically on these occasions. These are also the only times the core will touch this area.

Let us say we have a valid client structure. At some point, we will need to collect information from the client or write new information to the client.

The author found it useful to define the functions **foo_read** and **foo_write** for this. In some cases, it will be easier to call I2C functions directly, but many chips have some sort of register value idea that can easily be encapsulated:

```
int foo_read_value(struct i2c_client *client, u8 reg)
{
```

```
        if (reg < 0x10) /* byte-sized register */
                return i2c_smbus_read_byte_data(client, reg);
        else            /* word-sized register */
                return i2c_smbus_read_word_data(client, reg);
}


int foo_write_value(struct i2c_client *client, u8 reg, u16 value)
{
        if (reg == 0x10)        /* Impossible to write - driver error! */
                return -EINVAL;
        else if (reg < 0x10)    /* byte-sized register */
                return i2c_smbus_write_byte_data(client, reg, value);
        else                    /* word-sized register */
                return i2c_smbus_write_word_data(client, reg, value);
}
```

Of course, the function skeletons above should not be copied literally but must be modified and adapted according to your use.

The Linux I2C stack was originally written to support access to hardware monitoring chips on PC motherboards and is therefore used to integrate certain assumptions more appropriate to SMBus (and PCs) than to I2C. One of these assumptions was that most adapter and device drivers support the **SMBUS_QUICK** protocol to detect the presence of devices. Another reason was that devices and their drivers could be sufficiently configured using only such probe primitives.

As Linux and its I2C stack have become more widely used in embedded systems and complex components such as DVB adapters, these assumptions have become more problematic. Drivers for I2C devices that issue interrupts require more (and different) configuration information, as do drivers handling chip variants that cannot be distinguished by the protocol probe or require board-specific information to function correctly.

The system infrastructure, usually the board-specific initialization code or boot firmware, indicates the existing I2C devices. For example, there may be a table in the kernel or from the bootloader identifying I2C devices and relating them to board-specific configuration information regarding IRQs and other wiring artifacts, chip type, etc. This could be used to create **i2c_client** objects for each I2C device.

Drivers for I2C devices using this binding model work like any other type of driver in Linux: they provide a **probe()** method to bind to these devices and a **remove()** method to unbind them:

```
static int foo_probe(struct i2c_client *client);
static void foo_remove(struct i2c_client *client);
```

Remember that **i2c_driver** does not create these client descriptors. The handle can be used during **foo_probe()**. If **foo_probe()** reports success (zero, not a negative status code), it can save the handle and use it until **foo_remove()** returns. This binding model is used by most Linux drivers.

The **probe** function is called when an entry in the **table_id** name field matches the device name. If the **probe** function needs this input, it can retrieve it using:

```
const struct i2c_device_id *id = i2c_match_id(foo_idtable, client);
```

If you know for a fact that an I2C device is connected to a given I2C bus, you can instantiate that device by simply populating an **i2c_board_info** structure with the device address and driver name and calling **i2c_new_client_device()**. This will create the device, then the driver kernel will take care of finding the right driver and call its **probe()** method. If a driver supports different device types, you can specify the desired type using the type field. You can also specify an IRQ and platform data if necessary.

Sometimes, you know that a device is connected to a given I2C bus, but you do not know the exact address it uses. This happens, for example, on TV adapters, where the same driver supports dozens of slightly different models, and the I2C device addresses change from one model to another. In this case, you can use the **i2c_new_scanned_device()** variant, which is similar to **i2c_new_client_device()**, except that it requires an additional list of possible I2C addresses to probe. A device is created for the first responsive address in the list. If you expect multiple devices to be present in the address range, simply call **i2c_new_scanned_device()** that many times.

The call to **i2c_new_client_device()** or **i2c_new_scanned_device()** usually occurs in the I2C bus driver. You may want to save the returned **i2c_client** reference for later use.

The device detection mechanism has several drawbacks. You need a reliable way to identify supported devices (usually using dedicated, device-specific ID registers), otherwise, detection errors will occur, and things can go wrong quickly. Keep in mind that the I2C protocol does not include any standard way to detect the presence of a chip at a given address, much less a standard way to identify devices. Worse still, the lack of semantics associated with bus transfers means that the same transfer can be seen as a read operation by one chip and as a write operation by another chip. For these reasons, device detection is considered a legacy mechanism and should not be used in new code.

Each I2C device created using **i2c_new_client_device()** or **i2c_new_scanned_device()** can be unregistered by calling **i2c_unregister_device()**. If you do not call it explicitly, it will be called automatically before the underlying I2C bus itself is removed because a device cannot outlive its parent in the device driver model.

The following code shows an almost complete driver that is communicating with an I2C device:

- Include necessary header files for Linux kernel module development, such as module management (**module.h**), initialization (**init.h**), memory management (**slab.h**), I2C bus communication (**i2c.h**), delay functions (**delay.h**), and kernel-related functions (**kernel.h**):

```
#include <linux/module.h>
#include <linux/init.h>
#include <linux/slab.h>
#include <linux/i2c.h>
#include <linux/delay.h>
#include <linux/kernel.h>
```

- Define constants for the I2C bus number (**I2C_BUS_AVAILABLE**), the name of the slave device and driver (**SLAVE_DEVICE_NAME**), and the I2C address of the SSD1306 OLED display (**SSD1306_SLAVE_ADDR**):

```
#define I2C_BUS_AVAILABLE   (          11 )              // I2C Bus
that we have created
#define SLAVE_DEVICE_NAME   ( "BPB_DEVICE" )            // Device and
Driver Name
#define SSD1306_SLAVE_ADDR  (        0x3C )
```

- Declare static pointers to **i2c_adapter** and **i2c_client** structures, which will be used to handle the I2C adapter and the OLED display client device, respectively. They are initialized to NULL:

```
static struct i2c_adapter *etx_i2c_adapter      = NULL;
static struct i2c_client  *etx_i2c_client_oled = NULL;
```

- Defines a function **I2C_Write** that sends data to the I2C client device. It takes a buffer **buf** and its length **len** as parameters. Inside the function, the **i2c_master_send** function is called to perform the actual data transmission. The return value of the function indicates the success or failure of the operation:

```
static int I2C_Write(unsigned char *buf, unsigned int len)
{
    /*
    ** Sending Start condition, Slave address with R/W bit,
    ** ACK/NACK and Stop condtions will be handled internally.
    */
    int ret = i2c_master_send(etx_i2c_client_oled, buf, len);
    return ret;
}
```

- Defines a function **I2C_Read** that reads data from the I2C client device. It takes a buffer **out_buff** and its length **len** as parameters. Inside the function, the **i2c_**

master_recv function is called to perform the actual data reception. The return value of the function indicates the success or failure of the operation:

```
static int I2C_Read(unsigned char *out_buf, unsigned int len)
{
    /*
    ** Sending Start condition, Slave address with R/W bit,
    ** ACK/NACK and Stop condtions will be handled internally.
    */
    int ret = i2c_master_recv(etx_i2c_client_oled, out_buf, len);

    return ret;
}
```

- Defines a function **SSD1306_Write3** that writes data or commands to the SSD1306 OLED display. It takes a Boolean parameter **is_cmd,** to determine whether the provided data is a command or not. Inside the function, a control byte is constructed based on the value of **is_cmd**, and then the data is sent to the OLED display using the **I2C_Write** function:

```
static void SSD1306_Write(bool is_cmd, unsigned char data)
{
    unsigned char buf[2] = {0};
    int ret;

    if( is_cmd == true )
    {
        buf[0] = 0x00;
    }
    else
    {
        buf[0] = 0x40;
    }

    buf[1] = data;

    ret = I2C_Write(buf, 2);
}
```

- Defines the **SSD1306_DisplayInit** function, which initializes the SSD1306 OLED display. It sends a series of commands to configure various parameters and settings of the OLED display, such as turning the display off, setting the clock divide ratio, setting the multiplex ratio, setting the display offset, enabling the charge pump, setting the memory addressing mode, setting the contrast control, etc. Finally, it turns on the display in normal mode and returns 0 to indicate successful initialization:

```
static int SSD1306_DisplayInit(void)
{
    msleep(100);                    // delay


    /* Commands to initialize the SSD_1306 OLED Display */
    SSD1306_Write(true, 0xAE); // Entire Display OFF
    SSD1306_Write(true, 0xD5); // Set Display Clock Divide Ratio and
Oscillator Frequency
    SSD1306_Write(true, 0x80); // Default Setting for Display Clock
Divide Ratio and Oscillator Frequency that is recommended
    SSD1306_Write(true, 0xA8); // Set Multiplex Ratio
    SSD1306_Write(true, 0x3F); // 64 COM lines
    SSD1306_Write(true, 0xD3); // Set display offset
    SSD1306_Write(true, 0x00); // 0 offset
    SSD1306_Write(true, 0x40); // Set first line as the start line of
the display
    SSD1306_Write(true, 0x8D); // Charge pump
    SSD1306_Write(true, 0x14); // Enable charge dump during display
on
    SSD1306_Write(true, 0x20); // Set memory addressing mode
    SSD1306_Write(true, 0x00); // Horizontal addressing mode
    SSD1306_Write(true, 0xA1); // Set segment remap with column
address 127 mapped to segment 0
    SSD1306_Write(true, 0xC8); // Set com output scan direction,
scan from com63 to com 0
    SSD1306_Write(true, 0xDA); // Set com pins hardware configuration
    SSD1306_Write(true, 0x12); // Alternative com pin configuration,
disable com left/right remap
    SSD1306_Write(true, 0x81); // Set contrast control
    SSD1306_Write(true, 0x80); // Set Contrast to 128
    SSD1306_Write(true, 0xD9); // Set pre-charge period
    SSD1306_Write(true, 0xF1); // Phase 1 period of 15 DCLK, Phase 2
period of 1 DCLK
    SSD1306_Write(true, 0xDB); // Set Vcomh deselect level
    SSD1306_Write(true, 0x20); // Vcomh deselect level ~ 0.77 Vcc
    SSD1306_Write(true, 0xA4); // Entire display ON, resume to RAM
```

```
content display
    SSD1306_Write(true, 0xA6); // Set Display in Normal Mode, 1 =
ON, 0 = OFF
    SSD1306_Write(true, 0x2E); // Deactivate scroll
    SSD1306_Write(true, 0xAF); // Display ON in normal mode
    return 0;
}
```

- Defines the **SSD1306_Fill** function, which fills the entire SSD1306 OLED display with the specified data. It calculates the total number of pixels in the display (128 columns x 8 pages x 8 bits per page) and then iterates through each pixel, writing the data to the display using the **SSD1306_Write** function with false indicating data transmission:

```
static void SSD1306_Fill(unsigned char data)
{
    unsigned int total  = 128 * 8;  // 8 pages x 128 segments x 8
bits of data
    unsigned int i      = 0;
    for(i = 0; i < total; i++)
    {
        SSD1306_Write(false, data);
    }
}
```

- Defines the **probe** function (**etx_oled_probe**) for the OLED driver. When a new device is detected on the I2C bus, this function is called. It initializes the OLED display using the **SSD1306_DisplayInit** function and fills the display with a specified data pattern using the **SSD1306_Fill**. It then prints a message to the kernel log to indicate successful probing and returns 0 to indicate success:

```
static int etx_oled_probe(struct i2c_client *client,
                        const struct i2c_device_id *id)
{
    SSD1306_DisplayInit();
    SSD1306_Fill(0xFF);
    pr_info("OLED Probed!!!\n");
    return 0;
}
```

- Defines the **remove** function (**etx_oled_remove**) for the OLED driver. When the device is removed or the driver is unloaded, this function is called. It simply prints a message to the kernel log to indicate that the OLED display has been removed and returns 0 to indicate success:

```
static int etx_oled_remove(struct i2c_client *client)
{
    pr_info("OLED Removed!!!\n");
    return 0;
}
```

- Defines an array **etx_oled_id** of **i2c_device_id** structures, which provides a mapping between the device name (**SLAVE_DEVICE_NAME**) and its driver-specific identifier. This mapping is used by the kernel to match the detected device with the appropriate driver. The **MODULE_DEVICE_TABLE** macro registers this array with the kernel:

```
MODULE_DEVICE_TABLE(i2c, etx_oled_id);
```

- Defines the **etx_oled_driver** structure, which represents the I2C driver for the OLED display. It contains a nested struct driver field with the name set to the device name (**SLAVE_DEVICE_NAME**) and the owner set to **THIS_MODULE** to indicate that the module owns this driver. Additionally, it specifies the probe and remove functions (**etx_oled_probe** and **etx_oled_remove**, respectively) to be called when a new device is detected or removed. The **id_table** field is initialized with the array of device IDs (**etx_oled_id**) defined earlier:

```
static struct i2c_driver etx_oled_driver = {
        .driver = {
            .name    = SLAVE_DEVICE_NAME,
            .owner   = THIS_MODULE,
        },
        .probe          = etx_oled_probe,
        .remove         = etx_oled_remove,
        .id_table       = etx_oled_id,
};
```

- Defines an **i2c_board_info** structure named **oled_i2c_board_info**, which represents information about the OLED display board. It uses the **I2C_BOARD_INFO** macro to initialize the structure with the device name (**SLAVE_DEVICE_NAME**) and the I2C address of the SSD1306 OLED display (**SSD1306_SLAVE_ADDR**):

```
static struct i2c_board_info oled_i2c_board_info = {
        I2C_BOARD_INFO(SLAVE_DEVICE_NAME, SSD1306_SLAVE_ADDR)
    };
```

- Defines the module initialization function (**etx_driver_init**). It obtains a handle to the I2C adapter (**etx_i2c_adapter**) corresponding to the specified bus number (**I2C_BUS_AVAILABLE**) using **i2c_get_adapter**. If the adapter handle is obtained successfully, it creates a new I2C client device (**etx_i2c_client_oled**) using

i2c_new_device, passing the adapter handle and the board information. If the client device creation is successful, it adds the I2C driver (**etx_oled_driver**) to the system using **i2c_add_driver**. Finally, it prints a message to the kernel log indicating that the client driver has been added and returns 0 to indicate successful initialization:

```
static int __init etx_driver_init(void)
{
    etx_i2c_adapter     = i2c_get_adapter(I2C_BUS_AVAILABLE);
    if( etx_i2c_adapter != NULL )
    {
        etx_i2c_client_oled = i2c_new_device(etx_i2c_adapter, &oled_
i2c_board_info);
        if( etx_i2c_client_oled != NULL )
        {
            i2c_add_driver(&etx_oled_driver);
        }
        i2c_put_adapter(etx_i2c_adapter);
    }
    pr_info("Client Driver Added!!!\n");
    return 0;
}
```

- Defines the module **exit** function (**etx_driver_exit**). It unregisters the I2C client device (**etx_i2c_client_oled**) using **i2c_unregister_device** and then removes the I2C driver (**etx_oled_driver**) from the system using **i2c_del_driver**. Finally, it prints a message to the kernel log indicating that the client driver has been removed:

```
static void __exit etx_driver_exit(void)
{
    i2c_unregister_device(etx_i2c_client_oled);
    i2c_del_driver(&etx_oled_driver);
    pr_info("Client Driver Removed!!!\n");
}
```

Serial Peripheral Interface architecture

Serial Peripheral Interface (**SPI**) is widely used in embedded systems because it is a simple and effective interface: essentially a multiplexed shift register. Its three signal wires contain a clock (SCK, often in the range 1 to 20 MHz), a **Master Out, Slave In** (**MObSI**) data line, and a **Master In, Slave Out** (**MISO**) data line. SPI is a full duplex protocol;

for each bit shifted off the MOSI line (one per clock), another is shifted onto the MISO line. These bits are assembled into words of different sizes while traveling to and from system memory. An additional chip select line is typically active-low (nCS); four signals are normally used for each device, plus sometimes an interrupt.

An SPI is a synchronous serial interface technology introduced by Motorola. consists of a master device and one or more slave devices.

The central idea of SPI is that each device has a shift register that it can use to send or receive a byte of data. These two shift registers are connected together in a ring, with the output of one going to the input of the other and vice versa. One device, the master, controls the common clock signal that ensures that each register shifts a bit exactly as the other register shifts a bit out (and vice versa):

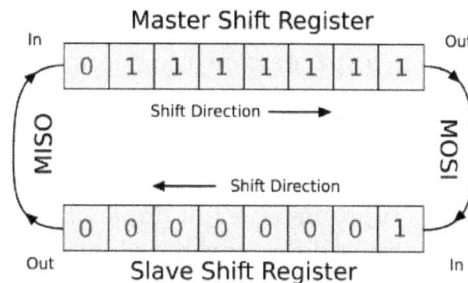

Figure 11.4: *The two shift registers interconnected*

SPI needs at least four wires. However, some recent devices also support 3-pin mode and 4-pin mode:

- **MOSI**: Master output, slave input
- **MISO**: Master Input Slave Output
- **SCLK**: Serial clock
- **SS/CS/CE**: Ointment Selection/Chip Selection/Chip Activation

The following figure details the electronic diagram between a master module and several slaves using an SPI bus:

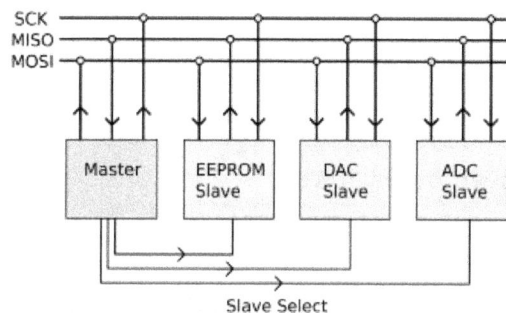

Figure 11.5: *Diagram of an SPI bus between a master and slaves*

The SPI bus features listed here provide a generalized interface for declaring SPI buses and devices, managing them according to the standard Linux driver model, and performing input/output operations. Currently, only "master" side interfaces are supported, where Linux communicates with SPI devices and does not implement such a device itself (The interfaces supporting the implementation of SPI slaves would necessarily be different).

The programming interface is structured around two types of drivers and two types of devices. A "controller driver" abstracts the controller hardware, which can be as simple as a set of GPIO pins or as complex as a pair of FIFOs connected to two DMA motors on the other side of the SPI shift register (maximizing the flow). Such drivers bridge the bus they are on (often the platform bus) and SPI and expose the SPI side of their device as a **spi_master** structure. SPI devices are children of this master, represented by a **spi_device** structure and made from **spi_board_info** structure descriptors, which are usually provided by board-specific initialization code. A **spi_driver** structure is called a "protocol driver" and is linked to a **spi_device** using normal driver template calls.

The I/O model is a set of queued messages. Protocol drivers submit one or more struct **spi_message** objects, which are processed and completed asynchronously. (Synchronous wrappers do exist, however.) Messages are constructed from one or more **spi_transfer** struct objects, each of which encapsulates a full-duplex SPI transfer. Various protocol tuning options are necessary because different chips adopt very different policies for how they use the bits transferred with SPI.

Statistics for **spi** transfers:

```
struct spi_statistics {
  spinlock_t lock;
  unsigned long messages;
  unsigned long transfers;
  unsigned long errors;
  unsigned long timedout;
  unsigned long spi_sync;
  unsigned long spi_sync_immediate;
  unsigned long spi_async;
  unsigned long long bytes;
  unsigned long long bytes_rx;
  unsigned long long bytes_tx;
#define SPI_STATISTICS_HISTO_SIZE 17
  unsigned long transfer_bytes_histo;
  unsigned long transfers_split_maxsize;
};
```

The SPI device driver in Linux is mainly managed by the SPI subsystem, and it is divided into 3 sections:

- **SPI core**: The SPI core provides APIs for defining basic data structures, registering, and handling the rollback of SPI controller drivers and device drivers. It is a platform-independent hardware layer, which hides differences from the physical bus controller downward and defines a unified access strategy and interface.

  It provides a unified interface upwards. So, the SPI device driver can send and receive data through the SPI bus controller. In the Linux kernel, the main SPI code is located in **kernel/drivers/spi/spi.c**.

- **SPI controller driver**: The SPI controller driver is the platform-specific driver. So, every SoC manufacturer has to write this driver for their platform or MCU. controllers These SPI controller drivers can be integrated into System-On-Chip processors and often support master and slave roles.

  These drivers touch hardware registers and may use DMA, or they may be GPIO bit bangers, requiring only GPIO pins. Its responsibility is to implement a corresponding read and write method for each SPI bus in the system.

  Physically, each SPI controller can connect multiple SPI slave devices. When the system is powered on, the SPI controller driver is loaded first. A controller driver is used to support reading and writing a specific SPI bus. So, this SPI controller driver is similar to the I2C adapter/bus driver.

  You can see all SPI controller drivers in **kernel/drivers/spi/**.

- **SPI protocol driver**: Each SPI bus controller can connect to multiple slave devices. This driver is used to communicate with specific devices via the SPI bus. This is similar to the I2C client driver.

Usage

To go into detail, let us look at an example of drivers using SPI messages:

- Include necessary header files for Linux kernel module development, such as module management (**module.h**), initialization (**init.h**), SPI usage (**spi.h**):

  ```
  #include <linux/module.h>
  #include <linux/init.h>
  #include <linux/spi/spi.h>
  #include <linux/delay.h>
  #include <linux/kernel.h>
  ```

- Define macros for the SPI bus number, chip select line, and bus speed:

  ```
  #define SPI_BUS 0
  #define SPI_BUS_CS1 0
  #define SPI_BUS_SPEED 1000000
  ```

- Declares a pointer to an **spi_device** structure, representing the SPI device:

```
static struct spi_device *spi_device;
```

- Defines the **probe** function, which is called when the SPI device is detected. Sets up the SPI device parameters, configures the device using **spi_setup**, and performs a simple **read**/**write** operation to verify communication. Prints messages to the kernel log and returns **0** on success or an error code on failure:

```
static int spi_device_probe(struct spi_device *spi)
{
    int ret;
    u8 tx[] = {0xAA};
    u8 rx[ARRAY_SIZE(tx)];

    spi->max_speed_hz = SPI_BUS_SPEED;
    spi->mode = SPI_MODE_0;
    spi->bits_per_word = 8;
    ret = spi_setup(spi);
    if (ret) {
        pr_err("spi_setup failed\n");
        return ret;
    }

    ret = spi_write_then_read(spi, tx, ARRAY_SIZE(tx), rx, ARRAY_
SIZE(rx));
    if (ret) {
        pr_err("spi_write_then_read failed\n");
        return ret;
    }

    pr_info("SPI device probed successfully\n");
    return 0;
}
```

- Defines the **remove** function, called when the SPI device is removed:

```
static int spi_device_remove(struct spi_device *spi)
{
    pr_info("SPI device removed\n");
    return 0;
}
```

- Defines an array of device tree IDs, specifying the compatible devices:

```
static const struct of_device_id spi_device_dt_ids[] = {
    { .compatible = "spi_device" },
    { }
};
```

- The **MODULE_DEVICE_TABLE** macro registers this array with the kernel:

```
MODULE_DEVICE_TABLE(of, spi_device_dt_ids);
```

- Defines the SPI driver structure, specifying the driver name, device tree match table, **probe** function, and remove function:

```
static struct spi_driver spi_device_driver = {
    .driver = {
        .name = "spi_device",
        .of_match_table = spi_device_dt_ids,
    },
    .probe = spi_device_probe,
    .remove = spi_device_remove,
};
```

- Initialize the driver:

```
static int __init spi_device_init(void)
{
    int ret;
    struct spi_master *master;

    master = spi_busnum_to_master(SPI_BUS);
    if (!master) {
        pr_err("spi_busnum_to_master failed\n");
        return -ENODEV;
    }

    spi_device = spi_alloc_device(master);
    if (!spi_device) {
        pr_err("spi_alloc_device failed\n");
        return -ENOMEM;
    }

    spi_device->chip_select = SPI_BUS_CS1;
    spi_device->max_speed_hz = SPI_BUS_SPEED;
```

```
    spi_device->mode = SPI_MODE_0;
    spi_device->bits_per_word = 8;
    spi_device->dev.platform_data = NULL;
    strlcpy(spi_device->modalias, "spi_device", SPI_NAME_SIZE);

    ret = spi_add_device(spi_device);
    if (ret) {
        pr_err("spi_add_device failed\n");
        spi_dev_put(spi_device);
        return ret;
    }

    ret = spi_register_driver(&spi_device_driver);
    if (ret) {
        pr_err("spi_register_driver failed\n");
        spi_unregister_device(spi_device);
        return ret;
    }

    pr_info("SPI device driver registered\n");
    return 0;
}
```

- Clean the driver before exiting:

```
static void __exit spi_device_exit(void)
{
    spi_unregister_driver(&spi_device_driver);
    spi_unregister_device(spi_device);
    pr_info("SPI device driver unregistered\n");
}
```

Serial architecture

To be properly integrated into a Linux system, serial ports must be visible as TTY devices from userspace applications. Therefore, the serial driver must be part of the TTY subsystem of the kernel. Until version 2.6, serial drivers were implemented directly behind the TTY kernel, and lots of complexity was involved. Since version 2.6, a specialized TTY driver, **serial_core**, facilitates the development of drivers; see **include/linux/serial_core.h** for the main definitions of **Serial_core**.

The line discipline that cooks the data exchanged with the **tty** driver. For normal serial ports, **N_TTY** is used.

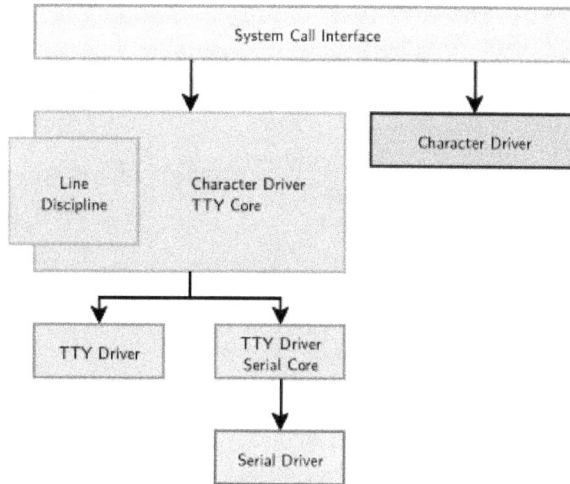

Figure 11.6: Linux serial architecture

To be properly integrated into a Linux system, serial ports must be visible as TTY devices from userspace applications. Therefore, the serial driver must be part of the TTY subsystem of the kernel. Until version 2.6, serial drivers were implemented directly behind the TTY kernel, and lots of complexity was involved. Since version 2.6, a specialized TTY driver, **serial_core**, facilitates the development of drivers; see **include/linux/serial_core.h** for the main definitions of **Serial_core**.

The line discipline that cooks the data is exchanged with the **tty** driver. For normal serial ports, **N_TTY** is used.

A data structure called **uart_driver** represents a driver:

- Unique instance for each driver
- **uart_register_driver()** and **uart_unregister_driver()**
- Example code from **drivers/serial/atmel_serial.c**:

```
static struct uart_driver atmel_uart = {
        .owner       = THIS_MODULE,
        .driver_name = "atmel_serial",
        .dev_name    = ATMEL_DEVICENAME,
        .major       = SERIAL_ATMEL_MAJOR,
        .minor       = MINOR_START,
        .nr          = ATMEL_MAX_UART,
        .cons        = ATMEL_CONSOLE_DEVICE,
```

```
};

static struct platform_driver atmel_serial_driver = {
        .probe       = atmel_serial_probe,
        .remove         = atmel_serial_remove,
        .driver         = {
                .name               = "atmel_usart_serial",
                .of_match_table         = of_match_ptr(atmel_serial_
dt_ids),
                .pm                 = pm_ptr(&atmel_serial_pm_ops),
        },
};
```

A data structure **uart_port** represents a port:

- One instance for each port (several per driver are possible)
- **uart_add_one_port()** and **uart_remove_one_port()**
- It can be allocated statically or dynamically
- Usually saved at **probe time ()** and not saved at **delete time ()**
- Most important areas:
  - **iotype**: I/O access type, typically **UPIO_MEM** for memory-mapped devices
  - **mapbase**: Physical address of registers
  - **irq**: The IRQ channel number
  - **membase**: The virtual address of the registers
  - **uartclk**: The clock frequency
  - **ops**: Pointer to operations
  - **dev**: Pointer to device (**platform_device** or other)

A data structure **uart_ops** contains pointers to operations:

- Linked from **uart_port** via **ops** field
- Important operations:
  - **tx_empty()**: Indicates whether the transmission FIFO is empty or not
  - **set_mctrl() and get_mctrl()**: Allow you to set and obtain modem control parameters (RTS, DTR, LOOP, etc.)
  - **start_tx() and stop_tx()**: To start and stop transmission
  - **stop_rx()**: To stop reception
  - **startup() and shutdown()**: Called when the port is open/closed

- ○ **request_port() and release_port()**: Request/release I/O or memory regions

  - ○ **set_termios()**: Modifies port parameters

- See detailed description in **Documentation/serial/driver**

The **start_tx()** method should start transmitting characters over the serial port. Characters to be transmitted are stored in a circular buffer, implemented by a struct structure **uart_circ**. It contains:

- **buf[]**: The character buffer

- **tail**: Index of the next character to transmit. After transmission, the tail must be

- updated using **tail = tail &(UART_XMIT_SIZE - 1)**

There are some utility functions on **uart_circ**:

- **uart_circ_empty()**: Indicates if the circular buffer is empty

- **uart_circ_chars_ending()**: Returns the number of characters remaining to transmit

From a **uart_port** pointer, this structure is accessible using **port->status->xmit**.

On receipt, usually in an interrupt handler, the driver must:

- Increment **port→icount.rx**

- Call **uart_handle_break()** if a BRK was received, and if it returns **TRUE**, ignore to the next character

- If an error occurred, increment **port->icount.parity, port→icount.frame, port->icount.overrun** depending on error type

- Call **uart_handle_sysrq_char()** with the received character, and if it returns **TRUE**, move to the next character

- Call **uart_insert_char()** with the received character and a status; this status is **TTY_NORMAL** if everything is fine, or **TTY_BREAK, TTY_PARITY, TTY_FRAME** in error case.

- Call **tty_flip_buffer_push()** to push data to the TTY layer

Usage

To go into detail, let us look at an example of drivers using a serial interface:

- Include necessary header files for Linux kernel module development, such as module management (**module.h**), initialization (**init.h**), serial usage (**serial_ core.h, serial_reg.h**), tty:

```
#include <linux/module.h>
#include <linux/init.h>
```

```
#include <linux/serial_core.h>
#include <linux/serial_reg.h>
#include <linux/tty.h>
#include <linux/tty_flip.h>
#include <linux/platform_device.h>
```

- Defines macros for the driver name, UART base address (example address for COM1), and IRQ number (example IRQ number for COM1):

```
#define DRIVER_NAME "simple_serial"
#define UART_BASE 0x3F8  // Base address for COM1 (example address)
#define UART_IRQ  4       // IRQ number for COM1 (example IRQ number)
```

- Defines a structure (**simple_serial_port**) that contains a **uart_port** structure, representing the UART port:

```
struct simple_serial_port {
    struct uart_port port;
};
```

- Declares a static instance of the **simple_serial_port** structure, representing the serial port managed by this driver:

```
static struct simple_serial_port simple_port;
```

- Defines the **simple_serial_startup** function, which is called to start up the serial port. It prints a message to the kernel log and returns **0**. Actual initialization steps should be added where indicated:

```
static int simple_serial_startup(struct uart_port *port)
{
    pr_info("%s: starting up\n", DRIVER_NAME);
    // Initialization steps to start up the serial port (e.g.,
enabling interrupts)
    return 0;
}
```

- Defines the **simple_serial_shutdown** function, which is called to shut down the serial port. It prints a message to the kernel log. Actual cleanup steps should be added where indicated:

```
static void simple_serial_shutdown(struct uart_port *port)
{
    pr_info("%s: shutting down\n", DRIVER_NAME);
    // Cleanup steps to shut down the serial port
}
```

- Defines the **simple_serial_tx_empty** function, which checks if the transmit buffer is empty and returns the status:

```
static unsigned int simple_serial_tx_empty(struct uart_port *port)
{
    // Check if the transmit buffer is empty
    return UART_LSR_THRE; // Transmitter Holding Register Empty
}
```

- Defines the **simple_serial_set_mctrl** function, which sets the modem control lines. The actual implementation should be added where indicated:

```
static void simple_serial_set_mctrl(struct uart_port *port, unsigned
int mctrl)
{
    // Set modem control lines
}
```

- Defines the **simple_serial_get_mctrl** function, which gets the modem control lines status:

```
static unsigned int simple_serial_get_mctrl(struct uart_port *port)
{
    // Get modem control lines status
    return 0;
}
```

- Defines the **simple_serial_stop_tx** function, which stops transmitting data and prints a message to the kernel log. The actual implementation should be added where indicated:

```
static void simple_serial_stop_tx(struct uart_port *port)
{
    pr_info("%s: stopping TX\n", DRIVER_NAME);
    // Stop transmitting data
}
```

- Defines the **simple_serial_start_tx** function, which starts transmitting data and prints a message to the kernel log. The actual implementation should be added where indicated:

```
static void simple_serial_start_tx(struct uart_port *port)
{
    pr_info("%s: starting TX\n", DRIVER_NAME);
    // Start transmitting data
}
```

- Defines the **simple_serial_stop_rx** function, which stops receiving data and prints a message to the kernel log. The actual implementation should be added where indicated:

```
static void simple_serial_stop_rx(struct uart_port *port)
{
    pr_info("%s: stopping RX\n", DRIVER_NAME);
    // Stop receiving data
}
```

- Defines the **simple_serial_enable_ms** function, which enables modem status interrupts. The actual implementation should be added where indicated:

```
static void simple_serial_enable_ms(struct uart_port *port)
{
    // Enable modem status interrupts
}
```

- Defines the **simple_serial_handle_irq** function, which handles interrupts for the serial port and prints a message to the kernel log. The actual implementation should be added where indicated:

```
static void simple_serial_handle_irq(struct uart_port *port)
{
    pr_info("%s: handling IRQ\n", DRIVER_NAME);
    // Handle interrupts for the serial port
}
```

- Defines a **uart_ops** structure (**simple_serial_ops**) that maps the UART operations to the functions implemented in the previous blocks:

```
static const struct uart_ops simple_serial_ops = {
    .startup        = simple_serial_startup,
    .shutdown       = simple_serial_shutdown,
    .tx_empty       = simple_serial_tx_empty,
    .set_mctrl      = simple_serial_set_mctrl,
    .get_mctrl      = simple_serial_get_mctrl,
    .stop_tx        = simple_serial_stop_tx,
    .start_tx       = simple_serial_start_tx,
    .stop_rx        = simple_serial_stop_rx,
    .enable_ms      = simple_serial_enable_ms,
    .handle_irq     = simple_serial_handle_irq,
};
```

- Defines a **uart_driver** structure (**simple_uart_driver**) that represents the UART driver, specifying the module owner, driver name, device name, major and minor numbers, and the number of devices managed by this driver:

```
static struct uart_driver simple_uart_driver = {
        .owner          = THIS_MODULE,
        .driver_name    = DRIVER_NAME,
        .dev_name       = DRIVER_NAME,
        .major          = 0,
        .minor          = 0,
        .nr             = 1,
};
```

- This block defines the module initialization function (**simple_serial_init**):

```
static int __init simple_serial_init(void)
{
        int ret;

        simple_port.port.iotype = UPIO_PORT;
        simple_port.port.iobase = UART_BASE;
        simple_port.port.irq = UART_IRQ;
        simple_port.port.uartclk = 1843200;
        simple_port.port.fifosize = 16;
        simple_port.port.ops = &simple_serial_ops;
        simple_port.port.flags = UPF_BOOT_AUTOCONF;
        simple_port.port.line = 0;

        ret = uart_register_driver(&simple_uart_driver);
        if (ret)
            return ret;

        ret = uart_add_one_port(&simple_uart_driver, &simple_port.port);
        if (ret) {
            uart_unregister_driver(&simple_uart_driver);
            return ret;
        }

        pr_info("%s: driver initialized\n", DRIVER_NAME);
        return 0;
}
```

- Remove the UART port and unregister the UART driver:

```
static void __exit simple_serial_exit(void)
{
    uart_remove_one_port(&simple_uart_driver, &simple_port.port);
    uart_unregister_driver(&simple_uart_driver);
    pr_info("%s: driver exited\n", DRIVER_NAME);
}
```

Peripheral Component Interconnect architecture

PCI Linux driver model restricts a device with a single driver. Linux drivers are loaded based on the PCI device ID and function. Once a driver is loaded, no other drivers for this device the vice can be loaded. Referring to *Figure 11.7*, if the root port hot-plug driver is loaded first, it claims the Root Port device. PCI Linux Driver Model, therefore, prevents support for multiple services per PCI Express port using individual service drivers.

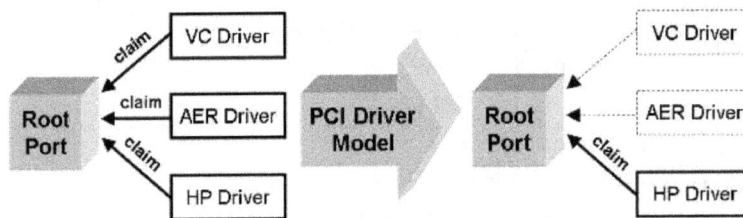

Figure 11.7: Service Drivers under the Linux PCI Driver Model

The PCI architecture was designed to replace the ISA standard, with three main goals: to achieve better performance when transferring data between the computer and its peripherals, to be as platform independent as possible, and to simplify the addition and removal of devices from the system.

The PCI bus achieves better performance by using a higher clock frequency than ISA; its clock runs at 25 or 33 MHz (its actual frequency being a factor of the system clock), and implementations at 66 MHz and even 133 MHz have also recently been deployed. Additionally, it is equipped with a 32-bit data bus, and a 64-bit extension has been included in the specification. Platform independence is often a goal in computer bus design, and it is a particularly important feature of PCI, because the PC world has historically been dominated by processor-specific interface standards. PCI is currently widely used on IA-32, Alpha, PowerPC, SPARC64, and IA-64 systems, as well as some other platforms.

What is most relevant to the driver writer, however, is PCI's support for automatic interface card detection. PCI devices are jumperless (unlike most older devices) and are automatically configured at boot time. Next, the device driver must be able to access the device configuration information in order to complete the initialization. This happens without the need for any verification.

Each PCI device is identified by a bus number, device number, and function number. The PCI specification allows a single system to host up to 256 buses, but since 256 buses are not enough for many large systems, Linux now supports PCI domains. Each PCI domain can host up to 256 buses. Each bus accommodates up to 32 devices, and each device can be a multifunction card (such as an audio device accompanied by a CD-ROM drive) with up to eight functions. Therefore, each function can be identified at the hardware level by a 16-bit address or key. However, device drivers written for Linux do not need to handle these binary addresses because they use a specific data structure, called **pci_dev**, to act on devices.

Newer workstations have at least two PCI buses. Connecting multiple buses in a single system is carried out using bridges, special PCI devices whose task is to connect two buses. The general layout of a PCI system is a tree where each bus is connected to a higher-layer bus, up to bus 0 at the root of the tree. The CardBus PC card system is also connected to the PCI system via bridges. A typical PCI system is shown in *Figure 11.8*, where the various bridges are highlighted.

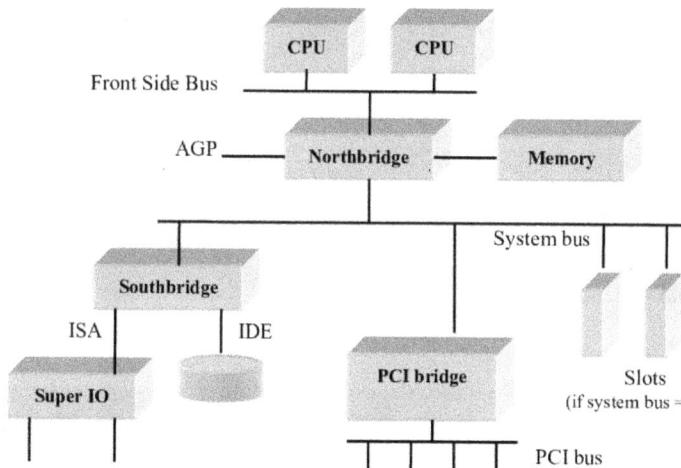

Figure 11.8: Layout of a typical PCI system

The 16-bit hardware addresses associated with PCI devices, although mostly hidden in the **pci_dev** struct object, are still occasionally visible, notably when device lists are used. One such situation is the output of **lspci** (part of the **pciutils** package, available with most distributions) and the arrangement of information in **/proc/pci** and **/proc/bus/pci**. The **sysfs** representation of PCI devices also shows this addressing scheme, with the addition of PCI domain information. When the hardware address is displayed, it can be displayed as two values (an 8-bit bus number and an 8-bit device and function number), three values (bus, device, and function), or four values (domain, bus, device, and function); All values are usually displayed in hexadecimal.

For example, **/proc/bus/pci/devices** uses a single 16-bit field (for easier parsing and sorting), while **/proc/bus/busnumber** splits the address into three fields:

Extract PCI Device Class, Vendor, and Device IDs:

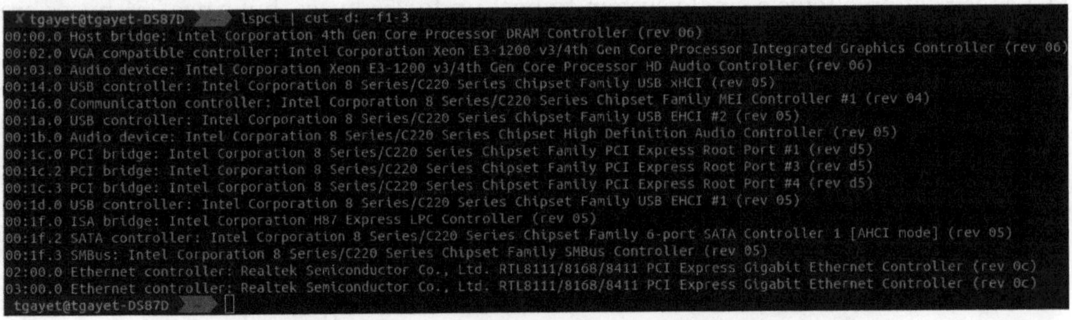

```
tgayet@tgayet-DS87D  lspci | cut -d: -f1-3
00:00.0 Host bridge: Intel Corporation 4th Gen Core Processor DRAM Controller (rev 06)
00:02.0 VGA compatible controller: Intel Corporation Xeon E3-1200 v3/4th Gen Core Processor Integrated Graphics Controller (rev 06)
00:03.0 Audio device: Intel Corporation Xeon E3-1200 v3/4th Gen Core Processor HD Audio Controller (rev 06)
00:14.0 USB controller: Intel Corporation 8 Series/C220 Series Chipset Family USB xHCI (rev 05)
00:16.0 Communication controller: Intel Corporation 8 Series/C220 Series Chipset Family MEI Controller #1 (rev 04)
00:1a.0 USB controller: Intel Corporation 8 Series/C220 Series Chipset Family USB EHCI #2 (rev 05)
00:1b.0 Audio device: Intel Corporation 8 Series/C220 Series Chipset High Definition Audio Controller (rev 05)
00:1c.0 PCI bridge: Intel Corporation 8 Series/C220 Series Chipset Family PCI Express Root Port #1 (rev d5)
00:1c.2 PCI bridge: Intel Corporation 8 Series/C220 Series Chipset Family PCI Express Root Port #3 (rev d5)
00:1c.3 PCI bridge: Intel Corporation 8 Series/C220 Series Chipset Family PCI Express Root Port #4 (rev d5)
00:1d.0 USB controller: Intel Corporation 8 Series/C220 Series Chipset Family USB EHCI #1 (rev 05)
00:1f.0 ISA bridge: Intel Corporation H87 Express LPC Controller (rev 05)
00:1f.2 SATA controller: Intel Corporation 8 Series/C220 Series Chipset Family 6-port SATA Controller 1 [AHCI mode] (rev 05)
00:1f.3 SMBus: Intel Corporation 8 Series/C220 Series Chipset Family SMBus Controller (rev 05)
02:00.0 Ethernet controller: Realtek Semiconductor Co., Ltd. RTL8111/8168/8411 PCI Express Gigabit Ethernet Controller (rev 0c)
03:00.0 Ethernet controller: Realtek Semiconductor Co., Ltd. RTL8111/8168/8411 PCI Express Gigabit Ethernet Controller (rev 0c)
tgayet@tgayet-DS87D
```

Figure 11.9: Extract PCI bus addresses

```
tgayet@tgayet-DS87D  cat /proc/bus/pci/devices | cut -f1
0000
0010
0018
00a0
00b0
00d0
00d8
00e0
00e2
00e3
00e8
00f8
00fa
00fb
0200
0300
tgayet@tgayet-DS87D
```

Figure 11.10: Display PCI device hierarchy

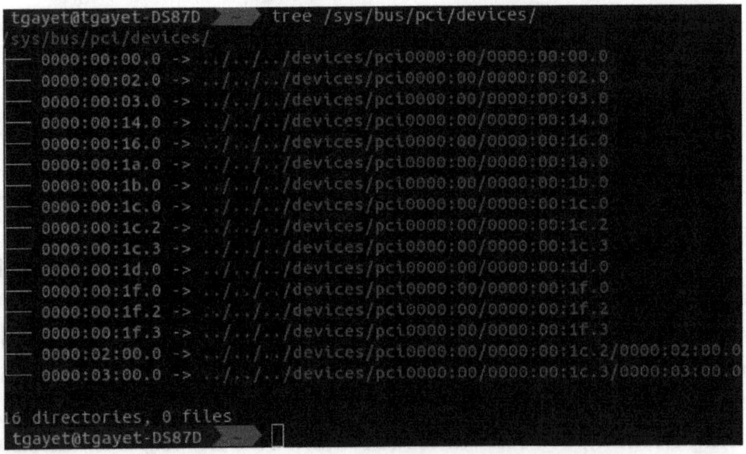

```
tgayet@tgayet-DS87D  tree /sys/bus/pci/devices/
/sys/bus/pci/devices/
├── 0000:00:00.0 -> ../../../devices/pci0000:00/0000:00:00.0
├── 0000:00:02.0 -> ../../../devices/pci0000:00/0000:00:02.0
├── 0000:00:03.0 -> ../../../devices/pci0000:00/0000:00:03.0
├── 0000:00:14.0 -> ../../../devices/pci0000:00/0000:00:14.0
├── 0000:00:16.0 -> ../../../devices/pci0000:00/0000:00:16.0
├── 0000:00:1a.0 -> ../../../devices/pci0000:00/0000:00:1a.0
├── 0000:00:1b.0 -> ../../../devices/pci0000:00/0000:00:1b.0
├── 0000:00:1c.0 -> ../../../devices/pci0000:00/0000:00:1c.0
├── 0000:00:1c.2 -> ../../../devices/pci0000:00/0000:00:1c.2
├── 0000:00:1c.3 -> ../../../devices/pci0000:00/0000:00:1c.3
├── 0000:00:1d.0 -> ../../../devices/pci0000:00/0000:00:1d.0
├── 0000:00:1f.0 -> ../../../devices/pci0000:00/0000:00:1f.0
├── 0000:00:1f.2 -> ../../../devices/pci0000:00/0000:00:1f.2
├── 0000:00:1f.3 -> ../../../devices/pci0000:00/0000:00:1f.3
├── 0000:02:00.0 -> ../../../devices/pci0000:00/0000:00:1c.2/0000:02:00.0
└── 0000:03:00.0 -> ../../../devices/pci0000:00/0000:00:1c.3/0000:03:00.0

16 directories, 0 files
tgayet@tgayet-DS87D
```

Figure 11.11: Display the PCI bus device tree

The three device lists are sorted in the same order since **lspci** uses **/proc** files as its source of information. Taking the VGA video controller as an example, 0x00a0 means 0000:00:14.0 when divided into domain (16 bits), bus (8 bits), device (5 bits), and function (3 bits).

The hardware circuitry on each peripheral board responds to requests for three address spaces: memory locations, I/O ports, and configuration registers. The first two address spaces are shared by all devices on the same PCI bus (i.e., when you access a memory slot, all devices on that PCI bus see the bus cycle at the same time). The configuration space, for its part, uses geographic addressing. Configuration requests only address one location at a time, so they never collide.

As for the driver, memory and I/O regions are accessed in the usual way via **inb**, **readb**, etc. Configuration transactions, on the other hand, are performed by calling specific kernel functions to access configuration registers. As for interrupts, each PCI slot has four interrupt pins, and each peripheral function can use one without worrying about how those pins are routed to the CPU. This routing is the responsibility of the IT platform and is implemented outside of the PCI bus. Because the PCI specification requires interrupt lines to be shareable, even a processor with a limited number of IRQ lines, such as x86, can accommodate many PCI interface cards (each with four pins). interruption).

I/O space in a PCI bus uses a 32-bit address bus (leading to 4 GB of I/O ports), while memory space is accessed with 32-bit or 64-bit addresses. 64-bit addresses are available on newer platforms. Addresses are supposed to be unique to a device, but the software can mistakenly configure two devices with the same address, making it impossible to access either one. But this problem never occurs unless a driver intentionally messes with registers it should not touch. The good news is that each memory and I/O address region offered by the interface card can be remapped using configuration transactions. That is, the firmware initializes the PCI hardware at system startup, mapping each region to a different address to avoid collisions. The addresses to which these regions are currently mapped can be read from the configuration space so that the Linux driver can access its devices without probing. After reading the configuration registers, the driver can safely access its hardware.

PCI configuration space consists of 256 bytes for each device function (except PCI Express devices, which have 4 KB of configuration space for each function), and the layout of configuration registers is standardized. Four bytes of the configuration space contain a unique function ID, so the driver can identify its device by looking up the specific ID of that device. In summary, each device card is geographically addressed to retrieve its configuration registers; the information in these registers can then be used to perform normal I/O access without the need for additional geographic addressing.

It is clear from this description that the main innovation of the PCI interface standard compared to ISA is the configuration address space. Therefore, in addition to the usual driver code, a PCI driver must be able to access the configuration space to save itself from risky probing tasks.

For the rest of this chapter, we use the word device to refer to a device function because each function on a multifunction card acts as an independent entity. When we refer to a device, we mean the tuple: domain number, bus number, device number, and function number.

The configuration registers PCI devices. All PCI devices have at least 256 bytes of address space. The first 64 bytes are standardized, while the rest are device dependent. *Figure 11.12* shows the layout of the device-independent configuration space:

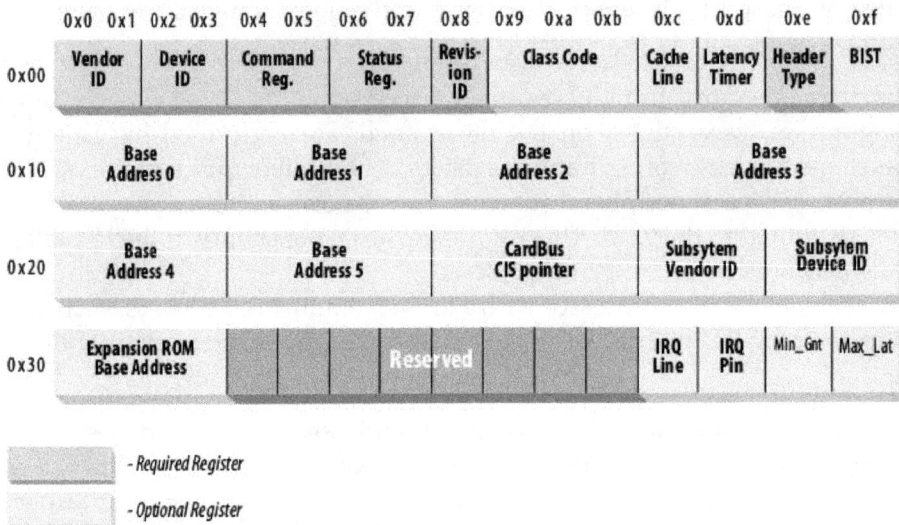

	0x0 0x1 0x2 0x3	0x4 0x5	0x6 0x7	0x8	0x9 0xa 0xb	0xc	0xd	0xe	0xf
0x00	Vendor ID · Device ID	Command Reg.	Status Reg.	Revis-ion ID	Class Code	Cache Line	Latency Timer	Header Type	BIST
0x10	Base Address 0	Base Address 1		Base Address 2		Base Address 3			
0x20	Base Address 4	Base Address 5		CardBus CIS pointer		Subsytem Vendor ID		Subsytem Device ID	
0x30	Expansion ROM Base Address		Reserved			IRQ Line	IRQ Pin	Min_Gnt	Max_Lat

- *Required Register*

- *Optional Register*

Figure 11.12: Standardized PCI configuration registers

Let us look at these registers in more detail:

- **Supplier ID**: This 16-bit register identifies a hardware manufacturer. For example, every Intel device has the same vendor number, 0x8086. There is a global registry of these numbers, maintained by the PCI Special Interest Group, and manufacturers must apply to have a unique number assigned to them.

- **Device reference**: This is another 16-bit register, selected by the manufacturer; no official registration is required for the device ID. This identifier is typically combined with the vendor ID to create a unique 32-bit identifier for a hardware device. We use the word signature to refer to the vendor and device ID pair. A device driver typically relies on the signature to identify its device; you can find the value to look for in the hardware manual of the target device.

- **Class**: Each device belongs to a class. The class register is a 16-bit value whose first 8 bits identify the "base class" (or group). For example, "Ethernet" and "Token Ring" are two classes belonging to the "Network" group, while the "Serial" and "Parallel" classes belong to the "Network" group and the "Communication" group. Some drivers may support multiple similar devices, each with a different signature, but all belonging to the same class. These drivers can rely on the class register to identify their devices, as discussed later.

o   Subsystem Vendor ID

o   Subsystem Device ID

These fields can be used for further identification of a device. If the chip is a generic interface chip with a local (integrated) bus, it is often used in several completely different roles, and the driver must identify the actual device it is communicating with. Subsystem identifiers are used for this purpose.

There are two helper macros that must be used to initialize a struct **pci_device_id** structure:

- **PCI_DEVICE (vendor, device)**: Creates a **pci_device_id** structure that matches only the specific vendor and device ID. The macro sets the **subvendor** and **subdevice** fields of the framework to **PCI_ANY_ID**.

- **PCI_DEVICE_CLASS (device_class, device_class_mask)**: Creates a **pci_device_id** structure that corresponds to a specific **PCI** class.

An example of using these macros to define the type of devices supported by a driver can be found in the following kernel files:

```
static const struct pci_device_id bypass_pci_id_table[] = {
    /* ChipIdea on Intel MID platform */
    { PCI_DEVICE(PCI_VENDOR_ID_INTEL, 0x0811), },
    { PCI_DEVICE(PCI_VENDOR_ID_INTEL, 0x0829), },
    { PCI_DEVICE(PCI_VENDOR_ID_INTEL, 0xe006), },
    {}
};
```

These examples create a list of **struct pci_device_id** structures, with an empty structure set to zeros as the last value in the list. This ID array is used in the **pci_driver** structure (described as follows), and it is also used to tell user space which devices this specific driver supports.

This **pci_device_id** structure should be exported to user space to allow hotplugging and module loading systems to know which module works with which hardware devices. The **MODULE_DEVICE_TABLE** macro accomplishes this.

An example is:

```
MODULE_DEVICE_TABLE(pci, i810_ids);
```

This statement creates a local variable called **_mod_pci_device_table** that points to the list of **pci_device_id** structures. Later in the kernel build process, the **depmod** program searches all modules for the symbol **_mod_pci_device_table**. If this symbol is found, it extracts the module data and adds it to the **/lib/modules/KERNEL_VERSION/modules.pcimap** file. After **depmod** completes, all PCI devices supported by kernel modules are listed, along with their module names, in this file. When the kernel tells the **hotplug** system that a new PCI device has been found, the **hotplug** system uses the **modules.pcimap** file to find the appropriate driver to load.

The main structure that all PCI drivers must create to be properly registered with the kernel is the struct **pci_driver** structure. This structure consists of several function callbacks and variables that describe the PCI driver to the PCI core.

Here are the fields in this structure that a PCI driver should be aware of:

- **const char *name;**: Name of the driver. It must be unique among all kernel PCI drivers and is normally set to the same name as the driver's module name. It appears in **sysfs** under **/sys/bus/pci/drivers/** when the driver is in the kernel.

- **const struct pci_device_id *id_table;**: Pointer to the **struct pci_device_id** table described earlier in this chapter.

- **int (*probe) (struct pci_dev *dev, const struct pci_device_id *id);**: Pointer to the probe function in the PCI driver. This function is called by the PCI core when it has a **pci_dev** structure that it thinks this driver wants to control. A pointer to the **pci_device_id** structure that the PCI core used to make this decision is also passed to this function. If the PCI driver claims the **pci_dev** structure passed to it, it should initialize the device correctly and return **0**. If the driver does not want to claim the device or if an error occurs, it should return a negative error value. More details on this feature will follow later in this chapter.

- **void (*remove) (struct pci_dev *dev);**: Pointer to the function that the PCI core calls when the **pci_dev** structure is removed from the system or when the PCI driver is unloaded from the kernel. More details on this feature will follow later in this chapter.

- **int (*suspend) (struct pci_dev *dev, state u32);**: Pointer to the function that the PCI core calls when the **pci_dev** structure is suspended. The suspend status is passed in the status variable. This feature is optional; a driver is not required to provide it.

- **int (*resume) (struct pci_dev *dev);**: Pointer to the function that the PCI core calls when resuming the **pci_dev** structure. It is always called after the suspension is called. This feature is optional; a driver is not required to provide it.

In summary, to create a proper **struct pci_driver** structure, only four fields need to be initialized:

```
struct pci_driver {
    const char              *name;
    const struct pci_device_id *id_table;
    int (*probe)(struct pci_dev *dev, const struct pci_device_id *id);
```

```
    void (*remove)(struct pci_dev *dev);
    int (*suspend)(struct pci_dev *dev, pm_message_t state);
    int (*resume)(struct pci_dev *dev);
    void (*shutdown)(struct pci_dev *dev);
    int (*sriov_configure)(struct pci_dev *dev, int num_vfs);
    int (*sriov_set_msix_vec_count)(struct pci_dev *vf, int msix_vec_
count);
    u32 (*sriov_get_vf_total_msix)(struct pci_dev *pf);
    const struct pci_error_handlers *err_handler;
    const struct attribute_group **groups;
    const struct attribute_group **dev_groups;
    struct device_driver    driver;
    struct pci_dynids       dynids;
    bool driver_managed_dma;
};
```

To register the **pci_driver** structure with the PCI kernel, a call to **pci_register_driver** is made with a pointer to the **pci_driver** structure. This is traditionally done in the module initialization code for the PCI driver:

```
static int __init pci_skel_init(void)
{
    return pci_register_driver(&pci_driver);
}


static void __exit pci_skel_exit(void)
{
    pci_unregister_driver(&pci_driver);
}
```

Usage

Let us look at an example of drivers using a PCI interface:

- Include necessary header files for Linux kernel module development, such as module management (**module.h**), initialization (**init.h**), serial usage (**serial_core.h, serial_reg.h**), **tty**:

```
#include <linux/module.h>
#include <linux/init.h>
#include <linux/pci.h>
#include <linux/io.h>
```

- Defines macros for the driver name, PCI vendor ID, and PCI device ID:

```
#define DRIVER_NAME "simple_pci"
#define PCI_VENDOR_ID_EXAMPLE 0x1234
#define PCI_DEVICE_ID_EXAMPLE 0x5678
```

- Defines an array of **pci_device_id** structures (**pci_ids**) that specify the devices supported by this driver. The **MODULE_DEVICE_TABLE** macro registers this array with the kernel:

```
static struct pci_device_id pci_ids[] = {
    { PCI_DEVICE(PCI_VENDOR_ID_EXAMPLE, PCI_DEVICE_ID_EXAMPLE), },
    { 0, }
};
MODULE_DEVICE_TABLE(pci, pci_ids);
```

- Defines a structure (**simple_pci_dev**) to represent the private data for the PCI device. It includes a pointer to the **pci_dev** structure and a pointer to the memory-mapped I/O base address:

```
struct simple_pci_dev {
    struct pci_dev *pdev;
    void __iomem *mmio_base;
};
```

- Defines the probe function (**simple_pci_probe**), which is called when a matching PCI device is found:

```
static int simple_pci_probe(struct pci_dev *pdev, const struct pci_
device_id *ent)
{
    struct simple_pci_dev *dev;
    int bars, err;

    dev = kzalloc(sizeof(*dev), GFP_KERNEL);
    if (!dev)
        return -ENOMEM;

    dev->pdev = pdev;
    pci_set_drvdata(pdev, dev);

    err = pci_enable_device(pdev);
    if (err)
        goto err_free_dev;
```

```
    bars = pci_select_bars(pdev, IORESOURCE_MEM);
    err = pci_request_selected_regions(pdev, bars, DRIVER_NAME);
    if (err)
        goto err_disable_device;

    dev->mmio_base = pci_iomap(pdev, 0, 0);
    if (!dev->mmio_base) {
        err = -EIO;
        goto err_release_regions;
    }

    pr_info(DRIVER_NAME ": device probed\n");
    return 0;

err_release_regions:
    pci_release_selected_regions(pdev, pci_select_bars(pdev,
IORESOURCE_MEM));
err_disable_device:
    pci_disable_device(pdev);
err_free_dev:
    kfree(dev);
    return err;
}
```

- Defines the remove function (**simple_pci_remove**), which is called when the PCI device is removed:

```
static void simple_pci_remove(struct pci_dev *pdev)
{
    struct simple_pci_dev *dev = pci_get_drvdata(pdev);

    pci_iounmap(pdev, dev->mmio_base);
    pci_release_selected_regions(pdev, pci_select_bars(pdev,
IORESOURCE_MEM));
    pci_disable_device(pdev);
    kfree(dev);

    pr_info(DRIVER_NAME ": device removed\n");
}
```

- Defines the PCI driver structure (**simple_pci_driver**), specifying the driver name, device ID table, probe function, and remove function:

```
static struct pci_driver simple_pci_driver = {
    .name = DRIVER_NAME,
    .id_table = pci_ids,
    .probe = simple_pci_probe,
    .remove = simple_pci_remove,
};
```

- Defines the module initialization function (**simple_pci_init**):

```
static int __init simple_pci_init(void)
{
    return pci_register_driver(&simple_pci_driver);
}
```

- Defines the module exit function (**simple_pci_exit**):

```
static void __exit simple_pci_exit(void)
{
    pci_unregister_driver(&simple_pci_driver);
}
```

Conclusion

In this chapter, we discussed the use of the different communication protocols needed to communicate with the different hardware components of a motherboard, whether on a serial or parallel bus. Most of them are historical with the serial bus. The parallel bus or centronic was not discussed because it no longer exists. However, other buses have succeeded to result in becoming means of communication that are increasingly greedy in terms of the volume of data to be transmitted.

In the next chapter, we will understand the different scheduling algorithms for managing processes, whether kernel or user.

Join our book's Discord space

Join the book's Discord Workspace for Latest updates, Offers, Tech happenings around the world, New Release and Sessions with the Authors:

https://discord.bpbonline.com

CHAPTER 12

Process Management

Introduction

This chapter will explain how the task scheduler (processes, threads, drivers, etc.) works. Furthermore, focusing on the kernel part, we will see how to manage kthreads, workqueues, etc.

Structure

The chapter covers the following topics:

- Tasks scheduling
- GNU/Linux and real-time
- Kthreads
- Workqueue
- Locks

Objectives

By the end of this chapter, you will be able to understand how task management is done in a GNU/Linux system.

In addition, we will see how to manage tasks within the Linux kernel in drivers.

Tasks scheduling

In GNU/Linux, task scheduling is handled by the kernel, which employs sophisticated algorithms to ensure that processes are executed efficiently and fairly. This presentation will delve into the intricacies of GNU/Linux task scheduling, exploring its core principles, mechanisms, and policies.

Process is an instance of a program in execution. A set of processes combined together makes a complete program. There are two categories of processes in Unix, namely:

- User processes are operated in unprivileged mode inside the userspace
- Kernel processes are operated in privileged mode inside the kernelspace

The lifetime of a process can be divided into several states, each with certain characteristics that describe the process. It is essential to understand the following states:

- The process is currently executing in user mode.
- The process is currently executing in kernel mode.
- The process is not executing, but it is ready to run as soon as the scheduler chooses it. Many processes may be in this state, and the scheduling algorithm determines which one will execute next.
- The process is sleeping. A process puts itself to sleep when it can no longer continue executing, such as when it is waiting for 1/0 to complete.
- The process is ready to run, but the swapper (process 0) must swap the process into the main memory before the kernel can schedule it to run.
- The process is sleeping, and the swapper has switched the process to secondary storage to make room for other processes in the main memory.
- The process returns from the kernel to user mode, but the kernel anticipates this and performs a context switch to schedule another process.
- The process is newly created and is in a state of transition; The process exists, but it is not ready to run or sleeping. This state is the starting state of all processes except process 0.
- The process has executed the exit system call and is in a zombie state. The process no longer exists, but it leaves a record containing an exit code and timing statistics for its parent process to collect. The zombie state i. the final state of a process.

Since a processor can only run one process at a time, at most one process can be in states 1 and 2. The two states correspond to the two execution modes, user and kernel.

The states that a process enters while working from start to finish are called process states. These are listed as follows:

- The process was just created by a system call and is not ready to run.

- **User running**: The process is running in user mode, which means it is a user process.

- **Kernel running**: Indicates the process is a kernel process running in kernel mode.

- **Zombie**: Process does not exist/is terminated.

- **Preempted**: When the process runs from kernel mode to user mode, it is said to be preempted.

- **Ready to run in memory**: This indicates that the process has reached a state where it is ready to run in memory and is waiting for the kernel to schedule it.

- **Ready to run, swapped**: The process is ready to run, but no empty main memory is present

- **Sleep, swapped**: The process has moved to secondary storage and is in a blocked state.

- **Asleep in memory**: The process is in memory (not transferred to secondary storage) but is in a blocked state.

The following figure shows the state transition diagram of a process under GNU/Linux:

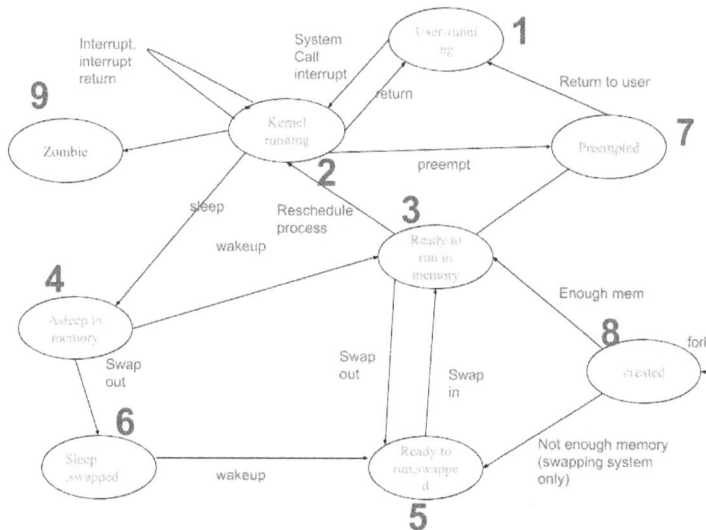

Figure 12.1: State-transition diagram for a process

The working of the process can be explained in the following stages:

- **Running by user**: The process is run by the user.

- **Kernel execution**: The process is allocated to the kernel and is, therefore, in kernel mode.

- **Ready to run in memory**: Additionally, after processing in main memory, the process is rescheduled to the kernel. That is, the process does not execute but is ready to execute as soon as the kernel schedules it.

- **Asleep in memory**: The process is asleep but resides in the main memory. He waits for the task to begin.

- **Ready to run, swapped**: The process is ready to run and be swapped by the processor into main memory, allowing the kernel to schedule its execution.

- **Sleep, swap**: The process is in a sleep state in secondary memory, leaving room for other processes to execute in main memory. She can resume once the task is accomplished.

- **Preempted**: The kernel preempts a running process for the allocation of another process while the first process switches from kernel mode to user mode.

- **Created**: The process has just been created but is not running. This is the starting state for all processes.

- **Zombie**: The process has been completed thoroughly, and the exit call has been activated. The process, therefore, no longer exists. However, it stores a statistical record of the process. It is the final state of all processes.

The scheduler is responsible for allocating CPU time to various processes running on the system. Its primary goals are to maximize CPU utilization, provide fair access to CPU resources, ensure system responsiveness, and support real-time processes where necessary. The Linux kernel employs the **Completely Fair Scheduler** (**CFS**) as its default scheduling algorithm, introduced in kernel version 2.6.23 to replace the older O(1) scheduler.

The CFS is designed to provide a fair distribution of CPU time among processes. Unlike traditional round-robin or priority-based scheduling algorithms, CFS does not use fixed time slices. Instead, it aims to ensure that every process gets a proportionate share of CPU time based on its weight or priority.

The following figure shows the link between the different scheduling policies:

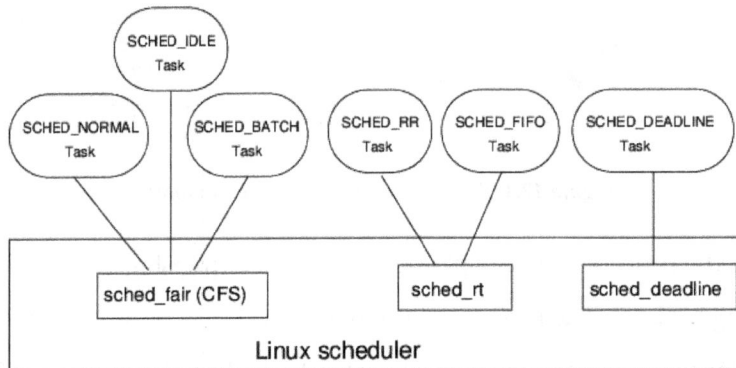

Figure 12.2: Family of Linux schedulers

The key concepts of CFS are as follows:

- **Virtual runtime (vruntime)**: CFS tracks the time a process has spent running using a metric called virtual runtime. Processes with lower vruntime values have higher priority for CPU access. The scheduler aims to balance the vruntime across all runnable processes.

- **Red-black tree**: CFS uses a red-black tree, a type of balanced binary search tree, to manage processes. Each node in the tree represents a process, with the tree organized by vruntime. The leftmost node, having the smallest vruntime, is selected for execution next.

- **Load balancing**: CFS includes mechanisms for load balancing across multiple CPUs or cores, ensuring that no single CPU is overloaded while others are idle.

Linux supports several scheduling policies to cater to different types of processes, including real-time and non-real-time policies.

The following figure shows data locality in single-process and multithreaded modes:

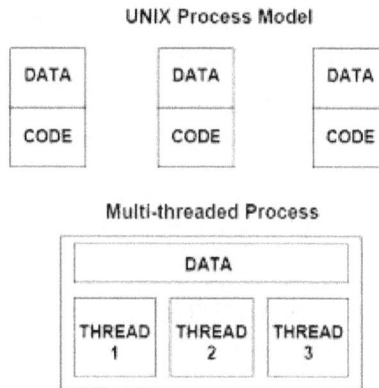

Figure 12.3: Single vs multithreaded mode

The non-real-time policies are as follows:

- **SCHED_NORMAL (or SCHED_OTHER)**: This is the default policy for regular, non-real-time processes. It uses the CFS to manage CPU time fairly among all processes.

    o **Description**: This is the default scheduling policy used for regular, non-real-time tasks. It utilizes the CFS to manage process scheduling.

    o **Characteristics**: Provides a fair share of CPU time to all processes, ensuring balanced and efficient use of CPU resources.

- **SCHED_BATCH**: This policy is intended for batch-processing jobs that do not require user interaction. It aims to maximize CPU throughput and minimize the impact on interactive processes by running batch jobs at a lower priority.

- o **Description**: This policy is intended for batch-processing jobs that do not require immediate user interaction.

- o **Characteristics**: Optimized for throughput rather than interactivity, processes under this policy run at a lower priority compared to interactive tasks, minimizing their impact on system responsiveness.

- **SCHED_IDLE**: Processes with this policy only run when the CPU has no other runnable tasks, making it suitable for very low-priority background tasks.

- **Description**: A real-time scheduling policy where the highest priority process runs until it either blocks or explicitly yields the CPU.

- **Characteristics**: Does not use time slices; a lower priority process will not run until higher priority processes have finished. Suitable for time-critical applications.

The real-time policies are as follows:

- **SCHED_FIFO (First-in, first-out)**: This policy is a real-time policy where the highest priority process runs until it either blocks or voluntarily yields the CPU. It does not use time slices, meaning lower priority processes may starve if a higher priority process is continuously runnable.

- o **Description**: A real-time scheduling policy where the highest priority process runs until it either blocks or explicitly yields the CPU.

- o **Characteristics**: Does not use time slices; a lower priority process will not run until higher priority processes have finished. Suitable for time-critical applications.

The following figure gives an example of scheduling with **SCHED_DEADLINE**:

First In, First Out (FIFO)

- ▫ First Come, First Served (FCFS)
  - • Very simple and easy to implement
- ▫ Example:
  - • A arrived just before B which arrived just before C.
  - • Each job runs for 10 seconds.

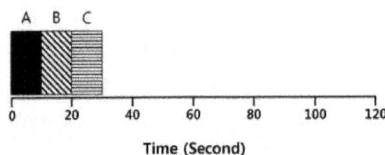

Avg turnaround time = 10+20+30/3 = 20 sec

Figure 12.4: Example of deadline scheduling

- **SCHED_RR (Round-Robin)**: Similar to **SCHED_FIFO** but with a time slice for each process. Processes of the same priority are cycled through in a round-robin manner, preventing starvation and ensuring that each real-time process gets periodic CPU time.

  o **Description**: It is similar to **SCHED_FIFO** but with time slices. Each process runs for a fixed time slice before moving to the next process of the same priority.

  o **Characteristics**: Ensures that processes of the same priority are periodically given CPU time, preventing starvation and providing predictable performance for real-time tasks.

The following figure gives an example of scheduling with **SCHED_RR**:

RR Scheduling Example

▫ A, B and C arrive at the same time.

▫ They each wish to run for 5 seconds.

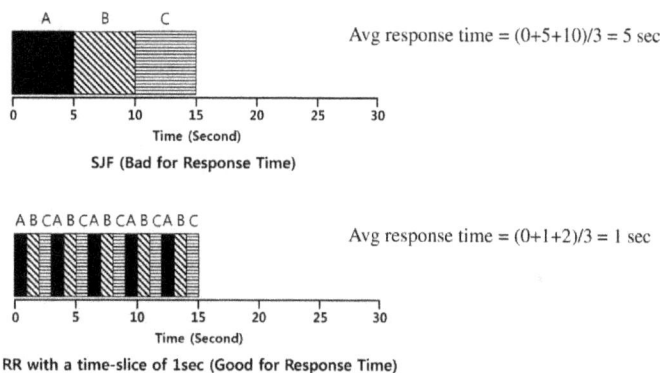

Figure 12.5: Example of Round Robin scheduling

- **SCHED_DEADLINE**: A real-time scheduling policy in Linux designed to guarantee that tasks are completed before specified deadlines. It schedules tasks based on parameters like runtime, deadline, and period, ensuring precise timing for applications with stringent timing requirements, such as multimedia processing or embedded systems.

  o **Description**: A more advanced real-time scheduling policy designed to guarantee that tasks are completed before a specified deadline.

  o **Characteristics**: Suitable for applications with stringent timing requirements, such as multimedia processing or embedded systems. Tasks are scheduled based on deadlines rather than priorities.

Real-time tasks have fixed priorities ranging from 1 to 99, with 99 being the highest priority. These priorities determine the order in which tasks are scheduled. Nice values for non-real-time/regular tasks use "nice" values to influence their scheduling priority. Nice values range from -20 (highest priority) to 19 (lowest priority). Higher nice values decrease priority, meaning the process gets less CPU time.

GNU/Linux task scheduling is a complex yet crucial component of the operating system, ensuring the efficient and fair allocation of CPU resources. The CFS represents a significant advancement in scheduling algorithms, providing equitable CPU time distribution. By understanding the various scheduling policies, priorities, and tools available, users and administrators can optimize system performance and manage processes effectively. Whether dealing with real-time applications or regular workloads, Linux's versatile scheduling capabilities cater to a wide range of requirements, ensuring robust and responsive system behavior.

Here are practical examples for launching a process with a specific nice value:

- Launch a process with a specific nice value:

  ```
  $ nice -n 10 myprocess
  ```

  o This command starts **myprocess** with a nice value of 10, giving it a lower priority compared to other processes with a default nice value of 0. The renice alters the scheduling priority of one or more running processes. The first argument is the priority value to be used. The other arguments are interpreted as process IDs (by default), process group IDs, user IDs, or usernames. Renice a process group causes all processes in the process group to have their scheduling priority altered. renice a user causes all processes owned by the user to have their scheduling priority altered.

- Changing the scheduling policy of a process to **SCHED_RR**:

  ```
  $ chrt -r -p 20 1234
  ```

  o This command sets the scheduling policy of the process with PID 1234 to round-robin with a priority of 20.

- Monitoring process scheduling:

  ```
  $ top
  ```

  o The top command provides a real-time view of running processes, including their priorities and scheduling policies.

Other utilities can be used for monitoring:

- **Top**: Real-time display of running processes, CPU, and memory usage.
- **Htop**: Interactive version of top with a better UI and mouse support.
- **Atop**: Advanced process monitoring with disk and network stats.
- **Btm**: Ustomizable graphical process/system monitor for the terminal, inspired by **gtop, gotop,** and **htop**.

- **Btop**: Modern and colorful command line resource monitor that shows usage and stats for processor, memory, disks, network, and processes.

- **Glances**: Cross-platform monitoring tool with detailed stats.

- **Ps**: Shows a snapshot of running processes.

- **Pgrep**: Searches for processes by name.

- **Pidstat**: Reports CPU usage of individual processes over time.

- **nice/renice**: Adjusts process priority dynamically.

GNU/Linux and real-time

GNU/Linux is not itself a **real-time operating system** (**RTOS**) in its standard form, but it can be adapted to meet real-time requirements through specific modifications and configurations.

Here is a detailed explanation of the capabilities and limitations of GNU/Linux in the context of real-time computing:

- **Features**:

    o The default Linux kernel is designed as a general-purpose operating system, optimized for overall performance, responsiveness, and flexibility across a wide range of applications.

    o Under standard Linux, the kernel is not fully preemptible, meaning that some kernel operations can block other processes, resulting in variable and sometimes high latencies.

    o The default scheduler (CFS) aims to provide a fair distribution of CPU time between processes, but it is not optimized for the strict timing guarantees required by real-time applications.

- **Boundaries:**

    o Latency in standard Linux can be unpredictable, making it unsuitable for difficult real-time applications where precise timing is essential.

    o The non-deterministic nature of task scheduling and interrupt handling in standard Linux can result in missed deadlines in time-sensitive applications.

To address the limitations of standard Linux for real-time applications, several extensions and fixes have been developed, such as the `PREEMPT_RT` patch.

The `PREEMPT_RT` patch is the largest effort to transform the standard Linux kernel into a real-time kernel.

Here is a list of its features:

- **Full kernel preemption**: The **PREEMPT_RT** patch makes almost all parts of the kernel preemptible, reducing peak latency.

- **Priority inheritance**: Implements priority inheritance to prevent priority inversion, ensuring that high-priority tasks are not unduly delayed by lower-priority tasks holding resources.

- **High-resolution timers**: Provides high-resolution timers for precise task scheduling.

- **Interrupt handling**: Converts most interrupt handlers to preemptible kernel threads, allowing them to be scheduled with real-time priorities.

The need for a real-time system is required for the following applications:

- Industrial automation

- Robotics

- Military (missile, highly constrained systems)

- Telecommunications

- Multimedia processing

- Medical equipment

Several Linux distributions include the **PREEMPT_RT** patch or other real-time enhancements to provide out-of-the-box support for real-time applications:

- **Red Hat Enterprise Linux for real-time (RHEL-RT)**: A real-time variant of **RHEL** that includes the **PREEMPT_RT** fix and other optimizations.

- **Ubuntu Studio**: Offers low-latency kernels suitable for real-time audio processing.

- **Fedora Jam**: A version of Fedora with a real-time core, geared toward audio production and other real-time workloads.

To set up a real-time task, you can follow these steps:

1. Download and install a Linux kernel with the **PREEMPT_RT** patch, or use a distribution that provides a real-time kernel, such as Fedora's real-time kernel.

2. Configure real-time scheduling by using the **chrt** tool to set a real-time policy:
   ```
   $ sudo chrt -f -p $99 (pgrep myrealtimeapp)
   ```

3. This sets **myrealtimeapp** to use **the SCHED_FIFO** policy with the highest priority.

4. Monitor and test by using the **cyclictest** tool to measure latency:
   ```
   $ sudo cyclictest -t1 -p 80 -n -i 10000 -l 10000
   ```

5. This command tests system latency, providing information about its performance in real time.

Kthreads

Kernel threads (kthreads) are special types of threads that run in the kernel space of the GNU/Linux operating system.

Unlike user-space threads, which are created and managed by user applications, kthreads are created and managed by the kernel itself.

They perform various kernel-level tasks that are essential for the functioning of the operating system.

Kthreads are used to execute functions that need to run in the background, independently of user-space processes. They handle tasks such as:

- Managing hardware interrupts
- Performing I/O operations
- Handling timers and timeouts
- Carrying out maintenance tasks
- Executing various subsystems' operations (e.g., network stack, file system operations)

The characteristics of kthreads are as follows:

- Kthreads operate in kernel mode, meaning they have direct access to kernel data structures and hardware resources.
- They are not associated with any user process and do not have a user context, making them ideal for tasks that need to run irrespective of user-space activity.
- The Linux scheduler treats kthreads similarly to user-space processes, scheduling them based on their priority and the system's load.

Kthreads are created and managed using specific kernel APIs. The most commonly used functions for kthread management include:

- **kthread_create()**: Creates a new **kthread** but does not start it immediately.
  - **Usage:**
    ```
    struct task_struct *kthread_create(int (*threadfn)(void *data),
    void *data, const char namefmt[], ...);
    ```
  - **Parameters:**
    - **threadfn**: function to be executed by the **kthread**.
    - **data**: Argument passed to the thread function.
    - **namefmt**: printf-style format string for the kthread's name.

- **wake_up_process()**: Starts a **kthread** that has been created but not yet started.

  o **Usage:**

  ```
  int wake_up_process(struct task_struct *p);
  ```

  o **Parameters:**

    ▪ **p: task_struct** pointer to the **kthread** to be started.

- **kthread_run()**: Convenience function that combines **kthread_create()** and **wake_up_process()**.

  o **Usage:**

  ```
  struct task_struct *kthread_run(int (*threadfn)(void *data),
  void *data, const char namefmt[], ...);
  ```

  o **Parameters**: Same as **kthread_create()**.

- **kthread_stop()**: Stops a running **kthread**.

  o **Usage:**

  ```
  int kthread_stop(struct task_struct *k);
  ```

  o **Parameters:**

    ▪ **k: task_struct** pointer to the **kthread** to be stopped.

Here is a simple example demonstrating the creation and management of a **kthread**:

```
#include <linux/module.h>
#include <linux/kernel.h>
#include <linux/kthread.h>
#include <linux/delay.h>

static struct task_struct *my_kthread;

int my_thread_function(void *data) {
    while (!kthread_should_stop()) {
        pr_info("Kernel Thread: Running\n");
        ssleep(5); // Sleep for 5 seconds
    }
    pr_info("Kernel Thread: Stopping\n");
    return 0;
}
```

```
static int __init my_module_init(void) {
    pr_info("Module Loaded\n");
    my_kthread = kthread_run(my_thread_function, NULL, "my_kthread");
    if (IS_ERR(my_kthread)) {
        pr_err("Failed to create kthread\n");
        return PTR_ERR(my_kthread);
    }
    return 0;
}

static void __exit my_module_exit(void) {
    kthread_stop(my_kthread);
    pr_info("Module Unloaded\n");
}

module_init(my_module_init);
module_exit(my_module_exit);

MODULE_LICENSE("GPL");
MODULE_AUTHOR("BPB");
MODULE_DESCRIPTION("A simple example of kthread usage");
```

Kthreads are a powerful feature of the GNU/Linux kernel, enabling the execution of background tasks at the kernel level.

They are crucial for various kernel operations, allowing the kernel to perform essential functions efficiently and independently of user-space processes.

Understanding and effectively utilizing **kthreads** is fundamental for kernel developers and for developing complex kernel modules that require background processing.

Workqueue

Workqueues are a powerful mechanism in the GNU/Linux kernel for deferring work to be done later, often in the context of a different kernel thread.

They provide a way to schedule tasks to be executed in a process context, which allows sleeping (blocking) operations that are not permitted in an interrupt context.

This makes **workqueues** suitable for tasks that need to be executed asynchronously but require the full capabilities of the kernel thread.

Workqueues serve several purposes in the kernel, including:

- **Deferring interrupt work**: Handling time-consuming tasks outside the interrupt context to avoid delaying the handling of other interrupts.

- **Scheduling tasks**: Allowing certain operations to be scheduled and executed later, improving the responsiveness of the kernel.

- **Context switching**: Performing operations that require sleeping or need to be executed in the process context rather than the interrupt context.

The key concepts are as follows:

- **Work struct (struct work_struct)**: Fundamental structure representing a single unit of work. Each work item is represented by this structure and includes a pointer to the function that should be executed.

- **Workqueue (struct workqueue_struct)**: A `workqueue` manages a pool of worker threads that execute the work items. The kernel maintains several default workqueues, but custom workqueues can also be created.

The Linux kernel provides APIs to create and manage workqueues and work items. Here are the primary functions and macros used:

- **DECLARE_WORK**: Declare and initialize a work item.

  o **Usage**:
    ```
    DECLARE_WORK(my_work, my_work_function);
    ```

  o **Parameters**:

    ▪ **my_work**: name of the work item.

    ▪ **my_work_function**: function to be executed when the work item is processed.

- **INIT_WORK**: **Purpose**: Initialize a work item dynamically.

  o **Usage**:
    ```
    struct work_struct my_work;
    INIT_WORK(&my_work, my_work_function);
    ```

  o **Parameters**:

    ▪ **my_work**: Work item to initialize.

    ▪ **my_work_function**: Function to be executed.

- **queue_work**: Queue a work item to be executed by the default `workqueue`.

  o **Usage**:
    ```
    bool queue_work(struct workqueue_struct *wq, struct work_struct *work);
    ```

- o **Parameters**:
    - ▪ **wq**: Workqueue to which the work item is submitted (usually a system default workqueue).
    - ▪ **work**: **work** item to be queued.

- **schedule_work**: Queue a work item to the system-wide workqueue.
    - o **Usage**:
    ```c
    bool schedule_work(struct work_struct *work);
    ```
    - o **Parameters**:
        - ▪ **work**: Work item to be queued.

- **create_workqueue**: Create a custom workqueue.
    - o **Usage**:
    ```c
    struct workqueue_struct *my_wq = create_workqueue("my_
    workqueue");
    ```
    - o **Parameters**:
        - ▪ **"my_workqueue"**: name of the workqueue.

- **destroy_workqueue**: Destroy a custom workqueue.
    - o **Usage**:
    ```c
    void destroy_workqueue(struct workqueue_struct *wq);
    ```
    - o **Parameters**:
        - ▪ **wq**: Workqueue to destroy.

Here is a simple example demonstrating the creation of a workqueue and the scheduling of a work item:

```c
#include <linux/module.h>
#include <linux/kernel.h>
#include <linux/init.h>
#include <linux/workqueue.h>

static struct workqueue_struct *my_wq;
static struct work_struct my_work;

void my_work_function(struct work_struct *work) {
    pr_info("Workqueue: Executing my work function\n");
```

```
}

static int __init my_module_init(void) {
    pr_info("Module Loaded\n");

    // Create a custom workqueue
    my_wq = create_workqueue("my_workqueue");
    if (!my_wq) {
        pr_err("Failed to create workqueue\n");
        return -ENOMEM;
    }

    // Initialize and queue the work item
    INIT_WORK(&my_work, my_work_function);
    queue_work(my_wq, &my_work);

    return 0;
}

static void __exit my_module_exit(void) {
    // Destroy the workqueue
    destroy_workqueue(my_wq);
    pr_info("Module Unloaded\n");
}

module_init(my_module_init);
module_exit(my_module_exit);

MODULE_LICENSE("GPL");
MODULE_AUTHOR("BPB");
MODULE_DESCRIPTION("A simple example of workqueue usage");
```

Workqueues in the GNU/Linux kernel provide a flexible and powerful mechanism for deferring tasks to be executed later in a process context.

They are essential for handling tasks that need to be performed asynchronously, especially those that cannot be executed in an interrupt context due to the need to sleep or perform blocking operations.

Understanding workqueues and how to use them effectively is crucial for kernel developers who need to manage background tasks efficiently.

Locks

The GNU/Linux kernel provides various lock mechanisms to ensure synchronization and prevent race conditions in the kernel space, especially when developing kernel drivers. Here is a detailed introduction to the different lock mechanisms available in the GNU/Linux kernel:

- Spinlocks are used for short critical sections where the lock holder is expected to release the lock quickly. They are called **spinlocks** because a thread trying to acquire the lock will **spin** in a loop, repeatedly checking if the lock is available.

    o **Basic spinlock:**
    ```
    spinlock_t my_lock;
    spin_lock_init(&my_lock);
    spin_lock(&my_lock);
    // critical section
    spin_unlock(&my_lock);
    ```

    o **Interrupt-safe spinlock**: Used when the code might be executed in an interrupt context.
    ```
    spinlock_t my_lock;
    unsigned long flags;
    spin_lock_irqsave(&my_lock, flags);
    // critical section
    spin_unlock_irqrestore(&my_lock, flags);
    ```

- **Mutexes** are used to protect data structures that can be accessed by multiple threads, ensuring that only one thread can access the critical section at a time. Unlike spinlocks, mutexes will put the thread to sleep if the lock is not available.

    o **Usage:**
    ```
    struct mutex my_mutex;
    mutex_init(&my_mutex);
    mutex_lock(&my_mutex);
    // critical section
    mutex_unlock(&my_mutex);
    ```

- **Read-write locks**: Locks that allow multiple readers or a single writer to access the critical section. They are useful for scenarios where reads are more frequent than writes. There are two types of locks:

- o **Read lock:**

```
rwlock_t my_rwlock;
read_lock(&my_rwlock);
// read-only critical section
read_unlock(&my_rwlock);
```

- o **Write lock:**

```
rwlock_t my_rwlock;
write_lock(&my_rwlock);
// write critical section
write_unlock(&my_rwlock);
```

- **Seqlocks** are designed for situations where data readers are more common than data writers. Writers get exclusive access while readers can proceed without locking, but they may have to retry if a writer is active. As with the read-write lock, there are two types of locks:

  - o **Writing:**

```
seqlock_t my_seqlock;
write_seqlock(&my_seqlock);
// write critical section
write_sequnlock(&my_seqlock);
```

  - o **Reading:**

```
unsigned int seq;
do {
        seq = read_seqbegin(&my_seqlock);
        // read critical section
} while (read_seqretry   (&my_seqlock, seq));
```

- **Completion** are synchronization mechanisms that allow one thread to wait for another thread to complete some task. They are often used for signaling between interrupt handlers and normal kernel code.

  - o **Usage:**

```
struct completion my_completion;
init_completion(&my_completion);

// In the waiting thread
wait_for_completion(&my_completion);
```

```
// In the signaling thread
complete(&my_completion);
```

- **Read-copy-update (RCU)** is a synchronization mechanism that allows readers to access data concurrently with writers, where writers make changes by creating new versions of the data structures. The lock mechanism also has two types:

  o **Reading:**
    ```
    rcu_read_lock();
    // read critical section
    rcu_read_unlock();
    ```

  o **Writing:**
    ```
    synchronize_rcu();
    ```

- **Semaphores** are used to manage access to resources, allowing a certain number of threads to access the critical section simultaneously.

  o **Usage:**
    ```
    struct semaphore my_sem;
    sema_init(&my_sem, 1);
    down(&my_sem);
    // critical section
    up(&my_sem);
    ```

- **Spinlocks with RCU** provide efficient mechanisms for read-mostly synchronization. It allows readers to access shared data without locks while writers make changes to the data structure without blocking readers.

  o **Usage:**

    ▪ **RCU read lock :**
    ```
    rcu_read_lock();
    // read critical section
    rcu_read_unlock();
    ```

    ▪ **RCU write lock:**
    ```
    spinlock_t my_spinlock;
    spin_lock(&my_spinlock);
    // update data structure
    spin_unlock(&my_spinlock);
    synchronize_rcu();
    ```

- **Big kernel lock (BKL) (Deprecated)** was a global lock used in older versions of the Linux kernel to provide mutual exclusion across the entire kernel. It has been deprecated and removed in modern Linux kernels.

These lock mechanisms are essential for ensuring data consistency and synchronization in the kernel space, particularly when developing kernel drivers.

Each lock type serves different purposes and is chosen based on the specific requirements of the task, such as the need for sleeping, the frequency of reads versus writes, and the criticality of the section being protected.

Understanding and correctly implementing these lock mechanisms is crucial for writing efficient and reliable kernel code.

Conclusion

In this chapter, we explained how schedulers work under Linux, the management of kthreads, workqueues, and many other things related to task management. Kernel threads (kthreads) in GNU/Linux are lightweight threads running in kernel space, allowing background execution of tasks independently of user processes.

Workqueues provide a structured way to defer work execution to dedicated kernel worker threads, enabling asynchronous processing while allowing sleeping operations.

For synchronization, various lock mechanisms exist: spinlocks are efficient for short critical sections but cause busy waiting, whereas mutexes and semaphores put threads to sleep when contention occurs, improving CPU efficiency.

Read-write locks optimize performance by allowing multiple concurrent readers while ensuring exclusive write access. Seqlocks and RCU are ideal for read-heavy workloads, enabling lockless reads with minimal contention.

Choosing the right synchronization primitive is crucial for performance, balancing efficiency, fairness, and responsiveness in kernel development.

In the next chapter, which will be the last, we will see how to debug and install the Linux drivers as well as the kernel itself.

## CHAPTER 13

Debugging GNU/Linux Kernel and Drivers

Introduction

This chapter of the book explains how to debug a new kernel or driver. To do this, several techniques will be studied. It is much more complicated to develop a driver in the running kernel space than from the user space. Indeed, the use of breakpoints is only possible from another machine via an execution via a serial or Ethernet cable. This is why probes have been created to avoid interference to a minimum.

The following figure shows us an overview of the different means used when debugging drivers in the GNU/Linux kernel:

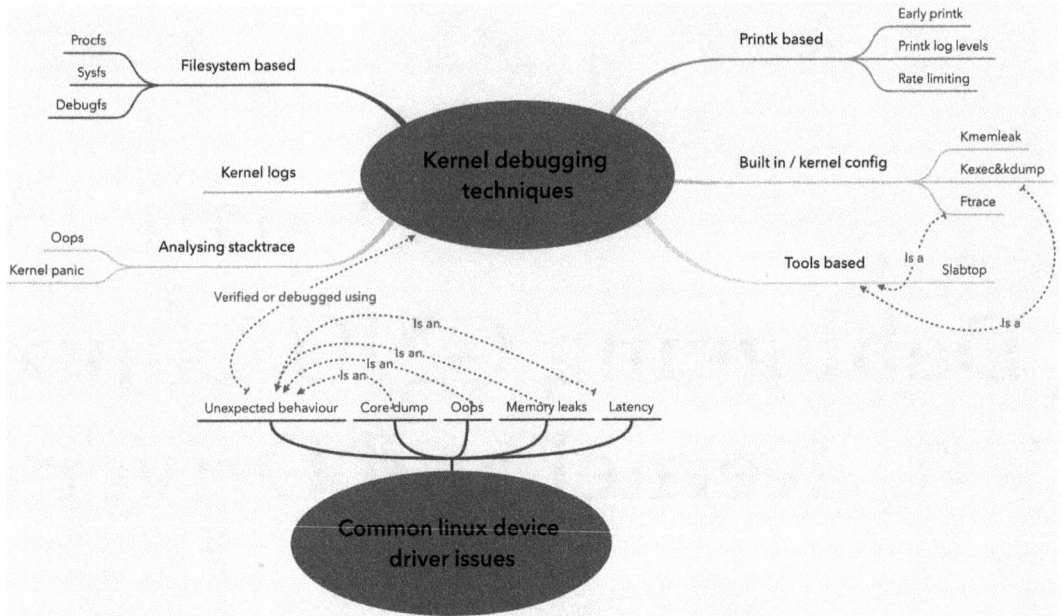

***Figure 13.1:** Summary of some debug investigation*

Structure

The chapter covers the following topics:

- GNU / Linux kernel debugging options
- Magic SysRq key
- Debugging by printing
- Dynamic debugging
- kgdb / kdb kernel debugger
- Kernel probes
- OOPS
- Profiling

Objectives

By the end of this chapter, you will be able to understand how to debug your drivers. Indeed, any software design can involve this step, especially since the kernel and the drivers operate in a privileged environment separated from the user's world. In addition, one wrong step can block and freeze the entire system.

GNU/Linux kernel debugging options

Debugging GNU/Linux kernels used in development mode requires enabling specific kernel configuration options.

These options improve the kernel's ability to provide detailed diagnostic information, facilitate run-time debugging, and help detect bugs.

These options are found in the *Kernel hacking* or *Kernel debugging* menu of your GNU/Linux kernel configuration tool. It is important to know, however, that some of these options are not usable on all architectures.

Here is a list of some important GNU/Linux kernel configuration options that are commonly used for debugging the kernel and drivers:

- **CONFIG_DEBUG_KERNEL**: Enables debugging options in the kernel; enabling it is mandatory but does not enable any other features.

- **CONFIG_DEBUG_SLAB**: Enables multiple validation mechanisms within the kernel's memory allocation functions to detect memory overflows and uninitialized memory access errors. Each allocated byte is initialized to 0xA5 before being returned to the caller and set to 0x6B upon deallocation. If these patterns appear in driver logs or kernel oops messages, they indicate specific types of memory corruption. When debugging is enabled, the kernel inserts sentinel values before and after each allocated memory block; any modification to these values signals a buffer overflow, triggering an exception. Additional advanced integrity checks are also enforced.

- **CONFIG_DYNAMIC_DEBUG**: Enables dynamic debug features, which allow debug messages to be enabled or disabled at runtime.

- **CONFIG_LOCKDEP**: Enables lock dependency checks, useful for detecting deadlocks and other locking problems in the kernel.

- **CONFIG_PROVE_LOCKING**: Extends `CONFIG_LOCKDEP` capabilities to prove locking correctness and find potential deadlocks at compile time.

- **CONFIG_DEBUG_PAGEALLOC**: When enabled, this removes entire pages from the kernel address space when they are freed. Note that this option can slow down the kernel considerably, but can also be useful in identifying certain types of memory corruption errors.

- **CONFIG_DEBUG_SPINLOCK**: Enables interception of operations on uninitialized spinlocks in the kernel and various other errors (such as unlocking a lock twice).

- **CONFIG_DEBUG_SPINLOCK_SLEEP**: When enabled, this option allows checking of sleep attempts while holding a spinlock. If an error is detected, it is possible to call a function that could potentially sleep, even if the initial call would not sleep.

- **CONFIG_INIT_DEBUG**: When this option is enabled, items marked with **_init** (or **_initdata**) are removed after system initialization or just after module loading. This allows checking of code that attempts to access memory at startup after initialization is complete.

- **CONFIG_DEBUG_INFO**: Causes the kernel to be built with full debug information included. You will need this information if you want to debug the kernel with **gdb**. You may also want to enable **CONFIG_FRAME_POINTER** if you plan to use **gdb**.

- **CONFIG_MAGIC_SYSRQ**: Activates the **"magic SysRq"** key.

- **CONFIG_DEBUG_STACKOVERFLOW**

- **CONFIG_DEBUG_STACK_USAGE**: When enabled, this helps detect stack overflows in the GNU/Linux kernel. The first option adds explicit overflow checks to the kernel, while the second forces the kernel to monitor stack usage and generate statistics available via the SysRq magic key.

- **CONFIG_KMEMCHECK**: Helps detect the use of uninitialized memory, which can catch subtle memory-related bugs.

- **CONFIG_DEBUG_MEMORY_INIT**: Ensures that memory allocations are explicitly initialized, helping catch issues related to the use of uninitialized memory.

- **CONFIG_DEBUG_PAGEALLOC**: Delays the reuse of freed memory to catch use-after-free errors.

- **CONFIG_SLUB_DEBUG**: Provides extensive checks and statistics for the SLUB allocator, useful for debugging SLUB memory issues.

- **CONFIG_KALLSYMS** : When enabled (under General Configuration/Standard Features), enables the generation of a list of symbols compiled and available in the static part of the GNU/Linux kernel; this option is enabled by default. This symbol information is used in debugging contexts such as for analyzing an oops, which can display a **stacktrace** with the kernel symbol addresses in hexadecimal only, which is not very useful if you do not have the mapping. It is also very useful when debugging via **kdb** or **kgdb**.

- **CONFIG_IKCONFIG**

- **CONFIG_IKCONFIG_PROC**: When enabled (in the General Configuration menu), this option causes the full kernel configuration state to be extracted from the kernel and made available via **/proc**. Usually, the list of options for a GNU/Linux kernel is known or available via the **.config** file located in the kernel sources themselves (see *Chapter 2, Introduction to the Linux Kernel*). They can, however, be useful if you are trying to debug a problem in a kernel built by someone else by performing a rebuild of the .config file, which can then be used to recompile a new kernel.

- **CONFIG_ACPI_DEBUG**: When enabled (under Power Management/ACPI) this option provides access to detailed information about **Advanced Configuration and Power Interface** (**ACPI**) debugging when an ACPI-related problem is suspected.

- **CONFIG_DEBUG_DRIVER**: Enables debugging information in GNU/Linux kernel drivers. This is often necessary or even essential to detect problems in low-level code close to the hardware.

- **CONFIG_SCSI_CONSTANTS**: When enabled (under Device Drivers/SCSI Device Support), this option enables the addition of information to detailed SCSI error messages.

- **CONFIG_FTRACE**: Enables function tracing infrastructure, allowing you to trace function calls in kernel code.

- **CONFIG_FUNCTION_TRACER**

- **CONFIG_FUNCTION_GRAPH_TRACER**: These options provide tracing of function calls and returns throughout the kernel, useful for performance analysis and debugging.

- **CONFIG_STACKTRACE**: Provides stack trace support in various parts of the kernel, helpful for diagnosing problems or crashes.

- **CONFIG_SCHED_DEBUG**: Offers verbose debug output from the scheduler, providing insights into scheduling behavior and potential issues.

- **CONFIG_DEBUG_LIST**: Helps detect problems in list handling by performing extra checks around linked lists.

- **CONFIG_BUG_ON_DATA_CORRUPTION**: Triggers a kernel BUG on detecting data corruption, which is critical for catching corrupt states early.

- **CONFIG_X86_DEBUG_FPU (for x86 architectures)**: Keeps track of FPU usage to catch FPU state corruption, especially in complex driver interactions.

- **CONFIG_ARM_UNWIND (for ARM architectures)**: Enables stack unwinding support on ARM, which is essential for producing stack traces.

- **CONFIG_KGDB**: Allows kernel debugging with **gdb** over serial or USB, providing a powerful interface to debug kernel problems interactively.

- **CONFIG_KASAN (Kernel address sanitizer)**: Detects memory errors such as buffer overflows or use-after-free vulnerabilities, which are crucial for driver development.

To understand how to activate options in your kernel, refer to *Chapter 2, Introduction to the Linux Kernel,* for more explanations.

Magic SysRq key

The magic SysRq key is a feature of the Linux kernel that provides a way to send commands directly to the kernel through the keyboard, which can be extremely helpful in situations where the system is unresponsive. This feature is often used for recovery and debugging purposes when the system encounters a severe crash or freeze.

The magic SysRq key is activated by a key combination on the keyboard. Typically, it involves the following keys:

- **Alt**
- **SysRq** (often shared with the Print Screen key)
- Another key represents a specific command.

Before you can use magic SysRq commands, you must ensure the feature is enabled in your Linux kernel. It can be enabled in two primary ways:

- **Kernel configuration**: When compiling the kernel, ensure that **CONFIG_MAGIC_SYSRQ** is enabled.

- **Runtime configuration**: Modify the **/proc/sys/kernel/sysrq** file to control the functionality:

  o Write **1** to enable all functions.

  o Write **0** to disable all.

  o Other values to selectively enable specific functions based on a bitmask.

To enable all functions at runtime, you can use:

```
$ echo 1 > /proc/sys/kernel/sysrq
```

To use these commands:

- Ensure that the SysRq functionality is enabled on your system, as seen previously.

- Remember that using some of these commands might lead to data loss (especially **b** and **o** without prior use of **s** and **u**).

- These commands are typically used when other, more standard tools and approaches fail, such as during system hangs or hardware-related freezes.

The commands provided by magic SysRq can be a last-resort toolkit for system administrators when dealing with unresponsive Linux systems.

Here are some commonly used magic SysRq key combinations and their effects. Press these keys while holding down the Alt and SysRq keys:

- **reisub**: A mnemonic for a sequence of commands to safely reboot a frozen system:

  - **r**: Switches the keyboard from raw mode to XLATE mode.

  - **e**: Send the SIGTERM signal to all processes except **init**.

  - **i**: Send the SIGKILL signal to all processes except **init**.

  - **s**: Synchronizes (sync) all mounted file systems, flushing their associated data caches to disk.

  - **u**: Remount all filesystems read-only.

  - **b**: Reboot the system immediately without syncing or unmounting disks.

- **b**: **Reboot**: Immediately reboots the system without unmounting or syncing filesystems.

- **c: Crash**: Causes a kernel crash by triggering a NULL pointer dereference, which can be useful for testing crash recovery and producing crash dumps.

- **d: Display all locked locks**: Shows all locks that are currently held.

- **e: SIGTERM**: Sends the SIGTERM signal to all processes except **init**, giving them the chance to terminate gracefully.

- **F: OOM Killer**: Invokes the Out Of Memory Killer to kill a process that is hogging memory and has not responded to the SIGTERM signal.

- **g: Generate a crash dump**: (on systems where **kdump** or a similar crash dumping mechanism is configured), triggers a crash dump.

- **h: Help**: Displays help. This shows all available SysRq keys and their actions.

- **i: SIGKILL**: Sends the SIGKILL signal to all processes except **init**, forcing them to terminate immediately.

- **j: Thaw filesystems**: Unfreezes all frozen filesystems, reversing the effect of the SysRq-s.

- **k: Secure Keyboard Entry**: Kills all programs on the current virtual console, used for secure login screens.

- **l: Show a stack backtrace for all active CPUs**: Display a stack trace for all active processors in the console.

- **m: Memory Information**: Displays current memory usage, which can be useful for diagnosing memory-related issues.

- **n: Nice level**: Sets all RT tasks to normal scheduling policy with static priority 0 (can be useful to recover from certain deadlocks).

- **o: Power Off**: Shuts off your computer immediately.

- **p: Show Regs**: Displays the current registers and flags to the console, useful for diagnosing problems or crashes.

- **q: Query other CPUs**: Shows the backtrace of all CPUs except the current one.

- **r: Turn off Keyboard Raw Mode**: Disables raw keyboard mode and sets it to XLATE mode helping to regain control of a keyboard in case of emergency.

- **s: Sync Disk**: Attempts to sync all mounted filesystems by flushing data to disk.

- **t: Task List**: Displays on the console the list of current tasks along with some associated information..

- **u: Unmount**: Attempts to remount all mounted filesystems in read-only mode.

- **v:** Use if ever the screen goes black by forcing the framebuffer to be restored.

- **w: Display Blocked Tasks**: Shows tasks that are blocked on resources, useful for deadlock diagnosis.

- **x: Used by Xen**: If you are running on a Xen hypervisor, the x key can be used for special Xen operations.

- **z: Freeze filesystems**: Freezes all filesystems, making them read-only without unmounting them.

Magic SysRq commands are potent tools, especially in system recovery or emergency scenarios where traditional methods fail. However, they should be used with caution as some commands (like the immediate reboot or kill commands) can result in data loss if filesystems are not properly synced or if processes are terminated abruptly.

Due to its powerful nature, magic SysRq access should be restricted, especially on systems with physical security concerns or multi-user environments. Adjusting the bitmask in **/proc/sys/kernel/sysrq** to enable only necessary functions is a recommended practice to balance utility and security.

Debugging by printing

Printing kernel traces within a Linux driver involves using specific kernel facilities designed for debugging and logging. Here are some of the most important and useful aspects to consider when you want to print kernel traces from within a Linux driver.

One of the differences with **printf** userspace is that **printk** allows you to classify messages based on their severity by assigning different logging levels, or priorities, to messages.

printk() messages can specify a log level. The format string is largely inspired by the **printf** that can be used in userspace and is still compatible with C99, although it does not support exactly the same parameters. It has some additions but also some limitations, such as the %n or floating-point conversion specifiers, which are not supported.

It remains the most straightforward method for logging in the kernel. It functions similarly to the user-space `printf()`:

Definition: `#define pr_info(fmt,arg...) \`

    `printk(KERN_INFO fmt,##arg)`

`Header: <printk.h>`

Usually, the log level is specified via a macro. So, there is one macro per log level type or priority. For example, **KERN_INFO** is one of the possible log levels of the message for an informative trace. Basically, the loglevel macro consists of a string, which is concatenated to the message text at compile time. This explains why there is no comma between the priority of a trace itself and the format string.

Here are two example `printk` commands, a debug message and a critical message:

`printk(KERN_DEBUG "We are here : %s:%i\n ", __FILE__, __LINE__);`

`printk(KERN_DEBUG "BPB driver | memory pointer: %p\n", ptr);`

There are eight possible log level strings, defined in the `<linux/kernel.h>` header. Here is a summary of them listed in order of decreasing severity (this table will remain an important asset to understand and master the addition of traces in your code):

Level	String	Alias	Description
KERN_EMERG	"0"	pr_emerg()	used for emergency messages, usually preceding an accident
KERN_ALERT	"1"	pr_alert()	alert situation requiring immediate action
KERN_CRIT	"2"	pr_crit()	critical situations, often linked to serious hardware or software failures
KERN_ERR	"3"	pr_err()	reporting an error condition in a device driver to signal a hardware difficulty for example or other.
KERN_ WARNING	"4"	pr_warn()	warnings of an annoying situation related to the kernel itself but less problematic than an error.
KERN_ NOTICE	"5"	pr_notice()	normal situations in the life of a driver, but nevertheless worthy of being mentioned. Most security-related messages are reported at this trace level
KERN_INFO	"6"	pr_info()	informational messages used by many drivers to display useful information about the hardware they find at boot.

Level	String	Alias	Description
KERN_DEBUG	"7"	pr_debug() and pr_devel() if DEBUG is defined	used to debug messages.
KERN_DEFAULT	"c"		The default kernel loglevel.
KERN_CONT	""	pr_cont()	"Continuation" line of log printing (performed only after a line without enclosing \n).

Table 13.1: Listing of the debug level within the GNU/Linux kernel

Adjusting the log level helps in managing the verbosity of log messages, which is particularly useful in production environments.

The log level of a **printk** macro specifies the importance of a message itself.

The kernel can decide whether or not to display a message immediately by printing it on the current console, taking into account its log level and the current **console_loglevel** itself defined via a kernel variable and modifiable via **procfs**.

With a message having a higher priority level and a lower log level, the message will be printed on the console.

If no logging level was specified, the message will be with the **KERN_DEFAULT** priority.

The current logging level or priority can be viewed with the following command:

```
$ cat /proc/sys/kernel/printk
4 4 1 7
```

This command displays a set of four logging levels: current, default, minimum, and finally, default at startup.

To modify the current logging level, simply write the desired level in **/proc/sys/kernel/printk**. For example, to select all debug messages on the console, simply use the **dmesg** command:

```
$ sudo echo 5 > /proc/sys/kernel/printk
```

The kernel traces can then be viewed from a terminal using the **dmesg** command:

```
$ sudo dmesg -w
```

```
[112647.597783] usb 4-1.1.2.3: Product: Patriot Memory
[112647.597785] usb 4-1.1.2.3: Manufacturer:
[112647.597786] usb 4-1.1.2.3: SerialNumber: 070A09B667673D49
[112647.601096] usb-storage 4-1.1.2.3:1.0: USB Mass Storage device detected
[112647.601294] scsi host8: usb-storage 4-1.1.2.3:1.0
[112648.617361] scsi 8:0:0:0: Direct-Access           Patriot Memory    PMAP P
Q: 0 ANSI: 6
[112648.617592] sd 8:0:0:0: Attached scsi generic sg3 type 0
[112648.617796] sd 8:0:0:0: [sdd] 60604416 512-byte logical blocks: (31.0 GB/28.
9 GiB)
[112648.617996] sd 8:0:0:0: [sdd] Write Protect is off
[112648.618000] sd 8:0:0:0: [sdd] Mode Sense: 45 00 00 00
[112648.618205] sd 8:0:0:0: [sdd] Write cache: disabled, read cache: enabled, do
esn't support DPO or FUA
[112648.652670]  sdd: sdd1
[112648.652962] sd 8:0:0:0: [sdd] Attached SCSI removable disk
[112648.913335] audit: type=1400 audit(1721489462.928:346): apparmor="DENIED" op
eration="open" class="file" profile="snap.firefox.firefox" name="/etc/fstab" pid
=8066 comm="firefox" requested_mask="r" denied_mask="r" fsuid=1000 ouid=0
```

Figure 13.2: Example of result using the dmesg command

Another way, using **dmesg**:

```
$ sudo dmesg -n 7
```

With this command, it is possible to specify to **dmesg** the log level to filter the display.

The Linux kernel provides a few mechanisms to handle rate limiting of log messages. The primary function used for this purpose is **printk_ratelimit()**. This function allows log messages to be printed only at a certain rate, helping to prevent the log buffer from being flooded with repetitive messages.

The **printk_ratelimit()** function is typically used in conjunction with the **printk()** function. Here is how you might see it used in a kernel module or driver:

```
if (printk_ratelimit()) {
        printk(KERN_INFO "This message is rate-limited!\n");
}
```

This code snippet will limit the frequency of log messages to the default values defined within the kernel, which are usually set to allow a burst of 10 messages and subsequently one message every 5 seconds. These parameters can be adjusted via the following **sysctl** settings:

- **/proc/sys/kernel/printk_ratelimit**: Sets the interval between kernel messages; the unit is seconds.

- **/proc/sys/kernel/printk_ratelimit_burst**: Sets the number of burst messages allowed before a limit applies and prevents a burst.

In practice, rate limiting is useful in scenarios where error conditions might cause many error messages to be logged in a short period. For example:

- Hardware errors that repeatedly trigger an interrupt.
- Network drivers that encounter frequent packet errors under specific conditions.
- File system errors due to disk issues might generate many similar log entries.

While rate limiting is useful for keeping logs manageable and preventing log-induced performance issues, it can also suppress important messages if not configured correctly. Developers must balance the need for information with the potential for log flooding. Developers must balance the need for information with the potential for log flooding.

In some scenarios, it might be beneficial to adjust rate limiting dynamically based on the state of the system. This is not directly supported by **printk_ratelimit()** but can be implemented by conditionally calling the function based on external factors.

For more sophisticated or adjustable logging mechanisms, developers might use dynamic debugging (**CONFIG_DYNAMIC_DEBUG**) or implement their own logging controls within their driver or module code, possibly using more complex criteria for when to log and when to withhold messages.

Overall, **printk_ratelimit()** is a simple and effective tool for controlling kernel log verbosity during runtime, helping to maintain system stability and performance even when potential logging storms occur.

Sometimes, especially during automated testing, it is very useful to insert messages into the kernel log buffer to annotate what is happening:

```
# echo "Start debugging" > /dev/kmsg
```

Of course, this message receives the default logging level, if you wish e.g. To issue a **KERN_DEBUG** message, you must use a special string representation of the logging level - in this case, **"<2>"**. The special string is different from the log level string used internally in the kernel, to make it easier to use from user space. The ASCII value of the log level is surrounded by brackets. (Historically, this was how the internal log level string was represented, so this format is retained for log messages submitted from **userspace** for backward compatibility):

```
# echo "<7>Start debugging (from userspace)" >/dev/kmsg
```

The message will appear like any other kernel message—there is no way to tell them apart!

Note: We are printing a kernel message from user space that is quite different than a printf() call.

If **/dev/kmsg** does not exist, it can be created with the following commands:

```
$ sudo mknod -m 600 /dev/kmsg c 1 11
```

By default, the device **/dev/kmsg** is owned by **root:root**, but the group can be changed with an admin group:

```
$ sudo groupadd admingroup
$ sudo chown :admingroup /dev/kmsg
```

Then we can increase the rights of **/dev/kmsg** for this group:

```
$ sudo chmod u=rw,g=rw,o=r /dev/kmsg
```

All **printk** messages are stored in a ring buffer, viewable via **dmesg**. This buffer has a fixed size, and older messages are overwritten by newer ones.

Commands like **dmesg**, **trace-cmd**, **ftrace**, and **perf** can be used for extracting and analyzing kernel logs and traces.

Dynamic debugging

Dynamic debugging allows to dynamically enable/disable debug messages when running the GNU/Linux kernel or drivers.

It uses the **pr_debug()** and **dev_dbg()** functions to display debug messages.

To do this, the **CONFIG_DYNAMIC_DEBUG** option must be enabled when configuring the kernel.

This dynamic debugging type is designed to allow enabling/disabling kernel code in order to obtain additional information about the kernel. If **CONFIG_DYNAMIC_DEBUG** is enabled, then all **pr_debug()/dev_dbg()** and **print_hex_dump_debug()/print_hex_dump_bytes()** calls can be enabled dynamically.

If **CONFIG_DYNAMIC_DEBUG** is not set, then **print_hex_dump_debug()** will be redirected to **print_hex_dump(KERN_DEBUG)**.

Dynamic debugging works by adding specific debugging statements into the kernel code. These debugging statements can then be controlled at runtime via a control file located in **/sys/kernel/debug/dynamic_debug/control**.

Each debugging statement in the source code is therefore modified to include a descriptor containing information about the file, line number, module, and function where it resides. These descriptors are then used to filter and control the output dynamically.

With **print_hex_dump_debug()/print_hex_dump_bytes()**, the format string is its argument **prefix_str** if the string is a constant or **hexdump** if **prefix_str** is obtained dynamically.

Dynamic debugging has even more useful features. Indeed, a simple query language allows debugging statements to be enabled or disabled by matching any combination of 0 or 1 of the following:

- Source file name
- Function name
- Line number (including line number ranges)
- Module name
- Format string

These macros allow for dynamic enabling and disabling of debug messages at runtime, reducing performance overhead when debugging is not needed.

Definition: Those macros are controlled via **/sys/kernel/debug/dynamic_debug/ control**, allowing fine-grained control over debug output:

```
#define pr_fmt(fmt) "%s:%s: " fmt, KBUILD_MODNAME, __func__ #define
pr_info(fmt, ...) eprintf(0, verbose, pr_fmt(fmt), ##__VA_ARGS__)

dev_dbg(dev, "Device-specific debug message: %d\n", value);

#define pr_info(fmt, ...) eprintf(0, verbose, pr_fmt(fmt), ##__VA_
ARGS__)
```

Control it at runtime via **/sys/kernel/debug/dynamic_debug/control**.

Use echo commands to enable/disable driver-specific messages, such as:

```
# echo -n 'file svcsock_bpb.c line 1603 +p' >
                                <debugfs>/dynamic_debug/control


# echo -n ' file   svcsock_bpb.c    line  1603 +p ' >
                                <debugfs>/dynamic_debug/control


# echo -n 'file svcsock_bpb.c line 1603 +p' >
                                <debugfs>/dynamic_debug/control
# echo "file drivers/usb/* +p" > <debugfs>/dynamic_debug/control


# echo 'file driver_bpb.c +p' > /sys/kernel/debug/dynamic_debug/control
```

Here is how to use dynamic debugging:

- **Access control file**: Navigate to **/sys/kernel/debug/dynamic_debug/**control. You may need root access to view and modify this file.

- **View current settings**: To see the current dynamic debug settings, you can use the cat command:

  `$ cat /sys/kernel/debug/dynamic_debug/control`

- **Modify settings**: To enable or disable debugging output for specific messages, you write commands to the control file. These commands can filter by source file, line number, module name, and function, and can either enable or disable the logging.

Examples, for enabling all messages in a particular source file:

```
$ echo 'file my_module.c +p' > /sys/kernel/debug/dynamic_debug/
control
```

- Disable all messages for a specific function:

```
$ echo 'func my_function -p' > /sys/kernel/debug/dynamic_debug/
control
```

The control file supports querying using a simple query language that matches descriptors. You can use these queries to refine which debug statements are enabled or disabled:

- **Filename**: file filename.c
- **Line number**: line 1234
- **Module**: module mymodule
- **Function**: func my_function

Developers can turn on debugging for just the part of the system they are interested in, reducing noise and overhead.

Since debugging can be turned off when not needed, there is minimal performance impact compared to having static debugging compiled into the kernel.

Debugging can be controlled without rebooting or recompiling the kernel, which is invaluable for debugging live systems or systems that are hard to reproduce.

Dynamic debugging is a powerful tool for Linux kernel developers, providing a versatile approach to managing kernel debug output in a controlled, on-demand fashion. This makes it an excellent choice for development and troubleshooting in both development and production environments.

kgdb/kdb kernel debugger

The kernel has two interfaces that interface with a GNU/Linux kernel that can be used for debugging: **kdb** and **kgdb**.

It is possible to use either of these debugging interfaces and even switch between them dynamically if you configure the kernel with the right options at compile time and run time.

kdb is a simplistic shell or command-line interface that you can use on a system console with a keyboard and/or serial console.

It can be used to inspect memory, registers, process lists, **dmesg,** and even set breakpoints to stop at a specific point in the kernel.

kdb is not a source-level debugger, although it is possible to set breakpoints and perform basic monitoring of kernel execution. **kdb** is primarily intended to perform analysis tasks to aid in development or diagnosis of kernel problems. So you can access some symbols by name in kernel builtins or kernel modules if the code was created with **CONFIG_KALLSYMS**.

kgdb (similar to **gdb-server**), on the other hand, is intended to be used as a debugger associated with a Linux kernel source code. It is used in conjunction with **gdb** (client) to debug a Linux kernel. The goal is that **gdb** can be used quite extensively to inspect memory and variables and browse call stack information in the same way that a userspace application developer would use **gdb** to debug an application. It is, therefore, possible to set breakpoints in the kernel code or dynamic modules and perform some limited execution steps.

To do this, two machines are required to use **kgdb**. One of these machines is a development machine where all the sources are located and where the compilations are performed, and the other is the target machine used to execute the kernel under development itself. Indeed, imagine using a breakpoint in the kernel that would halt the host OS if there were only one machine for development. The latter runs an instance of **gdb** on the **vmlinux** file dedicated to development (uncompressed) from the compilation that contains all the symbols; this image differs from the images used at boot, such as **bzImage**, **zImage**, **uImage**. With **gdb**, the developer specifies the Serial or IP connection parameters and then connects to the **kgdb** module. The type of connection a developer establishes with **gdb** depends on the availability of **kgdb input/output** (**I/O**) modules compiled as built-in modules or loadable kernel modules in the kernel of the test machine.

KDB

To use **kdb**, you need to enable it in the kernel configuration:

1. **Kernel hacking**:
   - [*] Kernel debugging
   - [*] Compile the kernel with debug info
   - [*] Provide Oops tracing for the kernel
   - [*] KGDB: kernel debugger
   - [*] Include kdb frontend for kgdb
   - [*] KGDB over Network (KGDBoE)

   Extract of kernel config:
   - CONFIG_KGDB=y
   - CONFIG_KGDB_SERIAL_CONSOLE=y
   - CONFIG_KGDB_KDB=y
   - CONFIG_KGDB_TESTS=y
   - CONFIG_NETCONSOLE=y

- CONFIG_NETPOLL=y

- CONFIG_NETPOLL_KGDB=y

2. Save the configuration and rebuild your kernel:

```
$ make
$ make modules
$ make install
$ make modules_install
```

3. Reboot your system with the new kernel. Add the following boot parameters to the GNU/Linux kernel command line to enable **kdb** over a serial line:

kgdboc=ttyS0,115200 kgdbwait

The explanation of the code is as follows:

- **kgdboc=ttyS0,115200**: Specifies the serial console for **kgdb**.

- **kgdbwait**: Stops the kernel and waits for the debugger to attach.

4. Once the system is booted, you can enter **kdb** by triggering a breakpoint:

```
$ echo g > /proc/sysrq-trigger
```

In **kdb**, you can use various commands to inspect the system:

- **bt**: Print the stack backtrace.

- **ps**: Display the current tasks.

- **lsmod**: List loaded modules.

- **dmesg**: Display the kernel message buffer.

- **go**: Continue normal execution.

KGDB

Follow the same steps as for **kdb** to enable **kgdb** in the kernel configuration.

You need two machines: the target (running the kernel to be debugged) and the host (running **gdb**).

Connect the target and host machines using a null-modem serial cable. On the target machine, specify the **kgdboc** parameter in the bootloader:

kgdboc=ttyS0,115200 kgdbwait

Or,

```
$ sudo modprobe kgdboc
$ sudo modprobe netconsole
```

```
$ sudo modprobe netpoll
$ sudo modprobe netpoll_kgdb
$ sudo echo "kgdboe=@eth0,192.168.1.100/,@192.168.1.50/" > /sys/module/
kgdboe/parameters/kgdboe
$ sudo echo g > /proc/sysrq-trigger
```

On the host machine, ensure you have **gdb** installed, then start **gdb** with the **vmlinux** file:

```
$ gdb /path/to/vmlinux
```

You can now use **gdb** to debug the kernel on the target machine:

- **break function_name**: Set a breakpoint.
- **continue**: Continue execution until the next breakpoint.
- **step/next**: Step through the code.
- **print variable**: Print the value of a variable.
- **bt**: Display the backtrace.

Connect to the target machine:

```
target remote /dev/ttyS0
```

Or,

```
target remote udp:192.168.1.100:6443
```

Set a breakpoint:

```
break do_fork
```

Continue execution:

```
continue
```

Step through code:

```
step
```

Inspect variables:

```
print some_variable
```

Display backtrace:

```
bt
```

Continue execution:

```
continue
```

By following these steps, you can effectively debug the Linux kernel using **kdb** and **kgdb**.

Kernel probes

Kernel probes, specifically Kprobes and Kretprobes, are powerful diagnostic tools in the Linux kernel that allow developers to dynamically examine and debug kernel behaviors. These tools are instrumental in identifying performance issues and bugs within the kernel without needing to restart the system or modify kernel code permanently.

There are two types of probes: kprobes and kretprobes (also called return probes).

A kprobe can be inserted on almost any kernel instruction. A kretprobes probe is triggered on the return of a specific function.

Kprobes-based instrumentation is packaged as a dynamic module. The **init** function of such a module installs one or more probes and the exit function removes them. A registration function such as **register_kprobe()** indicates where the probe should be inserted and also which handler should be called when the probe is used.

There are also **register_/unregister_*probes()** functions for registering/unregistering a set of ***probes**. These features can ease the unregistration phase when you need to unregister several probes at once.

Kprobes can probe most of the kernel except itself. This means that there are some functions that kprobes cannot probe. Probing a function may cause a recursive abort in case of a double fault, or a nested probe handler may never be called. Kprobes also maintains lists of functions as a blacklist. If you want to add a function to the blacklist, simply include **linux/kprobes.h** and use the **NOKPROBE_SYMBOL()** macro. Indeed, Kprobes will check the address of the given probe against the blacklist and refuse to register it if the given address is in the blacklist.

Kprobe

Kprobes allow you to monitor any kernel routine and collect debugging and performance information without interruption.

They are designed to be as non-invasive as possible, which makes them particularly useful for production systems where you cannot afford high overhead or risk of failure:

- **Functionality**: A Kprobe can be set on almost any instruction in the kernel space. When the kernel executes that instruction, the probe points trigger custom handler functions.

- **Uses**: Common uses include examining the state of data structures, tracking performance metrics, and logging specific events.

Kprobe data struct: The **struct kprobe** is defined in the Linux kernel headers, specifically in **<linux/kprobes.h>**. This structure encapsulates all the information needed to set up a probe, including where to place the probe, what handler functions to call, and optional data specific to the probe. Here is a breakdown of the primary fields within **struct kprobe**:

- **kprobe_addr:**

  - Type: `void *`

  - **Description**: The address at which to plant the kprobe. If `kprobe.symbol_name` is used, `kprobe_addr` is resolved to the address corresponding to the symbol name.

- **offset:**

  - Type: `unsigned long`

  - **Description**: Offset from `kprobe_addr` to place the probe. Used when probing an address within a specific function or area in memory.

- **symbol_name:**

  - Type: `const char *`

  - **Description**: Name of the symbol where the probe is to be placed. The kernel resolves this to an address during registration.

- **pre_handler:**

  - Type: `int (*)(struct kprobe *, struct pt_regs *)`

  - **Description**: Pointer to the function that will be called just before the probed instruction is executed.

- **post_handler:**

  - Type: `void (*)(struct kprobe *, struct pt_regs *, unsigned long)`

  - **Description**: Pointer to the function that will be called just after the probed instruction executes. The third argument contains the flags register content prior to the probe point being hit.

- **fault_handler:**

  - Type: `int (*)(struct kprobe *, struct pt_regs *, int)`

  - **Description**: Optional handler that is called if executing the probe causes a fault (such as a page fault). It can be used to handle specific errors or clean up if needed.

- **addr:**

  - Type: `unsigned long`

  - **Description**: Internally used to store the address where the probe was actually installed. This is typically set during the registration process.

- **opcode:**
  - ○ **Type**: `kprobe_opcode_t`
  - ○ **Description**: Stores the original opcode replaced by the breakpoint instruction. This is used internally to restore the original code during the removal of the probe.

- **flags:**
  - ○ **Type**: `kprobe_flags_t`
  - ○ **Description**: Flags for controlling various internal aspects of the kprobe's behavior.

The components of kprobes are as follows:

- **Probe points**: The specific locations in the kernel code where you attach your probes. These can be function names or specific addresses in the kernel.

- **Handler functions**: Custom functions you write that are called when the probe points are hit. There are typically two types:

  - ○ **Pre-handler**: Runs just before the probed instruction.

  - ○ **Post-handler**: Runs immediately after the probed instruction.

Define a kprobe: Specify the target function or address, and define a handler function:

```
#include <linux/kprobes.h>

static int handler_pre(struct kprobe *p, struct pt_regs *regs) {
    printk(KERN_INFO "Pre-handler: probe hit at %p\n", p->addr);
    return 0; // 0 means continue execution
}

struct kprobe kp = {
    .symbol_name = "do_fork",
    .pre_handler = handler_pre,
};
```

Register the kprobe:

```
int ret = register_kprobe(&kp);
if (ret < 0) {
    printk(KERN_INFO "Failed to register kprobe\n");
    return ret;
}
```

KRETPROBE

Kretprobes are a variant of Kprobes, focused on functions' return points.

They allow you to intercept the return from a kernel function, which is particularly useful for checking the status and outputs of functions after they execute:

- **Functionality**: A Kretprobe is attached to the entry of a function, and it automatically places a breakpoint at the return address on the stack. When the function returns, your handler function is called.

- **Uses**: It is commonly used for error checking and logging the results of kernel functions.

Define a Kretprobe: Set up a **kretprobe** and its handler function:

```
static int handler_ret(struct kretprobe_instance *ri, struct pt_regs *regs)
{
    printk(KERN_INFO "Return-handler: probe hit at %p\n", ri->rp->kp.addr);
    return 0;
}


static struct kretprobe rp = {
    .handler = handler_ret,
    .kp.symbol_name = "do_fork",
    .maxactive = 20, // Maximum instances of probed functions
simultaneously
};
```

Register the Kretprobe:

```
int ret = register_kretprobe(&rp);
if (ret < 0) {
    printk(KERN_INFO "Failed to register kretprobe\n");
    return ret;
}
```

The best practices are as follows:

- **Minimize impact**: Ensure that handler functions are as simple and fast as possible to minimize their impact on the system.

- **Safety and cleanup**: Always provide cleanup code to unregister probes when they are no longer needed or when the module is removed.

- **Error handling**: Properly handle potential failures during registration and setup.

Kprobes and Kretprobes offer a flexible and powerful mechanism for dynamic kernel analysis, making them invaluable tools for kernel developers and system administrators alike.

Kprobes and Kretprobes are instrumental for debugging and monitoring within the Linux kernel, but they come with their own sets of advantages and drawbacks.

The following is a table that summarizes these:

Feature	Kprobes	Kretprobes
Advantages	Can be attached to almost any point in the kernel code. Minimal overhead when not active. Does not require code modification.	Specifically useful for capturing data when functions return. Automatically handles saving and restoring register states.
Use cases	Monitor or intercept any kernel function or instruction. Useful for tracking down hard-to-find bugs.	Ideal for checking return values and post-execution state in functions. Useful in performance analysis after a function executes.
Flexibility	High flexibility with the ability to probe at virtually any kernel instruction.	Less flexible than Kprobes as they are only used at function return points.
Performance impact	Can slow down the system if used extensively or placed in frequently executed code paths.	Generally has a lower performance impact than Kprobes, but depends on the function's frequency and complexity.
Complexity	Requires understanding of the kernel's internal workings to use effectively.	Simpler to use for function exit monitoring but requires understanding of what data to capture after function execution.
Drawbacks	Can potentially destabilize the system if not used carefully. Overhead increases with the number of active probes.	Limited to function returns, offering less granularity than Kprobes. Can still impact performance if the function is critical.

Table 13.2: Comparison between kprobe and kretprobe

Some additional considerations are as follows:

- **Safety**: Both Kprobes and Kretprobes should be used with caution, particularly in production environments. Their intrusive nature means they can inadvertently affect system stability if used improperly.

- **Data collection**: Both methods allow for sophisticated data collection and are particularly useful in environments where standard debugging tools fall short, such as with systems that cannot be easily stopped or restarted.

- **Learning curve**: There is a significant learning curve associated with using these tools effectively. Understanding the kernel's architecture and behavior is crucial to make the most out of Kprobes and Kretprobes.

- **Development and maintenance**: As kernel versions evolve, maintaining and updating probe points may be necessary to align with changes in the kernel code and internal APIs.

Kprobes and Kretprobes are powerful tools that provide deep insights into the kernel's operation, making them invaluable for developers involved in low-level kernel development, debugging, or performance tuning.

OOPS

The **Out of Place State** (**OOPS**) in Linux is a diagnostic tool provided by the kernel to report a critical system error, usually due to a bug in the kernel or its modules. When an OOPS occurs, it does not necessarily crash the system like a kernel panic would, but it does indicate serious issues that could lead to instability or security risks.

An OOPS can be triggered by various issues within the kernel, such as:

- Dereferencing null or invalid pointers.

- Access violations within the kernel space.

- Bugs in kernel modules or drivers leading to illegal operations.

The following figure shows a memory crash of a process by displaying a detail of the current execution context as well as the `callstack`:

```
[12710.153112] oops init (level = 1)
[12710.153115] triggering oops via BUG()
[12710.153127] ------------[ cut here ]------------
[12710.153128] kernel BUG at /home/duck/Articles/linuxoops/oops.c:171
[12710.153132] invalid opcode: 0000 [#1] PREEMPT SMP PTI
[12710.153748] CPU: 0 PID: 5531 Comm: insmod
[12710.156191] RSP: 0018:ffffb41340e6fdd8 EFLAGS: 00010246
[12710.156849] RAX: 0000000000000019 RBX: ffffffffc1015040 RCX: 0000000000000000
[12710.157513] RDX: 0000000000000000 RSI: ffffffff83bc9d39 RDI: 00000000ffffffff
[12710.158171] RBP: ffff8d6101bd1d50 R08: 0000000000000000 R09: ffffb41340e6fc90
[12710.158826] R10: 0000000000000003 R11: ffffffff83f3d1e8 R12: ffffb41340e6fde0
[12710.159483] R13: 0000000000000000 R14: 0000000000000000 R15: 0000000000000000
[12710.160143] FS:  00007f6c290b31c0(0000) GS:ffff8d6411a00000(0000) knlGS:00000
[12710.160820] CS:  0010 DS: 0000 ES: 0000 CR0: 0000000080050033
[12710.161478] CR2: 0000000004134f0 CR3: 000000018be34005 CR4: 00000000003706f0
[12710.162156] DR0: 0000000000000000 DR1: 0000000000000000 DR2: 0000000000000000
[12710.162824] DR3: 0000000000000000 DR6: 00000000fffe0ff0 DR7: 0000000000000400
[12710.163474] Call Trace:
[12710.164129]  <TASK>
[12710.164779]  do_one_initcall+0x56/0x230
[12710.165424]  do_init_module+0x4a/0x210
[12710.166050]  __do_sys_finit_module+0x9e/0xf0
[12710.166711]  do_syscall_64+0x37/0x90
```

Figure 13.3: Example of oops in the kernel trace

Finally, there is also a parameter called **"oops_limit"** which indicates after how many oops a panic should occur. The default value is 10,000 (**https://docs.kernel.org/admin-guide/sysctl/kernel.html#oops-limit**).

When an OOPS occurs, the kernel generates a report that includes several important pieces of information to help diagnose the problem:

- **Type of error**: The report starts with a description of the error, such as a segmentation fault or a general protection fault.

- **Registers and flags**: It lists the state of CPU registers and flags at the time of the error.

- **Stack trace**: Provides a stack trace from the point where the error occurred, showing the path of execution that led to the fault.

- **Code segment**: Includes a snippet of the offending code where the error was triggered.

- **Kernel modules**: Lists loaded kernel modules and their states, which can help identify if a specific module is at fault.

- **Symbolic information**: If available, symbols are resolved to give human-readable names of functions and variables in the stack trace.

When an OOPS is generated:

- **Logging**: The details of the OOPS are logged into the system logs, which can be reviewed using tools like **dmesg** or **journalctl**.

- **System response**: Depending on the severity of the error and the kernel's configuration, the system may continue running, or specific functionalities might be disabled.

- **Crash dumps**: In some configurations, an OOPS can trigger a kernel crash dump (**vmcore**) to capture the full state of the memory, which is invaluable for comprehensive post-mortem analysis.

To debug an OOPS:

- **System logs**: Check the logs for the OOPS report and any other relevant messages before or after the incident.

- **Reproduction**: If possible, try to reproduce the issue under controlled conditions to better understand the triggers.

- **Kernel configuration**: Make sure the kernel is compiled with debugging symbols and without optimizations to enhance the quality of diagnostic data.

- **External tools**: Use tools like **kdump**, **crash**, and **gdb** to analyze the kernel state and the **vmcore** if available.

Kdump internally uses **kexec** to boot on a snapshot from a kernel whenever a system kernel memory dump needs to be performed, such as during a kernel panic. The system kernel memory dump is retained and remains persistent across reboots.

Kdump and kexec are currently supported on the following architectures: x86, x86_64, ppc64, ia64, s390x, arm, and arm64.

When the GNU/Linux kernel boots, it reserves a small section of memory for the memory dump kernel. This ensures that ongoing **direct memory access (DMA)** from the system kernel does not corrupt the memory dump kernel.

The **kexec -p** command loads the memory dump into this reserved memory area.

The following figure details the architecture of how **kdump** and **kexec** work:

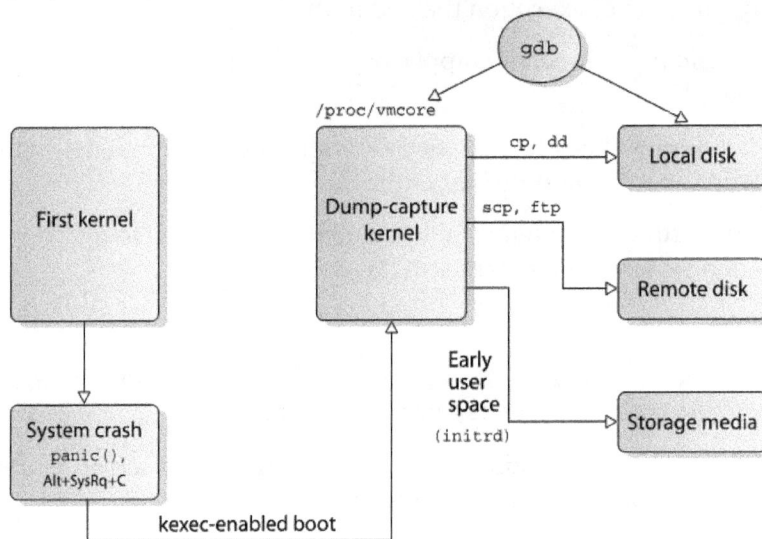

Figure 13.4: *Architecture of kdump and kexec*

On x86 machines, the first 640 KB of physical memory is needed at boot time, regardless of where the kernel is loaded. Therefore, **kexec** dumps this region just before rebooting into the memory dump.

Similarly, on PPC64 machines, the first 32 KB of physical memory is needed at boot time, regardless of where the kernel is loaded, and to support a 64 KB page size, **kexec** dumps the first 64 KB of memory.

All necessary information about the GNU/Linux kernel image is encoded in ELF format and stored in a dedicated memory area before a crash.

The physical address of the start of the ELF header is passed to the memory dump via the **elfcorehdr= boot** parameter. Optionally, the ELF header size can also be passed when using the following syntax: **elfcorehdr=[size[KMG]@]offset[KMG]**.

With a core dump, you can access the core image via **/proc/vmcore**. This exports the dump as a file in ELF format that you can write using file copy commands such as **cp** or **scp**. Additionally, you can use analysis tools such as **GNU Debugger** (**GDB**) and the Crash tool to debug such core dump files. This method ensures that the dump pages are correctly ordered and, therefore, usable.

The kernel core dump utility can be installed via the following command:

```
$ sudo apt install linux-crashdump
```

Note: As of Ubuntu 16.04, this GNU/Linux kernel core dump tool is enabled by default.

During installation, the following dialog boxes appear:

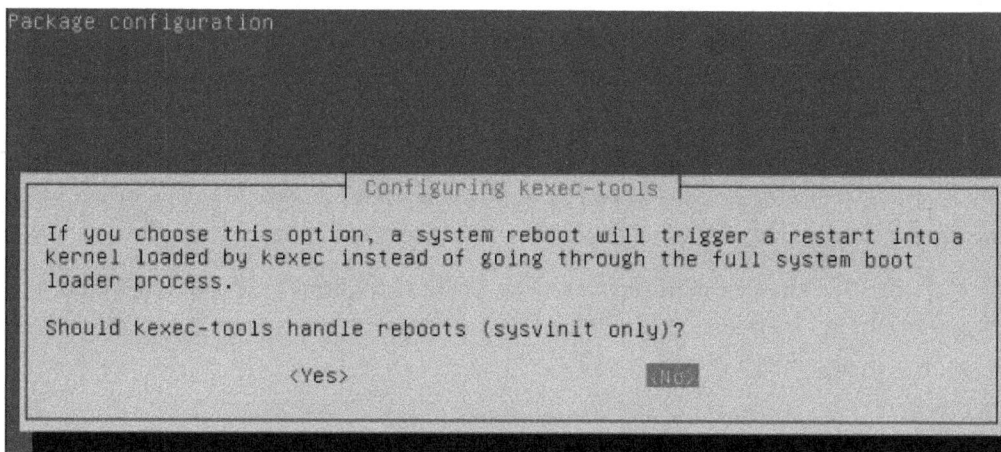

Figure 13.5: The kexec-tool activation

Select **Yes** to enable **kexec-tools** on all reboots:

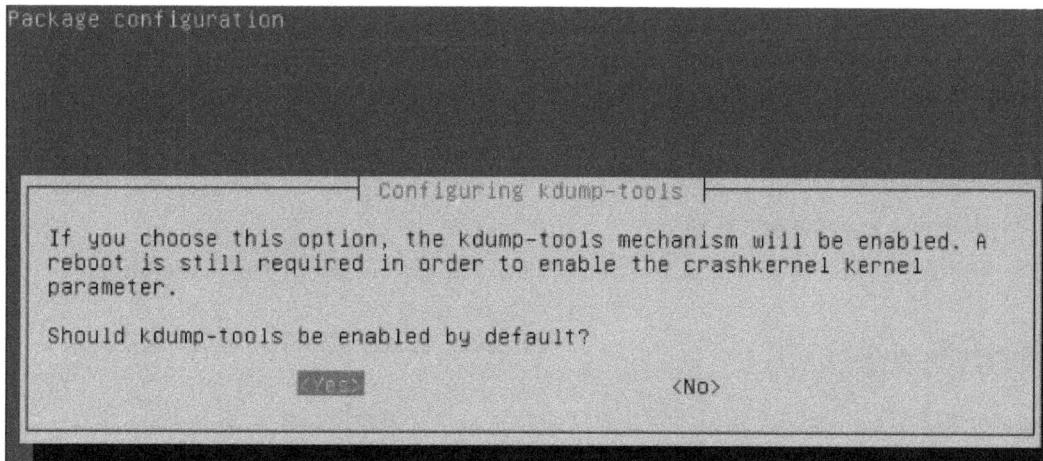

Figure 13.6: The kdump-tool activation

"Yes" must also be selected here to enable **kdump-tools**.

You can manually (re)enable the feature via the **dpkg-reconfigure kexec-tools** and **dpkg-reconfigure kdump-tools** commands. To do this, you will need to answer **"Yes"** to both questions.

It is also possible to edit the **/etc/default/kexec** file and set the parameters directly:

```
# Load a kexec kernel (true/false)
```

```
LOAD_KEXEC=true
```

Also, edit the **/etc/default/kdump-tools** file to enable **kdump** by including the following line:

```
USE_KDUMP=1
```

If no reboot has been performed since installing the **linux-crashdump** package, a reboot will then be necessary to enable it by passing the **crashkernel=** boot parameter. Upon reboot, **kdump-tools** will, therefore, be enabled and active.

Additionally, if you enable **kdump-tools** after a reboot, you will only need the **"kdump-config load"** command to enable the mechanism used with **kdump**.

The current state of **kdump** can be accessed via the **"kdump-config show"** command. It will display something like this:

```
DUMP_MODE: kdump
USE_KDUMP: 1
KDUMP_SYSCTL: kernel.panic_on_oops=1
KDUMP_COREDIR: /var/crash
crashkernel addr:
/var/lib/kdump/vmlinuz
kdump initrd:
/var/lib/kdump/initrd.img
current state: ready to kdump

kexec command:
/sbin/kexec -p --command-line="..." --initrd=...
```

After that, the core dump will be located in **/var/crash** for further investigation.

Profiling

Profiling a GNU/Linux kernel involves collecting and analyzing data about its performance to identify bottlenecks and optimize system performance.

Setting up the environment: Ensure that you have the necessary tools installed for profiling. Common tools include **perf, ftrace, systemtap**, and **bpftrace**:

```
$ sudo apt-get install linux-tools-$(uname -r) linux-tools-common linux-tools-generic
$ sudo apt-get install systemtap
$ sudo apt-get install bpfcc-tools bpftrace
```

The **perf** command:

The first command is **perf**. This is a powerful tool for profiling the Linux kernel and applications.

Start by collecting data with **perf**:

```
$ sudo perf record -a
```

Record kernel events such as CPU cycles, instructions, cache references, and more:

```
$ sudo perf record -e cycles -a sleep 10
```

Profile specific kernel functions:

```
$ sudo perf record -e probe:do_sys_open -aR
```

Use tracepoints to trace specific events in the kernel:

```
$ sudo perf record -e 'syscalls:sys_enter_*' -a
```

Record and analyze context switches:

```
$ sudo perf record -e context-switches -a sleep 10
```

Monitor and analyze page faults:

```
$ sudo perf record -e page-faults -a sleep 10
```

Monitor CPU usage for specific processes or system-wide:

```
$ sudo perf stat -a -- sleep 10
```

Profile memory access patterns:

```
$ sudo perf record -e mem_load_uops_retired.l3_miss -a sleep 10
```

Record and analyze branch mispredictions:

```
$ sudo perf record -e branch-misses -a sleep 10
```

Monitor L1 data cache misses:

```
$ sudo perf record -e L1-dcache-load-misses -a sleep 10
```

Trace specific instructions being executed:

```
$ sudo perf record -e instructions -a sleep 10
```

Trace kernel functions using kprobes:

```
$ sudo perf probe do_sys_open
$ sudo perf record -e probe:do_sys_open -a sleep 10
```

Get detailed tracing for specific functions:

```
$ sudo perf probe -x /path/to/vmlinux 'do_sys_open%return'
$ sudo perf record -e probe:do_sys_open -a sleep 10
```

Record hardware events:

```
$ sudo perf record -e r003c -a sleep 10
```

Create and use custom events for profiling:

```
$ sudo perf record -e 'cycles:u,instructions:u,cache-misses:u' -a sleep 10
```

Monitor idle CPU time:

```
$ sudo perf record -e cpu-idle -a sleep 10
```

Analyze specific kernel modules:

```
$ sudo perf probe -x /path/to/module.ko 'function'
$ sudo perf record -e probe:module:function -a sleep 10
```

Separate profiling of user and kernel space events:

```
$ sudo perf record -e cycles:u -a sleep 10 # User space
$ sudo perf record -e cycles:k -a sleep 10 # Kernel space
```

Add dynamic probes to trace kernel functions without recompiling:

```
$ sudo perf probe 'do_sys_open'
$ sudo perf record -e probe:do_sys_open -aR
```

This command records system-wide profiling data. Use *Ctrl+C* to stop recording.

Once data have been collected, it is possible to analyze it:

```
$ sudo perf report
```

View the call graph data in a visual format:

```
$ sudo perf report --call-graph
```

Get a detailed report of symbols in the kernel:

```
$ sudo perf report --symbols
```

To profile a specific workload:

```
$ sudo perf record -a -g -- your_command
```

The **-g** option captures call graphs (stack traces), which is useful for understanding the flow of execution.

Generate statistical profiles of various kernel metrics:

```
$ sudo perf stat -e cycles,instructions,cache-references,cache-misses -a
sleep 10
```

Profile the scheduler to analyze task scheduling and context switching:

```
$ sudo perf sched record
$ sudo perf sched latency
```

Analyze lock contention in the kernel:

```
$ sudo perf lock record
$ sudo perf lock report
```

Monitor the system in real-time to see which functions are consuming the most CPU time:

```
$ sudo perf top
```

The **ftrace** command:

The second command is **ftrace** and is a built-in Linux tracer for kernel functions.

Enable the desired tracers and set up the tracing:

```
$ echo function > /sys/kernel/debug/tracing/current_tracer
```

Start tracing:

```
$ echo 1 > /sys/kernel/debug/tracing/tracing_on
```

Stop tracing:

```
$ echo 0 > /sys/kernel/debug/tracing/tracing_on
```

View traces:

```
$ cat /sys/kernel/debug/tracing/trace
```

The **systemtap** command:

The third command is **systemtap** and allows you to write scripts to collect detailed kernel information:

1. Create a script:

   ```
   # myscript.stp
   probe kernel.function("vfs_read") {
       printf("vfs_read called by %s\n", execname())
   }
   ```

2. Run the script:

   ```
   $ sudo stap myscript.stp
   ```

The fourth command is **bpftrace**. It is used for advanced tracing using a high-level tracing language for GNU/Linux:

1. Create a script to trace read system calls:

```
# read_trace.bt
tracepoint:syscalls:sys_enter_read {
    printf("%s read called\n", comm);
}
```

Here are several kinds of scripts:

- **Trace file open events**: It traces all file open events in the system:

```
tracepoint:syscalls:sys_enter_openat
{
    printf("File open: %s by %s\n", str(args->filename), comm);
}
```

- **Trace TCP connections**: It traces TCP connections established on the system:

```
tracepoint:inet:inet_sock_set_state
/args->protocol == IPPROTO_TCP && args->newstate == TCP_ESTABLISHED/
{
    printf("TCP connection from %s to %s\n", ntop(args->sport),
ntop(args->dport));
}
```

- **Measure time spent in a function**: It measures the time spent in the **vfs_read** function:

```
kprobe:vfs_read
{
    @start[tid] = nsecs;
}

kretprobe:vfs_read
/@start[tid]/
{
    @time = hist(nsecs - @start[tid]);
    delete(@start[tid]);
}

END
```

```
{
    print(@time);
}
```

- **Monitor disk I/O latency**: It monitors disk I/O latency for read operations:

```
tracepoint:block:block_rq_issue
{
    @start[args->sector] = nsecs;
}

tracepoint:block:block_rq_complete
/@start[args->sector]/
{
    @latency = hist(nsecs - @start[args->sector]);
    delete(@start[args->sector]);
}

END
{
    print(@latency);
}
```

- **Track memory allocations**: It tracks memory allocations greater than a specified size:

```
tracepoint:kmem:kmalloc
/args->bytes > 1024/
{
    printf("Large allocation: %d bytes by %s\n", args->bytes, comm);
}
```

- **Count system calls**: It counts the number of system calls made by each process:

```
tracepoint:raw_syscalls:sys_enter
{
    @syscalls[comm] = count();
}

interval:s:5
{
    print(@syscalls);
}
```

- **Trace context switches**: It traces context switches and prints the process names involved.

```
tracepoint:sched:sched_switch
{
    printf("Context switch: %s -> %s\n", str(args->prev_comm),
str(args->next_comm));
}
```

- **Monitor page faults**: It monitors page faults per process.

```
tracepoint:vm:vm_fault
{
    @faults[comm] = count();
}


interval:s:10
{
    print(@faults);
}
```

- **Measure function latency**: It measures the latency of a specific kernel function.

```
kprobe:do_sys_open
{
    @start[tid] = nsecs;
}


kretprobe:do_sys_open
/@start[tid]/
{
    @latency = hist(nsecs - @start[tid]);
    delete(@start[tid]);
}


END
{
    print(@latency);
}
```

- **Track network packet transmission**: It tracks network packet transmission and prints the packet size:

```
tracepoint:net:net_dev_xmit
{
    printf("Packet transmitted: %d bytes by %s\n", args->len, comm);
}
```

These scripts are a good starting point for profiling different aspects of the Linux kernel. You can modify them to suit your specific needs or create new scripts based on the examples provided.

Run the script:

`$ sudo bpftrace read_trace.bt`

Once you have collected data using the tools above, analyze it to find performance bottlenecks. Look for the following:

- **High CPU usage**: Identify functions or processes consuming excessive CPU time.

- **I/O bottlenecks**: Check for slow I/O operations and their causes.

- **Memory usage**: Identify memory-intensive operations.

- **Lock contention**: Look for locks causing significant waiting time.

Different profiling techniques can be used in several use cases:

- Optimization or refactoring of the code causing the bottlenecks; hardware upgrades may be considered if the bottlenecks are related to them

- Adjustment of kernel parameters to better adapt its operation

Document the profiling process, findings, and optimizations made. Share the results with relevant stakeholders to ensure transparency and collaborative improvement.

Here is a typical profiling workflow:

- **Identify the problem**: Notice the performance issue (e.g., high CPU usage).

- **Collect data**: Use perf to record profiling data (CPU consumption, memory usage, disk usage (I/O), network usage in/out)

- **Analyze data**: Use the perf report to identify functions with high CPU usage.

- **Trace specific functions**: Use **`ftrace`** or **`bpftrace`** to get detailed traces of problematic functions.

- **Implement changes**: Optimize the identified bottlenecks in the kernel or application code.

- **Verify improvements**: Profile again to ensure the changes improved performance.

By following these steps, you can effectively profile and optimize the Linux kernel for better performance.

Conclusion

In this chapter, we explained how to develop a driver with breakpoints but also probes injected at specific points to avoid being too intrusive on drivers that are running. This step is crucial in case of a problem or bug but also serves to ensure that the driver works nominally (traces).

This concludes this book on the GNU/Linux kernel and its drivers. We hope you enjoyed reading it and developing your own drivers.

Join our book's Discord space

Join the book's Discord Workspace for Latest updates, Offers, Tech happenings around the world, New Release and Sessions with the Authors:

https://discord.bpbonline.com

Index

www.ingramcontent.com/pod-product-compliance
Lightning Source LLC
Chambersburg PA
CBHW061740210326
41599CB00034B/6743